Building
Bridges

Building Bridges

UCEA's First Two Decades

Jack Culbertson
Professor Emeritus
The Ohio State University

The University Council for Educational Administration

For information address:

 The University Council For Educational Administration
212 Rackley Building
University Park, Pennsylvania   16802-3200

Printed in the United States of America

ISBN 1-55996-159-7

Cover design by Robinson C. Smith.

To Mary Virginia, Margaret, Karen, and Douglas

For good or evil our interests and our erudition are grounded in the age in which we live, and the justice of our view of the past is moderated by the contemporary angle which can never be wholly removed.

Richard McKeon

Contents

Preface

During the twenty-two years I served as executive director of the University Council for Educational Administration (UCEA), at least a dozen professors suggested that I should eventually write a book on some aspect of the UCEA enterprise. Professors Richard Wynn and Willard Lane of the universities of Pittsburgh and Iowa, respectively, were the first to propose the idea. About 1969 Wynn encouraged me to do an historical study of the changes in training programs for school administrators which UCEA universities had wrought. About 1970 Lane, UCEA's immediate past president, noted that it was a "mystery" to him and to others how so many UCEA programs had emerged since the completion of the 1969-74 plan. He urged me to explain and illustrate how such programs were conceived, launched, and brought to fruition.

In 1981 Jean Hills of the University of British Columbia and I had a conversation about the meaning of "development" both in relation to UCEA professors and to their universities. We agreed that the functions of the developer differed markedly from those of the administrator. Near the end of the conversation Hills suggested that I use the UCEA experience to probe the problem more thoroughly. He proposed that the outcome might be a systematic treatment of the role of developers and a delineation of the functions they perform.

In between Wynn's and Lane's suggestions and that of Hills' were additional ones. More than one professor proposed that I write a book about the ablest UCEA leaders with whom I had worked. A few told me that a general history of UCEA needed to be written. One advocated that the crucial stages in UCEA's growth and maturation should be depicted and explained. The rise and fall of the "theory movement," the meaning of leadership in a far-flung organization of "elite" universities, and the problem of cooperatively navigating UCEA through seas of inter-university competition were other subjects which piqued the interests of leading UCEA professors.

When I left UCEA in June of 1981, I was more weary than I had

i

anticipated, and I was satiated with my two decades of intense experience there. My immediate motivation was to find renewal in a fresh domain of activity. In a post at The Ohio State University I found that desired domain in the field of history. In a newly developed course I focused upon the hundred-year quest (1875-1975) of school leaders and professors to achieve a sound knowledge base and to develop effective training programs for school administrators. I also studied the origins and development of school management as a field of practice. As I read about the early growth of school management in the Massachusetts Bay Colony, I identified a more general problem which fascinated me greatly, namely: how John Cotton, John Winthrop, and other colonial leaders employed divine, liberal arts, "scientific," and experiential knowledge to build a new community in the "Devil's Territories."

The idea of an historical study of UCEA lay dormant until 1988. Philip West of Texas A & M University caused me to re-consider the idea during a meeting of the National Council of Professors of Educational Administration (NCPEA) in Kalamazoo, Michigan. In our extended discussion he encouraged me to write the history. Stimulated by the conversation, I subsequently thought more carefully about undertaking the work. I had the commitment needed to take on the task. Yet I wondered if I had the requisite detachment to write about UCEA in ways which would meet reasonable standards of objectivity. Since I had had seven years to distance myself from the 1959-81 period, I decided to move ahead.

In fairness I should reveal that some professors have questioned my capacity to write an accurate account of UCEA's history. For example, when I told a small group about my plans, one individual, a former president of UCEA, responded skeptically, "Are *you* the one to write the history?" Certainly, the professor's question was relevant. During my long UCEA tenure I had faced considerable controversy and over time had opposed the views of many professors. Whether or not I could fairly treat views which were contrary to my own was a reasonable question. In writing the book I have kept in mind the professor's question.

Books inevitably reflect the biases of their authors—sometimes brightly and sometimes glimmeringly. In this book careful readers will recognize that my focus upon developments related to UCEA's official mission (i.e. the improvement of training programs for educational administrators) has caused me to concentrate more upon the dynamics of change than upon maintenance. If the book's dominant focus had been upon the dynamics of organizational maintenance, its story would have differed from the one told on the pages which follow.

A second example of bias is related to UCEA's major means for improving training, namely: knowledge. My critiques of the tenets underlying a hoped-for science of administration can be viewed as biased, since they are rooted in a humanistic rather than a scientific view of knowledge. This view has given me a fruitful perspective for detecting shortcomings inherent in scientific knowledge, in the same way that those who adhere to scientific tenets of knowledge are in a favorable position to identify weaknesses in my views.

I have sought to diminish the negative effects of bias in several ways. First, I have included, when feasible, interpretations of UCEA developments which are counter to my own. At various points, for instance, I have shown how the readings of UCEA events by professors departed from my own. I have also provided detailed descriptions of some of my major biases. In Chapter Twelve, for instance, I have delineated my beliefs about the nature of knowledge and how these beliefs meshed with my UCEA experiences. Finally, I have outlined in Chapter One selected pre-UCEA educational and professional experiences which have informed my outlook. Hopefully, this information will provide readers with insights into the perspectives which influenced my work at UCEA as well as the conclusions contained in this book.

While crafting the volume, I have intermittently reminded myself that those who write autobiographically are subject to the well-known human tendency to depict themselves more favorably than they depict others. This tendency is expressed in at least two ways: by the people, agencies, events, and conditions authors choose to treat, and by the way they interpret the chosen content. Although readers will undoubtedly find passages in this book which seem designed to serve the author's interests more than the general interest, I hope that such passages will be relatively few in number.

Since history is many-sided, and an author must choose one side for examination, every book's content is severely constrained by its focus. The study which follows looks at the practice of inter-university cooperation—a practice which the book clearly demonstrates can generate outcomes which have wide-ranging impacts. For almost seven decades dozens of higher education institutions have employed inter-institutional cooperation to pursue stipulated goals. Yet I am unaware of a published in-depth study of the cooperative work of a particular organization, although more general treatments of the subject are available. The twenty-two years I observed and participated in inter-institutional cooperation offers a time span sufficiently long in duration to warrant an in-depth study.

A prerequisite of inter-university cooperation was effective bridge building. In the end the most crucial bridges built were those which effectively linked knowledge to cooperative, inter-university practice. Notably, the practice of inter-university cooperation was one angle in a triangle of practices. The training of educational administrators in universities and the administration of educational organizations, especially schools, were the two other angles. The results of inter-university cooperation within UCEA could not be fully evaluated without probing the degree to which its outcomes affected training in universities. Chapter Four, for example, describes four rationales for incorporating content from the humanities into training programs. To evaluate these four rationales, which emanated from several UCEA development endeavors, I had to assess the degree to which scholars in universities used the rationales, and what impacts the uses had upon training programs. On the other hand, the rationales were all explicitly related to premises about the practice of administration. Thus, bridges had to be built between and among the three classes of practice.

Knowledge-action relationships differed for each of the three practices. Essential to the practice of inter-university cooperation were ideas which could give direction, form, and content to UCEA endeavors in research, development, and dissemination. Relevant to the practice of training were ideas and knowledge-based products (e.g. instructional materials) which could be used to update or re-design preparatory programs for administrators. Decisions about administrative practice were informed in part by educational and management ideas acquired from training experiences.

Before UCEA could construct bridges between knowledge and inter-university practice, it had to build antecedent bridges. Some had to be constructed between scholars as, for example: those which enabled professors of educational administration to mesh their diverse but related talents in ways which produced unified action; those which helped social scientists or experts in the humanities join with professors of educational administration in cooperative research, development, or dissemination programs; and those which brought together scholars and thoughtful practitioners from different nations in new developmental endeavors. Often bridges had to be built between and among already existing agencies before needed relations between knowledge and practice could be forged as, for example, those between UCEA universities and leading school systems. Sometimes UCEA had to create new agencies before needed bridges between knowledge and practice could be built. (See chapters Seven and Nine). Paradoxically, all bridges which facilitated cooperation had to be built within a context of intense inter-university competition.

The distinguished historian, Oscar Handlin, once observed: "It is difficult enough, and achievement enough, to get the record straight." The difficulty of constructing an accurate factual account from the written record is so vast that one can only strive to reach Handlin's ideal. In addition, when writers rely upon their memories and/or the memories of others for information, they must deal with another set of obstacles, as they strive "to get the record straight."

In my quest for accuracy I have stayed as close as I could to the written word. Fortunately, the information recorded about UCEA's actors, decisions, actions, publications, successes, and failures is relatively abundant. One day while taking stock of the numerous boxes of UCEA documents in my study, I remembered a remark made by a UCEA Executive Committee member in the 1970s. As he entered the room shortly before the Executive Committee meeting was to begin, he carried a bound volume of 185 pages of materials prepared largely by the UCEA staff. Holding the document aloft, the new committee member exclaimed, "I know that the Executive Committee members are supposed to be informed about the decisions they are to make, but this is ridiculous!" The volume apparently signaled to the UCEA decision-maker information "over-kill." Yet as I sought to understand UCEA's past, it and the scores of others like it constituted a prized bonanza. So did the numerous other documents about UCEA.

The book contains considerable information which is rooted in memory. One class of such information is that which I was relatively sure but not absolutely certain that I had remembered accurately. This class typically consisted of oral reports from secondary sources about individuals or events. While writing the book, for example, I remembered hearing early in my tenure that Hollis Moore, who had served as Executive Secretary of the Committee for the Advancement of School

Administration in the last half of the 1950s and the early 1960s, was the son of a Texas school superintendent. I also remembered someone telling me in the early sixties that the Australian professor, William Walker, had obtained his Ph.D. from the University of Illinois in 1958. In introducing readers to Hollis Moore and William Walker I wanted to use the information just noted. However, it was subject to two types of error. First, I might have remembered it inaccurately. Second, the reports I remembered could have been in error. When I wrote to Kenneth McIntyre of the University of Texas and to William Walker of the University of New England in New South Wales, I obtained evidence that the reports and my memories were in fact accurate.

As a rule, it was relatively easy to confirm or invalidate remembered information obtained from secondary sources about individuals or events. Sometimes I did encounter obstacles. I remembered that a well-known scholar had written an unpublished paper in the late 1960s for a seminar in Australia. Since I needed the paper, I called the author to see if he could send it to me. The scholar's initial responses when I described the paper's content, was that he had not written it. Fortunately, he later found it in his files and sent me a copy. Occasionally, the problems were such that the accuracy of remembered statements from secondary sources could not be validated. If I were relatively certain that my memories of such statements were correct, I tended to use them. I did so because of evidence gained from experience in validating remembered information. The accumulated evidence revealed that my recall of those statements, about which I was relatively sure I had remembered correctly, was usually accurate (four errors in 50 test cases).

Another class of information was that which I remembered but was uncertain of my memory's accuracy. For example, when I was writing Chapter Three, I needed to refer to the 1959-60 name of the University of Iowa's professional education unit. I was unsure whether the unit was a department or a college of education, although I leaned toward the former. However, when Iowa's Professor Jerry Kuhn wrote in August, 1989, he informed me that the unit was a college. By the time I had obtained experience in validating a dozen such cases, I knew that when I was uncertain about the correctness of a remembered item, it was often inaccurate. In such cases I used memories only as beginning points for further investigation.

The final class of information encompassed items I remembered, but whose accuracy I could not validate. Information of this type I typically obtained directly from experience rather than from oral reports about events or individuals. It was obtained largely from conversations and from group discussions. (e.g. meetings of the UCEA Board of Trustees). No audio or written records were developed about statements made or actions taken in such exchanges. In addition, many of the participants who produced the remembered items are no longer alive.

Included in the book, then, are numerous unvalidated reports of vividly remembered statements about individuals and events. Since psychologists have demonstrated that simplification, selectivity, and creativity can affect recall, I am sure that my reported memories suffer from some distortion. I have taken the precaution of including only those items which were the most deeply etched upon my memory. By sharing many of the memories over the years with UCEA associate directors and others, I have also reinforced and kept them alive.

Since the book's chapters are not all ordered chronologically, some comments about their sequencing and content are in order. In addition to describing briefly my early professional and educational background, Chapter One delineates: the opportunity UCEA afforded me in 1959, its problematic nature, and its attending conditions. Chapter Two depicts the origins of UCEA and describes the struggle UCEA's founders, who were among the field's most outstanding leaders, engaged in as they transferred an evolving dream into a reality. Chapters Three to Six, respectively, encompass the following time periods: 1959-64; 1964-69; 1969-74; and 1974-81. The four chapters describe selected UCEA programs enacted in the respective time periods, assess their effects, and explore why some succeeded while others failed. As a group, the chapters shed light on UCEA's life stages: beginnings, early development, growth, and institutionalization. Depictions of these stages are accompanied by information about the ever-changing professional and societal contexts which affected UCEA, its member universities, and its program offerings.

Chapters Seven, Eight, and Nine deal with large-scale programs whose durations extended beyond those encompassed in given five-year periods. The titles of the chapters highlight their content: "Reach Across the Seas," "The Monroe City Simulation," and "The Partnership." Chapters Ten, Eleven, and Twelve all cover the entire 1959-1981 period. Chapter Ten explores why and how UCEA's thirty associate directors contributed significantly to the continuing renewal of UCEA. Chapter Eleven describes and assesses UCEA's initial dual governance structures, the dissatisfactions which brought changes in these structures, and how governance decisions affected UCEA's programs. Chapter Twelve depicts some of the learnings acquired during my twenty-two year tenure at UCEA. These learnings relate, among other things, to inter-university cooperation and the problem of trust, to ethical decision-making, and to paradoxes I confronted as a user of knowledge.

Readers may wonder why certain UCEA programs are not featured in the book. Because of imposed limits on the book, criteria for including and excluding content had to be utilized. Only those activities which were directly related to public school administration made the final draft. Thus, such programs as UCEA's five year effort (1969-74) to improve the training of non-public school administrators, and its 1974-79 programs to advance the training of higher education leaders were eliminated. I also chose to include programs whose results shed light on perennial issues (e.g. the nature of theory, theory-practice relationships, the content of training programs, the role of the social sciences in inquiry). Strewn on UCEA's 1959-81 landscape were aborted programs, "still born" programs, uncompleted programs, and programs which suffered from "slippages." For the most part such endeavors are not included in the book. However, the whys and wherefores of program failures are probed at various points. In Chapter Three, for example, analyses are made of several aborted programs. In Chapter Eight an effort is made to explain why nine of nineteen development teams failed to achieve "Monroe City" simulations, while the remainder successfully did so.

I have received much help in crafting this book. I am especially indebted to several individuals and agencies for providing me copies of valued materials. I express much appreciation to Patrick Forsyth, Executive Director of the University Council for Educational Administration, and his staff for sending me more than 10,000 pages of copied source materials. Included were the minutes of all the 1959-81 meetings of the UCEA Interim Committee, the Board of Trustees, the Executive Committee, the Plenary Session, and the Partnership Co-ordinating Committee. Other examples of helpful items were UCEA five year plans, annual reports, and the voluminous materials prepared for UCEA's numerous governance meetings.

From Patrick Forsyth came another valuable service. Taking the two discs on which the manuscript was stored, he managed all the prosesses required to bring the book to fruition. I thank him and his staff for their good help.

I am also in debt to Robert Kinsinger, a former officer of the W. K. Kellogg Foundation, and to his staff. Through their help I received copies of all the 77 annual reports prepared in the 1950s by directors of the eight university centers responsible for the ten year, nationwide Cooperative Program in Educational Administration (CPEA). Without the annual reports and associated papers I could not have written a major part of the chapter, "Roots." Richard Miller, Executive Director of the American Association of School Administrators (AASA), and his staff also mailed me source materials which informed the "Roots" chapter. Containing descriptions of AASA's pioneering efforts to professionalize the school superintendency during the 1940s and 1950s, these primary sources not only added to my understanding but also spared me from repeating erroneous statements I had gleaned from published secondary sources. Thus, I am grateful to Richard Miller and his staff.

To my spouse, Mary Virginia, and my two daughters, Margaret and Karen, I express warm appreciation. As readers of the initial draft of the book, they provided numerous observations and analytical comments which enabled me to re-write unclear passages, alter awkwardly stated sentences, and add needed information. Their suggestions also helped me re-think certain portions of several chapters.

Three able professionals who read and reacted to the book's second draft deserve much approbation: Donald Willower, Professor of Educational Administration, Pennsylvania State University; Robin Farquhar, President, Carleton University in Ottawa, Canada; and H. Warren Button, a specialist in educational history at the University of Buffalo. The thoughtful critiques and the constructive suggestions provided by the three scholars were extremely helpful.

I am also grateful to a number of individuals who have read and provided suggestions for improving particular chapters. Offering detailed comments on the chapters, "Research Across the Seas," were the Australian leader and scholar, William Walker; Thomas Wiggins, Professor Emeritus, University of Oklahoma; and Patrick Lynch, Professor Emeritus, Pennsylvania State University. I also express appreciation to former UCEA associate directors who provided specific reactions to the chapter entitled "The Renewers:" Grace Butler, Vice

President, Faculty Affairs, University of Houston; Terry Eidell, Executive Director of the Appalachia Educational Laboratory; and Kenneth St. Clair, Professor Emeritus, Oklahoma State University.

I am indebted to Samuel Popper, Professor Emeritus of the University of Minnesota, for special assistance. A thorough reader and careful examiner of the penultimate draft of the manuscript, he offered me sound suggestions for improving the text—suggestions which I greatly appreciate, especially those in the section on the humanities in Chapter Four.

The combined list of those who have sent me fugitive papers, unpublished reports, re-prints, and vitas, and those who have responded to specific questions via extended memos, letters, and telephone conversations is a long one. Although I cannot recognize all of them individually, I can and do express appreciation to them as a group.

Although I express appreciation to those who have reacted to all or parts of the manuscript, I must assume full responsibility for whatever factual errors, flawed interpretations, or inaccurate generalizations appear on the pages of this book.

Personnel at UCEA's headquarters not only provided me bounteous assistance, but they also contributed indirectly to this book. The important work of UCEA's associate directors is recognized in Chapter Ten. The many Ohio State doctoral students who served as staff assistants also provided UCEA ideas and energetic actions. Thus, I give thanks to Richard George, the first assistant (1959-60), to Barbara Hurdzon, the last assistant (1975-76), and to all the others who served during the 1960-75 period. Those who typed letters and manuscripts, handled subscriptions for journals, shipped instructional materials, helped produce UCEA publications, and in many other ways enhanced UCEA's performance deserve recognition. Special appreciation is expressed to Harriet Ferrell who served as my secretary for most of my 22 years at UCEA. Others who worked for many years at UCEA were Sandy Conyers and Margaret Tossey. To them and to all the other clerical staff who advanced UCEA's work I offer sincere thanks.

Finally, I would be remiss if I did not share my deep feelings of gratitude to those in a much larger group, namely: the professors, graduate students, school administrators, and others who worked with me in many settings during the 1959-81 period to build, nurture, and sustain UCEA. Without their help and the support of the agencies they represented, there would be no history of UCEA to write.

1

An Unexpected Choice

"Two roads diverge in a wood, and I—I took the one less traveled by."

Robert Frost

Shortly before noon on May 22, 1959, after teaching a class in educational psychology at the University of Oregon, I strolled homeward. Six blocks later I arrived at a Dutch Colonial house situated near a picturesque millrace. Upon entering our barn-red home I greeted Mary Virginia, my wife, and spoke with our two daughters, Karen and Margaret, who were three and one year old, respectively. After a brief visit we seated ourselves around the dining table for a valued interlude of lunch and conversation.

During the previous days we had talked about the impending move from our home on the millrace to an apartment in far-away New York City. With the help of Paul Jacobson, Dean of the School of Education at the University of Oregon, I had obtained a leave of absence to spend 1959-60 at Teachers College, Columbia University. At Teachers College I was to work with Daniel Griffiths, Norman Fredriksen, and John Hemphill on the first research project sponsored by the budding University Council for Educational Administration (UCEA). With support from the U.S. Office of Education, the project's directors hoped to determine criteria which would differentiate successful from unsuccessful school principals.[1] Weeks earlier we had obtained an apartment near Teachers College for the upcoming year. More recently we had learned that a professor of economics from the University of Virginia, who planned to spend 1959-60 at the University of Oregon, hoped to occupy our home on the millrace.

Suddenly a ringing phone interrupted our conversation. On answering it, I learned that Walter Anderson, Dean of the School of

1

Education at New York University and President of the UCEA Board of Trustees, was calling. A very friendly man who was widely known in the field, Anderson had served as president of the Association for Supervision and Curriculum Development and the American Association of Colleges for Teacher Education, and as the elected head of the National Conference of Professors of Educational Administration (NCPEA).[2] Straightaway he reported that the Board of Trustees had decided earlier in the day to offer me the UCEA executive directorship post. Since I had never imagined, even in my most unfettered fancies, that the UCEA offer would come my way, I was dumb struck. Apparently sensing my difficulty, Anderson asked if I would like to speak to my dean, Paul Jacobson, who was a member of the UCEA Board of Trustees. Jacobson, who was unusually generous in helping members of his staff advance professionally, suggested that I look at the proffered position. When I expressed concern about my 1959-60 commitment to those at Teachers College, he assured me that Daniel Griffiths would release me from the obligation. At that point I decided to explore the opportunity.

Exploratory Conversations

Within ten days I flew eastward. My first stop was at the Columbus, Ohio, airport where John Ramseyer greeted me. Director of the Cooperative Program in Educational Administration (CPEA) at The Ohio State University, Ramseyer soon shared with me his deep interest in UCEA's future development. While I was dining with him and his wife, Zoa, at the Jai Lai Restaurant, he thoughtfully responded to my queries about UCEA problems and potentialities. Among other things, he described UCEA's recent move from Teachers College, Columbia, to Columbus, and noted that Ohio State would provide needed office space, furniture, equipment, and conference rooms. In subsequent months I learned that UCEA leaders selected the Columbus headquarters in part because of John Ramseyer. An altruistic individual who valued the cooperative ethic, he was esteemed by colleagues, both locally and nationally.

The next morning, after visiting UCEA's offices in Page Hall on the well-known "Oval," I left for Washington, D.C., where I spent several hours with Hollis Moore, Executive Secretary of the Committee for the Advancement of School Administration (CASA). Supported by the

W. K. Kellogg Foundation and sponsored by the American Association of School Administrators (AASA), the Committee, among other things, disseminated information about research and training accomplishments attained by leaders in the eight CPEA centers. Housed in higher education institutions, the eight centers reached from Harvard to Stanford and from the University of Texas to the University of Chicago. The son of a Texas school superintendent and a former associate editor of *The Nation's Schools*, Moore was recognized as an aggressive young leader knowledgeable about developments in the field.

An ex officio member of UCEA's Board of Trustees, Moore was well informed about the new organization. As an outsider, he could more easily be critical of UCEA than could insiders. In selecting members, the UCEA Board, he contended, had looked more favorably on eastern than on western universities. In 1958 the Board had selected 33 universities, and in 1959 had added another. Five were far western universities: California at Berkeley, California at Los Angeles, Oregon, Stanford, and Washington State. Only one was selected from the Rocky Mountain area (Colorado), one from the Plains region (Nebraska), and one from the southwest (Texas). Six were southern institutions: Auburn, Florida, Georgia Peabody, Kentucky, North Carolina, and Virginia. The midwest claimed ten universities: Chicago, Illinois, Iowa, Michigan, Michigan State, Minnesota, Missouri, Northwestern, Ohio State, and Wisconsin. Ten appeared on the eastern list: State University of New York at Buffalo, Columbia (Teachers College), Harvard, New York University, Pennsylvania, Pennsylvania State, Pittsburgh, Rutgers, Syracuse, and Temple. Even though the bulk of the nation's population resided east of the Mississippi River, Moore argued that the west was under-represented.

Although Moore believed that UCEA could have a positive influence on training, he wondered if the elite universities in UCEA could effectively address the immediate and on-going needs of school administrators. He emphasized that the new director of UCEA would encounter difficulties. Yet he encouraged me to accept the post. He also assured me that CASA would be supportive of UCEA's efforts.

On the following morning I met with Finis Engleman, Executive Secretary of the AASA. Having served as a school administrator, a college president, and a state commissioner of education, Finis not only appreciated the practice and study of school administration, but also had a keen interest in improving both of them. Aware that he had played a role in the early discussions of UCEA, I solicited his views about the organization's potential. His reactions, though brief, were largely positive. At the end of the conversation he assured me that if I should decide to take the position, he would discuss matters more fully during the summer, since he had agreed to teach courses at the University of Oregon in July and August.

In late morning I left Washington for New York City to visit with professors at Teachers College, Columbia—UCEA's original home. Leaders there, especially Daniel Davies, had led in articulating the need for UCEA and had helped nurture national support for its development. With the assistance of staff at Teachers College, UCEA had already sponsored two national seminars for professors, one at The University of Chicago, on administrative theory, and the other at Harvard, on the case method of instruction.

On reaching Teachers College, I learned that John Norton, head of the Department of Educational Administration and Guidance, was preparing to leave for the airport. Director of the Research Division of the National Education Association earlier in his career, he had also led in establishing the influential Educational Policies Commission in the 1930s. His secretary suggested that I come immediately to his office.

When I arrived, he informed me that he only had five minutes. Waving me toward a comfortable chair behind his desk, he seated himself near the door. Pointing his finger at me, he energetically observed: "Young man, the field cannot move ahead unless professionals are willing to stick their necks out." His initial observation served as a text for a vivid, five-minute sermonette. Beginning with the thesis that younger professionals were too concerned about personal security, he concluded by stressing the virtues of risk-taking. He then rose abruptly, shook hands, and quickly made his way out the door. As he departed, I was disappointed that I had not obtained his views about the questions which I had brought to his office. At the same time I recognized that his message, though unsought and unexpected, was relevant to my impending decision.

When I went to see Daniel Davies, coordinator of the CPEA Center at Teachers College, I learned that he was out of town. As an undergraduate major in physics and chemistry at Harvard, he had obtained his B.A. in 1933. Caught in the Great Depression, he obtained a teacher's certificate at St. Thomas College in Scranton, Pennsylvania, and began to teach. After obtaining an Ed.D. degree from Teachers College,

Columbia, in 1946, he became a professor there. Because he was an active CPEA, NCPEA, and UCEA leader, his absence disappointed me.

After leaving Davies' office I contacted Daniel Griffiths' secretary who assured me that Dan would see me the next day. Already a well-known author, Griffiths had joined the staff in educational administration at Teachers College in 1956, after serving at the New York State College for Teachers at Albany for four years. From 1957 to 1959 he had worked part-time as Director of Research for UCEA. A former high school teacher of mathematics and science, and an instructor in the course, "Problems of Physical Science," at Colgate University, he saw in UCEA a means for making research more scientific, and training programs more rigorous. Highly critical of established training and research practices, he spoke optimistically about UCEA.

At the end of our visit I asked Dan a question which had puzzled me when I was assessing impressions gleaned from previous explorations. UCEA's executive director, I had concluded, would face two over-riding, though related challenges. On the one hand, there was the intellectual challenge of understanding the substantive research and training issues in the field, and of helping conceptualize needed goals and programs. On the other, there was the political challenge inherent in the conflicting expectations of leaders within and without the geographically far-flung universities which comprised UCEA. Thus, I asked Dan whether he thought the challenge of UCEA would be more substantive or more political. He smiled faintly, thought for a few seconds, and answered: "Both." Although his answer was an uncharacteristically equivocal one, I accepted it at face value. However, the issue continued to puzzle me. I was concerned more about whether I could deal effectively with the political dimensions of UCEA than about whether I could address its substantive problems.

Education as Preparation

As I flew homeward, I wondered more than once why the UCEA Board of Trustees had asked me to become the organization's executive director. In a way it seemed incongruous that an assistant professor should be expected to take on what seemed to be an imposing responsibility. During the journey I thought about my previous educational and professional experiences and about their implications for my impending decision.

My formal education had begun in the Appalachian foothills of southwest Virginia in a one-room school. After moving from one grade to another with some "skips" along the way, I finally graduated from Nickelsville High School, along with six other seniors. In the fall of 1935 I enrolled at Emory and Henry College, where I studied professional education, psychology, and related subjects for two years. When I had completed "practice teaching" in the spring of 1937, I applied for a "Normal Professional Certificate." Upon receiving the certificate from the state, I possessed the formal certification needed to begin a teaching career.

After spending five years as a teaching principal in five different elementary schools in two southwest Virginia counties, I returned to Emory and Henry to complete the requisite work for a B.A. degree. Very soon I began for the first time to become a serious student. Subjects I found especially stimulating were English literature, psychology, and the history of education. The most appealing of all the subjects I studied were French and German, especially the latter. Undergirding my interest in languages was the deep respect I had for Professor "Harry" Garnand, the college's most popular language instructor. After conversing with him one day in his large, book-filled office, I decided that I wanted eventually to become a professor of languages.

At Emory and Henry I capitalized on an array of learning opportunities outside the formal classroom. Shortly after my return to the college, for instance, I began to participate in the Hermesian Literary Society, an organization which sponsored student debates and extemporaneous speaking. Several months later I found myself on the debating team and began traveling to colleges in the region to address the issue of the year: resolved that a United Nations Association should be established. At one stop the team would debate the positive side of the question and at another the negative. I found it much more challenging to argue the negative side of the issue.

Following my debating experiences, members of the honorary forensic fraternity, Tau Kappa Alpha, invited me to join the organization. During the two-week period of initiation, some of the most vivid events of my years at Emory and Henry occurred. I was unexpectedly asked, for instance, to make a fifteen-minute extemporaneous speech to the fraternity's members on "The Effects of the Gargoyles of Notre Dame de Paris on Continental Morals." While ascending the podium to talk about "effects", I recognized the challenge before me: I did not know what a gargoyle was! Bravely plunging ahead, I persevered for fifteen minutes. At the end Woodrow Flanary, a lecturer and advisor of the fraternity, wryly remarked: "Now I know what filibustering is." So did I!

After graduation I taught high school mathematics and biology for one year and then entered Duke University to study German and French and to prepare for a teaching career in higher education. Since I had obtained an assistantship in the German department, I had the opportunity to work closely with Professor Clement Vollmer, who headed the program. Initially, I found myself at a disadvantage, since he conducted all of his classes in German. The three courses I had taken at Emory and Henry, which had emphasized reading more than speaking, left me ill-prepared to follow class discussions. Fortunately, I got acquainted with George Grasty, a fellow student, who later taught German at the University of California in Los Angeles. At meal times each day we conversed in German. A fluent speaker of the language, he helped me greatly to get up to speed.

As I progressed in the study of literature, I came in contact with German thinkers whose writings stimulated my interest in philosophy. The works of Johann Friedrich Schiller, for example, helped me begin to think seriously, for the first time, about esthetic and moral issues. When I chose a problem for the M.A. thesis early in the second year, I decided to examine the origins and development of Schiller's esthetic-moral ideas, especially his proposition that beauty can make human beings more moral. While writing the thesis, I studied the philosophy of esthetics with Professor Katherine Gilbert. That year I also discovered that issues bearing upon the nature of knowledge challenged and puzzled me immensely.

Several months before I had completed the M.A. degree, I began to doubt whether I wanted to devote my life to the teaching of languages. As I delved into philosophy, I found myself interested more in pursuing substantive issues than in mastering the languages in which the issues were embedded. The study of problems related to knowledge took me into the domain of psychology, a field which, for good reasons, had first resided in departments of philosophy. After several months of uncertainty about what I should do, I enrolled in the department of psychology where I began the third year of my education at Duke. During the year I also taught German to students who were pursuing doctorates in such fields as math, history, philosophy, and psychology, and who were preparing for language exams.

Duke's department of psychology was blessed with outstanding professors. Donald Adams and Karl Zener had studied with Kurt Lewin and other Gestalt psychologists in Germany. As translators of eight of Lewin's seminal papers, they had led in diffusing the great psychologist's early theories and experimental studies into the United States.[3] Both were committed Gestalt psychologists and were great admirers of Kurt Lewin. As the senior faculty members, they strongly influenced the intellectual climate of the department. When Kurt Lewin, then a professor at the University of Iowa, died about mid-year, Duke's stunned staff members were saddened; they had lost an irreplaceable friend, and their field had lost one of its most creative scholars.

The most exciting course I took was on systems of psychology. Taught by Sigmund Koch, 29 years of age and a brilliant scholar, the course spanned functional, Gestalt, psychoanalytic, associationist, and behavioral psychology. Koch was already planning a multi-volume work on psychology which he would later edit. A highly critical thinker, he aspired to assess the idea of psychology as a science. Envisaging a large-scale project, he wanted leading scholars to address issues which transcended individual systems of psychology. Among other things, he hoped to show that the core generalizations offered by diverse schools of thought were similar in meaning, though stated in different technical languages.[4] The meanings of motivation in the differing systems, for instance, were comparable, he presumed, though stated in different jargon.

In the course on systems of psychology Professor Koch asked each student to select a system, to choose one of its outstanding representatives, and then to do a critique of the major works of the chosen representative. I decided to study the system elaborated by Kurt Lewin. His thought appealed to me for two reasons. First, he, more than other distinguished psychologists, had thought carefully about the nature of knowledge. For example, he had studied the uses physical scientists had made of scientific theory and method, and had elaborated some of the implications for his field. The second reason for my choice was that the Gestalt conception, as compared to the conceptions of other systems, seemed more encompassing and defensible. Yet I could not help but question the optimistic belief of Gestalt psychologists that they could achieve a science of human behavior.

When I read Lewin's monograph on *The Conceptual Representation and the Measurement of Psychological Forces,* I was taken by the range of his theoretical formulations, by his extensive use of symbolic logic, and by his employment of deductive thinking. That he valued theory highly and saw in physics the ideals needed to guide psychological research is evident in the following passage (Lewin, 1938, p.4):

> Psychology at the moment is rich with more or less new 'general approaches.' However, more important for psychology today than general approaches is the development of a type of 'Theoretical Psychology' which has the same relations to 'Experimental Psychology' that 'Theoretical Physics' has to 'Experimental Physics.'

While writing the paper for Professor Koch I was unaware that Duke's psychology department was strongly influenced by the scientific philosophy which Herbert Feigl, fifteen years earlier, had labeled "logical positivism." More than thirty years later, while studying the impact of logical positivism upon the social sciences and the field of educational administration, I came to see that psychologists were more influenced by the tenets of the new philosophy than were sociologists and political scientists. Further, the psychologists, Clark Hull and Kurt Lewin, had constructed the most elegant and advanced hypothetico-deductive systems in their field—systems which were the hallmarks of logical positivism. I also learned that Kurt Lewin was a member of the Society for Scientific Philosophy (Gesellschaft fuer wissenschaftliche Philosophie) in Berlin, at the same time that Rudolph Carnap, Herbert Feigl, Otto Neurath, and other scholars in Vienna were elaborating the propositions of logical positivism (Joergensen, 1951, p.48). The views of science which emanated from Berlin and Vienna were closely linked. However, since Lewin's views, in contrast to those of the Vienna scholars, were tempered by much experimental work, his philosophy of science was less grandiose than the more famous one spawned in Vienna.

The brand of psychology I studied quenched to some degree my thirst for greater insight into epistemological issues. However, my experiences at Duke, while intellectually exciting, led me to a far-reaching decision. After considerable introspection, I realized that the application of ideas was for me more satisfying than simply studying them. The time had come, I decided, to turn away from the pursuit of psychology and philosophy. My immediate inclination was to return to public school work. However, when Professor Vollmer informed me that Marshall College was looking for an instructor in German, I reluctantly applied for the post. Following a long bus ride, I discussed the position with Marshall professors. After rejecting the proffered post, I retraced my steps, some months later, to another teaching principalship in Tazewell County, Virginia.

In August, 1949, after spending two years as a teaching principal in Tazewell County in southwest Virginia, I moved across the continent to a junior high school in El Centro, California. At the end of my first year as a California teacher, I opted to attend summer school at the University of California in Berkeley. I also learned that the College of the Pacific (now the University of the Pacific) was offering a one-week philosophy institute at Lake Tahoe, Nevada, just prior to the Berkeley summer school. Since the event's theme appealed to me, I enrolled immediately. When I arrived, scholars from Deweyan, Thomist, personalistic, and other schools of thought were ready to present their perspectives. One unexpected but useful activity was summarizing on a three-by-five card the essence of each of the assigned essays we read during the week. I also well remember luncheon conversations with faculty members, especially with T. V. Smith, a provocative thinker and former congressman, who was a professor of poetry, politics, and philosophy at Syracuse University.

An unforeseen but fateful event occurred on the second day of the institute. At 8:15, while standing in the breakfast line, I met Mary Virginia Pond, my spouse-to-be. Appropriately, the institute's theme was "Human Destiny"! When the two of us attended subsequent sessions at Lake Tahoe, the director always introduced us as a living example of what a philosophy institute could do for its enrollees!

In the fall of 1953 I left my administrative post in Santa Barbara County, California, which I had held for two years, and entered the doctoral program in school administration at Berkeley. Serving as an assistant to the able and distinguished professors, Theodore Reller and Edgar Morphet, was the highlight of the first year. As an assistant I performed such tasks as preparing exams, evaluating them, reading term papers, and conferring with students enrolled in a "core" course on school administration. The course, which lasted throughout the year, attracted approximately 65 students. Focusing upon problems and issues, it encompassed such topics as vocational education, private schooling, church-state relationships, curriculum, personnel administration, educational governance, and school finance. I learned much from observing the differing styles of Reller and Morphet, both of whom were outstanding teachers. Reller was an articulate and enthusiastic lecturer, while Morphet leaned more toward group discussion. As a listener to lectures, a reader of numerous references, and a participant-observer in the discussions, I acquired new insights into administration.

During the first year at Berkeley the resident students launched an informal weekly seminar with encouragement from Professor Howard Bretsch. At the end of each session we determined the problem to be addressed at the next session. Usually one or two students were responsible for introducing the problem to be examined. Sometimes we chose to visit educational settings in the area. I remember well a discussion we had in Palo Alto with Ralph Tyler, Director of the Center for Advanced Study in the Behavioral Sciences. Through the informal seminar we learned much from one another.

My colleagues in the doctoral program were usually able students. Two individuals I remember well were Paul Lapp and John Corbally. When Paul Lapp arrived at Berkeley from the Lutheran Synod in St. Louis, he had already acquired a Master's degree in education and a divinity degree. Possessor of a restless mind, he was often seen reading theological treatises immediately before the start of classes. After two years at Berkeley he completed the Ph.D. at the age of 22 and then enrolled in the Semitic language program at Johns Hopkins University. Two years later he obtained his second doctorate and accepted a post at Harvard.

John Corbally enrolled at Berkeley after serving as a teacher and high school principal in the state of Washington. As one of the 65 students in the course in which I served as an assistant, he quickly demonstrated his abilities. In fact, the staff suggested that he exit the course at the end of the first semester and take work in disciplines outside the school of education. After completing the Ph.D. degree, he joined the department of educational administration at The Ohio State University. About 1960 he moved into university administration at Ohio State where he held a variety of leadership posts. Later he served as president of two higher education institutions: Syracuse University and the University of Illinois.

Some of the Berkeley experiences deepened my interest in the complex problems of preparing educational leaders. A conference on "Related Disciplines and the Study and Teaching of Educational Administration" proved to be very exciting. Sponsored by the Stanford

Cooperative Program in Educational Administration (CPEA) and implemented by Professor Reller, the conference featured papers, for example, by Harvard and Oregon social scientists on the "Bay City" and
"Valley City I" studies, respectively. For the first time I clearly saw how
the social sciences could be used to study problems of the field.
Professors and students at Berkeley also had opportunities to discuss
issues with their counterparts at Stanford. At one of the sessions I
offered a paper on needed improvements in preparatory programs. In
my second year, with encouragement from Edgar Morphet, I prepared
a paper on "The Problem of Certifying School Administrators" for
participants in a Western States conference on "Certification."

In the spring of 1954 the University of Oregon CPEA Center invited
Stanford and Berkeley each to nominate a graduate student to participate in its two interdisciplinary seminars scheduled for the upcoming
summer. When Professor Reller asked if I could participate, I immediately said, "Yes." I was not disappointed. The two seminars, in
different ways, provided unique opportunities to think seriously about
the uses of the social sciences in the practice and the study of educational administration.

One of the seminars dealt with administrative behavior. Typically
staffed by a clinical psychologist, a sociologist or political scientist, a
professor of business or public administration, and Paul Jacobson,
Dean of the School of Education, the seminar featured the case method
of instruction. As the students and professors analyzed cases from
diverse perspectives, the prominent role which values played in decision-making was tellingly displayed. The experience caused me to
question whether the so-called "is-ought" dichotomy, which I had read
about the previous year at Berkeley, could be maintained in social
science inquiry. Because the case method encouraged the application
of knowledge, it strongly appealed to me. The seminar enabled me to
observe how social scientists brought to bear their concepts and methods upon problems of practice.

The second seminar, which focused upon the scope and the methods of the social sciences, was usually staffed by an economist, a
sociologist, a social psychologist, a political scientist, an anthropologist,
and by Donald Tope, Director of the Oregon CPEA Center. Aimed at
providing students an overview of the basic concepts and methods of
the social sciences, the seminar featured lectures, small-group discussions, and extensive readings. Its wide-ranging content proved to be

stimulating. It also helped me identify issues related to the use of social science content in training programs. I wondered, for example, which of the many social science concepts were of greatest value to prospective educational leaders, and whether criteria could be developed to separate the more valuable from the less valuable ones.

At the end of the summer Paul Jacobson invited me to his office and noted that the staff, after observing me during the summer, had concluded that I "was a bright young man." He suggested that I do the dissertation research on my return to Berkeley and then join the faculty in school administration at the University of Oregon. One idea we discussed was that I might take the lead in writing a book based upon the case method as used in the interdisciplinary seminar on administrative behavior. The idea, which was closely linked to my pedagogical and research interests, stirred my imagination.

The most important learnings of the last year at Berkeley came from the dissertation experience. In my readings I had found that administrators typically spend as much as three-fourths of their time preparing, receiving, interpreting, and transmitting messages. This finding stimulated me to think about a dissertation topic. To expand my understandings I read references on semantics, rumor analysis, two-person communication, small group processes, organizational communication, mass communication, non-verbal communication, and cybernetics. After several false starts, I undertook, with the aid of my dissertation advisor, Howard Bretsch, to evaluate selected methods for studying organizational communication within a large city high school. Utilizing the "living in" technique, I spent a minimum of six hours a day in the school for a period of more than three months. During the summer of 1955 the dissertation committee members approved the results. Having accepted Paul Jacobson's offer of an assistant professorship some months earlier, Mary Virginia and I readied ourselves to return to the University of Oregon.

My formal education had provided opportunities, then, to study such varied subjects as languages, philosophy, psychology, the social sciences, education, and school administration. Even though I had moved from one field to another and had delayed a firm fix on a career goal, I did not feel I had wasted time. My encounters with diverse subject matters likely buttressed the belief that I could cope with substantive issues within the UCEA context.

The Issue of Professional Experience

Although I had acquired wide-ranging teaching, administrative and professional experiences in diverse settings, they seemed less pertinent to the projected UCEA role than did the educational experiences described above. In 1937 I had begun my career as a teaching principal in a two-room elementary school in the Appalachian foothills of southwest Virginia, the place of my birth. As principal, I taught fourth, fifth, sixth, seventh, and eighth grade students, while Jesse Lee Boatright, my colleague, taught "primer," first, second, and third grade students. Aptly called Riverview, the school rested less than sixty feet from a hundred foot wide river which more than once, after periods of heavy rain, threatened to drive us from the building.

As the second day of school ended, a group of parents appeared. They were very concerned that some of their children had graduated from Riverview the previous year but could not continue their schooling. The closest high school was ten miles distant from the Riverview community. Since they did not want their children to walk 20 miles daily, especially in wintry weather, they asked if I would teach a "special" eighth grade class. When I explained that work in such a class could not later be transferred to another school, they were not deterred. As an eager young teacher, I acceded to their entreaty. They then promised to pay me a dollar a month for each student taught. When four students enrolled later in the week, my sixty-dollar-a-month salary was boosted by seven percent! One of the new students was 15 years old, another 16, one 17, and the fourth 18, while I, five weeks earlier, had turned 19.

For one who had labored on a farm from an early age, the experiences gained in the rural Riverview community were indeed exhilarating. Trying to teach effectively more than 30 dissimilar students each day proved to be more challenging than suckering tobacco, shocking wheat, or shucking corn. Living from Monday to Friday each week throughout the year with one of Riverview's respected families provided a special window on the community and its people. I became acquainted with many Riverview parents, and occasionally I had "supper" and stayed over night in the home of a student. Even though the teaching was marred by my inexperience, the community seemed to appreciate it. I was especially touched on the last school day in December, when every student brought me a Christmas gift.

Fortunately, from my perspective, Scott County officials assigned me to a different two-room school in each of my first four years of teaching. From Riverview I went to Lane, then to Mt. Hagan, and finally to Strongs. In all cases I was a teaching principal. Understanding another community each year, familiarizing myself with a group of students I had not met, and getting acquainted with a set of parents I had not seen were enjoyable experiences. Each community offered its own opportunities. In one locality I worked as a clerk in a country store from 3:30 to 6:30 p.m., Monday through Friday, and in another I spent a similar time period in a country store competing with the community's best checkers players.

As I traveled homeward each week for fours years, I became more familiar with parts of my native county. When I left Mt. Hagan, for instance, I walked twelve miles westward before reaching my father's farm. However, when I left Strongs each Friday in the subsequent year, I traveled northeast for eleven miles. As I walked homeward past scattered houses, I enjoyed seeing the hills, rivers, creeks, and springs. I also observed barking dogs, multi-colored birds, startled rabbits, and running colts. During the return walks on Sunday, I saw many of the same sights but from another direction.

After four years in Scott County I moved to the nearby county, Tazewell, and became a teaching principal of a six-room school. There I had my first opportunity to experience life in a small town. Located on top of a tall ridge, the town possessed a school, church, teacherage, physician's office, store, restaurant, and bowling alley, all located within 300 yards of each other. Elizabeth Fox, one of the bright seventh-grade students there, after accidentally discovering my address thirty years later, would write that she had obtained a doctoral degree and was a professor at the University of Alabama.

The teaching and administrative experiences gained in the five diverse communities of two Virginia counties broadened my horizons. As a central link between and among students, teachers, and parents, I had many learning opportunities. I observed that most parents in all five communities placed a special value on schooling, even though their own education was generally limited. Most were eager to see their children obtain a sound education. Convinced that schooling was a very significant enterprise, I firmly decided to devote my life to the field of education. Toward that end, after five formative years of experience, I left the county, though not permanently, to complete work for a B.A. degree at Emory and Henry College.

After attaining the degree, I went to Winston-Salem, North Caro-lina, and began teaching biology and math in a large suburban high school. I found myself in a setting which differed radically from the ones I had experienced in the Appalachian foothills. For the first time each morning I had available a newspaper and each day a range of options afforded by movie theaters, libraries, city transportation, and other urban offerings. The attitudes of my adolescent students differed markedly from those of the rural students I had known earlier. They were more likely to challenge the teacher's authority. Nor did I hear parents call me "professor", as I had in rural Virginia.

For unknown reasons, on a wintry night in 1944, the Mineral Springs High School burned to the ground. Administrators, teachers, and students were faced with a crisis. However, in a couple of weeks carpenters had partitioned the high school gymnasium into small classrooms. Thus, schooling soon resumed, though in two daily shifts. Inevitably, the learning of the students suffered. Nevertheless, the experience demonstrated that citizens and educators could adapt quickly to unexpected and destructive circumstances.

Shortly after the fire occurred, I obtained a job working from three to eleven on Saturdays in a local radar factory. Laboring on one of several mass production lines, along with more than two dozen others, I took part in making, assembling, and packaging radar parts. The tasks were routine and therefore not very edifying. However, the environ-ment in which I worked fascinated me. I enjoyed observing and interacting with those who were engaged in processes of production. More valuable were opportunities to see factory managers function as trouble shooters and as supervisors.

After teaching one year at the Mineral Springs High School, I entered Duke University to study for the Master's degree. Following my work at Duke and two additional years in Tazewell County, Virginia, as a teaching principal, I moved to California where I taught social studies at the Wilson Junior High School in El Centro. Located in the desert about 12 miles north of the Mexican border, the city afforded novel surroundings with its hot summer temperatures, rare rainfalls, and unusual flowers and foliage.

I was struck by the diversity of the city's people. During my two-year stay in El Centro I met only two adults who were native-born citizens of the city. Represented among the 180 students I taught were Caucasians, Mexican Americans, African Americans, Chinese, Japanese,

Korean, and other Orientals. In teaching and managing six highly heterogeneous groups each day, I had to use all the wit, skill, and knowledge I possessed. In fact, my two years of instructing El Centro's eighth graders proved to be the most demanding teaching assignment of my life. At the same time I had rewarding opportunities to work with a well educated and able staff in a school system which supplied teachers with an array of books, films, and other teaching materials.

Having decided I needed experience working with a school board before I entered a doctoral program, I drove to Los Angeles during my second year to visit with placement personnel in the California Teachers Association. After I explained my objective, the counselor asked if I could wait some years for a superintendency or was I "in a hurry?" When I indicated I wanted to move quickly, he suggested that I seek a post in one of California's small school districts. When I accepted his advice, he agreed to assist me in obtaining a position. In the spring of 1951 I traveled to Santa Barbara County to interview for a superintendency-principalship in the Ellwood Union School District. Following the interview the school board offered me the position which I accepted.

Working with the district's school board from 1951 to 1953 proved to be enlightening. Among the board members I remember best were a housewife who was intensely interested in the district's welfare; an executive of the Signal Oil Company who had very firm views about schooling; and a farmer who owned much land and had a large family. Because of its oil deposits and fertile farm lands the district was a very wealthy one. However, the expenditure decisions of the school board were, by my lights, conservative. As independent thinkers, the board members did not hesitate to reject my recommendations. I soon learned the importance of discussing the major elements of proposals with board members before formalizing them.

After acquiring the doctorate from the University of California in Berkeley in 1955, I accepted an assistant professorship in the School of Education at the University of Oregon. My four years of university experience differed markedly from that acquired in public school settings. Since I taught only two or three classes daily, I spent most of the time as a student. As I prepared to teach such varied courses as educational psychology, school finance, supervision, administrative behavior, and curriculum, I read extensively. As a writer of articles and crafter of a book, I became immersed in large bodies of literature. In helping prepare the book, for instance, I spent months investigating the history of the case method and its uses in law, business, and public administration. In designing a new course on the "Theory and Practice of Communication," I read works in many disciplines. Thus, students during the first week of the course discussed the simple semantic theses in Irving Lee's book, *How to Talk with People*, while in the last week they probed the complex ideas about cybernetics, elaborated by Norbert Wiener in *The Human Use of Human Beings*.

Leading the inter-disciplinary seminar on administrative behavior each summer was the most cherished professional experience the University of Oregon provided me. Not only did I have copious opportunities to learn about the case method of instruction, but I also gained new insights into the relationships between and among administrative facts, social science concepts, and societal values. Both types of learning were linked to my deep interest in applying knowledge to problems of practice. Certainly, the social scientists who served as staff members for the seminar extended and deepened my education. I remember well, for example, the teaching style exhibited by Robert Dubin. An eminent sociologist and author of the highly influential *Human Relations in Administration*, he was a thoughtful analyst and a skillful provocateur of group discussion.

The locations, the contexts, and the content of my professional experiences, then, were varied. A practitioner in diverse settings, I had taught in four states, in three widely-separated regions, and in rural and suburban schools. Having instructed elementary, junior high, senior high, undergraduate, and graduate students, I had worked at all levels of education. I had also acquired some administrative experience along the way. Yet the experiences I had obtained seemed far removed from those projected in the UCEA context. I presumed, in other words, that UCEA's national environment would differ substantially from the local settings in which I had worked, and that UCEA functions, particularly the political ones, would deviate sharply from those I had previously performed. Thus I was uneasy about my ability to cope with the political dimensions of UCEA.

Making the Decision

When I landed in Eugene, Oregon, following the long flight from New York, I was confronted with two inharmonious tendencies. On the one hand, I was emotionally excited by the UCEA prospect. The potential and uncertainty of the projected endeavor offered an immense challenge. On the other hand, when I thought about the task of developing and leading a new national organization, I became more cautious. While my emotions were pushing me strongly toward the new position, my thoughts were causing me to hesitate.

After recounting my experiences and ideas about the previous week's events to Mary Virginia, I asked for her thoughts on the choice before us. She emphasized that the impending decision should be made on the basis of what would be most professionally rewarding. In other words, if I chose to accept the position, she would be supportive. Her response, as I saw it, was a generous one. Acceptance of the post would require her to move away from friends in the pleasant setting of Eugene and to leave behind a western family heritage which reached back to the California Gold Rush and spanned four generations.

When I reported my experiences to Paul Jacobson, he asked if I planned to accept the position. I indicated that I was leaning in that direction, but that I wanted to consider it for a few more days. If I did take the post, Dean Jacobson suggested that he could get me a two-year leave of absence. Noting that there was a risk in the UCEA opportunity, and that the building of a new institution was not an easy endeavor, he stressed that an extended leave would provide me good insurance. Little did I realize at the time that seven years later I would still be on leave from the University of Oregon!

In the next few days I talked about the new post with a number of professors, including Vincent Ostrom, a political scientist. An active and able participant in the Oregon CPEA Center, he had worked during the 1950s with students and professors of educational administration on a number of research endeavors. When I told him about the new opportunity, he asked if I had reservations about it. I noted that I was unsure about my capacities to deal with the political aspects of the new endeavor. My uncertainty, he replied, was understandable, given the special character of the new organization. However, he emphasized that there was only one way to answer the question meaningfully, namely: to accept the post and to test my political savvy in future UCEA endeavors. His response, which was undoubtedly influenced by his strong commitment to John Dewey's pragmatic philosophy, was for me a liberating one.

Another person I sought out was Egburt Wengert, a professor of public administration who was very familiar with the Inter-University Case Development Program in his field. During the past several years he had often assisted me, especially in relation to the case book I was preparing with the help of Paul Jacobson and Theodore Reller. After I described my impending career choice, he stressed that promoting cooperation among professors and institutions of higher education was an important and needed function. In his own field beneficial outcomes had come, he attested, from inter-university cooperation. Although he encouraged me to accept the position, he did so with a definite qualification, namely: that I should not remain in the post for more than four or five years. Although inter-university cooperation had high value, higher education institutions, he explained, had not yet found ways to reward adequately those who promoted and advanced it. The major rewards, he contended, still went to effective competitors. At the time I did not fully understand his observations. However, later when I saw more clearly the dominant role which competition played in university life and in relations between universities, I understood his point. Yet I also found that cooperation had its own rewards.

Before the week ended I told Paul Jacobson I would accept the two-year leave. During the summer I served as co-ordinator of the inter-disciplinary seminar on "Administrative Behavior" for the last time. Early in August I also finished the final work on the book, *Administrative Relations: A Case Book*. The summer was filled with considerable emotional turmoil. On the one hand, I frequently felt sad about the prospect of leaving the university, colleagues with whom I was working, and students whom I was teaching. On the other hand, I was so excited about impending tasks that I had trouble at times concentrating on immediate ones. I continued to find time to think about potential UCEA objectives and projects. In mid-summer I arranged a brain-storming session in which Finis Engleman, Paul Jacobson, Donald Tope, and Keith Goldhammer participated. In July I also selected William Coffield, an associate professor of education at Auburn University, to serve as UCEA's first associate director.

In mid-August Margaret, Karen, Mary Virginia, and I, after seeing our belongings loaded into a moving van, drove eastward. Traveling through the mountains and deserts of Oregon, into and through Idaho, and over the Rockies, we reached the Great Plains and, thereafter, made our way through Nebraska, Iowa, Missouri, Illinois, Indiana, and Western Ohio to Columbus. As we departed Eugene, we were not in a joyous mood. We were keenly aware that we were putting a great distance between ourselves and our immediate friends. Adding to our family's dismay was another event. A few hours earlier we had given our cherished family dog, "Buddy," to an Oregonian. Yet as we made our way eastward on a road we had never traveled, we saw new sights. On arriving in Columbus I felt that even more novel and expansive vistas lay ahead.

Notes

1. See Hemphill, J. K., Griffiths, D. E., & Frederiksen, N. (1962). *Administrative performance and personality.* New York: Teachers College Press, Columbia University.

2. In checking biographical information included in this and subsequent chapters, I have used the following references: Cook, R. C. (Ed.). (1968). *Who's Who in American Education.* Hattiesburg, MS: Who's Who in American Education, Inc.; Bradfield, R. (Ed.). (1974). *Who's Who in Education.* London: Mercury House Reference Books; Ohles, J. F. (Ed.). (1978). *Biographical dictionary of American educators.* Westport, CT: Greenwood Press; Jaques Cattell Press. (Ed.). (1974). *Leaders in education.* New York: R. R. Bowker Company; Calkins, R. W. (Ed.). (1970). *Who's who in American college and university administration.* New York: Crowell-Collier Educational Corporation; Cook, R. C. (1964). *Presidents and deans of American colleges and universities.* Nashville, TN: Who's who in American education, Inc.; Cattell, J. (1949). *American men of science: A biographical directory.* Lancaster, PA: The Science Press; Willette, T. J. (Ed.). *Biographical directory of the American Psychological Association.* (1975). Washington, DC: The American Psychological Association; and Jaques Cattell Press. (Ed.). (1983). *American men & women of science.* New York: R. R. Bowker Company.

3. See Lewin, K. (1935). *A dynamic theory of personality.* (D. K. Adams & K. E. Zener, Trans.). New York: McGraw-Hill Book Company, Inc.

4. Many years transpired before the project was fully conceived and implemented. The initial plan for seven volumes fell short by one. For more details see Koch, S. (Ed.). (1959-1963). *Psychology: A study of science.* (Vols. 1-6). New York: McGraw-Hill Book Company, Inc.

References

Joergensen, J. (1951). The development of logical empiricism. *Encyclopedia of Unified Science*, II (9), 1-100.

Lewin, K. (1938). The conceptual representation and the measurement of psychological forces. *Contributions to Psychological Theory*, I (1), 1-233.

2

Roots

When the oaktree is felled, the whole forest echoes with it; but a hundred acorns are planted silently by some unnoticed breeze.

Thomas Carlyle

UCEA's formation and early programs were influenced by American and European ideas. Views expressed in the late 1940s by officers of the W. K. Kellogg Foundation and by members of the American Association of School Administrators (AASA), for example, helped shape UCEA's mission statement. On the other hand, adapted versions of ideas generated by a group of scholars in Vienna, Austria, provided essential content for UCEA's first Career Development Seminar. The seminar's content in turn influenced some of UCEA's future programs.

The first exchange between AASA and foundation leaders took place in November, 1947. Two of the AASA travelers to Battle Creek, Michigan—the home of the foundation—were school superintendents Hobart Corning of Washington, D. C. and Herold Hunt of Kansas City, Missouri. Professors John Norton of Teachers College, Columbia, and Alfred Simpson of Harvard were present as was Henry Hill, President of George Peabody College for Teachers. Accompanying the committee was Worth McClure, AASA's executive secretary. Envisaging an extensive AASA commission study, the group believed that they could identify ways and means to improve the recruitment and training of superintendents as well as the conditions of their service.

About the time of the Battle Creek meeting the editor of *The School Executive* observed, with good reason, that AASA was "the one nationwide organization which devotes its energies to the improvement of school administration" (*The School Executive*, 1947, p.5). Ten months before the meeting AASA through its "Planning Committee" had elaborated a vision for a decade of action. Headed by Willard Goslin, Superintendent of Schools in Minneapolis, the committee highlighted the need for a professionalized superintendency. To help meet this need, the committee called upon AASA to "influence the training of superintendents on university campuses and in other areas by taking an active part in standardizing preparatory courses for school administration" (Moore, 1957, p.2).

Behind the report were several AASA concerns. One was the rapid growth in schools coupled with a limited supply of administrators. Another was the heavy pressures on superintendents. Shortly after AASA issued its report, Virgil Rogers, Superintendent of Schools in Battle Creek, Michigan, outlined 38 pressures including keeping "taxes down regardless of the effect on education," dealing with demands "from teachers' associations," and coping with "pressures from fanatic or ultrapatriotic groups or individuals" (Rogers, 1950, pp 37-38).

Ironically, about the time Rogers set forth his inventory of pressures, Willard Goslin, the leading elaborator of AASA's ten-year improvement plan, fell victim to right-wing pressure groups in Pasadena, California. During Goslin's first year as Pasadena's school superintendent in 1948-49, a group of disgruntled citizens attacked his "modern pragmatic" approach to education (Hulburd, 1951, p. 58). After defeating a tax levy, the group continued its anti-Goslin campaign. Goslin's opponents widely distributed the article "Progressive Education *Increases* Juvenile Delinquency", written by Allen Zoll, founder of the National Council for American Education. Located in New York City, the Council's mission was to eradicate "Socialism, Communism, and all forms of Marxism from schools and colleges of America, and to stimulate sound American education" (p.88). By November 1950, the city of Pasadena was in such a turmoil that four of its five school board members voted to discharge Goslin.

Superintendents saw in professionalization a means which could help them cope with pressures and problems. It could, they believed, make superintendents more competent and instill greater public confidence in schooling. However, professionalization could not be left to universities. As one superintendent noted (Berkhof, 1949, p. 51): "Professionalization ... is an ideal which can be achieved only through persistent and consistent effort. It never will be achieved unless we as administrators take an interest in achieving it."

Mission and Mode of Operation: Origins

When the AASA committee arrived in Battle Creek, the foundation's president, Emory Morris, and its education director, Hugh Masters, had already concluded that training programs for school superintendents needed improvement. Seeing leadership as "a prerequisite to human progress," they, as grant-monitors, had found problems in the "administration of county health departments, the management of hospitals, and the organization and conduct of public school systems" (Kellogg Foundation, 1979, p. 90). Thus, they perceived a need for "improved leadership and better preparation for leadership" (p.50).

Given the shared belief by AASA and foundation leaders in the need for improved training, the group's problem was to determine the course of action which would best meet the need. Foundation officials had reservations about the proposed commission study. While AASA could identify needed changes through a study, it could not implement them, because superintendents were trained in colleges and universities. Thus, foundation personnel some months later proposed that five regional meetings be conducted to explore further how the superintendency might be improved. Proposed conferees were school administrators, professors, and state and federal school officials. AASA leaders agreed to sponsor and implement the meetings.

When AASA and foundation leaders reviewed the results of the five meetings, they found strong "grass roots" support for a major project to improve school leadership. Moving away from a study, foundation officers decided to invest in action programs conducted in selected university centers. When they asked for help in launching the centers, AASA leaders formed a "Development Committee." Headed by Herold Hunt, the new superintendent of schools in Chicago, the committee first screened the proposals which universities had submitted and then recommended those they deemed most promising.

The foundation provided support initially for five university centers. Launched in 1950-51, they were located at The University of Chicago, George Peabody College for Teachers, Harvard University, Teachers College, Columbia University, and the University of Texas. A year later the foundation made grants to Stanford, Ohio State, and Oregon. During the 1950-55 period the foundation invested $3,347,567 in the eight university centers. In 1955 it granted an additional $2,393,642 to the eight centers for the 1955-1959 period.

As a group, the CPEA centers blanketed the nation. The first five served much larger regions than did the three funded in 1951-52. The territories served by the Texas, George Peabody, and Chicago centers encompassed three-fourths of the states. At the other extreme was the Ohio center which served only its native state. Most center directors engaged leaders from national organizations in their activities. They found, for instance, that the National Conference of Professors of Educational Administration (NCPEA)--now the National Council of Professors of Educational Administration--provided a valuable link into the higher education community.[1]

Significantly, the name of the nationwide initiative--the Cooperative Program in Educational Administration (CPEA)--was first used by foundation officials (Moore, 1957, p. 71). Notably, it made clear that the target of change had shifted and broadened. Improving programs for preparing educational administrators generally, rather than for superintendents specifically, had become the aim of the CPEA centers. Thus, the aim of one center was "reconstructing the program of preparation of educational administrators in the light of new needs and demands. . ." (The Ohio State CPEA Center, 1952, p. 4), while the "fundamental objective" of another was better educational leadership "through improved preparation programs for educational administrators" (Southern States CPEA Center, 1951, p.55).

Not only did the aim provide a continuing focus for CPEA's developmental activities, but also it found its way into a new organization. The writers of UCEA's by-laws later decided that the new organization's aim should be "the improvement of the professional preparation of administrative personnel in the field of education."

Implicit in CPEA's title was another core belief held by foundation officials, namely: that lasting results can best be realized through "cooperative problem-solving" (Kellogg Foundation, 1942, p. ix). A related belief was that projects designed to "contribute the greatest good to the largest number" should involve leaders from "the entire community" (Kellogg Foundation, 1942, p. ix). Directors of the eight centers put the beliefs of foundation leaders into effect through a variety of "grass roots" strategies.

To achieve CPEA objectives through "cooperative problem solving," regional leaders created new inter-institutional arrangements. Thus, the Southern States CPEA established its regional association of professors of educational administration, and the Stanford CPEA its Pacific

Southwest regional association. CPEA directors documented the broad participation of leaders in center projects, usually via tables, in their annual reports to the foundation. Thus, the foundation, two decades after CPEA ended, reported that most "state departments of education became actively engaged in the project, and so did the majority of the more than 1000 school systems as well as an additional 144 colleges and universities" (Kellogg Foundation, 1979, pp. 32-22). Understandably, UCEA's articles of incorporation stipulated that it should pursue its mission through "inter-university cooperation."

Both CPEA and UCEA were influenced, then, by a set of beliefs expressed by AASA and W. K. Kellogg Foundation leaders in the late 1940s. First, the quality of school administration needed to be improved; second, quality could best be enhanced by upgrading programs for preparing school administrators; and third, the most desirable means for effecting improvements was cooperative problem solving.

Training and Research at Mid-Century

When AASA and foundation leaders met in Battle Creek in 1947, professors across the nation were giving little thought to improved preparation for school leaders. During the 1942-47 period they did not publish a single article on training in either *The School Executive* or *The Nation's Schools*, two of their major publication outlets. There were reasons for the relative lack of self-consciousness about their training roles. In November, 1947, AASA's history reached all the way back to 1866, but NCPEA, the organization for professors, was less than three months old. When 72 professors from 43 institutions gathered at NCPEA's first meeting in 1947, most reportedly had "known one another almost solely as names: on the title pages of textbooks, in the programs of association meetings of one kind or another, in the catalogs of institutions of higher learning" (Flesher and Knoblauch, 1957, p. ix). Three years later, however, two NCPEA professors testified with good reason that their "group was turning the spotlight on themselves and their institutions" (Davies and Flesher, 1950, p. 44).

During the 1947, 1948, and 1949 NCPEA annual sessions, professors recognized the escalating pressures for change.[2] Stimulated in part by the presentations of leading school administrators, they expressed positions on a range of training issues.[3] One NCPEA theme was that community and professional leadership is even more important than effective administration. School leaders could not set sound directions for education unless they understood "both the background and the nature of the social order" (Marshall, 1947, p. 22).

What were the key features of school administrator training and inquiry when the CPEA centers were initiated? One way of examining this question is to look at the characteristics of the literature which professors read and utilized in training programs. Obviously, a thorough answer to the question lies beyond the bounds of this chapter. However, by taking, as a starting point, my experiences as a student of school administration during the summers of 1950, 1951, and 1952, pertinent observations can be offered.

A few weeks before the W. K. Kellogg Foundation announced its far-reaching decision in August, 1950, I had completed a course on the school principalship at the University of California's School of Education at Berkeley. The text for the course was *The Principal at Work*. Authored by Professor George Kyte, who also taught the course, the text had three notable features. First, it was filled with specific procedures to guide the work of principals. The chapter on "Preparing the Close of School," for instance, included an exemplary principal's "bulletin." The bulletin described how teachers should handle records, lockers, the "Friday program," and other end-of-the-year matters (Kyte, 1941, pp. 226-228). Second, the book advocated "democratic" administration. The principal, it noted, should "be a democratic and dynamic leader" (p.16) and "teacher participation ... must predominate" (p.273). Third, the author stated that the principal, when acquiring information about the community and the school, should use "primarily the survey technique" (p. 33)—a technique then used mostly by professors to recommend ways for improving education in particular school systems.

Most other contemporary texts on school administration exhibited the same features as did Professor Kyte's. Eminently practical in orientation, the most popular ones were short on facts and long on statements about what administrators ought to do. The first textbook to reach a fourth edition, for instance, was especially notable for its specificity. Written by Ward Reeder of Ohio State, it contained chapters on such topics as "School-Supply Administration" and "Administration of Textbooks" (Reeder, 1951). A well-written book, it was read widely by school administrators.

Texts were beginning to appear which offered students a broader look at leadership and administration. In 1950 Arthur Moehlman of the

University of Michigan was completing a revision of a text which opened as follows (Moehlman, 1951, p. viii): "Education does not hang free in space: it operates continuously within organized cultural patterns." Drawing upon the works of such anthropologists as Franz Boas and Margaret Mead, this author, in one of his chapters, documented education's intimate links with culture. The textbooks of the late 1950s would be more like Moehlman's than Reeder's.

During the three Berkeley summer schools I took courses on school finance, school buildings, school law, personnel administration, and state school administration. Texts for such courses were informed by administrative experience, data and opinion obtained from surveys and questionnaire studies, and descriptions of particular school practices. An exception was the course on law in which a copy of the codified school laws of California was used as a text.

When I wrote term papers at Berkeley, there were no journals devoted specifically to school administration. As a result, I relied upon general purpose journals. The oldest was *The American School Board Journal*, founded in 1891. Although designed for school board members, the journal was read by many school superintendents. Founded in 1915, *Educational Administration and Supervision* was an academically oriented journal. Although it concentrated largely upon teaching, learning, and curriculum issues, it at times published articles on school administration. In 1947, for instance, only two of its 76 articles dealt with educational administration per se.

The journals most widely read by professors and school administrators in 1950 were *The School Executive* and *The Nation's Schools*, which were founded in 1927 and 1928, respectively. In 1946 Walter Cocking, a former school superintendent and dean at the University of Georgia, became editor of *The School Executive*. As editor, he continually sought to build bridges between ideas and practice and between school administrators and professors. *The Nation's Schools* was edited during the 1940s by Author Moehlman, a former research specialist in the Detroit public schools and a professor at Michigan. A respected teacher, Moehlman disseminated ideas about many facets of education and school administration.

A content analysis of all the 1940-49 issues of *The School Executive* uncovered three types of articles. One focused upon aspects of school experience. In the latter half of the forties, under a recurring column called "Leadership: Study Incident," such sub-titles as "A Troublemaker

Joins the Staff," "A Principal's Principal," and "The School Scrooge" appeared. Although linked to facts from experience, such articles contained many value judgments.

A second type of article was the essay. Titles written by individual professors included "The Joys of Administration" and "Leadership: What Is It?" Such essays were usually more conceptual than the first type of article. Typically two to four pages in length, they offered busy school administrators concepts and opinions. The third type of article was informed by information obtained from questionnaire studies, school surveys, and interviews. Published much less frequently, these articles usually offered recommendations for improving school practices. Their authors easily moved back and forth between facts and values.

Both texts and articles in the late 1940s, then, focused much more upon what school administrators ought to do than upon the realities of practice. Thus, the concept of theory was often equated with such terms as "principle" and "guideline." In one article, for instance, theory was equated with the recommendations of a school survey (*The Nation's Schools*, 1948, p.26).

Although NCPEA leaders openly criticized training programs, they ignored the quality of their research. To be sure, some stressed the need for more research. However, they were not yet ready to analyze critically their own inquiry. Deeply inured in the traditions of survey and experienced-based research, they seemingly lacked the needed perspectives and concepts to transcend prevailing practices. Arthur Rice, editor of *The Nation's Schools* and a frequent reader of manuscripts written by professors, was more critical. Affirming the need for "more effective communication between the administrator and those who seek to help him," he gently suggested that "more attention should be given . . . to improving the professional literature in administration" (*The Nation's Schools*, 1950, p. 31).

At the time of the 1947 Battle Creek meeting, then, professors were comfortably following established traditions in training and inquiry. However, by utilizing their newly-established organization, NCPEA, they had by 1950 formulated an array of recommendations for improving preparatory programs. However, they ignored the quality of their research and publications. Thus, it was left to CPEA leaders to implement new approaches to research and, with the help of social scientists, to bring fresh views about knowledge needed by the field.

Influential CPEA Themes

Shortly after the CPEA began, Arthur Rice wrote (*The Nation's Schools*, 1950, p. 31): "the dream of the American Association of School Administrators—that the job of the school superintendent can be put on a truly professional basis—is now a building project." Rice also reported that Herold Hunt had declared that "the CPEA project is one of the most thrilling things the AASA has ever embarked upon. I believe it will do for school administration what the Flexner report did for medicine" (p.31).

In their decade-long quest to improve training, CPEA directors fell far short of fulfilling the expansive dreams of AASA leaders. The traditions in research, training, and administration were so firmly set that CPEA personnel, even with intensive effort, could not effect radical improvements in the field. Nevertheless, they wrought changes which had long range import for school administration. In addition, they carried out unsuccessful ventures which still offer lessons for those who would learn from their struggles.

In reading and re-reading the 77 CPEA annual reports submitted to the W. K. Kellogg Foundation in the 1950s, one is impressed with the scope of the centers' activities. The successes and failures of CPEA centers deserve thorough study. However, the present discussion will be limited to brief depictions of outcomes which influenced UCEA's early programs. Three which had notable impacts upon programs for improving training were: greater use of critique and of well defined training concepts; the development and use of new case materials; and new ways of applying the social sciences in training.

CPEA professors seemingly found it easier to be critical of training during their inter-university meetings than during discussions in their "home" departments. In any case, regional groups of professors at times looked at their training programs very critically. Group analyses were often informed by the work of individuals. Kenneth McIntyre of the Texas center offered trenchant critiques, for example, of the relatively low academic abilities of students enrolled in school administration programs. Such critiques helped open gates to change.

Professors in most centers generated concepts to help analyze and redesign their training programs. The Teachers College Center developed three such concepts: "man," "job," and "setting." Another illustrative set was developed through the George Peabody Center.

Rooted in the idea of "competency patterns," three concepts had extensive use: "theory," "job," and "know-how."

Although these and other CPEA concepts had obvious limitations, they provided change agents with helpful tools. Professors used the man-job-setting ideas, for instance, to identify and assess linkages among leadership qualities, job functions, and administrative situations. And southern professors undertook via the "critical incident technique" to identify significant job tasks performed by business and personnel administrators in school systems. Some professors also used the concepts to evaluate newly-designed "competency" programs.[4]

Case development and use, the second CPEA training outcome, was influenced by instructional practices in schools of business and public administration. Two CPEA centers invested substantial energy and resources in case development and use.[5] Not surprisingly, Harvard was one of these centers. Long known as the citadel of case instruction, Harvard's use of the method reached all the way back to 1870, when Professor Christopher Langdell introduced it to Harvard Law School students. In 1919 professors began using cases in Harvard's business school and in the 1930s in its public administration program. Drawing upon resources immediately available to them, CPEA personnel at Harvard developed an array of cases in educational administration, tested and analyzed their uses, and disseminated the results.[6]

The Oregon Center also assigned priority to case development and use. Influenced more by the practices of professors of public administration, the faculty was aided initially by Egburt Wengert, an Oregon professor of public administration. In fact, the Oregon faculty used several public administration cases in its first seminars, an experience which highlighted the need for case development in school administration. Professor Wengert, an active participant in the Inter-University Case Program on public administration, shared his own case development experiences with professors and students of school administration. Selected cases were published along with the methods used to apply social science content to them.[7]

In 1950 Hugh Masters, a former school superintendent and the education director of the W. K. Kellogg Foundation, stated that an "extremely important aspect of this project (CPEA) has been the insistence that the preparation of the educational leader must draw heavily upon the basic social sciences, . . ." (quoted in *The Nation's Schools*, 1950, p. 33). CPEA center leaders, albeit to differing degrees, took Masters' view seriously. By nurturing relationships between professors of school administration and social scientists, the centers' leaders found new purposes and places for social science content in training. Arguably, CPEA's greatest impacts upon training were wrought through newly formed links with social scientists.

Given the marked psychological and organizational distances which separated social scientists and professors of school administration at mid-century, the foundation's charge was not easily met. A popular mechanism used initially to facilitate dialogue between the two groups was the multi-disciplinary committee. Teachers College had its "University Council of Advisors," Stanford its "All-University Committee," and Chicago its "Executive Committee." Some committee members were highly distinguished scholars. Serving at Teachers College was the renowned sociologist, Robert Merton; at Stanford Ernest Hilgard, the influential psychologist; and at Chicago the prolific student of public administration, Leonard White. The Chicago committee's purpose was similar to that of other centers: "to make use of the . . . knowledge and resources of such social sciences as economics, political science, psychology and sociology" (Midwest Administration CPEA Center, 1951, p. 1).

CPEA leaders incorporated the social sciences into training in varied ways. All sent students to social science departments to take established or specially developed courses. They also provided social science content by designing their own courses on such subjects as "Administrative Theory" and "Decision-Making." Some affected joint appointments of social scientists in schools of education and social science departments. Several experimented with inter-disciplinary seminars. Harvard, influenced by the medical school model, appointed social scientists to posts in its school of education.

While all of the above arrangements produced beneficial results, none was without flaws and most, after the cessation of foundation support, fell by the wayside. Even though the inter-disciplinary seminar at Oregon, an expensive endeavor, continued for almost a decade after the CPEA effort ceased, it could not in the end be institutionalized. Joint appointments also proved to be unstable, given the difficulties social scientists encountered in serving two masters. Almost all the social scientists appointed to posts in schools of education soon returned to their "home" departments. Two options for students did survive and had continuing uses: taking existing social science courses and enrolling in courses with social science content designed by professors of educational administration.

By the mid-fifties social science concepts were making their way into new textbooks.[8] Moving away from the hortatory statements of an earlier era, the new books contained more analysis and explanation. Theories of organization such as the "social process" one (Getzels, 1952) slowly made their way into the new texts. One result was fresher and more challenging training content for students. Another was newly acquired professorial perspectives.

As bridges were built between the social sciences and school administration, perceptible changes in research also took place. One result was more conceptually-based inquiry. Harvard researchers spent months formulating concepts to undergird the Bay City inquiries as did the southern designers of the Cheatham County research. In the early CPEA years Oregon scholars instituted several seminars to facilitate concept clarification. Through the seminars they defined such concepts as "community decision-making" and "leadership" with sufficient clarity to guide their research endeavors.

Stanford CPEA scholars, among others, gave inquiry a greater quantitative emphasis as, for example, in their research on the selection of school administrators. Led by the well-known psychologist, Arthur Coladarci, the research drew upon data developed over time on the verbal intelligence, knowledge of contemporary affairs, authoritarianism, values, and vocational interests of 600 school personnel. When doctoral students studied relationships between the results of varied tests and peer ratings, for instance, they could settle neither for qualitative statements nor for the simple statistics of an earlier era. As a result, such terms as "analysis of variance" made their way into the literature.

Another notable feature of CPEA inquiry was its emphasis upon programmatic research. The Southern States Center had its "Cheatham County," Harvard its "Bay City," and Oregon its "Valley City I" and "Valley City II." Such localities served as laboratories in which researchers, over a period of years, carried out inter-related studies. Although programmatic research had limited impact upon the cumulation of knowledge, it offered a sensible alternative to the practice of isolated and unrelated inquiries.

One other notable outcome of CPEA research was a new breed of professor. That the new breed benefited the field is evident from the scholarly works of able professors who received their training in CPEA centers. Examples would be Oregon's Keith Goldhammer, Chicago's James Lipham, Harvard's Oliver Gibson, Teacher's College's Laurence Iannaccone, and Tennessee's Ralph Kimbrough. These professors were in a better position than were their predecessors to make use of the social sciences and to advance theory-based inquiry.

A New Conception of Science

More than fifty professors from twenty leading universities traveled by car, train, and plane to Chicago on November 10, 1957, to take part in a seminar. Jointly sponsored by The University of Chicago and the fledgling UCEA, the seminar was entitled "Administrative Theory in Education." Not only did the three-day affair afford attendees an exciting intellectual experience, but also it proved to be a special event in the history of the field. Featuring leading scholars from CPEA universities, the seminar's central message was that there was a great need to develop theory in the field and to begin building a science of administration. The seminar had an unforeseen impact. It helped spawn what later came to be known as the "theory movement."

Informing the seminar's messages were simplified and attenuated versions of a relatively new philosophy of science. Differing markedly from the scientific tenets which positivists and pragmatists had elaborated and which leading researchers had employed earlier in the century,[9] the tenets offered the field fresh possibilities. Twenty-five years earlier Herbert Feigl, an exponent of the new philosophy, had named it "logical positivism." The epistemological tenets were forged in Vienna, Austria, a location which, according to one scholar, "provided propitious conditions for the development of an empirical attitude" (Neurath, 1935, p. 8). Originating in a seminar begun by Moritz Schlick of the University of Vienna in 1923, the tenets would stir the minds and emotions of scholars worldwide.[10] Schlick, who had obtained a doctorate in physics, had written a book on the philosophical significance of Albert Einstein's theory of relativity. His seminar attracted scientifically educated philosophers as well as scientists and mathematicians who were interested in philosophy. Among the members of the "Vienna Circle" were Otto Neurath, Rudolph Carnap, Herbert Feigl, Friedrich Waismann, and Viktor Kraft.

In the early years the Circle convened weekly in Vienna's coffee houses where its members analyzed ideas related to their interests. Works stressing that the road to knowledge is marked by empirical modes of inquiry appealed to them strongly. Examples were the writings of Auguste Comte, the "Father of Positivism," and those of the Scottish philosopher, David Hume. Appearing nearly a century before Schlick began his seminar, Comte's works had a strong impact upon the Vienna scholars. Some of the Comtean theses which were adopted by the logical positivists were: theological and metaphysical thinking are "useless digressions," while positivistic thinking can produce laws; to insure that thinking is informed by facts, positivists must subordinate their imagination to observations; and natural science methods can and should be applied to the study of social and human phenomena (Culbertson, 1981, pp 29ff).

Exciting the Vienna Circle scholars even more than Comte's ideas were Bertrand Russell's new propositions about the role of symbolic logic in scientific inquiry. Russell contended that the new logic could be employed to reorder language and, in turn, to reform traditional views about inquiry. The ideas in Ludwig Wittgenstein's *Tractatus Logico-Philosophicus* were also very compelling. Wittgenstein's book, according to Stephen Toulmin, "was one of the founding documents from which the new positivism. . . took its departure; . . . it was Wittgenstein who provided the channel by which Russell's work on mathematical logic and philosophy exerted its full influence on Schlick and his other colleagues" (Toulmin, 1969, p. 27).

In 1929 the Circle published a slender brochure entitled *The Scientific Conception of the World.*[11] The booklet contained the basic beliefs of the Vienna Circle—beliefs upon which the edifice of logical positivism was built. Negatively stimulated by the ill-defined abstractions which pervaded prevailing philosophies as well as most of the sciences, they passionately argued that all metaphysical, theological, and ethical statements were the stuff of poetry and myth, not science. Their "scientific conception" was in effect a declaration of independence from such statements as "the primary influence in the world is the unconscious," "God lives in the heavens," and "individuals ought to tell the truth." Scholars could not derive from such sentences "observation statements" about the empirical world. The witty Otto Neurath developed an *index verborum prohibitorum* which contained such words as "mind," "motive," and "spirit." As a self-appointed monitor of the Circle's discussions for a period, he uttered the word "metaphysical" each time he heard woolly-headed terms expressed. However, Schlick, noting that Neurath's actions were disruptive, asked him to desist.

Very early, then, the Vienna Circle scholars resolved to cure the serious "disease" which they believed sorely afflicted philosophy and science. One of Wittgenstein's statements became a guiding ideal (quoted in Neurath, 1973, p. 304): "What can be said at all, can be said clearly." They saw in *logical analysis* a needed means for treating the loathsome malady of traditional philosophy. By employing symbolic logic, they could construct statements as precise as those in mathematics. In so doing they could overcome the defects of language and of human prejudice.

A basic belief undergirding the Vienna Circle's "scientific world-conception" was that "there is knowledge only from experience" (Neurath, 1973, p. 309). Yet its members also believed that research begins with a theoretical model and ends in a test of its validity. Theory, in other words, is indispensable to science. For the European thinkers, physics was the only scientific discipline which was largely free of metaphysical, theological, and ethical thinking. Thus, they turned to physics and to mathematics for fitting exemplars of theory. Since "theory," as used in traditional writings, had multiple meanings, they substituted the concept of "hypothetico-deductive system" for theory. Joined in such a system were two radically different domains: the symbolic world of mathematics and the "real" world of experience. The systems, then, were unique intellectual creations.

Hypothetico-deductive systems were composed of disparate layers of thought. In the highest or most abstract layer were analytic statements of logic (i.e. axioms or postulates). These statements were "axiomatised" similarly to mathematical ones as, for example, axioms about such geometrical elements as points and lines (Neurath, 1973, p. 314). At the next layer were theorems, while "concepts of the experience" resided at the lowest layer (p.309). The system provided a framework within which the cherished method of *logical analysis* could be applied. Neurath described the process as follows (p. 309):

> Since the meaning of every statement of science must be statable by reduction to a statement about the given, likewise the meaning of any concept—must be statable by step-wise reduction to other concepts, down to the concepts of the lowest level which refer directly to the given.

The system of axioms was "cut loose from all empirical applica-tion" (Neurath, 1973, p. 11). The meaning of the "primitive" concepts in the axioms was fixed or defined, not by their content, but by their mutual relationships. As the objects to which the concepts in axioms referred were defined by objects in the next layer of the system, a movement toward empirical meaning was set in motion which pro-ceeded toward experimental research designs and "observation state-ments." As the creators of the systems moved from the abstract to concrete expressions, they used symbolic logic at each step along the way.

The goal of inquiry, the Circle affirmed, is unified science. This goal, which could best be pursued through *"collective efforts, "* would facilitate a "search for a total system of concepts" which would "harmo-nize the achievements of individual investigators in their various fields . . . " (Neurath, 1973, p. 306). By achieving a unified science, scholars could seek "a neutral system of formulae" and a "symbolism freed from the slag of historical languages . . ." (p.306). Even the social sciences, which suffered from much contradictory and fuzzy thinking, could be cleansed and take their place alongside the natural sciences. This message was a reassuring if not a beguiling one for social scientists.

Neurath's slender brochure enabled the Circle's basic ideas to move far beyond the Vienna coffee houses. In 1929 a Congress was held in Prague, where members of the Circle presented ideas on mathemat-ics and logic, and a similar Congress convened in Koenigsberg the next year. Moritz Schlick spoke to the Seventh International Congress of Philosophy in Oxford, England, in 1930, on "The Future of Philosophy." During his address he observed (Schlick, 1947, p. 747-748): "Our view of the nature of philosophy will be generally adopted in the future." Philosophers would then be "searching for clarity"—not teaching systems of thought (p.748). Soon after Schlick made his address, some of the Circle's ideas reached Australia. Still, no place was more hospitable to the ideas than was the United States. Herbert Feigl later noted that in the U. S. there was "a *zeitgeist* thoroughly congenial to our Viennese position" (Feigl, 1968, p. 645). No scholars embraced the new philosophy more warmly than did social scientists. One expert con-cluded that its impact upon the behavioral sciences was "enormous" (Scriven, 1969, p. 197).[12]

The Circle's ideas had the greatest and the most immediate impact upon the discipline of psychology. Notably, psychologists played a major role in diffusing the new philosophical concepts about science into the field of educational administration. Thus, it was no accident that half of the presenters at the Chicago seminar on "Theory" were leading psychologists who had played distinctive roles in CPEA centers.

Psychologists in the 1930s and 1940s were searching for a scientific research methodology. In addition, the Circle scholars, given their commitment to physical or observable referents, vehemently rejected the "introspectionists" in psychology and embraced the "behaviorists." Notably, there were many more behaviorists in psychology than in other disciplines.

By 1940 the psychologist, Clark Hull, and his colleagues had set forth a hypothetico-deductive system in their *Mathematico-Deductive Theory of Rote Learning*. Conforming closely to the standards of the Circle scholars, the system was constructed with the aid of an expert in symbolic logic. It contained 18 postulates which its authors equated with natural laws. From the 18 postulates were derived 44 theorems. The system was used to advance research on learning. Yet its creators encountered vexing problems. For example, they could not ensure that the number of postulates in the system was the correct one. Consequently, the accuracy of lower order statements could be questioned.[13] Still the system provided psychologists with fresh possibilities and an influential application of logical positivistic concepts.

Another important source from which professors acquired ideas about logical positivism was the applied field of public administration. The single most important source was the first edition of Herbert Simon's book, *Administrative Behavior*, which was written in the mid-forties. In his book Simon revealed his heavy debt to the logical positivists whose ideas he had "accepted as a starting point" in building his decision-making theory (Simon, 1947, p. 45). His book had an immense influence not only upon political science but also upon the applied field of public administration. A few years before the 1957 seminar took place in Chicago, one eminent scholar in his monograph, *The Study of Public Administration*, included a section on the "Impact of Logical Positivism" (Waldo, 1955, p. 43ff). In his work he gave Herbert Simon full credit for introducing to "the literature of public administration the doctrines of the school of thought known as logical positivism" (p. 43). After discussing the import for public administration of the "is" and "ought" categories, "pure" science, and other concepts, he observed (p. 45):

One can do no more than guess at the long-term affect of logical positivism on the study of public administration. *Administrative Behavior* has certainly been a widely read and influential work, and all one can say of the present situation is that it has set strong currents flowing counter to those predominant in the forties.

Shortly after Simon's book appeared, a group of scholars assessed the new tenets of science at a debate sponsored by the American Political Science Association. Attracting both political scientists and professors of public administration, the debate featured multiple speakers, pro and con. Among the speakers who supported the tenets was Herbert Simon; one of the opponents of the tenets was Charner Perry of The University of Chicago. In a paper titled "The Semantics of Political Science," he questioned the new ideas (Perry, 1950, p. 398):

Social knowledge has indeed been greatly extended and improved in the last two hundred years; but so far as I know there have been no important contributions in the field resulting from the application of scientific method. The zeal for science has probably been quite important as a motivating force but as a guide to investigation it has been almost, if not completely, sterile.

Perry's views elicited strong reactions. The logical positivist, George Lundberg of the University of Washington, was one who attacked Perry's ideas in a paper entitled "The Semantics of Charner Perry." Offering a variation on a theme of the Vienna scholars, he noted (Lundberg, 1950, p. 414): "I find his (i.e. Perry's) discussion very much more revealing as an *example* of his own semantic difficulties than as an analysis of the actual semantic problems frustrating the development of a science of political behavior."

Most of the 50 plus professors of educational administration who attended the 1957 seminar were already aware that there was ferment in psychology and public administration, and that the ferment was spilling over into their own field. A few months earlier the groundbreaking book, *Administrative Behavior in Education*, had appeared. Edited by Roald Campbell and Russell Gregg (1957), the book contained new ideas about theory and science. For example, the two chapters written by Andrew Halpin and Daniel Griffiths were harbingers of things to come. Writers of the book's chapters made 23 references to Simon's book—eight more than were made to any other author cited (Culbertson, 1981, p. 40). The second and third largest number of citations were to works written by two influential psychologists who were presenting papers at the Chicago seminar: Andrew Halpin and Jacob Getzels. Fourteen out of 16 authors of chapters were professors of educational administration. However, the authors they cited most frequently were in departments outside their fields.

Since many if not most of the attendees at the 1957 seminar had already read some of the writings of Simon, Getzels, or Halpin, they were prepared to listen to the eight distinguished presenters. Among other things, the presenters would make more explicit certain logical positivistic ideas which were often implicit in the literature, give examples of applications of these ideas, and advocate that professors use them to develop theory and to build a science of administration.

As a student of the history of science and a leading disseminator of the new concepts of science, the Vienna scholar, Neurath, had anticipated that some of his colleagues would "regret the 'trivialized' form that these matters inevitably take on spreading" (Neurath, 1973, p. 316). Certainly, the logical positivistic ideas which reached the Chicago seminar were attenuated and adapted versions of their original expressions. Having traveled across national and disciplinary boundaries on their way to Chicago, some of the ideas had fallen by the wayside, while others had been altered to meet perceived needs in particular contexts.

The psychologist, Andrew Halpin, and the sociologist, James Thompson, were the two Chicago presenters who defined the new tenets and recommended their use. Halpin, a member of the Chicago CPEA Center, was respected for his research attainments and his felicitous writing skills. While pursuing a B.A. degree at Columbia, and a Ph.D. at Cornell, he had learned about logical positivism. The impact upon him, he reported, "was strong enough to have stayed with me for half a century" (personal correspondence, March, 1980). Thompson was Director of the Administrative Science Center at the University of Pittsburgh, the only such agency in the U.S. A year earlier he had become the first editor of the *Administrative Science Quarterly*.

Both Halpin and Thompson stressed an idea emphasized by the Vienna scholars: namely, that science and inquiry are highly dependent upon theory.[14] Raw data could provide "for electric light sockets and wall switches," but not "for the wiring which relates them, and we remain in the dark" (Thompson, 1958, p. 27). Needed was "theory" from which hypotheses could be derived and tested. Opting for the Vienna view that theory suffers from too many meanings, Halpin proposed that "hypothetico-deductive system" might replace the term "theory." He clarified the concept by quoting Feigl's popular definition (Halpin, 1958b, p. 71): "a set of assumptions from which can be derived by purely mathematico-deductive procedures, a larger set of empirical laws."

Halpin and Thompson devoted little attention to methods for developing hypothetico-deductive systems. Yet their stated views about scientific method meshed with those of the Vienna scholars. Thompson, for example, noted that theories must "meet the test of internal logic" (Thompson, 1958, p. 21). He also stated that "deductive reasoning" was an important source of "modern developments" (p. 34). In another passage he stressed the need to begin with a postulate and "to arrive by logical steps at more specific propositions" (p. 34). "Concepts. . . in logical systems" needed to be expressed through "operational" definitions (p. 35). While both Thompson and Halpin underlined the importance of logical analysis, neither author referred to the power or the use of symbolic logic.

The Circle's railings against fuzzy-headed thinking did not reach Chicago. Neither metaphysical nor theological ideas were mentioned. The enemy at the seminar was "naked empiricism" (Halpin, 1958a, p. xv). The logical positivists' distinction between fact and value or "is" and "ought" questions *did* reach Chicago. Quoting Neal Gross, Halpin made clear that "ought" statements reside outside science (1958b, p.3): "Theory must be concerned with how the superintendent *does* behave, not with someone's opinion of how he *ought* to behave."

The Vienna idea of a unified science also stopped short of Chicago. However, inherent in the concept of administrative science—was a partial application of the idea of unified science. Thompson noted that "a theory adequate for educational administration must be able to encompass" all fields of administration (Thompson, 1958, p. 31). To achieve such a theory, it would be necessary to acquire, develop, and order knowledge from all fields of administration. In addition, professors from the various domains of administrative study would have to cooperate and communicate with one another. Such requirements meshed with those set forth by the Vienna scholars for realizing a unified science.

Both Halpin and Thompson agreed that a science of administration would have to be rooted in the social and behavioral sciences, because the latter were the major repositories of existing theories. This belief was also supportive of the concept of unified science. A unified science would feature general theories of administration, while preserving the in-ought dichotomy. However, by aligning their fields with other fields of administration, Thompson and Halpin made it easier for their followers to ignore the aims of schooling and the policies needed to realize these aims.

Roald Campbell, Director of the Chicago CPEA Center, did argue that school administration had unique qualities. A distinguished leader who had served on the staff of the CPEA center at Ohio State before he moved to the University of Chicago, Campbell would later be elected president of the American Educational Research Association. Lacking a framework for comparatively analyzing the diverse species of administration, Campbell's "special case" arguments for school administration were not entirely compelling.

Following Halpin's and Thompson's presentations, three psychologists, a sociologist, and a professor of educational administration each delineated a generic theory. The first one was set forth by Talcott Parsons, the world-renowned "grand" theorist. As a Harvard sociologist, Parsons had gained a reputation for his abstract theories of social systems. They encompassed the structure of societies, on the one hand, and the world of small groups, on the other. In his "General Theory of Formal Organizations" three concepts were featured: "technical," "managerial" and "institutional" systems.

Jacob Getzels, a psychologist at The University of Chicago, set forth a "social process" theory of administration. In presenting his theory he acknowledged his indebtedness to Talcott Parsons with whom he had studied at Harvard. Getzels' theory, elaborated in its initial form five years earlier, was the first of its kind in the field (Getzels, 1952). With the help of Egon Guba he had continued to refine it. Getzels' model and the research it generated enabled the Chicago CPEA Center to become a leader in theory development.

Carroll Shartle's theory of "Behavior in Organizations" reflected his experience as Director of the Personnel Research Board at The Ohio State University. During the previous decade the Research Board had sponsored varied studies of leadership in military, industrial, educational, and other organizations. Thus, his theory was designed to guide research in all types of organizations.

John Hemphill outlined a theory of group leadership. Selected in the late 1940s by Carroll Shartle to conduct studies of leadership in military organizations, Hemphill soon began constructing a theory to guide his research. With the help of his colleague, Arthur Coons, he had formulated the well-known concepts of "initiation" and "consideration" and had helped construct the widely used Leadership Behavior Description Questionnaire (LBDQ). Hemphill concentrated primarily upon carefully defining such constructs as "group," "leadership acts," and "interaction."

Daniel Griffiths was the only professor of educational administration to set forth a theory. Fifteen months earlier he had chaired the first meeting of the NCPEA interest group on "Theory." Recipient of a Ph.D. in school administration from Yale University, he had already become a forceful proponent of theory-based research. If Jacob Getzels and Andrew Halpin played the leading roles in diffusing concepts about theory *into* the CPEA network, Griffiths led in disseminating the ideas *within* the larger field. Through his lucid thinking and pointed writings he became a leader of the "theory movement." Focusing upon decision-making, Griffiths' theory contained three major, three minor, and one "converse" proposition.

To what extent did the theories in Chicago adhere to the standards the Vienna scholars had set forth? Halpin observed that Hemphill's theory was "hypothetico deductive in character" (Halpin, 1958a, p. xiii). Certainly, Hemphill's definitions of the concepts in his theory were arrived at through systematic and logical analysis. However, the relationships between and among the concepts were not clearly specified. Getzel's social process theory adhered much more closely to the ideals of hypothetico-deductive systems than any of the other theories. Its well defined and logically ordered concepts had already spawned hypotheses which had been tested in military and educational organizations. Getzels summarized succinctly his theory in the following mathematical equation: $B=f(R \times P)$ — (behavior is a function of role times personality). The equation underlined the fact that Getzels' theory possessed logical, precise, and parsimonious properties.

Parsons' theory also was notable for its logical construction. Because its major concepts (i.e. "technical," "managerial," and "institutional" systems) were precisely defined and well integrated, they facilitated deductive reasoning. One of his propositions was that the three systems of organizations operate more independently in school systems than in military or industrial organizations. From the theory could also be deduced hypotheses about the relationships of the three postulated systems to their external environments.

Even though Shartle and Griffiths were able to express their theories in mathematical symbols, their creations fell short of the Vienna standards. The logic underlying Griffiths theory was more implicit than explicit. The relationships among the concepts in Shartle's formulation were very loose—a condition which may help explain why he called his offering a "framework" rather than a theory.

Not only did Parsons' and Getzels' formulations best reflect the ideals of the Vienna scholars, but their two seminal theories also had a *much* greater impact upon the field than did those of the other three. Getzels' theory was used by scores of scholars in the U.S., Canada, and other nations. Parsons' systems concepts also appeared and re-appeared in many publications in the field.

Had Neurath attended the Chicago seminar, he likely would have had mixed feelings about the attenuated and altered forms in which the ideas of the Vienna scholars were expressed. For example, the superficial treatment of hypothetico-deductive systems would have disappointed him, while the importance assigned to theory development might have pleased him. As one who had worked hard to advance the concept of unified science, he likely would have regretted strongly the fact that the concept was not mentioned in Chicago. However, the discussion of administrative science would have reassured him, since it reflected some movement toward a unified science.

That the ideas presented in Chicago were altered and even distorted is not the main point to be made. Rather, the significant point is that the ideas helped set a new direction for the field. At least three reasons shed light on why the seminar had a strong impact. First, the new concepts of science provided tools for those who were dissatisfied with the status of inquiry, and who wanted to change it. In the ideas he advocated Andrew Halpin saw the means for addressing the empty "empiricism" of the time. Years later Daniel Griffiths stated the appeal of the seminar's ideas in a related but different way (Griffiths, 1979, P. 12): "It seemed to me that the logical positivist approach was the proper antidote for the self-serving testimonials, the pseudotheories of Mort and Sears, and the plain nonsense that constituted the field of educational administration."

A second reason why the new tenets of science were appealing was that they gave fresh hope to the attendees at the 1957 seminar. The promised land of science, they had been told, could bring them and their field new benefits. The knowledge gained from pursuing a science of administration could strengthen their teaching, research, and the practice of educational administration. Their elevated hopes were reinforced by such statements as the following (Thompson, 1958, p. 39): "Eventually our theories of administration may lead practice rather than follow it, and in time . . . contribute significantly to the behavioral sciences."

A third reason why the attenuated tenets of logical positivism were attractive stemmed from their psychological appeal. As professors in an applied field, the Chicago attendees were targets of criticism, especially from those in the scientific communities of universities. Historically, members of schools or departments of administration were "forced to defend themselves against charges that they were operating trade schools" (Thompson, 1958, p. 38). Thus, the clear call for theory-based inquiry and for a science of administration opened a way for seminar participants to stifle their critics and to enhance their status. Over time an administrative science would enable them to overcome the negative images which had long afflicted their inquiry.

The ideas transmitted in Chicago had their effects. Leading professors adopted the ideas and put them to work. They also advocated that others utilize the ideas. Soon Daniel Griffiths transmitted his views about theory and inquiry in: *Administrative Theory* and in *Research in Educational Administration.*[15] In a half dozen years the so-called "theory movement" emerged—a development which reflected the impact of the Chicago presentations. Department heads and deans in UCEA universities began recruiting professors who understood theory-based inquiry, while courses on "Administrative Theory" were launched in numerous UCEA universities.

The ideas presented at the seminar also influenced UCEA's subsequent activities. For example, readers of the UCEA book *Educational Research: New Perspectives* will see that the concept of theory-based inquiry left its mark on a number of the book's chapters. Later the tenets would serve as a negative stimulus. At a UCEA Career Development Seminar, for example, Joseph Schwab offered a trenchant critique of logical positivistic theory (Schwab, 1964).

Signals in the seminar's immediate environment already foreshadowed one of the dilemmas which would face single-minded pursuers of a science of administration. During the seminar there repeatedly appeared on the *Chicago Tribune*'s front pages articles about Sputnik II.

The "earth moon," traveling with its canine companion, Laika, had streaked daily across Chicago's western skies. Negative judgments about science education in the U.S. abounded in print as did calls for its improvement. What ought the schools to do about science education was the question. Ironically, the seminar speakers, as scientists, had ruled out the study of such "ought" questions. Even the Chicago presenters did not escape the is-ought dilemma. As scientists, they rejected the study of "ought" questions; as leaders, they recommended that the field "ought" to develop a science of administration.

Organizational Roots

The beginnings of UCEA as an actuality can be traced to a symposium sponsored by the Teachers College CPEA Center in November, 1954. Designed to evaluate the center's progress, the symposium was led by Daniel Davies, the center's director. An important outcome of the two-day session was a "recommendation to continue and extend the cooperative association of institutions" begun earlier at Teachers College.[16] A few months later Daniel Davies met with the education director of the W. K. Kellogg Foundation, Hugh Masters. In their meeting, as Davies remembers it (personal telephone conversation, January, 1989), Masters proposed that plans for cooperation be moved from a regional to a national level. In March, 1955, the idea of a "national association of institutions" was endorsed by the Council of Associated Colleges, a 16 university offspring of the Teachers College CPEA Center. Later when Davies proposed that the foundation support the "further development" of an association, officials of the W. K. Kellogg Foundation awarded Teachers College the needed funds.

In November, 1956, Teachers College sponsored an "exploratory conference" to assess further the idea of developing a national association. Chaired by Virgil Rogers, former president of the American Association of School Administrators (AASA) and Dean of the School of Education at Syracuse University, the conference attracted leaders from 31 prominent U.S. colleges and universities. Also present were Finis Engleman, AASA's executive secretary, and Walter Cocking, editor of *The School Executive*.

In opening the conference Hollis Caswell, President of Teachers College, stated that the session's purpose was "to discuss ways and means of strengthening and helping one another in meeting our present problems." While stressing the "tremendous possibilities in a plan of inter-university cooperation," he warned that the "working patterns of operation would not be easy to develop." Daniel Davies emphasized that the proposed concept of inter-university cooperation "must be tested rigorously by you, . . . before it can proceed further."

The assembled leaders first discussed a report of a committee headed by John Ramseyer of The Ohio State CPEA Center. The issue which gained most attention was that of purpose. The committee had offered two options for discussion: "to develop a concept of educational administrative statesmanship" and "to develop a program of basic research." Hollis Caswell added three other alternatives: "the best possible selection and preparation of personnel for leadership roles in schools," "advancement of knowledge of goals and procedures in administration," and "arrangements which will allow professorial staff to keep up to date." Most of the purposes probed during the day were variations on Ramseyer's and Caswell's ideas. However, at the end of the session the group, still generating purpose statements, was not yet ready to make limiting decisions.

Before the body adjourned, the chair appointed a committee on organization and another on purpose. Heading the organization group was Paul Jacobson, Dean of the School of Education at the University of Oregon. Serving with him were two former elected heads of NCPEA: William Arnold and Russell Gregg, of the universities of Pennsylvania and Wisconsin, respectively; Daniel Davies, head of the Teachers College CPEA Center; and Robert Fisk, Dean of the School of Education at the University of Buffalo. Leading the committee on purpose was John Norton, head of the Department of Educational Administration and Guidance at Teachers College. Working with him were Laurence Haskew and Truman Pierce, education deans at Texas and Alabama Polytechnic Institute, respectively.

Perhaps because the report on purpose captured well the previous day's discourse, it received little attention. However, there was a keen interest in finding a name for the new organization. Among the options floated during the day were "Cooperative Center for Educational Administration," "Educational Administration Clearing House," "Cooperative Council for Educational Administration," and "National Council of Administrative Leadership."

The committee on organization raised another question: what relationship should adhere between the organization's central unit and

its member universities, especially its "home" university? The committee made clear that the "council shall be independent of the institution
near which it is located." Implicit in the statement was an old CPEA
problem: how could university leaders who had long competed with
one another for money, status, power, and students trust one another in
cooperative endeavors? In the Middle Atlantic Region, for instance, the
problem came into play at the very first meeting of the Council of
Associated Colleges when a professor asked (Middle Atlantic CPEA
Center, 1951, p.6): "Are we really going to be participating partners in
this project, or are we expected to 'coo' while Teachers College 'operates'?" Such distrust, which had previously prevailed in regional
networks, was surfacing at a national level. As receivers of a foundation
grant to bring a new national organization into being, Teachers College
personnel, in the eyes of other conferees, had special advantages.· Years
would pass before UCEA leaders could craft a working solution to this
delicate problem.

At the end of the conference the body decided that a council should
be established. The conferees also agreed that an interim committee
should be appointed to direct its establishment. Agreeing to serve on
the committee were Walter Anderson, New York University; Francis
Chase, Chicago; Laurence Haskew, Texas; Paul Jacobson, Oregon;
Francis Keppel, Harvard; William Odell, Stanford; Truman Pierce,
Alabama Polytechnic Institute; John Ramseyer, Ohio State; and Virgil
Rogers, Syracuse. Among America's most outstanding educational
leaders, all were well equipped to design and launch UCEA. Appointed as executive officer for the committee was Daniel Davies.

During the next year the committee met on three occasions. At its
February 17, 1957, meeting it determined that the organization's name
should be the University Council for Educational Administration
(UCEA). Four days later 32 university representatives officially approved the chosen name. In the board's discussion of membership
criteria John Ramseyer suggested that the "principle tests" should be
"whether the institution had the resources (funds, facilities and staff) to
carry on significant research in educational administration, and whether
the institution had demonstrated an interest in such research" (IC Min,
2/17/57, p. 21).[17] Although the group recognized a need for "objective"
membership criteria, it decided to deal with immediate applications on
an *ad hoc* basis.

The problem of "inter-university relationships" aroused the most concern at the December, 1956, and November, 1957, meetings. Committee members were apprehensive about the leadership role of Teachers College. At the group's first meeting Francis Chase warned that the committee "should not set up a giant super-structure nor should they set up a center which would function separate from the universities" (IC Min, 12/17/56, pp. 1-2). Worried about possible competition for funds between the UCEA central unit and member universities, two deans noted that they would not be able to raise funds for the new organization.

At its November, 1957, meeting the committee discussed possibilities for altering the "center" concept. Haskew, noting that "all of the money might end up at Teachers College," proposed that the fund-raising roles of universities and foundations be clarified (IC Min, 11/13-14/57, p.5). Chase indicated that "UCEA should not go to a power center." Rather, it would be better to locate it in Cleveland, St. Louis, or Colorado (p.10). Paul Jacobson, making a more sweeping suggestion, recommended "an independent organization located in the central part of the country, one which was incorporated, detached from a university, and with a central staff" (p.4). Francis Keppel suggested that "symbolism was very important and that because of this the UCEA should leave Teachers College" (p.7).

The second day's discussion turned more positive. William Odell, noting that "we need more than something which threatens us," stressed the necessity for "personal involvement and real dedication to the UCEA" (IC Min, 11/13-14/57, p.8). Haskew recounted recent successes, and Jacobson asserted that the UCEA should certainly remain at Teachers College until July 31, 1959. When the group agreed to submit a proposal to the W. K. Kellogg Foundation, Walter Anderson asked if it could be submitted under UCEA auspices. Davies answered "Yes" and volunteered to draft a proposal for Interim Committee review. After accepting Davies' idea, the group decided that the committee should be replaced by an elected Board of Trustees. It then determined through a drawing of lots that Laurence Haskew, Francis Keppel, and William Odell should be the first members to be replaced.

When committee members expressed concerns about Teachers College's role, Davies and Griffiths listened silently. Later, when Davies informed Hollis Caswell, President of Teachers College, that he "sensed a certain degree of resistance on the part of some, if not all," of the Interim Committee members to "having the center at TC," President

Caswell replied, "If that is the case, put it up to vote. Let them decide" (personal correspondence, September 1988). The likely loss of the center must have disappointed Teachers College personnel. However, as leading progenitors of the UCEA idea, Teachers College professors wanted to see it flourish. By accepting altered conceptions of the enterprise, they helped ensure its survival.

While the committee was struggling to resolve organizational issues, UCEA launched its first programs. A seminar at Chicago on "Theory" and one at Harvard on the "Case Method" engendered both satisfaction and enthusiasm. Beneficiary of a major government grant, the UCEA "criteria of success" project generated hope for the future. Staff-designed proposals to increase scholarship monies and to improve state departments of education created interest, as did two proposals submitted by member universities: one on school finance from Northwestern, and another on historical inquiry from Pennsylvania State. When confronted with doubt, committee members more than once reminded themselves of the outcomes UCEA had already attained.

At an April, 1958, meeting of all university representatives Virgil Rogers asked committee members for comments. Francis Chase observed that while "some of the Interim Committee meetings were frustrating," UCEA had "developed quickly since its last Plenary Session," and that its prospects were "extremely pleasing" (PS Min, 4/2/58, p.2). Recognizing the "generosity of Teachers College, Columbia," he pointed to its use of foundation funds for UCEA's development, its making available uncommitted 1958-59 funds to UCEA, and the public statement that the college "did not want special consideration as the home of the UCEA" (p.3).

Following Chase's comments the Plenary Session examined a proposed set of UCEA by-laws and a certificate of incorporation. Presented by Anderson, Norton, Pierce, and Rogers, the documents contained ideas approved in previous meetings. For instance, the articles of incorporation noted that UCEA "should promote, through inter-university cooperation, the improvement of the professional preparation of administrative personnel in the field of education." After approving both documents, Plenary members elected Russell Gregg, University of Wisconsin; John Norton, Teachers College; and Theodore Reller, California at Berkeley; to the Board of Trustees.

Between the 1958 and 1959 Plenary sessions the Board of Trustees resolved additional issues. In May of 1958 Paul Jacobson reported that four universities had submitted applications to host the UCEA: Northwestern, Ohio State, Pittsburgh, and Teachers College, Columbia. After a lengthy discussion the Board decided to locate UCEA at Ohio State. John Norton then moved that the president "be instructed to complete negotiations for the transfer of the UCEA from Teachers College to Ohio State" (B Min, 5/15-17/58, p.1).

At the Board's November, 1958, meeting Walter Anderson, President of UCEA, read a letter from Daniel Davies. After declining the executive directorship of UCEA, Davies wrote: "I am proud to be counted among all of you who have helped transform the dream of an inter-university group furthering research and development in the selection and preparation of educational administrators into reality" (B Min, 11/12-13/58, p.5). Jacobson led the group in a standing vote of appreciation for Davies' role in UCEA. Later the Board offered the executive directorship to Daniel Griffiths.

In February, 1959, at the third UCEA Plenary Session, Maurice Seay, Education Director of the W. K. Kellogg Foundation, asserted that the foundation "wants everyone to take . . . membership in . . . UCEA seriously. If the UCEA is a low priority on various campuses, then a big mistake has been made..." (PS Min, 2/19/59, p.3). Later in the meeting Walter Anderson reported that Daniel Griffiths had decided against accepting the post of executive director. He also requested that new nominations be submitted to members of the selection committee— Walter Anderson, John Norton, and John Ramseyer.

At its meeting in May, 1959, the Board of Trustees officially accepted the foundation grant. Having attained financial support, a set of by-laws, and a new home for UCEA's central unit, the leaders had completed the first phase of UCEA's development. Even though they at times, when faced with unsettling issues, had succumbed to competitive pressures, they had continued to cooperate. Daniel Davies, with the help of Hugh Masters, had projected an initial vision which caught the field's attention. However, leaders from other universities had to state and restate firmly that a "center for educational administration" was not the right means for facilitating the inter-institutional pursuit of the vision. Needed was a central unit which was at least one step removed from the powerful competitive forces which moved UCEA universities. After many months and much effort the group finally devised and approved such a unit.

Notes

1. At one point officials of the W. K. Kellogg Foundation considered asking NCPEA rather than AASA to help implement the CPEA effort. See Flesher, W. R., & Knoblaugh, A. L. (1957). *A decade of development in educational leadership.* Austin, TX: The National Conference of Professors of Educational Administration, p. 18.

2. For pertinent NCPEA references see Flesher, W. R., & Knoblaugh A. L. (1957). *A decade of development in educational leadership.* Austin, TX: The National Conference of Professors of Educational Administration.

3. For a synthesis of the positions taken at the 1947, 1948, and 1949 meetings see Miller, V. (Ed.). (1951). *Toward tomorrow's profession of school administration.* Austin, TX: National Conference of Professors of Educational Administration. For reports on the conclusions developed by early conferees see *The School Executive.* (1949). Essential elements for the preparation of the school administrator. 67(7), 58-62; *The School Executive.* (1949). Educational leaders—Their function and preparation, 68(7), 62-70; and Davies, D. R., & Flesher, W. R. (1950). A look at the school administrator's job. *The School Executive,* 69(110), 43-52.

4. For a description of the competency concepts see Southern States CPEA Center. (1955). *Better teaching in school administration.* Nashville, TN: McQuiddy Printing Co. For a comprehensive report on the work of the Southern States CPEA, plus a 21-page annotated bibliography, see Pierce, T. M., & Albright, A. D. (1960). *A profession in transition.* Nashville, TN: Southern States Cooperative Program in Educational Administration.

5. Individual professors at most CPEA centers as, for example, at Stanford, Teachers College, and Texas, developed and used cases.

6. See Sargent, C. G., & Belisle, E. L. (1955). *Educational administration: Cases and concepts.* Boston: Houghton Mifflin Co.

7. See Culbertson, J. A., Jacobson, P. B., & Reller, T. L. (1960). *Administrative relationships: A casebook.* Englewood Cliffs, NJ: Prentice-Hall, Inc.

8. For one example see Griffiths, D. E. (1956). *Human relations in school administration.* New York: Appleton-Century-Crofts, Inc.

9. For more than a century conceptions of science have significantly influenced inquiry in the field. However, the conceptions have changed as one era has given way to another. For details see Culbertson, J. A. (1988).

A century's quest for a knowledge base. In N. J. Boyan (Ed.), *Handbook of research on educational administration* (pp. 3-26). White Plains, NY: Longman, Inc.

10. Viktor Kraft has traced the early development of the Vienna Circle and outlined some of the key concepts and tenets of logical positivism. See Kraft, V. (1953). *The Vienna Circle: The origin of neopositivism.* New York: Philosophical Library. For a more thorough and probing analysis of logical positivism see Achinstein, P., & Barker, S. F. (Eds.). (1969). *The legacy of logical positivism.* Baltimore: The Johns Hopkins Press.

11. The author of the 1929 brochure is not listed. However, the record makes clear that the brochure was written by Otto Neurath with editorial help from Rudolph Carnap, Hans Hahn, and others. Therefore, Neurath is listed as its author.

12. For one account of the initial dissemination of logical positivistic ideas into America see Feigl, H. (1968). The Wiener Kreis in America. *Perspectives in American History,* II, 630-673. For a depiction of the diffusion of the ideas within Europe and beyond, see Joergensen, J. (1951). The development of logical empiricism. *International Encyclopedia of Unified Science,* 2(9), 1-100.

13. See Hull, C. L., et al. (1940). *Mathematico-deductive theory of rote learning.* New Haven, CT: Yale University Press.

14. For Halpin's, Thompson's, and the other seminar papers see Halpin, A. W. (Ed.). (1958). *Administrative theory in education.* New York: The Macmillan Company.

15. For details see Griffiths, D. E. (1959). *Administrative theory.* New York: Appleton-Century-Crofts, Inc.; Griffiths, D. E. (1959). *Research in educational administration.* New York: Bureau of Publications, Teachers College, Columbia University.

16. All unreferenced quotations related to the founding of UCEA are taken from a mimeographed paper emanating from the Teachers College CPEA Center. Entitled "Report of Cooperative Center for Educational Administration Conference," the paper's author is unknown.

17. References to the minutes of UCEA's governance meetings in this and in subsequent chapters are abbreviated as follows: Interim Committee minutes (IC Min); Board of Trustees minutes (B Min); Executive Committee minutes (EC Min); Plenary Session minutes (PS Min); and Partnership Coordinating Committee minutes (PCC Min).

References

Berkhof, W. L. (1949). Professionalism. *The Nation's Schools*, 43(4), 50-51.

Campbell, R. F., & Gregg, R. T. (Eds.). (1957). *Administrative behavior in education*. New York: Harper & Brothers Publishers.

Culbertson, J.A. (1981). Antecedents to the theory movement. *Educational Administration Quarterly*, XVII(1), 25-47.

Davies, D. R., & Flesher, W. R. (1950). A look at the school administrator's job. *The School Executive*. 69(11), 43-52.

Feigl, H. (1968). The Wiener Kreis in America. In D. Fleming & B. Bailyn. (Eds.)., *Perspectives in American History*. 2, 630-673.

Flesher, W. R., & Knoblauch, A. L. (1957). *A decade of development in educational leadership*. Austin, TX: The National Conference of Professors of Educational Administration.

Getzels, J. W. (1952). A psycho-sociological framework for the study of educational administration. *Harvard Educational Review*. 22(4), 235-246.

Griffiths, D. E. (1979). CADEA in retrospect. An unpublished paper presented to a meeting of the Collegiate Association for the Development of Educational Administration in Albany, New York.

Halpin, A. W. (1958a). Introduction. In A. W. Halpin (Ed.), *Administrative theory in education* (pp. xi-xiv). New York: The Macmillan Company.

Halpin, A. W. (1958b). The development of theory in educational administration. In A. W. Halpin (Ed.), *Administrative theory in education* (pp.1-19). New York: The Macmillan Company.

Hulburd, D. (1951). *This happened in Pasadena*. New York: The Macmillan Company.

Kellogg Foundation, W. K. (1942). *The W. K. Kellogg Foundation: The first eleven years*. Battle Creek, MI: Trustees of the W. K. Kellogg Foundation.

Kellogg Foundation, W. K. (1979). *The first half century: 1930-1980*. Battle Creek, MI: Trustees of the W. K. Kellogg Foundation.

Kyte, G. C. (1941). *The principal at work*. Boston: Ginn and Company.

Lundberg, G. A. (1950). The semantics of Charner Perry. *The American Political Science Review*, XLIV(2), 414-422.

Marshall, J. E. (Ed.). (1947). *Developing leaders for education*. Austin, TX: The National Conference of Professors of Educational Administration.

Middle Atlantic CPEA Center. (1951). *Annual report*. New York: Teachers College, Columbia University.

Midwest Administration CPEA Center. (1951). *Annual report: The first year of the Midwest Cooperative Program.* Chicago: The University of Chicago.

Moehlman, A. B. (1951). *School administration: Its development, principles, and function in the United States.* Boston: Houghton Mifflin Company.

Moore, Jr. H. A. (1957). *Studies in school administration.* Washington, DC: American Association of School Administrators.

Neurath, O. (1935). *Le développement du cercle de Vienna et l'avenir de l'empirisme logique.* Paris: Librairi Scientifique Herman et Cie.

Neurath, O. (1973). *The scientific conception of the world.* In M. Neurath and R. S. Cohen (Eds.), *Empiricism and sociology* (pp. 301-318). Dordrecht-Holland: D. Reidel Publishing Company.

Perry, C. (1951). The semantics of political science. *The American Political Science Review,* XLIV(2), 374-414.

Reeder, W. G. (1951). *The fundamentals of public school administration.* New York: The Macmillan Company.

Rogers, V. M. (1950). Administrators are under fire. *The School Executive,* 70(1), 37-38.

Schlick, M. (1947). The future of philosophy. In D. J. Bronstein, Y. H. Krikorian, & P. P. Wiener (Eds.), *Basic problems of philosophy* (pp.730-748). New York: Prentice Hall, Inc.

Schwab, J. J. (1964). The professorship in educational administration: Theory--art--practice. In D. J. Willower & J. A. Culbertson. (Eds.), *The professorship in educational administration* (47-70). Columbus, OH: University Council for Education Administration.

Scriven, M. (1969). Logical positivism and the behavioral sciences. In P. Achinstein & S. F. Barker (Eds.), *The legacy of logical positivism* (pp. 195-209). Baltimore, MD: The Johns Hopkins Press.

Simon, H. A. (1947). *Administrative behavior.* New York: The Macmillan Company.

Southern States CPEA Center. (1951). *Annual report: Cooperative program in educational administration.* Nashville: George Peabody College for Teachers.

The Nation's Schools. (1948). Current theories of administration illustrated in La Grange survey. 41(1), 26.

The Nation's Schools. (1950). AASA-Kellogg project. 46(5), 31-35.

The Ohio State CPEA Center. (1952). *Annual report: Cooperative program in educational administration.* Columbus, OH: The Ohio State University.

The School Executive. (1947). We salute the American Association of School Administrators. 67(3), 5.

Thompson, J. D. (1958). Modern approaches to theory in administration. In A. W. Halpin (Ed.), (1958). *Administrative theory in education* (pp. 20-39). New York: The Macmillan Company.

Toulmin, S. E. (1969). From logical analysis to conceptual history. In P. Achinstein, & S. F. Barker (Eds.), *The legacy of logical positivism* (pp. 25-53). Baltimore: The Johns Hopkins Press.

Waldo, D. (1955). *The study of public administration*. New York: Doubleday and Company, Inc.

3

Beginnings

"The beginning is the most important part of the work."

Plato

About ten days after arriving in Columbus I traveled to Buffalo, New York, to take part in the National Conference of Professors of Educational Administration (NCPEA). Held on August 23-28, 1959, the conference's theme was "Administrative Training and Executive Development in Other Fields." As leaders from business, government, and hospital administration made their presentations, I arrived at an idea for a UCEA activity which was later implemented: visits by groups of UCEA professors to selected "Lighthouse" training programs in their regions. During the visits they would exchange ideas with specialists engaged in preparing executives for particular types of organizations. At the NCPEA meeting I also obtained much advice about what UCEA might do to improve training and advance research. The sessions spawned a variety of suggestions. They ranged all the way from raising "big money" for professorial research to the promotion of one professor's newly written textbook.

Since NCPEA members had elected me to their Executive Committee the previous summer, and I was to become UCEA's executive director within a week, I had dual roles to perform at the conference. At times I felt awkward because of the concerns some professors had about NCPEA-UCEA relationships. Near the end of the conference John Ramseyer, an Ohio State professor, introduced me as UCEA's new executive director. Aware of the prevailing unease about UCEA, Ramseyer stressed that I was an "objective" problem-solver. After the introduction I made a few comments. Immediately thereafter John Benben of Northern Illinois University arose and angrily expressed his views. Directing his ire chiefly at UCEA's "elite" image, he decried the exclusionary membership policy which kept many NCPEA professors outside the organization.

Since I had acquired some insight into the NCPEA culture during the three previous conferences, I was not surprised at Benben's reactions. An unusually hospitable organization, NCPEA warmly welcomed all comers. Noted for its family atmosphere, its constant bent was toward inclusion. Thus, when the "elite" UCEA appeared on the scene, many of NCPEA's members did not like the message they received, namely: they could not belong to the organization because their institutions did not meet UCEA's standards. Reflected in John Benben's passionate remarks, then, were attitudes shared by other NCPEA professors. Also reflected in his angry words was a special problem: how could more wholesome relations between UCEA and NCPEA professors be realized? Judging the problem to be a significant one, I began to analyze it. Three months later I recommended seven policy guidelines to the UCEA Board of Trustees for ameliorating NCPEA-UCEA relations.

Issues Encountered During University Visits

On September 1, 1959, Associate Director William Coffield and I began our labors in UCEA's headquarters at Ohio State.[1] A former chemistry teacher and a supervising principal in Mobile, Alabama, Bill had been schooled in quantitative research during his doctoral work at Iowa. In 1959-60 he spent one-third of his time working on the UCEA-sponsored "Criteria of Success" project, and the other two-thirds in a staff role. While in Columbus the two of us had many informal debates on research and training issues. Our exchanges were lively, in part because we often disagreed. At times Bill would teasingly tell me that I should listen to him carefully, because he was more nearly representative of the professoriate than was I! The searching exchanges helped prepare us for upcoming UCEA events.

Keenly aware that we were in a new and far-flung organization, and that we had no neatly crafted strategies for pursuing its mission, we decided to visit, jointly or singly, during 1959-60 most if not all of the 34 universities in UCEA. Since professors were to be the major implementers of UCEA programs, we needed to establish and maintain close links with them. During the visits we met with staffs and talked individually with all professors who were available. We also conversed with deans of education and, in some institutions, with professors in related disciplines. On the visit to Harvard, for instance, Neal Gross, the sociologist, warned me not to "oversell" the social sciences to the field. After each visit we recorded on audio tapes the information we had obtained about professors' talents, interests, aspirations, and accomplishments.

Not infrequently we received unexpected messages. Many of them pinpointed what would prove to be perennial problems. During one string of visits I listened at length to two angry administrators of higher education: Ralph Cherry, Dean of the School of Education at the University of Virginia, and Ralph Rackley, Dean of the College of Education at Pennsylvania State. Because planners of a conference on UCEA research policy held in, 1958-59, had excluded representatives from their universities, they were visibly upset. When I later reviewed the record, I learned that the UCEA Board, after asking each member university to nominate a conference candidate, had chosen 13 attendees from a list of 28 nominees. Both deans felt strongly that UCEA research policy was of such fundamental import that representatives from all institutions should have a say in its formation.

The message from the two deans provided food for thought for one who would often be involved in determining participants in UCEA endeavors. Very early I resolved that equity would play a prominent role in such choices. However, in the years ahead I would encounter the anger of individual professors and even of staffs who had felt the pain of exclusion from projects in which they wanted to participate. UCEA's elite status enhanced the perceived value of participation, at the same time that it added to the discontent of those excluded from circles in which they wanted to sit. Limited time and resources, incomplete information, and the press for mission attainment would make it difficult always to hold high the ideal of equity.

While I was visiting a university in New York, the influential head of the department of educational administration there pinpointed another issue. Early in the meeting he asserted that he and his staff would not be sharing valued ideas: "We do not have anything against you, Culbertson. We only want to ensure that our ideas are not stolen." Although the concern about the "stealing of ideas" receded somewhat with time, two decades later it was still much alive in the professoriate. Seemingly spawned by inter-institutional distrust and by intense competition among university professors for funds, faculty, and fame, the press to protect esteemed ideas often interfered with UCEA's efforts to nurture cooperative action.

While visiting the University of Iowa in 1960, I met with Elmer Peterson, Dean of the College of Education. After expressing hope that UCEA would prosper, he shared with me his concerns about UCEA membership fees. First, he was not sure that his university would continue to approve the expenditures, especially since the fee would increase from $100 in 1959-60, to $500 in 1963-64. Second, he was worried that professors in other departments of the college would object to his providing special support to professors of educational administration. These concerns of the midwestern dean would be expressed again and again by other deans in the years ahead.

During the visits professors made clear that they valued UCEA. Belonging to an organization of the nation's leading universities afforded them a unique status. Excited by knowledge already acquired at UCEA seminars, many looked forward to working on projects with professors from other universities. At the same time some worried about UCEA's ultimate success. Thus, during visits we were intermittently asked, "Can UCEA survive?" Soon I developed a response which I subsequently repeated many times: "If UCEA is effective in pursuing its important mission, it will survive; if not, it will not deserve to endure." The survival question did not go away. At a 1973 planning meeting, for instance, two widely known professors predicted that UCEA would not last another five years.

In November, 1959, Bill Coffield and I traveled to Battle Creek, Michigan, to meet with Maurice Seay, the W. K. Kellogg Foundation's director of education. Arriving in late afternoon, we went directly to his home. Soon afterward he showed us a photograph of a group of elementary school students sitting in front of a one-room Kentucky school. Assuring us that he was one of the students in the photograph, he promised us an extra drink if we could identify him. Bill and I scrutinized the picture carefully. However, we failed to identify Maurice. Even though we flunked the exercise, it proved to be a good icebreaker. We soon were animatedly talking about our respective educational and social experiences in the south.

During the dinner hour the conversation took a more serious turn. After sharing some thoughts about his work at The University of Chicago, Maurice Seay spoke about his role in monitoring the eight university centers which comprised the foundation-supported Cooperative Program in Educational Administration (CPEA). In turn, Bill and I reported impressions gleaned from university visits and talked about their import for UCEA endeavors. Near the end of the evening Maurice shared with us some unexpected observations which, as I recall, went as follows:

> Most of the foundation's investments are safe ones. Making such investments can be compared to stepping out the door, walking around the corner, and depositing money in a bank. We know there will be a return. However, the UCEA investment is different. We encountered serious problems in getting the project off the ground. UCEA leaders had much difficulty in agreeing on a mission and in choosing a home for the new organization. More seriously, they at times distrusted one another. We want the two of you to know that the UCEA investment, as we see it, is a very risky one. We also want you to know that if the endeavor fails, we will not hold it against you.

Although I had heard others say that the UCEA enterprise was a risky one, I had not expected to hear it from Maurice Seay. However, I valued his candid communication and his reassuring attitude.

Inter-University Cooperation: Purposes and Patterns

Within weeks it became clear that the over-riding immediate *and* five-year challenge was that of developing mission-related programs. Only through such programs could valued outcomes be produced. However, the information which professors were transmitting to us about their interests, while valuable, provided an insufficient base for designing programs. Concepts had to be generated to guide program development. We quickly recognized that excessive time spent "on the road" could be detrimental to program development. Thus, I immediately became enmeshed in a never ending UCEA struggle: achieving and maintaining a balance between external engagements and internal thinking about objectives and programs.

Another important question soon arose. What means did the UCEA staff have for influencing mission-related change? The essential one, it seemed, was ideas. However, an early barrier to the translation of ideas into programs was that my concepts of inter-university cooperation were murkily defined. I recognized that cooperation called for a broadened perspective on human benefit, an altruistic rather than an egoistic attitude on the part of its practitioners, and the bringing of others into the foreground. Because these features struck me as noble ones, the ethic of cooperation appealed to me strongly. However, I was unclear about the operational meanings of UCEA cooperation.

In 1959-60, as I perused the *New York Times*, I noticed that reports on newly created consortia in higher education were appearing more frequently. The missions of the new consortia varied. Some planned to cooperate in the exchange of information, others in sharing libraries, professors, or instructional technologies, and still others in research or development. The aspirations of UCEA's founders, it seemed clear, were neither small nor timid. They wanted their new creation to go beyond the exchange of information and to perform the much more complex tasks of inter-university development and research.

To learn that UCEA was a part of a larger movement, and that cooperative initiatives in higher education were in a distinct uptrend, was both reassuring and exciting—reassuring in that leaders were assigning a higher priority to cooperation, and exciting in that UCEA, as the only *nation-wide* consortium of which I was aware, offered unusual experimental opportunities. Such opportunities motivated me to think seriously about two questions: why pursue inter-university cooperation, and what patterns of cooperation might best advance dissemination, development, and research?

The rationale for inter-institutional cooperation which I had heard stated was that universities as a group could do things together that they could not do separately. While the statement seemed sensible, it did not satisfy me. To envisage the potential in inter-university cooperation more clearly, I examined the subject in an essay published in the UCEA Annual Report of 1962-63. In the essay I proposed that inter-university cooperation might help advance large scale research and development, facilitate the spread of innovations in higher education, and deploy human resources more efficiently.

Technological development in industry and research in the natural sciences, I noted, had moved beyond the work of single individuals to that of large-scale cooperative endeavors. Given the complexity of social and educational problems, "small scale and isolated approaches to the solution of problems and/or the advancement of knowledge..." needed to be "supplemented by more encompassing, ... and long-range efforts;" further, the UCEA laboratory of inter-university cooperation could provide "an excellent ground for developing and testing large-scale organizational ... " efforts (Culbertson, 1963, p. 4).

In the essay I stated that universities in "the next few decades will be faced" with a great "need to adapt, to change, and to become more effective. . ." (Culbertson, 1963, p. 6). Whether in fact they adapted would be "determined in part by their openness to . . . ideas and by the opportunities available to their personnel for learning and innovation" (p. 6). A cooperative organization which could "bind talent to talent, by putting capable individuals interested in similar problems in communication with one another," could facilitate an examination of the status quo, the development of needed innovations, and some insurance of their use (p. 9).

Founded decades before the jet age, the earliest higher education consortia's members were located near one another: For instance, the five which made up the Claremont Colleges, a consortium founded in 1925, were all within the same square mile (Bernard, 1962, p. 40). Such consortia helped ensure that colleges used one another's libraries and staff more efficiently. Though UCEA leaders were widely dispersed, they were faced with "rising enrollments, rising costs, increasing scarcity of personnel, heightened competition for resources. . ." (Culbertson, 1963, p. 3). Another potential outcome of cooperation, then, was greater efficiency, especially in nurturing, developing, and deploying UCEA's large reservoir of human resources.

It was one thing to project fruitful outcomes, and another to conceive patterns of cooperation to attain them. Eight weeks into the job, at a meeting in Washington, DC, I set forth my initial thoughts on such patterns (*UCEA Newsletter*, 1(2), 203). Subsequently, I had copious opportunities to refine and test what became five relatively distinct patterns. Two patterns, labeled decentralized and centralized, were defined in terms of organizational locus. Three—individual, group, and institutional—highlighted the primary participating agents.

In the *decentralized* pattern professors in one UCEA university coordinated a project, while those from other universities took part in it. Especially helpful in the exchange of information, this pattern was employed early to implement UCEA Career Development Seminars and institutes on "New Methods and Materials." It was also used to facilitate cooperative research in a project headed by Daniel Griffiths whose staff included professors from New York University, Illinois, and Rochester.[2] Later the pattern proved helpful in the development of new journals. In the decentralized type of operation the UCEA central staff initiated or enabled others to initiate projects, recommended them to the UCEA Board, and helped disseminate and extend the outreach of their products.

The pattern had its advantages: it provided those in sponsoring universities valued experiences and outcomes, and it freed the central staff from time consuming coordination demands. At times it facilitated project funding, since some federal agencies could not by law provide grants to UCEA. Since the pattern did not deviate markedly from university traditions, it was also easily grasped and accepted. However, when it was used to facilitate research, non-participants sometimes felt that the research project belonged to the sponsoring university rather than to UCEA. Thus, the pattern sometimes activated competitive rather than cooperative instincts.

A second pattern, which contrasted sharply with the one just described, was highly *centralized*. Both the co-ordinators and the implementers of the project resided at UCEA's headquarters. Through a federal grant, obtained in 1964, to implement the "Articulated Media Project", the pattern was tested. Located in an office near that of UCEA's regular staff, the project's implementers, among other things, designed a computer based simulation and a negotiations game.

The pattern had its strengths. Project staff members were protected from the many demands placed upon professors. In addition, they had an advantage, given their central location, in disseminating project outcomes. The computer based simulation, for instance, was demonstrated to scores of professors at three UCEA universities. However, because the pattern made limited use of inter-university cooperation, it had a distinct flaw. Some, feeling that the project did not belong to professors, argued that it should have been implemented in a UCEA university. Other problems arose, because the three able staff members, who were employed to implement the project, had neither met one another, before they came to UCEA, nor had they had a role in conceiving the endeavor. As a result, they never achieved a fully unified view of the project's mission.

The central agents in the other three patterns of cooperation, as already noted, were *individuals, groups,* and *institutions*. In the first pattern individual professors, working independently in their respective universities, performed mission-related developmental tasks. One product they developed was case studies depicting decision problems. Another was audio recordings of their "best lectures." Through the Case Studies Program, initiated in 1959-60, and the Best Lecture Series, launched in 1961-62, they prepared dozens of cases and lectures which were disseminated within and beyond UCEA.

This relatively simple pattern facilitated development by *individuals*. Since its outcomes were clear cut, and large quantities of products were not expected, it made limited demands on the central unit. Among other things, the staff wrote developmental guidelines, recruited referees to evaluate the materials created, edited written products, established distribution systems, publicized the products, and encouraged research on their uses. Enabling individuals to pursue specified purposes, the pattern did not suffer, as did other patterns, from exclusionary tendencies. All professors willing to abide by project guidelines could volunteer to pursue stipulated developmental objectives. However, in contrast to other patterns, it did not provide them opportunities to cooperate with professors from other universities. Their cooperation was largely with the UCEA staff.

The next pattern was designed to advance the work of *groups*. Enabling teams of professors to develop ideas or products, the pattern was used to advance the work of task forces in 1961-62 and, several years later, to simulate the Madison School District. Its most far-reaching use began in 1969 with the development of the "Monroe City" simulation. In this project numerous teams, made up of professors from different UCEA universities, sought to create particular sets of materials. The simulated Wilson High School, for instance, was developed by such a team.

The group pattern's greatest strength lay in its capacity for advancing large scale, development programs. No one university could have begun to construct the many disparate components of the Monroe City simulations. In the latter project about 190 professors from upwards of 40 universities worked cooperatively, over a six-year period, to bring the simulations into being. The pattern, a flexible one, also enabled other patterns to be integrated into its operation. By disseminating information about the simulations through approximately 70 institutes sponsored mostly by universities, it employed the *decentralized* pattern. By involving 16 professors in the preparation of 16 "background" booklets on such facets of Monroe City as its power structure and its demography, the project used the *individual* pattern. In addition, the pattern constituted a powerful dynamic for change. Professors not only acquired and used the simulations they developed, but also they persuaded others to adopt them.

The group pattern, as compared to others, made much greater demands upon the central staff. There was an ever present press for concepts to guide the Monroe City project and to move it from one phase to another. As teams completed simulations, the staff co-ordinated the work of other professors who critically read materials, previewed media products, or tested them in classrooms. Following needed revisions, the central staff, as the only ones familiar with all the simulated materials, edited documents and facilitated the reproduction of audio-recordings, films, film strips, and videotapes.

Because the group pattern was geared toward large scale development, it engendered more bottlenecks, slippages, and outright failures than did other patterns. Spread among many activities, the mishaps occurred fairly frequently and brought delayed, and at times, failed efforts. Thus, the pattern sheds considerable light upon the problems of large scale inter-institutional development (see Chapter Eight).

The third pattern was designed to facilitate the work of teams in different UCEA *institutions*. Although the latter pattern was conceived early in the life of UCEA, immediate attempts to implement it ended in failure. In the early sixties, for instance, its potential was discussed with officials at the Carnegie Foundation in a proposed study of the politics of education. To be conducted by three teams of professors and graduate students of political science and educational administration in three UCEA universities, the project, as proposed, would have enabled each team to work on a particular component of a larger program of inquiry. Unfortunately, the project failed to attract needed support, possibly because its proposed activities were not well defined.

In the 1970s the institutional pattern was finally employed in two federally funded projects. One, involving 31 institutions of higher education, was directed at the integration of training programs for general and special education administrators. The other, a six-university project, developed training materials for enhancing women's equity in educational administration. In the latter project each university had its own development team which intermittently met with the other university teams. Each team produced a set of materials which complemented sets created by the five other teams.

The major advantage of the institutional pattern, especially as implemented in the 31-university consortium, was its capacity for changing university programs. The primary units of change in the consortium were departments of educational administration and special education. In each of the 31 institutions one professor of general and one professor of special education administration sought in varied ways to effect joint learning experiences for their students. Inter-university teams of professors assisted local change agents, for example, through the implementation of regional seminars for students in the two departments and through the creation of new training materials (see Chapter Five). The primary functions of the patterns previously discussed were to develop products and/or knowledge and to transmit them for use. In contrast the institutional pattern, by addressing UCEA's mission directly rather than indirectly, altered training programs. Significantly, the pattern combined the efforts of external change agents (i.e. central project staff) with those of internal change agents (i.e. the two-professor teams).

The institutional pattern incorporated into its structure and operations most of the other patterns. In the six-university women's equity project, for example, the decentralized, individual, and group patterns were all utilized (see Chapter Six). Because the institutional pattern included some but not all universities in projects, it activated feelings of exclusion and opposition among some non-participants. Professors who opposed the purposes of the two projects would have been happier, in other words, if they could have pursued their own prized objectives in a different consortium. The pattern also brought forth the reverse problem. Some in non-participating universities valued the objectives of the projects and were upset because their universities were uninvolved.

In sum, then, the need for clearly defined patterns of cooperation quickly became apparent. Five patterns were conceived and tested. Departing least from university traditions, the decentralized pattern was used frequently. The centralized pattern, which was the least rooted in inter-university cooperation, was used only a few times. Requiring close cooperation between the central staff and participating professors, the other three patterns—individual, group, and institutional—provided flexible, versatile, and effective means for facilitating inter-university cooperation and for attaining mission-related outcomes.

Seminars and Simulations

When I became UCEA's executive director, the organization already had some on-going programs. The most widely known was the

Career Development Seminar. Three such seminars, all offered by private universities, were implemented before UCEA became an official entity. The first, sponsored by The University of Chicago in November, 1957, was entitled, "Toward the Development of a Theory of Educational Administration;" the second, held at Harvard University in February, 1958, explored "Case Methods;" and the third, offered by Northwestern University in November, 1958, focused on "Community Analysis and Administrative Decision-Making." The seminars were designed to improve the professional competence of UCEA professors as well as to challenge contemporary thinking and practice.

As a participant in UCEA's first three seminars, I found them to be exciting, in part because they brought fresh concepts into the field. Although some professors wanted to change the seminars, almost all valued the learnings they afforded and wanted them to have a prominent place on the programmatic landscape of UCEA. Twenty-five of these seminars were offered during my 22 years at UCEA. From the fall of 1959 to the spring of 1964, the following were scheduled:

"Government of Public Education for Adequate Policy Making," University of Illinois, November, 1959.

"Development of Criteria of Success in School Administration," Teachers College, Columbia, May, 1960.

"Values: A Key Variable in the Administrative Complex," The Ohio State University, November, 1961.

"Communication," Stanford University, April, 1962.

"Common and Specialized Learnings for Personnel Preparing for Different Administrative Positions," Michigan State University, November, 1962.

"The Economics and Politics of School Finance," Syracuse University, May, 1963.

"Educational Administration: Philosophy in Action," University of Oklahoma, November, 1963.

"The Professorship in Educational Administration," The Pennsylvania State University, May, 1964.

The published proceedings of the seminars constituted a new resource for the field. The best ones provided professors and graduate students ground-breaking concepts and perspectives. Notably, the seminars were financed by the sponsoring universities.

Another important on-going program was the "Criteria of Success" project which was led by Daniel Griffiths of Teachers College, Columbia, and John Hemphill and Norman Frederiksen of the Educational Testing Service. Directed initially at defining the job of school administrators and at developing an instrument for selecting them,[3] the project's uses of simulation attracted much attention.[4] By gathering extensive information on an actual suburban community and its school system, the research team simulated the "Jefferson Township" system, the "Whitman School" within Jefferson, and an array of decision problems which Whitman's new school principal, "Marion Smith," faced. In so doing the researchers brought to the field a novel research context and a unique set of training materials.

The first task of the 232 "principals" of Whitman during the research phase of the project was to get acquainted with the Jefferson community. In so doing they viewed a film and a film strip, studied a written community survey, and read school board policies. They then examined, among other things, a school census, teacher personnel records, test scores, a staff handbook, data on class size, a staff roster, and a description of Whitman's intricate, informal web of staff relationships. As principals, the 232 "Marion Smiths" made decisions about accumulated problems found in three different "in-baskets" on their desks. Illustrative items were a note from a teacher protesting the methods another teacher was using to teach fractions, a memo from the superintendent about bicycle riding, a note from a teacher about a student who was unable to do class work, and a letter from a mother which contended that the class in which her child was enrolled was progressing more slowly than were other classes. Whitman principals also observed kinescopes showing selected teachers at work and then evaluated their effectiveness. The principals made decisions about problems presented to them by their secretaries through audio-recordings and participated in a group problem-solving situation. Finally, they aided the researchers by providing detailed notes on their choices.

Professors quickly recognized that the simulation had import for training school administrators. In the summer of 1959, even before the project was completed, Hollis Moore at Stanford, and Luvern

Cunningham at Chicago, offered workshops in which trainees made decisions as Whitman's school principal. In the spring of 1959 Harold McNally and Richard Wynn at Teachers College, Columbia, began planning a fall clinic on simulated problems. Given such developments, the UCEA staff immediately faced the following question: what initiatives might best serve professors' burgeoning interests in simulation?

In October, 1959, a group met in Chicago to explore the question. Participating were those from Chicago, Stanford, and Teachers College, who had used the simulations; Daniel Griffiths and Norman Frederiksen who, with others, had created the simulations; Laurence Iannaccone of Washington University, who had done the Whitman faculty study; and Hollis Moore, Executive Secretary of the Committee for the Advancement of School Administrators (CASA). From the deliberations came four objectives which the UCEA Board approved one month later: a funded project to study the instructional effects of simulation; the simulation of Jefferson positions other than the Whitman principalship; experimental uses of the Whitman materials by four to six additional universities; and a monograph on simulation to be published jointly by UCEA and CASA.

In January, 1960, Daniel Griffiths, Norman Frederiksen, Bill Coffield, and I wrote a proposal to study the instructional effects of simulation on 450 students in 10 universities, and submitted it to the U.S. Office of Education. After learning four months later that federal officials had rejected the proposal, we abandoned the research objective. However, we did attain the other three objectives. In May, 1960, UCEA and CASA published the monograph, *Simulation in Administrative Training*.[5] Subsequently, Luvern Cunningham, University of Minnesota, Donald Erickson, University of Chicago, and Conrad Briner, Claremont Graduate School, simulated the Jefferson High School principalship. Norton Beach and Daniel Griffiths of Teachers College created the Jefferson superintendency, and Felix McCormick at Teachers College simulated the Jefferson business manager post.

In the spring of 1961, after several discussions with publishers, Daniel Griffiths concluded that the commercial distribution of the simulated materials was not feasible. He then submitted the materials to the UCEA staff to see if we might find ways of disseminating them. Believing that the simulations had unique instructional potential, the staff developed a distribution plan. In the fall of 1961, the Board of Trustees decided that UCEA itself should distribute the materials on a non-profit basis to member and non-member institutions.

Because the demand for the Whitman materials was greater than we anticipated, the UCEA mimeograph machine during the first five months of 1961 was often overworked. Instead of reproducing simulations for six universities, we provided them for twenty. Within five months the UCEA staff, with the help of Ohio State students, reproduced and assembled approximately 660,000 pages of written materials. Richard George, UCEA's administrative assistant, managed the operation. However, since all of us spent time on the project, we sometimes wondered if we were expending our energies wisely. Nevertheless, our work enabled numerous professors and about 600 student to experience the Whitman School simulation during the summer of 1961. More significantly, the effort set in motion a series of events which by 1975 had made UCEA the nation's leading developer and distributor of simulated administrative positions, functions, and problems.

The UCEA Board of Trustees, recognizing that most professors were unfamiliar with simulation materials, enacted a "training-for-use" requirement. To meet the requirement professors typically attended a UCEA Institute on "New Methods and Materials for Preparing School Administrators."[6] After previewing the Jefferson materials and making decisions as "principals" of Whitman, attendees saw professors demonstrate methods for using the simulations. Ten institutes were conducted during the 1961-64 period. By 1980 the number of institutes sponsored by UCEA had passed the 100 mark. Professors also demonstrated various simulations to national audiences. For instance, Richard Wynn, University of Pittsburgh, and 15 additional professors demonstrated the Whitman simulation to approximately 3800 principals at the 1963 annual meeting of the National Education Association's Department of Elementary School Principals.

The Search for "Big Money"

Enabling professors to use simulations was not the only UCEA program the staff pursued. Before we arrived in Columbus, the UCEA Board had already approved for implementation three additional endeavors: a national fellowship program to recruit able educational leaders into preparatory programs; a study of the purposes and functions of state departments of education; and a case development program. Daniel Davies and Daniel Griffiths had already initiated a search for funds to support the fellowship program and the study of state departments of education. However, the case development program, only recently approved, was yet to be defined.

In pursuing the three projects I soon found myself in the special world of foundations. As an intermediary between foundations and UCEA, I encountered perplexing issues. Fortunately, Francis Keppel, Dean of the School of Education at Harvard, chaired the committee on fellowship funds. About a dozen years earlier at the age of 31 and with only a B.A. degree, Keppel had become dean of Harvard's school of education. When I met him in 1959, he was by my lights an outstanding educator and the most successful procurer of foundation funds among deans of education in the United States.[7] As UCEA sought funds during its early years, he provided me very helpful advice and accompanied me on several visits to different foundations.

The funding committee under Keppel's leadership decided to seek immediate fellowship aid from foundations and to encourage the federal government to address long range needs through a national fellowship program. In November, 1959, Keppel and I explored the fellowship idea with Lester Nelson of the Ford Foundation, who encouraged us to prepare a proposal for subsequent review.

Later in the month I submitted a proposal for a five year, five million dollar, fellowship program to the UCEA Board which approved it in principle. In the spring of 1960 the funding committee met with foundation officials. Serving on the committee with Francis Keppel were John Fischer, a former school superintendent in Baltimore and a candidate for a doctorate at Teachers College, and three deans of education: Paul Jacobson, Oregon; Virgil Rogers, Syracuse; and Lindley Stiles, Wisconsin. Foundation officials Clarence Faust, Philip Coombs, Lester Nelson, and Paul Woodring attended the meeting.

Foundation officials agreed that the proposal addressed an important problem. However, they questioned whether fellowships were the best means of ameliorating it. They also raised three additional questions. Was the fellowship program designed to recruit students into *existing* preparatory programs the soundest initiative? How would UCEA allocate fellowship funds among its universities? Who would determine the recipients of fellowship aid and the universities they attended? At the end of the discussion foundation officials agreed to take the proposal under consideration.

In the spring of 1960, at the suggestion of Francis Keppel, I met with Lawrence Derthick, U.S. Commissioner of Education, to discuss the fellowship idea. As a former school superintendent in Chattanooga, Tennessee, and a recent president of the American Association of School Administrators (AASA), he was keenly aware of the need for able school executives. When he suggested that his immediate staff examine the idea, we agreed to meet with him and his associates Homer Babbidge, Jr., Ralph Flynt, Peter Muirhead, and Wayne Reed, in June, 1960. Representing UCEA at the meeting were John Fischer and Herold Hunt. Hunt, a former superintendent of schools in Chicago, was a professor of educational administration at Harvard.

At the June meeting the group agreed to support the concept of federal aid to improve pre-service and in-service programs for school administrators. The Commissioner asked me to take the lead in writing a specific proposal and in the process to confer with Finis Engleman, Executive Secretary of AASA, and with Edgar Fuller, Executive Secretary of the Chief State School Officers. He also asked Ralph Flynt, Assistant Commissioner for Legislative and Program Development, to assist me in the undertaking. Finally, the group agreed that the proposal, if accepted, should be inserted in one of the titles of the National Defense Education Act.

In September, 1960, the participants in the June meeting plus Finis Engleman and Edgar Fuller met to examine the written proposal. Projected was a five-year, 21-million dollar investment in fellowships and about 12 million dollars for leadership institutes and related in-service endeavors. Encountering little objection to the proposal, Commissioner Derthick asked Ralph Flynt to translate the ideas into legislation. Although Flynt later searched for a congressional sponsor, he did not find one. However, by the mid-sixties, through a broadened interpretation of the National Defense Education Act, future school leaders were receiving federal fellowship aid to support their doctoral work. After President John Kennedy appointed Francis Keppel U.S. Commissioner of Education in 1962, in-service education for school administrators received a special boost. Under Keppel's leadership substantial support for in-service education was realized.

In July, 1960, Philip Coombs informed me that the Ford Foundation had decided not to support the fellowship proposal. The problem of training, he wrote, needed "to be looked at in total rather than dealt with in pieces" (official correspondence, July 15, 1960). Expressing his interest in effecting a "large breakthrough in the whole field of educational administration," he wanted to explore investments in a small number of "pilot" university programs. On October 6, 1960, Francis Keppel and I met with Philip Coombs, Clarence Faust, and Lester Nelson of the Ford Foundation to clarify Coombs' stated interest. At the meeting foundation leaders again made clear their opposition to fellowship aid for recruits who would enroll in *existing* university programs. Coombs also stressed that a breakthrough in preparation could not be achieved by using existing concepts of training. When I asked if UCEA might recruit six to eight outstanding thinkers to elaborate new directions in training and to present their ideas at a national conference, the foundation leaders quickly agreed to provide UCEA a $25,000 grant to implement the idea.

The foundation's rejection of the fellowship proposal sent a sober message to those who had dreamed about "big money" for UCEA. The message was further reinforced when several potential donors declined to support the large-scale study of state education agencies. Conversations held during and after UCEA's searches for "big money" revealed that there were unofficial as well as official reasons why the projects failed. For one thing, UCEA had no record or experience in conducting multi-million dollar, inter-university projects. For another, all the experienced fundraisers and project implementers were in member universities rather than in UCEA's central headquarters. Third, the project was scheduled for the 1961-66 period; however, UCEA's future was only fully assured through 1964.

Perhaps the most serious barriers to the acquisition of large grants were political ones. For decades leaders in UCEA's elite institutions had competed intensively with one another for external monies. Even UCEA's founders were greatly concerned that some UCEA institutions would garner more than their share of external grants. Thus, when foundation leaders asked about how the fellowship funds would be allocated among students and universities, they pinpointed a major political problem. None of us offered a satisfactory solution to it. Not surprisingly, we later heard that foundation officials were skeptical about the central staff's capacity to "stand up" to its 40 autonomous and powerful university "bosses."

Implicit in Philip Coombs' desire to invest in a small number of university training programs was a dilemma: how could the UCEA Board and staff members, who were expected to serve all member universities, help only a few acquire grants? During the 1961-64 period UCEA did find ways to serve the interests of some funding agencies while affording its members equality of opportunity. In 1961-62 the staff informed all UCEA Plenary members about the Russell Sage Foundation's interest in providing grants to sociologists to study problems in school systems. About ten universities submitted proposals of which three were funded. In 1963-64 UCEA informed each member university that officials in the National Institute of Mental Health wanted to fund a few innovative proposals for improving the training of school administrators. Later the officials decided to support two proposals from among the dozen they received. The University of Chicago and the University of New Mexico were awarded approximately $800,000 to carry out new training initiatives. The options used by Russell Sage and National Institute officials did not mesh with the practices of most funding agencies. Typically, officials in such agencies preferred to work directly with grantees—not through intermediaries.

Early R and D Initiatives

While searching for external funds, we were also assessing UCEA's internal resources, especially the human ones, and exploring how they could be deployed and developed. In 1959-60, while conversing with more than 200 professors during visits to universities, Bill Coffield and I were at times overwhelmed by UCEA's disparate voices. However, we soon perceived in the midst of the diverse expressions patterns of interest which stretched across institutions. One re-occurring question, for instance, was the following: in university training programs what content should be studied by those preparing for particular positions (e.g. the principalship) only, and what content should be studied by all prospective school administrators?

At the end of 30 university visits we had identified eight areas of interest. Four were linked to preparation: common and specialized learnings for elementary, secondary and general administrators; social science content in training; field experiences; and new instructional methods and materials. The other four reflected research interests: communication in organizations; the politics of education; the selection of school administrators; and staff utilization. About 80 professors representing most of UCEA's universities had expressed strong interests in at least one of the eight areas.

In the summer of 1960, we made plans to activate eight task forces to address each of the eight interests. Between November 9, 1960, and February 7, 1961, all of the task forces met. One planned outcome was that all participants in the meetings would be able to share and examine ideas about innovative training practices or about completed, on-going, or proposed inquiry. A second planned outcome was that each task force would identify crucial problems in its domain of interest and elaborate a set of objectives to guide its future activities.

At each of the eight meetings participants shared ideas and probed crucial problems. However, they were unable to define objectives to guide future ventures. Some were unsure they could fulfill future commitments. Most did not see how to mesh their interests with the interests of others. All seemed more comfortable in exchanging current ideas than in projecting new initiatives. When I expressed regret at the end of a meeting about our inability to achieve follow-up objectives, one professor quickly answered: "Don't worry about us. We have located new sources of information, made valuable contacts, and enjoyed the experiences of the last two days." Such outcomes were indeed salutary. However, since UCEA was expected to produce R and D outcomes for the field, I felt I had failed.

Afterwards, I recognized that it was unrealistic to expect a group of diverse professors, who had come together for the first time, to delin-eate acceptable follow-up objectives. Clearly, the staff needed to structure discussions about objectives more effectively. Had we asked each group to advise UCEA on desirable follow-up objectives, the discussions would likely have been freer and more fruitful. Another alternative would have been for the staff to formulate specific alterna-tives for discussion. The task force on field experiences, for example, might have been asked to evaluate which of the following outcomes would be most useful to the field: case studies of "light house" field experiences; a set of guidelines to encourage the development of new field experiences; or a synthesis of concepts and findings about field experience. Subsequently, we would use these two tactics and others to help professors achieve viable objectives. Our first experiences with task forces highlighted both the necessity and the difficulty of achieving acceptable R and D objectives. To succeed we had to conceive outcomes which meshed with the aspirations of diverse individuals, projected benefits for the field, and the organizational constraints of UCEA.

After additional reflection the staff did find ways to continue the task forces on preparation. At Michigan State University, in 1962, 16 scholars presented papers at a Career Development Seminar on "Com-mon and Specialized Learnings for Personnel Preparing for Differing

Administrative Positions."[8] Some months later at a conference held at the University of Alberta, such leading social scientists as Robert Agger, W. W. Charters, Jr., Neal Gross, Paul Lazarsfeld, and Solon Kimball presented papers on the relevance of their respective disciplines to the study of administration.[9] The field experience task force prepared a monograph which was published in 1963.[10] Finally, some of the training materials recommended by the task force on "New Instructional Materials and Methods" were subsequently developed. The task force on "Social Science Content in Training Programs" functioned throughout the 1960s. The other three task forces ended their work in 1963.

Unable to attain objectives for three of the four research task forces, we had to abort them. Thanks largely to Associate Director Stephen Hencley, the task force on the "Politics of Education" did continue. Recipient of a Ph.D from The University of Chicago, Steve had earlier held the following school positions in the Canadian province of Alberta: teacher, supervising principal, principal, and superintendent. He was a versatile conceptualizer and a quick performer of UCEA tasks. In developing a proposed cooperative study of community change and education, he employed social science theories he had acquired during his doctoral studies. Designed to test the efficacy of the "group" pattern of inter-university cooperation for facilitating large-scale research, the proposed project was funded with a grant of $30,000 from the Cooperative Research Program of the U.S. Office of Education. In the summer of 1963 six political scientists, four professors of educational administration, and a sociologist convened for three weeks at the University of Oregon. Before they came together, the 11 scholars had summarized available knowledge about community change and the politics of education. Their mission at Oregon was to conceptualize a large scale research plan.

Steve Hencley directed the 1963 project. Toward the end of its second week he called from Oregon to report that the 11 professors had decided, after intensive debate, against an inter-university, large-scale research project. The major stumbling block, he reported, was the group's inability to achieve a conceptual framework acceptable to its members. After years of study, the different scholars had already committed themselves to preferred theories or frameworks. To contemplate substituting their individual frameworks for a common one was an unpalatable idea. Most believed that the small islands of extant political theory were so widely separated that it simply was not feasible to build conceptual bridges among them.

Since my hopes for generating large-scale research were high, I was deeply disappointed by Steve's report. However, the inability of the 11 able scholars to formulate a research plan underlined the need for a reassessment. Clearly, my earlier hopes for large scale research did not mesh with the results produced by the scholars in Oregon. We had expected more of "scientific" theory than it could deliver. In the future it seemed UCEA should pursue simpler, less expansive, and more focused research projects than the Oregon venture. Fortunately, the project did produce useful outcomes. By testing an untested concept we gained new insight. In addition, the 11 scholars prepared a book on local politics and education which provided new content for both professors and students.[11]

Shortly before the Oregon project was funded, I began pursuing another research idea. Originating in a conversation I had with Paul Cullinan, then a graduate student in educational administration at The Ohio State University, the idea had to do with taxonomic inquiry. Earlier Andrew Halpin had written and spoken disparagingly about the prevailing uses of taxonomies in the field. However, Paul Cullinan contended that taxonomies had played a crucial role in the development of biological knowledge. The question, then, was whether or not taxonomies, as defined by biologists, might be employed to advance knowledge in educational administration.

In 1962, Associate Director Kenneth St. Clair and I agreed that UCEA should find ways of conducting and evaluating taxonomic inquiry. A former high school and community college director of music, Ken had earned a doctoral degree at the University of Texas. His quick witticisms brought smiles and laughter to the central office, and his distinctive writing style enlivened UCEA's annual reports and other publications. Initially, the two of us were unclear about who might direct a taxonomy project. After assessing the alternatives, we asked Daniel Griffiths about his interest in the idea. When he responded positively, Paul Cullinan and I drafted a paper on taxonomic inquiry and flew to Chicago where Griffiths was taking part in a conference. After reading our paper Dan asked whether a single or a multiple set of concepts should guide the inquiry. When I suggested that multiple sets seemed preferable, Dan agreed to prepare a formal proposal. Later the U.S. Office of Education awarded a $110,000 grant to New York University to implement the proposal. Cooperating with Dan in the research were professors from several UCEA universities.[12]

In 1961-62, we planned a program to assess the state of research in the field and to set forth new strategies to improve inquiry. The end result was the twenty-two chapter book, *Educational Research: New Perspectives.*[13] Since its chapters were first presented as seminar papers at the University of North Carolina, The University of Chicago, and the University of California at Berkeley, their authors profited from several critiques. Supported by the Cooperative Research Program of the U.S. Office of Education, the book represented UCEA's initial study of research in the field. It was also the first of many books which I, with the help of others, would conceptualize while at UCEA.

Program Planning and Risk

At its meeting on February 21, 1962, the Board of Trustees decided that UCEA should develop a plan for the 1964-69 period. During the next four months Steve Hencley and I produced an initial draft of the desired plan. Assisting us was Glenn Immegart, UCEA's assistant director. Earlier in his career Glenn had served as a teacher and an elementary school principal in Ohio. While performing as UCEA's assistant director, he was completing his doctoral work at The Ohio State University.

The five year plan's proposed goals and programs were examined and refined by the UCEA Board at its June, 1962, meeting, and in subsequent months by about 200 professors at eight, two-day regional meetings. Such experiences provided me a special perspective on planning. Not fully satisfied with the process of ordering program activities around a goal structure, I began to look for other organizing concepts. Since the objectives of some programs seemed much more difficult to achieve than others, the concept of risk entered the picture. Two questions seemed especially salient. First, could I find categories for classifying actual and projected programs in relation to risk? Second, given risk-related categories, would they be helpful in generating programs and in determining priorities?

After grappling with the questions for months, I found that the concepts of "blue chip," "growth," and "speculative" investments helped me think about program risks. A blue chip program, it seemed, would have a well-established record and a demonstrated capacity to provide attractive dividends to professors. The risks in such a program, in other words, would be limited. Early in UCEA's life the Career Development Seminar and the institutes on "New Methods and Materials" became blue chip programs. Easily implementable in relatively brief time periods, usually without external resources, the programs proved to have value. Blue chip programs tended to include dissemination but exclude R and D efforts.

At the other extreme were "speculative" programs. Although risky, these programs had considerable leverage for effecting change. If successful, they could have widespread, substantial, and continuing impact upon the field. Large in scope, a speculative program required a minimum of five years and typically more to unfold. Breakers of tradition, these programs sparked controversy. The greater the controversy generated, the higher the risk of failure.

In each five year period, beginning in the 1964-69 period, UCEA initiated one "speculative" program. During the 1964-69 period UCEA launched a long-range program designed to help internationalize the field. (see Chapter Seven). In UCEA's 1969-74 plan the simulation of a large urban school system became the high-risk program. Developing an international partnership of UCEA universities and leading school systems constituted the speculative program for 1974-79.

UCEA "growth" programs fell between the "blue chip" and the "speculative" ones. More expansive than the blue chip programs, most took at least three years to complete. Directed at specific targets of change, they usually elicited opposing views about their prospects. Since growth programs differed in their degrees of risk, they could be categorized as either "conservative" or "aggressive." Early examples of "conservative growth" programs would be the UCEA case development effort, the recorded "Best Lectures" series, and the updating of the Jefferson simulations. The "aggressive growth" programs were more complex and risky. Producing filmed cases was more chancy than preparing written cases. Institutionalizing a computer-aided system to help women and minority graduates acquire administrative positions was more hazardous than implementing a task force endeavor. Aggressive growth programs, in other words, had more ambitious objectives, more complex sets of activities, longer time horizons, and more imposing tasks than did conservative growth programs. When effective, they also had much more impact.

What was the major benefit of the "risk" categories? Perhaps it was their capacity to suggest important planning questions. In a given five-year plan what portions of UCEA's programs should be "blue chip," "growth," and "speculative"? Given the press for tangible results, should not most programs be "blue chips" ones? On the other hand, would not such an emphasis be an overly safe if not a stultifying one? If leaders eschewed high-risk programs, would not UCEA's long-range potential for success be severely constrained? In probing such issues I concluded that priority, measured in terms of staff time, should be assigned to "growth" and "speculative" programs. Translated into more specific terms, I aimed at the following allocations of staff time: "blue chip" programs—two-fifths; "growth" programs—two-fifths; and "speculative" programs—one fifth. Judgments about the risks inherent in given programs were inevitably subject to staff debate. However, the planning priorities encouraged high levels of performance by UCEA staff members.

Notes

1. In this and in other chapters I have relied on numerous facts from the following sources: *UCEA Newsletter* (1959-1974); *UCEA Review* (1974-1981); UCEA annual reports (1959-1969); minutes of UCEA's Board of Trustees, Executive Committee, Plenary Session, and Partnership Coordinating Committee; and the voluminous materials prepared for UCEA's differing governance meetings.

2. See Griffiths, D. E. (Ed.). (1969). *Developing taxonomies of organizational behavior in education administration.* Chicago: Rand McNally & Company.

3. See UCEA staff paper. (Undated). Criteria of success in school administration. New York: Teachers College CPEA Center, p. 1.

4. For the final report see Hemphill, J. K., Griffiths, D. E., & Frederiksen, N. (1962). *Administrative performance and personality.* New York: Bureau of Publications, Teachers College, Columbia.

5. For details see Culbertson, J. A., & Coffield, W. H. (Eds.). (1960). *Simulation in administrative training.* Columbus, OH: University Council for Educational Administration.

6. The first four were called "workshops." All subsequent ones were labeled "institutes."

7. For one account of Keppel's achievements as dean of the school of education at Harvard, see chapters 9 and 10 in Powell, A. G. (1980). *The uncertain profession: Harvard and the search for educational authority.* Cambridge, MA: Harvard University Press.

8. See Leu, D. J., & Rudman, H. C. (Eds.). (1963). *Preparation programs for school administrators: Common and specialized learnings.* East Lansing, MI: College of Education, Michigan State University.

9. See Downey, L. W., & Enns, F. (Eds.). (1963). *The social sciences and educational administration.* Edmonton, Alberta: The University of Alberta.

10. See Hencley, S. P. (Ed.). (1963). *The internship in administrative preparation.* Columbus, OH: University Council for Educational Administration, and Washington, DC: Committee for the Advancement of School Administration.

11. See Cahill, R. S., & Hencley, S. P. (Eds.). (1964). *The politics of education in the local community.* Danville, IL: The Interstate Printers & Publishers, Inc.

12. See Griffiths, D. E. (Ed.). (1969). *Developing taxonomies of organizational behavior in education administration.* Chicago: Rand McNally & Company.

13. See Culbertson, J. A., & Hencley, S. P. (Eds.). (1963). *Educational research: New perspectives.* Danville, IL: The Interstate Printers & Publishers, Inc.

References

Bernard, R. J. (1962). The Claremont colleges. In J. J. Wittich (Ed.), *College and university interinstitutional cooperation* (pp. 40-46). Princeton, NJ: College Center of the Finger Lakes.

Culbertson, J. (1963). Efficiency, large-scale research and innovation through inter-institutional cooperation. In J. A. Culbertson & K. St. Clair (Eds.), *UCEA Annual Report* (pp. 1-11). Columbus, OH: University Council for Educational Administration.

4

Transference

"Responsibility is like a string we can only see the middle of.
Both ends are out of sight."

William McFee

The major challenge of the 1959-64 period—the invention and
delivery of valued UCEA programs—continued throughout the 1964-
69 cycle. However, it was attended by a further challenge: ensuring that
UCEA attained the independence needed to pursue its mission beyond
1969. To meet the latter challenge leaders would have to transfer the
responsibility for financing UCEA from the W. K. Kellogg Foundation
to member universities. Stephen Hencley and I began thinking about
a strategy to effect the transfer in the fall of 1961, when we met with
Maurice Seay of the W. K. Kellogg Foundation. During the meeting we
learned that the foundation might provide UCEA a grant for the 1964-
69 period. If the grant could be attained, and if UCEA could continue
to generate valued outcomes, the chances for an effective transfer of
responsibility to universities would be greatly enhanced.

At the February 21, 1962, meeting of the UCEA Board we reported
that Maurice Seay was interested in receiving a second UCEA proposal.
We also suggested that UCEA should soon begin planning for another
five-year time span. Paul Jacobson proposed that "the UCEA central
staff prepare a preliminary . . . five year plan of operations for the
consideration of the Board of Trustees at the June meeting" (B Min, 2/
21/62, p. 2). The Board accepted Jacobson's suggestion.

During the next three months Steve and I produced a "preliminary" plan which provided a focus for the June meeting. President
Van Miller began the meeting by welcoming new board members
Roald Campbell, Chicago; James Harlow, Oklahoma; and Thomas
James, Stanford. He also welcomed Kenneth St. Clair, who would
soon replace Stephen Hencley as UCEA's associate director. Vet-
eran UCEA Board members in attendance were Daniel Griffiths,

New York University; Howard Jones, Iowa; Richard Lonsdale, Syracuse; and Truman Pierce, Auburn.

Following a review of the proposed 1964-69 goals and programs, President Miller invited board members to outline additional initiatives. Richard Lonsdale stressed the need for new programs to prepare metropolitan school leaders; Howard Jones called for special activities to serve younger professors; and Daniel Griffiths proposed that UCEA launch a national research center. The Board also approved a proposed set of follow-up activities, including the development by each UCEA university of its own five year plan.

In July and August, the staff expanded the planning statement. Entitled *A Five-Year Plan to Improve Preparatory Programs for School Administrators*, the 152-page document was sent to 460 professors in 43 UCEA universities. Professors in each university were asked to evaluate the plan, to elaborate ideas for improving it, and to begin developing their own five year plans. Between October 25 and December 11, selected professors from each university attended one of eight regional meetings. Chaired by UCEA board members, the meetings attracted about 25 individuals on average. Attendees assessed goal statements and identified the proposed programs which needed to be extended, revised, or curtailed. After adding their own program ideas, participants agreed to send the UCEA staff an initial report on their departments' five year plans by January 31, 1963.[1]

In February the staff summarized the research endeavors and program improvements, which members of departments in UCEA universities wanted to undertake, and the commitments departments had made to help carry out staff proposed, inter-institutional programs. The 69 page summary revealed that UCEA universities had made 330 commitments, either "firm" or "potential," to help UCEA achieve its 1964-69 goals. For example, to help realize goal II—"pioneering and implementing substantial changes in preparatory programs"—eight universities planned to implement new internship programs. In pursuing goal V—"providing professors opportunities for assessing new developments and concepts"—24 universities made commitments to finance and conduct a Career Development Seminar or an institute on "New Methods and Materials." To achieve goal VII—"organizing and communicating . . . knowledge pertinent to school administration"—48 professors volunteered to help implement a new UCEA abstracting service, while six universities offered to help launch a new journal. Such commitments suggested that the transfer of responsibility for supporting UCEA was already under way. To be sure, most of the potential and some of the firm commitments were never fully met. However, UCEA leaders fulfilled many of their promises. In addition, they helped execute numerous unanticipated programs which emerged in the latter part of the 1960s.

In May, 1963, the UCEA Board unanimously approved a revised five year plan. They also accepted Roald Campbell's motion that UCEA aim at "gradually increasing membership payments, in order to contribute evidence of the increasing independence of the University Council for Educational Administration" (B Min, 5/8-10/63, p. 5). Finally, the Board approved a proposal prepared for the W. K. Kellogg Foundation. Some months later Maurice Seay reported the foundation's decision to provide UCEA a $361,000 grant for the 1964-69 period.

Descendency of the Theory Movement

During the 1964-69 time span the major influences on research, training, and practice in school administration differed markedly from those which had prevailed in the previous decade. The high hopes for theory development, which the 1957 UCEA Career Development Seminar had helped generate, soon began to wane. In fact, Andrew Halpin, a theory movement leader, tough-mindedly questioned the sufficiency of the hoped-for theories, as the decade began (Halpin, 1960, p. 5):

> The administrator's doubt is justified; there is indeed something missing. The fault is that the scientist's theoretical models of administration are too rational, too tidy, too aseptic. They remind us of the photographs in magazines devoted to home decorating—the glossy pictures of dramatic and pristine living room interiors.

Near the end of the 1959-64 period Joseph Schwab of the University of Chicago rendered a more penetrating critique of theory. To pinpoint the type of theory he was addressing, Schwab offered several illustrative definitions, including the one offered by Herbert Feigl (Schwab, 1964, p. 56): "a set of assumptions from which can be derived by purely logico-mathematical procedures, a set of empirical laws." Achieving in the "foreseeable future" a sufficing theory of administration, as defined by Feigl, was, in Schwab's view, a "manifest impossibility;" further, the "pursuit of such theory" was "an uncritical aping of the wrong model" (p. 55).

The "impossibility" of attaining a scientific theory stemmed, Schwab attested, from the magnitude and diversity of the factors which affected school administration. The equations in physics, he noted, typically involved three to five factors (e.g. energy and mass). Biologists could cope with seven to nine. In the social sciences only a small class of theories, characterized by Schwab as "monuments of complexity and ingenuity," were in existence (Schwab, 1964, p. 57). Prevailing models in economics, for example, involved 50 to 200 terms. However, the number of factors affecting school administration, according to Schwab's explicit calculations, ranged from 4,000 to 50,000. They were so abundant and so complex that neither computers nor mathematical equations could capture them.

Even the most ingenious theories of decision-making suffer, Schwab argued, from the ills of abstractness. Abstract theories "are like pyramidal tents. The more ground they try to cover, the taller, that is the more abstract, they must be; and the more abstract they are", the farther they are removed from the complexities of action (Schwab, 1964, p. 61). Practitioners who use the "inelegant naked eye of experience and commonsense" are keenly aware of theory's distance from practice (p. 59).

Although Schwab vehemently rejected highly abstract theory, he did not disavow all types of theory (Schwab, 1964, p. 55):

> . . . I have no argument against a body of administrative knowledge, which resembles a physiology of form, "The function of the organ X is Y." I would similarly have no objection to a body of knowledge which imitated an anthropology which asserts the minimum indispensable functions of a culture and then proceeds to describe the diverse ways in which diverse cultures perform these functions. I would not for one moment impugn the enormous value, so mistakenly belittled by Halpin, of well-constructed taxonomic schemes, such as . . . the complex . . . schemes of botany and zoology. Indeed, it is precisely such relatively incoherent, atomized, bread-and-butter kinds of general knowledge which I would commend to the attention of investigators concerned with administration.

Since school administration did not possess well developed theories of the type Schwab opposed, he was in a sense fighting a straw man.

Nevertheless, he provided the field a penetrating and useful critique of the type of theory advocated at UCEA's 1957 Career Development Seminar and extolled the value of lower order theories. His message, then, was a constructive if sobering one.

Critical analyses such as that offered by Joseph Schwab helped fuel the growing skepticism about the viability of attaining theories applicable to all types of administration. However, the turbulent events of the 1964-69 period likely contributed even more to the eclipse of the theory movement. During the period school administrators experienced enormous pressures, as society's leaders increasingly saw in education an indispensable tool for attaining important national goals. At the end of the sixties I sought to summarize the grand aspirations which "New Frontier" and "Great Society" leaders had articulated for education (Culbertson, 1969, p. 9):

> The American school system... came to be viewed, more than ever before, as an instrument for achieving . . . significant national goals. Practical leaders saw in education a versatile and potentially effective weapon in the war on poverty; a force for helping to break down the walls of segregation and a medium for resolving conflicts between the races; a ladder for the culturally deprived to climb to higher status and greater opportunity; a developer of the manpower skills and the "conceptual capital" necessary to fuel an ever-growing and technologically advanced economy; and a major contributor to the increasingly intricate security and defense systems of the nation.

The federal government, armed with a new and extensive system of subsidies and grants, influenced school administrators in powerful ways. The Elementary and Secondary Education Act of 1965 enabled federal agencies to funnel large amounts of money to local school systems. Designed to facilitate the attainment of national goals, the funds spawned novel problems for school leaders. For instance, in public school systems there were frequent conflicts between central office personnel responsible for federally-supported projects and those responsible for traditionally-funded programs. Conflicts between school administrators and officials in voluntary, municipal, and state agencies also emerged.

The federal influence was only one of a number of forces which buffeted school systems during the 1964-69 cyle.[2] UCEA's programs reflected the new influences. Career Development seminars, for instance, dealt with such topics as change, racial unrest, teacher-administrator conflict, and new computer technologies:

"Change Perspectives," Auburn University, October, 1964.

"Computer Concepts and Educational Administration," University of Iowa, April, 1965.

"Administering the Community College in a Changing World," State University of New York at Buffalo, October, 1965.

"Collective Negotiations and Educational Administration," University of Arkansas, April, 1966.

"Educational Administration: International Perspectives," University of Michigan, October, 1966.

"Urban Education and the American Negro: The Development of Public Policy," Harvard University, March, 1967.

"Knowledge Production and Utilization in Educational Administration: Role Emergence and Reorganization," University of Oregon, October, 1967.

"Management Systems for Educational Organizations," Syracuse University, April, 1968.

The concepts presented in UCEA's 1964-69 programs emphasized application more than theory development. This emphasis can be seen in analyses of "system concepts," for example. When Daniel Griffiths first presented these concepts to a UCEA audience earlier in the decade, he offered a promising "model" or theory to guide inquiry (Griffiths, 1963). However, at a 1966 UCEA task force meeting on "Systems Analysis in Educational Administration" the concepts were viewed as tools for analyzing objectives, for developing plans, and for managing organizations. UCEA professors, who attended the University of Minnesota task force meeting, applied systems concepts in decision exercises. Similar themes prevailed at the Career Development Seminar held at Syracuse University in 1968. Such papers as "Planning, Programming, Budgeting Systems" and "Management Support Systems and Operations Analysis" reflected the bent toward application. As practitioners acquired systems concepts from texts and training courses, they used them to address problems ranging from the routing of school buses to the management of time.[3]

Another concept the turbulent period brought to the fore was that of "change." UCEA encouraged professors to examine this widely used concept from different perspectives. At the Auburn University seminar on "Change Perspectives" the "philosophical aspects of change" were elaborated (*UCEA Newsletter*, V(4), 4). At a seminar held a year later at the State University of New York at Buffalo, presenters focused on such societal changes as urbanization, new developments in economics, and occupational shifts, along with their implications for community college leadership.

At a conference in Washington, D.C., in 1965, I delivered a paper on "Organizational Strategies for Planned Change in Education." In the paper I described a proposed "National Institute" for studying change. Afterward David Clark and Egon Guba of Ohio State told me they would like to implement the proposed endeavor. I agreed to recommend that UCEA sponsor the institute, if needed funding could be obtained. About a year later, after moving to Indiana University, Clark and Guba obtained a planning grant from the Charles F. Kettering Foundation to launch the institute. Although the UCEA and Indiana staff failed to institutionalize the initiative, its activities continued into the 1970s. Its major accomplishments were investigations of the change process and the preparation of new personnel to study change. The institute's leaders tried hard to implement inter-university research projects, but they were unable to do so.

A New Watchword: Knowledge Utilization

Forces in the turbulent external environments of school systems and universities affected other UCEA programs. When the UCEA Task Force on the "Social Sciences and the Preparation of Educational Administrators" first met in the fall of 1960, its participants were psychologists, sociologists, and professors of school administration. As they analyzed the issues before them, they looked largely at variables internal to school systems. Theories of administrative and organizational behavior were their essential tools. However, at task force meetings in the 1964-69 cycle, specialists in the economics and politics of education participated—domains which dealt largely with problems in settings external to educational institutions.

As interests shifted from internal to external problems, the task force identified a vexing question: what criteria should be used to select social science content for training school leaders? The task force decided that a book should be written on the criterion problem. In the introductory chapter Associate Director Mark Shibles and I described four starting points for analyzing relevance: social science theories, a social science discipline, administrative problems, and the career objectives of trainees (Culbertson and Shibles, 1973, pp. 8-28). A former teacher of government and world history in Maine and Connecticut, Mark had obtained a Ph.D. at Cornell University. His multi-disciplinary studies at Cornell enabled him to examine the relevance question from various perspectives.

The book's authors used the four perspectives to derive criteria for selecting social science content. Each perspective generated several instructional objectives which served as criteria. From a liberal arts perspective a scholarly discipline could be used to enhance reasoning abilities, sharpen analytical skills, and provide students modes of inquiry which would make them more effective decision makers. The problems-based perspective offered a different set of instructional objectives as, for example, helping trainees understand and resolve "administrative problems." Professors sometimes used the case method to pursue this objective. For example, the UCEA film, "The Conference," dramatized a problem of conflict involving a teacher, department head, and school principal. As students applied concepts of small group theory to the filmed problem, they gained insight into the dynamics of three-person conflict.

The book also showed how professors used the differing sets of criteria to select social science content for training programs. The following chapters, respectively, explored content selection from a career based, a problems based, a discipline based, a theory based, and an integratively based view of relevance (Culbertson et al., 1973):

> "The Social Sciences and the Preparation of Educational Administrators at Harvard and Chicago" by Joseph Cronin, Secretary of Education, Commonwealth of Massachusetts, and Laurence Iannaccone, University of California at Riverside.
>
> "Social Science Concepts and Collective Negotiations" by John Horvat, Indiana University.
>
> "Discipline-Based Content: The Economics of Education" by Harry Hartley, University of Connecticut.

"Content Selection is Organizational Theory and Behavior in Education" by James Lipham, University of Wisconsin.

"Educational Administration and Social Science: An Integrative Approach" by Donald Willower, Pennsylvania State University.

The book provided a map for exploring a relatively new territory. However, the map was a primitive one. The criteria and their applications constituted a first rather than a last step toward resolving a complex problem. Nevertheless, the book's authors provided perspectives and criteria which can still be used by those who would systematically grapple with the relevance problem.

The 1967 Career Development Seminar on "Knowledge Production and Utilization" reflected the altered outlooks of scholars perhaps better than any UCEA program of the period. Presented at the University of Oregon, its content differed markedly from that of the seminar on "Administrative Theory" held a decade earlier. While the latter seminar called for a science of administration, the Oregon seminar focused upon effective ways of using knowledge. The 1957 seminar was held at the University of Chicago, the citadel of theory development. The 1967 seminar was held at the University of Oregon which, two years earlier, had obtained funding for the first federally supported research and development center on educational administration.

Financial support for research in 1967 contrasted sharply with that which had prevailed in 1957. The Elementary and Secondary Education Act of 1965 (ESEA) not only dramatically increased federal support for research, development, and dissemination in state and local education agencies, but it also expanded greatly the R and D funds available to higher education institutions. Between 1957 and 1967 the budget of the Bureau of Research of the U. S. Office of Education increased from $1,020,000 to $99,600,000 (Gaynor, 1969, p. 59). Among the new outcomes was a network of research and development centers and a complex of regional educational laboratories.

As noted earlier, six eminent social scientists and two leading professors of educational administration presented the major papers in Chicago. That the leadership roles of these eight presenters differed from those of the presenters at the 1967 seminar is evident from the latter's names and organizational affiliations:

Norman Boyan, Director, Division of Educational Laboratories, United States Office of Education.
Launor Carter, Senior Vice President, Systems Development Corporation.
Keith Goldhammer, Dean, School of Education, Oregon State University.
Egon Guba, Director, National Institute for the Study of Educational Change, Indiana University.
Ronald Havelock, Project Director, Center for Research on the Utilization of Knowledge, University of Michigan.
Richard Schmuck, Research Associate, Center for the Advanced Study of Educational Administration, University of Oregon.
Sam Sieber, Bureau of Applied Social Research, Columbia University.

Of the Oregon presenters only Egon Guba was a major contributor to the theory movement. Having helped Jacob Getzels refine the renowned "social process" theory, Guba was in a position to describe the reactions he and Getzels had received when they presented the theory to school administrators in the 1950s (Guba, 1968, pp. 37-38):

"What you say seems to make some sense, although I'm not sure I really know what you're talking about. Why don't you fellows come down out of your ivory tower and tell us about your ideas in language that we can understand? How about showing us how to apply those ideas on the "firing line'?

"Well, " we would say, "practice is hardly our concern. We don't know what the practical problems are. It's up to you administrators who have to deal with these problems every day to make the application. ... If applications are to be made, they would ask who is better to make them than the minds that developed those ideas in the first place?"

Implicit in such reactions, Guba concluded, was an important question: If "ivory tower" professors and "unlearned" administrators cannot jointly ensure the effective use of knowledge, what other agents or agencies are needed to resolve the problem? The question was at the center of the Oregon discussions. Boyan, for example, proposed that the utilization of knowledge would be strengthened only when educational development became a rewarded activity. Carter called for a new profession of social and educational engineering, while Havelock cogently described the important roles which "linkers" could perform in facilitating effective knowledge use.[4]

The Oregon seminar delineated promising paths toward the effective use of knowledge. However, the number of UCEA professors who worked intensely to reduce the theory-practice gap—a gap which the Oregon presenters perceived as an expansive one—was relatively small. Only a scattering of universities offered courses on knowledge utilization. At the same time almost every UCEA university had offerings on theory. In 1969 the final draft of the first widely used text on theory was completed (Owens, 1970). No comparable text on knowledge utilization would soon appear. However, the issues probed at the Oregon seminar would become increasingly salient. As the seventies would unfold, concerns about the theory-practice gap would become more intense, as would pressures on funding agencies to see that research was used in practice.

Reality Oriented and Computer Based Simulations

The growing press for more effective knowledge utilization supported UCEA's 1964-69 efforts to develop and disseminate new simulations. The most notable ones were revisions of the Jefferson Township simulations, a computer based simulation, a negotiations game, and "reality" simulations of non-suburban schools.

By 1965 the Jefferson Township simulations were becoming obsolete. Such filmed objects as automobiles and clothing were taking on an air of unrealism. In addition, the school management problems of 1965 differed from those of the late 1950s. Notably, an estimated 16,000 trainees in about 95 institutions had experienced one or more of the Jefferson simulations (*UCEA Newsletter*, 7(5), p. 2). In the spring of 1966 the U. S. Office of Education awarded UCEA a grant of $68,865 to perform the task. Assisting the development team were UCEA associate directors Donald Anderson and Terry Eidell. A former teacher of mathematics in a Minnesota high school, Donald had also served five years as a high school principal before obtaining a Ph.D. from the University of Minnesota. The unusual rapidity of his walk into the office each morning signaled his eagerness to do UCEA's work! Terry Eidell, as an undergraduate, studied engineering before switching to education. Later he taught high school physics and chemistry. Still later he obtained his doctorate from Pennsylvania State. At UCEA he was strongly committed to scientific research.

The "Madison School System" provided the setting for revising the Jefferson simulations. Richard Wynn, University of Pittsburgh, constructed the general background materials (i.e. a 197 page survey, three filmstrips, a legal code, and a general policy handbook). Others who served on the Madison team, and the simulations they developed were: Thurston Atkins, Teachers College, Columbia (Edison Elementary Principalship); Hugh Laughlin, Ohio State (Madison Secondary Principalship); Glenn Immegart, Rochester (The Madison Superintendency); Ben Harris, Texas (Assistant Superintendent for Instructional Services); and Walter Hack, Ohio State (Assistant Superintendent for Business Management).

In the summer of 1967, about a year after the project began, UCEA professors were using the new simulations. Those employing the elementary principalship, for instance, had information on the Edison School (e.g. a tape recorded description of each of Edison's teachers, a staff evaluation report, and an outline of the curriculum) along with materials on the Madison School District (i.e. three filmstrips, a 197 page survey, a policy handbook, and a legal code). Decision making problems were presented in two in-baskets, each with 25 items, a case study, and a film depicting the instructional methods used by an Edison teacher. UCEA professors utilized the five Madison simulations for seven years. However, the Madison materials also became obsolescent. In the mid-seventies another team of professors would replace them with the "Adam School District" simulations.

In the spring of 1964, UCEA obtained a $201,211 grant from the U. S. Office of Education to plan and develop some prototypes of new training materials. Called the Articulated Media Project (AMP), its training materials were the only ones developed entirely by UCEA central staff members. Heading the AMP effort during its first year was Edwin Bridges who had earned a Ph.D. at The University of Chicago. Strongly interested in applying knowledge to practice, he had earlier served as a high school teacher, counselor, and principal. When Edwin accepted a professorship at the end of his first year, Associate Director Loren Downey took his place. After serving as an elementary teacher and school principal in Oregon, Loren had entered the doctoral program at the University of Arizona where he specialized in the study of change. He brought to UCEA strong interpersonal skills and a keen awareness of latent barriers to change.

UCEA associate directors Paul Cullinan and Robert Ruderman were also members of the AMP staff. A former Catholic priest, Paul had served as a central office administrator in a Catholic school system in southeastern Ohio. Thirty-four years of age, he had obtained a Ph.D. at Ohio State where he demonstrated a strong interest in research. Twenty-eight years of age, Robert Ruderman had taught in one of New York City's elementary schools before he entered the doctoral program at Indiana University. There he studied media and instructional systems while serving as an instructor. An incisive thinker, he brought to UCEA a range of knowledge related to AMP's objectives. Rounding out the AMP staff was John Horvat, project assistant. A student in the doctoral program at Ohio State, John had earlier taught science for four years in the Columbus, Ohio, school system. Quickly recognized for his teaching skills, he served as a "television teacher" during his last three years in Columbus.

The AMP prototype which departed most from the Jefferson Township materials was a computer based simulation. Designed and developed by Robert Ruderman with help from Paul Cullinan, the simulation was demonstrated to UCEA professors in the spring of 1967 at the universities of Chicago, Pennsylvania, and Utah. Stored in Boston at Bolt, Bernaek, and Newman, Inc., the simulation was transmitted to professors at the three sites via teletypewriter consoles. After learning about the rationale for the computer simulation and the background information incorporated into it, professors made decisions about selected simulated problems. Afterwards, they evaluated the potential of the simulation for use in training and in research.

The computer simulation was an innovative one. However, few professors had the requisite motivation, skill, and equipment to adopt it for use. Subsequent UCEA experiences made clear that many more professors preferred to use "reality" simulations than computerized ones. The former afforded professors greater opportunity to pursue objectives which meshed with their individual teaching styles and values. "Reality" simulations invited them to be creative. However, computerized simulations demanded much more creativity from their developers that they did from their users.

The other simulations UCEA developed in the 1964-69 time span went beyond the Jefferson Township ones in several ways. During the period UCEA built its first simulated management games. One of these was developed by John Horvat in the AMP project. Focusing upon "Collective Negotiations", the game provided players data about the school system and the community in which it was set. Also provided were officially stated positions on 16 "bargaining" issues (e.g. pupil-staff ratios, salary, administrative appointments) by the community's school board and the school system's teachers association. Other items included were rules to guide the negotiations process, forms on which to state the terms of agreements, and criteria for rating the final settlements made. Also offered were instructions for using the Bales method for analyzing the interactions of the players. A timely instructional tool, the game helped trainees acquire insights into "negotiations" and social interaction.

UCEA also made available two games developed by Robert Ohm and Thomas Wiggins of the University of Oklahoma. Designed to help trainees acquire skills in conflict resolution, each game featured a sequence of decisions. One focused upon conflict between a department head and a teacher, while the second dealt with conflict between two teachers. Since the design of the exercise was shaped by gaming theory, both games provided trainees insights into the theory as well as into the practice of conflict resolution.

Finally, professors used the Jefferson procedures to simulate decision problems in other contexts. The Shady Acres simulation, developed by Kenneth McIntyre, University of Texas, was set in a rural context. Hugh Laughlin, Ohio State, created the small town "Midville High School Principalship." Lamar Johnson, at UCLA, simulated a community college presidency, while Kenneth McIntyre simulated a school board meeting in which attendees made decisions about such issues as high school marriages and a controversy over library books. Such developments provided fresh experiences for new groups. They also helped demonstrate that an effective innovation can have widespread and continuing impacts upon a field.

UCEA Develops Two Journals

During the 1964-69 period UCEA launched initiatives which were relatively independent of the immediate forces which were buffeting universities and school systems. Designed to test ideas which differed from those underlying traditional university practices, the programs were more forward looking. Only two of the half dozen such initiatives of the period will be addressed in this chapter: the launching of new journals and the pioneering of novel ways of using the humanities in preparatory programs.

As crafters of the intial draft of UCEA's 1964-69 plan, Stephen Hencley and I proposed that UCEA launch two new journals—one devoted to publishing the results of inquiry and the other to providing abstracts of articles from social science and educational journals. From the proposals for new journals came the first issues of the *Educational Administration Quarterly* in 1965 and the *Educational Administration Abstracts* in 1966. The idea for the *Abstracts* was derived from my own experiences with widely scattered social science journals and from the growing use by professors of social science content. Some weeks after drafting the idea, I shared it with Richard Carlson, Daniel Griffiths, and Richard Lonsdale during a meeting of the commission responsible for planning the 1964 Yearbook of the National Society for the Study of Education. The indifferent response I received surprised me. I soon learned that precisely defined initiatives produced more feedback than did general ideas.

Professors of school administration in the 1950s did not have a scholarly journal they could call their own. During the decade various leaders had called for better ways to diffuse scholarly ideas. The emergence of UCEA with its emphasis upon improved inquiry further reinforced the need for a scholarly journal. The staff proposal, then, was linked to perceived needs in the scholarly community and to UCEA's desire to advance research, development, and dissemination.

In the spring of 1962, the UCEA Board implicitly accepted the proposal for an abstracting service. However, the proposal for a scholarly journal sparked controversy. During the exchange Daniel Griffiths suggested that a committee be appointed to assess the feasibility of a new journal. President Van Miller then requested that Roald Campbell, Daniel Griffiths, and I "investigate the problem and report to the UCEA Board of Trustees" (B Min, 6/14-15/62, p. 6). Three years earlier Griffiths had expressed the need for a journal which would disseminate "the very best that is available in research and theory" (Griffiths, 1959, p. 57), and Campbell had worked hard for many years to improve the dissemination of research findings.

At the fall, 1962, board meeting Campbell, Griffiths, and I recommended that the Board of Trustees seriously consider the publication of a journal to provide a forum for research reports and articles (B Min, 11/14-15/62, p. 5). The proposal prompted skeptical reactions. Early in the discussion Thomas James turned to me and asked, "Do you know what you are getting yourself into?" Back of the question was a sincere concern, as I perceived it, for both UCEA and me. He then proceeded to make two points. First, there was not enough fresh content to justify a new journal. Second, existing journals provided adequate space for unpublished ideas.

James Harlow, who owned a printing company, spoke at length about spiraling costs and the economics of publishing. Doubtful about attracting large numbers of subscribers, he and other board members hesitated to saddle UCEA with a financial problem. A proposal for an "occasional" rather than a periodic journal failed to gain support. Finally, President Miller, rather than pressing for immediate action, asked me to prepare a more specific statement for the next meeting.

In May 1963, the staff convened two advisory committees, one to address issues related to abstracting and the other to offer advice on a scholarly journal. Chairing the committee on abstracting was Richard Wynn of the University of Pittsburgh. Also present were William Wayson and Paul Halverson, Syracuse; Alan Thomas, Chicago; Robert Marker, Iowa, and Marvin Kurfeerst, Pittsburgh. After reviewing staff suggestions, the committee agreed upon the purposes of the abstracts, the journals to be abstracted, the type of abstract needed, and the clients to be served. However, the committee failed to resolve three issues: the criteria for selecting articles to be abstracted, the indexing system to be used, and the medium for transmitting the abstracts. Marvin Kurfeerst precipitated much discussion by making a strong case for "machine" retrieval systems.

A few days later the advisory committee on the scholarly journal convened. In attendance were Roald Campbell of Chicago; Fred Enns and Gordan Mowat of Alberta; and Van Miller of Illinois. Also present was Archibald Shaw, former editor of *Overview* (successor to *The School Executive*) and Associate Secretary of the American Association of School Administrators. The committee decided that the journal should be directed principally at scholars; encompass administration in public and non-public schools and higher education institutions; and diffuse research findings, analytical studies, and conceptual pieces.

At its spring meeting in 1963, the UCEA Board approved the advisory committee's recommendations on the scholarly journal and asked the staff to develop an operational plan for its fall meeting. The Board also approved a staff recommendation that pilot work be undertaken in 1963-64 to resolve the unresolved abstracting problems (i.e. content standards, indexing, and delivery systems).

Six months later the staff presented to the Board a seven page plan for the journal and a recommendation that Roald Campbell be appointed as its first editor. The group approved a motion by Thomas James that Roald Campbell be designated as editor of the new journal (B Min, 11/6-7/63, p. 6). During the meeting four editorial board members were chosen: Charles Benson, Harvard; Van Miller, Illinois; Arthur Reeves, Alberta; and Richard Wynn, Pittsburgh. Later Clyde Blocker, President of Harrisburg Area Community College in Pennsylvania, joined the editorial board.

Months passed before UCEA leaders found a name for the new journal. Initially, they favored "Journal of Educational Administration." However, a year earlier the enterprising William Walker had chosen that title for a new journal published at the University of New England in Australia. In the end the name, *Educational Administration Quarterly*, was selected with some ambivalence. In the first issue Editor Campbell announced that the *Quarterly* would serve "all who would inquire about the nature of administration in education, its commonality with administration in general, its unique characteristics, its conceptual development, its empirical testing" (Campbell, 1964, p. iii). For 16 years the phrase, "Published Three Times Per Year," appeared in each issue. Finally, the phrase faded into history when editor Glenn Immegart, supported by the UCEA Executive Committee, expanded the journal to four issues.

To help professors explore criteria for selecting articles to be abstracted, I invited the editor of *Sociological Abstracts*, Leo Chall, to meet with a group of abstracters in February 1964. Chall began by observing that even though half of the articles in sociology were "crap", his service abstracted all of them. An aim of his *Abstracts* was to mirror the state of scholarship in sociology, both good and bad. Abstracters were expected to abstract, not to censor content. He attested that leading sociologists were responsible for upgrading the content of their discipline—not abstracters.

The UCEA challenge of selecting content differed from that in sociology in part because of the diverse population of journals to be abstracted. Most social science articles were not directly related to educational administration regardless of their quality. Thus, UCEA formulated two types of standards: those for judging relevance and those for assessing quality. The categories for classifying abstracts were used to determine relevance. Indicators of quality were fresh thoughts and/or new findings.

During May and June 1964, twelve professors abstracted, classified, and assembled content from twelve journals. Two months later most of them convened in New York City to assess results. Dissatisfied with the indexing system, they wanted a framework in which to fit and order the categories used to classify abstracts. After some discussion I suggested that Talcott Parsons' concepts of "technical," "managerial," and "community" or "institutional" systems might give better order to the categories. After illustrating how the suggestions might work, I was deservedly taken to task for distorting the meanings of Parsons' concepts. However, out of the discussion came three major categories for ordering more specific ones: "Tasks of Administration," "Administrative Processes and Organizational Variables" and "Societal Factors Influencing Education." These three categories and a fourth, "Preparation Programs for Educational Administrators," appeared in the first issue of the *Abstracts*.

In 1964-65, arrangements were made with professors at the Center for the Advanced Study of Educational Administration at the University of Oregon to assume editorial responsibility for the abstracts. Serving as general editors were Jean Hills and John Croft, young staff members in the new center. Helping them was the managing editor, Joanne Kitchel. Members of the "Editorial Commission" coordinated the work of abstracters and edited abstracts. Serving on the first commission were: Carl Dolce, Harvard; E. D. Duryea, Syracuse; Keith Goldhammer, Oregon; Howard Jones, Iowa; Marvin Kurfeerst, Pittsburgh; John Parsey, Michigan State; and Michael Thomas, Texas.

Published in the spring of 1966, the first issue contained abstracts from fifty-two journals whose titles ranged alphabetically from *Administrative Science Quarterly* to *Transaction*. In the issue the editors noted that "just as it takes money to make money, it also takes knowledge to make knowledge" (Hills and Croft, 1966, p. iii). In pointing to uses of the abstracts, the editors observed (Hills and Croft, 1966, p. iv): "Some recipients of knowlege may invest it in the production of new knowledge; others may 'spend' it in the solution of practical problems; and still others may 'lend' it to students who, in turn, either 'invest' it or 'spend' it." After years of labor the abstracting service was at last a reality!

Helping editors, editorial board members, abstracters, and printers produce, disseminate, and institutionalize the two journals proved to be a more demanding task than I had anticipated. The problems identified by the UCEA Board which related to the *Quarterly*—the short supply of articles, the limited revenues from subscriptions, and escalating publishing costs—proved to be perennial ones. Other problems were conflicts, occasionally, between some editors and printers, as well as between UCEA Board members who wanted to contain costs, and editors who desired to expand or improve a journal. The sparse results produced by numerous promotional efforts were frustrating. I also at times encountered the anger of professors whose manuscripts to the *Quarterly* had been rejected. Often I conversed constructively with these professors. However, when they adamantly asserted that they would *never* submit another article to the *Quarterly*, there was little left to say.

Editors Roald Campbell at The University of Chicago (1963-66) and Van Miller at Illinois (1967-72) worked valiantly and with limited success to encourage practitioners to write for the *Quarterly*. As students of educational policy, the two editors had a keen appreciation for theory-practice relationships. They also struggled with the problem of scarce content. At one of his early editorial meetings Van Miller plaintively observed that the "cupboard was bare." However, in a few years the problem was less troublesome.

The editors who followed Campbell and Miller were Don Carver, Illinois (1973-75); Daniel Griffiths, New York University (1975-79)[5]; and Glenn Immegart, Rochester (1979-85). These editors had obtained their doctorates later than had Campbell and Miller. Younger in outlook, they focused less on the interests of practitioners than did their predecessors. In his study of the *Quarterly*'s first fifteen years, Roald Campbell concluded that "the conceptual, theoretical and analytical thrust had received additional impetus in recent years" and that the quality of the journal's recent articles were superior to that of earlier ones (Campbell, 1979, p. 16).

During and after the advent of the *Abstracts* I had the opportunity to work with the following editors: John Croft, Jean Hills, and Joanne Kitchel, Oregon; William Knill, Alberta; Roy Harkins, North Carolina; Peter Cistone, Ontario Institute for the Study of Education, Toronto; and Philip West, Texas A & M. Editors of the *Abstracts* had to cope with complex coordination functions and with frequent turnovers of abstracters. Carrying out central office tasks were UCEA associate directors who served ex officio on the journal's editorial commissions. In the earlier years of the *Abstracts* Donald Anderson, Robin Farquhar, and Alan Gaynor provided help; in the middle years Rodney Pirtle, Jackson Newell, and Paula Silver; and in the latter part of my tenure Peter Hackbert, Martin Finkelstein, and Ellen Herda.

Moving journals intermittently from one university to another had beneficial results. Most editors, after wrestling with their tasks for years, typically lost their zest. As new editors came forward, they brought unjaded outlooks and fresh motivations to their tasks. Aspiring to put their own stamps on UCEA's journals, they often helped renew both the format and the content of the organs.

The *Quarterly* helped establish, I believe, higher and more explicit standards of scholarship. I observed that when authors had their manuscripts published, they were spurred to undertake additional inquiry. Most of the writers whose manuscripts were rejected found instructive the critiques which editors gave them. The *Abstracts* provided the field a unique reference. By involving hundreds of professors in abstracting, it also served as an international staff development project. On my visits to universities I could see the impact of the journals. It was a pleasure to observe professors and students animatedly discussing ideas obtained from the latest issue of the *Quarterly* and to hear graduate students recount how they had used the *Abstracts* in writing papers.

When I left UCEA in 1981, I had mixed feelings about the journals. I was delighted that the *Quarterly* was in the process of living up to its original name with a fourth issue. I was also pleased that after tens of thousands of advertisements and letters, it was financially self-supporting. During my last year Philip West and I gave a report to the UCEA Board on the state of the *Abstracts*. Even though its quality and coverage had reached new heights under Phil's editorship, it was not yet self-supporting. None of us was happy with its infirm financing.

Four Uses of The Humanities

In the 1964-69 time span UCEA tested uses of the humanities in preparing school administrators. Earlier I had asked James Harlow, Dean of the School of Education at Oklahoma, to present a paper on the humanities at a seminar supported by the Ford Foundation. His ideas were rooted in the following premises (Harlow, 1962, p. 62):

> ... Public, wide-scale education is not a given in any social order; it is a creation. It comes into being as the servant of social purpose. Its content and processes are altered to accommodate changes in those purposes. And education itself bears most intimately upon the formation and revision of the purposes which it in turn is required to serve.

Suggesting that school leaders are both developers and servants of educational purpose, Harlow asserted that it "follows necessarily that one of the principal emphases in the training of educational administrators—possibly the critical emphasis—must be . . . on educational purpose and the processes" of its definition (Harlow, 1962, p. 63). No amount of "empirical description of schools of management, regardless of frame of reference," he affirmed, could supply the necessary insights about purpose (p. 63). Only the humanities offered the requisite concepts and modes of thought.

Though Harlow had studied science and engineering, he had a deep appreciation for the humanities. His paper contained the most carefully reasoned rationale that the field had produced for using the humanities in preparation. Following his presentation I talked with him about probing the role of the humanities in greater depth. Subsequently, he reported that the University of Oklahoma was prepared to finance and sponsor a seminar on "Educational Administration—Philosophy in Action."

The seminar's major presenters were philosophers.[6] Carlton Berenda, head of the Philosophy Department at Oklahoma, developed the thesis that imagination and creativity are distinctively human qualities. Harold Broudy of Illinois depicted the tensions leaders feel when they are caught between the options of standing firm on principle and taking flight from conflict. Recognizing the dire effects of inadequate responses, he affirmed (Broudy, 1965, p. 53): "Without efficiency in coping with conflict, the enterprise will collapse dramatically; without a strong commitment to a value hierarchy, the enterprise dies more quietly and gradually but no less surely." Implicit in Professor Broudy's ideas was a second rationale: the humanities offer concepts and modes of thought for analyzing and coping with conflicting values.

Ohm and Monahan set forth another rationale for using the humanities which was linked to their belief that one "direction for further inquiry derives from the comforting convention, . . . that administration is more of an art than a science" (Ohm & Monahan, 1965b, p. 107). Thus, a third rationale was centered in the belief that artists and other practitioners must understand and be effective in the processes of creativity.

Charles Keller, Director of the Charles Hays Fellows, offered a fourth rationale for using the humanities. Stressing the liberalizing capacities of literature and philosophy, he proposed that the humanities, by impelling us to answer such basic questions as "Who am I?

Where am I going? . . . What do I believe? Why?" could make us more human (quoted in Ohm & Monahan, 1965a, p. vii).

At UCEA seminars, then, scholars delineated four rationales for using the humanities. They were rooted in the following concepts: purpose setting, conflicting values, adminstration as an art, and the liberalizing capacities of literature and philosophy. Although the rationales had abundant implications for preparatory programs, they were far removed from the actions of most professors. Thus, the big task lay ahead: employing the rationales to effect actual changes in programs. To help professors carry out this task the University of Virginia, as a part of its 1964-69 plan, supported a task force on the humanities. At a 1965 task force meeting 14 professors from 10 UCEA universities focused upon "action programs." Professors in half of the 10 universities later experimented with uses of the humanities. A half dozen professors not present at the meeting also launched new endeavors. Robin Farquhar led the UCEA effort by elaborating concepts, promoting idea exchange, nurturing innovations, and diffusing the results attained. Earlier an honors student in English at the University of British Columbia, Robin had served as a teacher, counselor, and department head in a Canadian secondary school. After acquiring a Ph.D. from The University of Chicago, he joined the UCEA at the age of 27 and displayed superior abilities.

William Monahan moved from Oklahoma to Iowa in 1965. Two years later he and his Iowa colleague, Willard Lane, began experimenting with the use of humanistic content in training. Employing the idea of administration as an art, they assumed that the outcomes of artistic leadership are not unlike those of novelists, sculptors, or composers. In other words, creative attainments represent wholes whose parts are ordered and arranged in unique patterns. Requiring disciplined analysis and synthesis, the attainments also reflect the visions of their creators.

Lane and Monahan reasoned that school leaders might understand creativity better by studying poems, novels, paintings, and other artistic products, by discussing the nature of creative processes with successful artists, and by thinking about the import of insights gleaned for leadership. They also asked students to engage in artistic pursuits. Instead of writing a dissertation, students took on more daunting tasks. Philip West wrote a novel for his culminating doctoral experience. In his novel he depicted conflicts which principal, "Richard Mobley" faced at "Providence High." Michael Sexton, another Iowa student, graphically depicted educaton in a Denver high school through photographs with accompanying commentary. His work was later published under the title *Who is the School?*

The Iowa initiative, however, was unable to compete effectively with established practices. Dependent upon able students courageous enough to travel new paths, the program was not institutionalized. Had it been linked more closely to creative school leaders through internships, it might have been more acceptable. Yet the two Iowa professors took the field into new territory. In addition, West and Sexton in their professorial roles continue to employ the humanities.

Preparing administrators to grasp and to cope with value conflicts was the most widely used rationale. Within the rationale were at least three sub-rationales. At the most concrete level were conflicts in specific decisions. A school principal responsible for deciding whether or not a teacher deserved tenure might find that half of the school's faculty supported the teacher while half did not. Students often probed this type of conflict through case analysis. Since well crafted cases were more the products of art than of science, they provided concrete situations to which concepts from the humanities could be applied.

At the next level were conflicting values which transcended specific decision problems as, for example, those associated with compromise versus non-compromise and equity versus inequity. At a UCEA seminar in 1962 I described how the humanities might be used to probe this level of conflict.[7] Delineated were seven examples of fundamental value conflicts along with a relevant novel, drama, or essay for each conflict. Should administrators, for example, consistently conceal information from staff, or should they always be entirely candid? Henrik Ibsen in his novel, *The Wild Duck*, dealt with this dilemma by dramatizing the consequences of total truth telling. Another example was George Bernard Shaw's *Major Barbara*, a drama which showed how power derived from great wealth can produce great social benefits. His work illuminates the contrasting values which undergird efficient power and inefficient virtue.

Several professors at the seminar later implemented adapted versions of the ideas I presented. In a new seminar at Harvard, Rodney McPhee and his students analyzed the value conflicts depicted by selected novelists. Using philosophical works, Keith Goldhammer at Oregon asked his students to describe the views of human beings and of society which were set forth in the writings of pragmatists, scientists, instrumentalists, and existentialists, among others. An objective of the two-quarter seminar was to enable leaders to decide which views about human beings and society they valued most highly.

A third level of conflict was associated with purpose setting. When leaders aim at setting new directions for schooling, they inevitably confront opposing views. Those who derive and articulate wise purposes from concepts of the "good" society and of "good" human beings, and who gain support for those purposes, exhibit supreme leadership. The Goldhammer seminar constituted an important first step in constructing such a bridge between societal and educational purposes. Other UCEA professors also found ways of addressing aspects of the problem.[8]

No program during the 1964-69 period consistently placed priority on the use of the liberal arts rationale. However, federally funded programs emerged at Florida and Tennessee which focused secondarily on liberalizing objectives. In the Florida program led by Ralph Kimbrough and Michael Nunnery, a new humanities seminar was offered primarily to alert "students to the . . . significance of conflicting values" and secondarily to provide "experience in the liberal arts. . ." (Farquhar, 1970, p. 27). During the first year students pursued the two purposes by studying works from world literature. According to student evaluations, the seminar achieved its secondary objective but not its primary one. The second year, when a professor of religion focused on problems of ethics, the seminar was judged to be more effective in realizing its primary purpose.

The Tennessee program, designed to serve younger trainees, had 18 different components. One, led by Charles Achilles, featured humanistic content. During the program's first year the humanities component focused on liberalizing objectives. In subsequent years it moved away from these objectives and concentrated more on educational purpose setting and ethical problems posed by value conflicts. Its content was the most eclectic of all the 1964-69 humanities programs within UCEA. Staffed by a novelist, drama director, and columnist along with professors of school adminstration, curriculum, institutional research, history, educational philosophy, religion, and art, the program afforded students a full-day, four-week experience. Trainees viewed dramas enacted at the university's Summer Playhouse, read and discussed novels, and analyzed essays and poems ranging, for example, from Plato's *Republic* to the writings of Emily Dickinson.

As the program unfolded, it focused more and more on value analysis. Believing that "administration is really humanism made operational through analysis and awareness of . . . values" (Achilles & Gentry, 1969, p. 37), the program's leaders concentrated more on human experience than on humanistic content. Significantly, about 33 percent of the first year participants perceived the humanities component to be the most valuable of all the 18 they experienced.

In sum, UCEA professors refined and tested four rationales for using the humanities. The rationale—administration as an art—was employed most thoroughly at Iowa. The leader's need to cope with value conflicts—the most popular of the four rationales—was used in about 10 universities. Although professors tested the purpose setting rationale to a degree, they never fully implemented it. Designers of programs in about six universities employed the liberalizing aims of the humanities. However, this rationale proved to be the least viable of the four. The pressures to pursue practice related objectives and to offer well established school courses (e.g. law, finance and theory) tended to push the rationale aside.

Although several of the initiatives survived the 1960s, almost all eventually faltered and failed. Bridges between humanistic thought and decision-making in schools were neither easy to build nor easy to traverse. In fact, program innovators themselves were caught between two disparate value systems. One, which resided in humanities departments, placed high value on inquiry and dialogue. The other, which inhabited school settings, pushed teachers and school administrators toward choice and action. To conceive clearly how the two systems might be joined in educational endeavors required imagination. To involve individuals, from the disparate systems, in effective learning experiences was an even more daunting endeavor. At the Oklahoma seminar James Harlow had pointed to the great distance between "excellent ideas", as guides to action, and actual university programs composed of "hard units of time, staff, and reference materials, of real live students who come with certain preconceptions and predilections" (Harlow, 1965, p. 95). Most existing courses and program requirements were tightly structured to achieve means-oriented objectives. In the competition between efficiency oriented and humanistic content, the latter was at a disadvantage.

Even though the innovators were not able to ensure a firm place for the humanities through permanent changes in programs, they did effect immediate and long term changes in training. In some cases they stimulated and helped other professors take up the cause. For example, George Chambers instituted a course on the humanities at Iowa, with the support of Willard Lane. In other cases professors continued to employ the humanities in new situations. For instance, Charles Achilles, as of this writing, was preparing to institute a ten-day, annual seminar on the humanities, for doctoral students at the University of North Carolina in Greensboro. Significantly, some of the students, who took part in the experimental programs, and who later became professors, have continued to utilize knowledge they acquired. For example, Philip West, a graduate of the Iowa program, was, at the time of this writing, regularly offering a course at Texas A. and M. on the "Leadership Functions of Literature."

Notably the four rationales for employing the humanities in training still stand. They offer resources to those who would dare to prepare school leaders to be more artful and creative, more aware of values and value conflicts, more visionary about purpose, and more perceptive about the human condition. They also provide starting points for those who would develop new or more refined rationales and who would test them in training programs.

During the development of UCEA's 1979-84 plan, there was a resurgence of interest in the humanities. In 1980, Charles Achilles of Tennessee, Samuel Popper of Minnesota, and I, among others, conferred about launching an endeavor which would go beyond the efforts of the 1960s. However, when I left UCEA, I had to place the hoped-for program on a list of "unfinished" projects.

Loyal to UCEA and deeply interested in the humanities, Samuel Popper made an individual commitment to continue the project. One outcome of his effort was the book, *Pathways to the Humanities in School Administration* (Popper, 1990).[9] The volume is the most comprehensive one yet written in our field on the uses of the humanities in training.

The book is informed by Sam's intensive, two-decade search for pathways. The search has led him through many collaborative endeavors with professors in the Department of Classics as well as in the Department of Art History at Minnesota. One result was a seminar which was cross-listed in the departments of school administration and classics. In addition, Sam and selected colleagues developed, conducted, and evaluated a six-session seminar on the humanities for practicing school administrators.

The fourth edition of Sam's book -- *Pathways to the Humanities: Administrative Leadership* -- will appear in 1994. In the book ideas developed by Chester Barnard, Niccolo Machiavelli, Talcott Parsons, and Philip Selzick are connected to decisions and actions depicted in the works of Dante, Shakespeare, and Sophocles, among others. For example, Barnard's concept of "executive authority" is linked to the royal actions of King Creon in *Antigone*, the 2400 year old classic written by Sophocles. This affinity of the humanities with core concepts in the sociology of organization is demonstrated in seven sections of the book. As a collection, the seven parts pinpoint and illuminate creative attributes of leadership -- attributes which are critical to institution building.

Professor Popper hopes that his book will motivate others in school administration to find their own pathways. He emphasizes that those who enter new pathways will need "tactical inventiveness." Such inventiveness will more easily occur among professors who exhibit a mastery of the literature in their field and an awareness of the rich sources of content in the multi-faceted humanities. Professor Popper's book reflects such mastery and awareness.

Transference: A Decisive Act

Planning for the 1969-74 period began at a UCEA Board meeting in Chicago. Providing a focus for the discussion was a lengthy two-part paper which I had prepared and sent to the Board earlier. The paper's first section, entitled "Retrospect," contained a summary and an evaluation of UCEA's first decade of operation. The second part, labeled "Prospect," set forth potential 1969-74 "adaptations" in UCEA's "goals, programs, structures, membership, staff and finances" (B Min, 5/4-6/67), p. 2). One of the problems discussed was that UCEA would not be able to function in the post-1969 period, unless those in its member universities assumed the full responsibility for its basic financial support. The decade-long support of the W. K. Kellogg Foundation was coming to an end.

One year later the UCEA Board approved the 1969-74 plan and appointed a Support Commission to suggest ways to finance UCEA in the future. Apppointed to the commission were Willard Lane, UCEA President; Luvern Cunningham, UCEA Vice-President; Kenneth McIntyre, UCEA past President; Roald Campbell, University of Chicago; Daniel Griffiths, New York University; James Harlow, President, West Virginia University; and Theodore Reller, California at Berkeley.

The Support Commission recommended to the Board that special UCEA staffing posts be created for professors. It also proposed "that the central office should endeavor to obtain general support rather than rely upon support from special projects" and that "such support should come from the member universities" (B Min, 1/13/69, p. 2). The UCEA Board decided to examine thoroughly the proposals at its May meeting.

As professors recognized the need for increased university support, they began to re-evaluate UCEA's governance structure. From UCEA's inception Plenary members from each university had possessed limited powers. Their most important tasks were to elect Board members and approve annual budgets and changes in membership fees. Discontented with their restricted decision roles, some resented the centralized control of the "strong" UCEA Board and staff. The impending increase in fees stirred new concerns in Plenary members. If universities were to pay UCEA's bills, their representatives, they argued, should have a stronger voice in policy making.[10]

At its May, 1969, meeting the Board approved plans for new UCEA staffing patterns. Three patterns, which were designed to provide learning experiences for professors, were approved: UCEA fellows, UCEA Associates, and UCEA Affiliates. These patterns and how professors used them are described and evaluated in the next chapter.

In 1968-69, the annual UCEA membership fee for universities was $1,000. Members of the UCEA Support Commission had suggested that the payments might be doubled during the 1969-74 period. At the May, 1969, Board meeting President Willard Lane of Iowa, a strong UCEA supporter, contended that the organization deserved a higher level of support. Clifford Hooker of Minnesota moved that the following fee structure be instituted: $1,750 per institution in 1970-71; $2,000 in 1971-72 and in 1972-73; and $2,500 in 1973-74. Hesitant about approving the motion, the Board postponed a decision until its November meeting.

At the November meeting the Board officially approved Hooker's earlier motion. Since the Plenary Session had the legal responsbility for approving all changes in membership costs, it had the final say on fee increases. Already scheduled for a December 7-10 Plenary Session was a vote on the proposed changes in fees. As Board members looked toward December, they sought to build a good case for the recommended increase in membership payments.

On December 7, 1969, Plenary representatives from 46 UCEA universities registered at Stouffer's Inn in Columbus, Ohio. Planned to serve multiple objectives, the Plenary Session featured special presentations as well as policy discussions. On the morning of December 8, for instance, Barbara Sizemore, the Superintendent of the

Woodlawn Experimental District, Chicago Public Schools, spoke on "Educational Leadership for the Black Community: Perceptions of an Experienced Adminstrator."

Following the presentation and the ensuing discussion, President Willard Lane spoke at some length about UCEA's financial problems and the reasons for the recommended changes in membership payments. Donald Willower, Pennsylvania State, moved that the proposed changes in membership fees be approved. After a lengthly discussion Forbis Jordan, Auburn, moved to amend the motion to require the payment to remain $2,000 in 1973-74. However, his amendment failed for want of a second. The question was called, and 38 representatives voted in favor of the motion, five voted against it, and three abstained. Thereafter, some complained because they were offered a single option rather than alternative ones. Toward the end of the meeting Leon Ovsiew, Temple, made a motion that the Board of Trustees and staff seek alternative sources of funds, so that the fee might later be reduced. Plenary Session members unanimously approved the motion.

The votes denoted that UCEA leaders, with much forethought, had formally transferred the responsibility of supporting UCEA from the foundation to the universities. Yet their courageous action created considerable distress among those at the Columbus meeting. Truman Pierce, one of UCEA's founding committee members and its second president, poignantly described the problem the increased fees created for him and his colleagues. His university's president had already made clear that he would not approve more than a $2,000 membership fee. Thus, Auburn's only option was to drop out of UCEA. Not surprisingly, some Plenary members began calling the Board's motion on the fees "Hooker's Snooker." The vote on the membership payments, then, was not a firm or final sign of UCEA's institutionalization. Unseen but imminent forces would press professors to return the issue of membership fees to UCEA governance agendas in the 1970s.

Notes

1. For a summary of the first draft of UCEA's 1964-69 plan see Culbertson, J. A., & St. Clair, K. (1963). *UCEA annual report: 1962-63* (pp. 30-34). Columbus, OH: University Council for Educational Administration.

2. For descriptions of other forces and their impact upon school

organization and administration, see Culbertson, J., Farquhar, R. H., Gaynor, A. K., & Shibles, M. R. (1969). *Preparing educational leaders for the seventies.* Columbus, OH: University Council for Educational Adminstration.

3. For an early text on the subject see Banghart, F. W. (1969). *Educational systems analysis.* New York: The Macmillan Company.

4. All of the seminar papers are available in Eidell, T. L., & Kitchel, J. M. (Eds.). (1968). *Knowledge production and utilization in educational administration.* Eugene, OR: Center for the Advanced Study of Education Administration, University of Oregon.

5. Daniel Griffiths has acknowledged the important role Bryce Fogarty played in editing the *Quarterly*: "the de facto editor was Professor Bryce Fogarty." See the *UCEA Review.* (1989). 1989 marks 25th anniversary of *The Educational Administration Quarterly,* 30(2),1-5.

6. See Ohm, R. E., & Monahan, W. G. (Eds.). (1965). *Educational administration—Philosophy in action.* Norman, OK: The College of Education, The University of Oklahoma.

7. See Culbertson, J. (1963). Common and specialized content in the preparation of administrators. In D. J. Leu & H. C. Rudman (Eds.), *Preparation programs for school administrators: Common and specialized learnings* (pp. 34-60). East Lansing, MI: College of Education, Michigan State University. In delineating the conflicts I drew upon MacIver, R. M. (Ed.). (1956). *Great moral dliemmas in literature, past and present.* New York: Harper and Brothers.

8. For a thorough review of the literature and descriptions of pertinent experimental uses of the humanities see Farquhar, R. H. (1970). *The humanities in preparing educational administrators.* Eugene, OR: The ERIC Clearinghouse on Educational Administration.

9. For an insightful review of the first edition of Samuel Popper's *Pathways* publication see Willower, D. J. (1988). Essay reviews. *Educational Administration Quarterly,* 24(2), 222-224.

10. Changes in governance are described more fully in Chapter Eleven.

References

Achilles, C. M., & Gentry, T. (1969). The administrator as man: Humanities in educational administrator education. In C. R. Blackmon (Ed.)., *Changing behaviors and values: The educational administrator in*

American society (pp. 22-38). Lafayette, LA: National Conference of Professors of Educational Administration.

Broudy, H. S. (1965). Conflicts in values. In R. E. Ohm & W. G. Monahan (Eds.), *Educational administration—Philosophy in action* (pp. 42-55). Norman, OK: The College of Education, The University of Oklahoma.

Campbell, R. F. (1964). The editor's desk. *Educational Administration Quarterly*, 1 (1), iii-iv.

Campbell, R. F. (1979). A critique of the *Educational Administration Quarterly*. *Educational Administration Quarterly*, 15 (3), 1-19.

Culbertson, J. (1969). The federal force in education. In J. Culbertson, R. H. Farquhar, A. K. Gaynor, & M. R. Shibles. *Preparing educational leaders for the seventies* (pp. 9-29). Columbus, OH: University Council for Educational Administration.

Culbertson, J., Farquhar, R. H., Fogarty, B. M., & Shibles, M. R. (Eds.). (1973). *Social science content for preparing educational administrators*. Columbus, OH: Charles E. Merrill Publishing Company.

Culbertson, J., & Shibles, M. R. (1973). The social sciences and the issue of relevance. In J. Culbertson et al (Eds.), *Social science content for preparing educational leaders* (pp. 3-32). Columbus, OH: Charles E. Merrill Publishing Company.

Farquhar, R. H. (1970). *The humanities in preparing educational administrators*. Eugene, OR: ERIC Clearinghouse on Educational Administration.

Gaynor, A. K. (1969). Research and development in education. In J. Culbertson, R. H. Farquhar, A. K. Gaynor, & M. R. Shibles. *Preparing educational leaders for the seventies* (pp. 102-103). Columbus, OH: University Council for Educational Administration.

Griffiths, D. E. (1959). *Research in educational administration*. New York: Bureau of Publications, Teachers College, Columbia University.

Griffiths, D. E. (1963). Some assumptions underlying the use of models in research. In J. A. Culbertson & S. P. Hencley (Eds.), *Educational research: New perspectives* (pp. 121-140). Danville, IL: Interstate Printers and Publishers, Inc.

Guba, E. G. (1968). Development, diffusion and evaluation. In T. L. Eidell & J. M. Kitchel (Eds.), *Knowledge production and utilization in educational administration* (pp. 37-63). Eugene, OR: Center for the Advanced Study of Educational Administration, University of Oregon.

Halpin, A. W. (1960). Ways of knowing. In R. F. Campbell & J. M. Lipham (Eds.), *Administrative theory as a guide to action* (pp. 3-20). Chicago: Midwest Administration Center, University of Chicago.

Harlow, J. G. (1962). Purpose-defining: The central function of the school administrator. In J. Culberston & S. P. Hencley (Eds.), *Preparing administrators: New perspectives* (pp. 61-71). Columbus, OH: University Council for Educational Administration.

Harlow, J. G. (1965). Implications for the preparation of educational administrators. In R. E. Ohm & W. G. Monahan (Eds.), *Educational Administration -- Philosophy in action* (pp. 94-105). Norman, OK: The College of Education, The University of Oklahoma.

Hills, R. J., & Croft, J. C. (1966). Editorial introduction. In R. J. Hills & J. C. Croft (Eds.), *Educational Administration Abstracts.* 1 (1), iii-iv.

Ohm, R. E., & Monahan, W. G. (1965a). Introduction. In R. E. Ohm & W. G. Monahan (Eds.), *Educational administration -- Philosophy in action* (pp. vii-ix). Norman OK: The College of Education, University of Oklahoma

Ohm, R. E., & Monahan, W. G. (1965b). Next steps. In R. E. Ohm & W. G. Monahan (Eds.), *Educational administration -- Philosophy in action* (pp. 106-108). Norman OK: The College of Education, University of Oklahoma.

Owens, R. G. (1970). *Organizational behavior in schools.* Englewood Cliffs, NJ: Prentice-Hall, Inc.

Schwab, J. J. (1964). The professorship in educational administration: Theory – art – practice. In D. J. Willower & J. A. Culbertson (Eds.), *The professorship in educational administration* (pp. 47-70). Columbus, OH: University Council for Educational Administration.

5

Adaptation

"It is provided in the essence of things, that from any fruition of success, no matter what, shall come forth something to make a greater struggle necessary."

Walt Whitman

As the 1969-74 period began, the editors of the respected journal, *Daedalus*, were preparing to publish a series of essays on "The Embattled University." The authors of the essays would contend that America's most distinguished universities were near or in a state of crisis.[1] Powerful student protests at Cornell, Columbia, Harvard, Ohio State, Wisconsin, California at Berkeley, and many other universities had uncovered disturbing questions. In addition, influential citizens, including legislators who appropriated monies for universities, had reacted angrily to the "uncontrolled" and at times violent actions of students.

Paradoxically, U. S. universities, though "embattled," were the envy of leaders in many other countries. Valuing the changes new knowledge had wrought in agricultural, medical, and industrial arenas, these leaders firmly believed that U. S. universities were superior to their own. In contrast, protesting students were outraged by the actions of higher education institutions which, as they saw it, were supporting the "establishment." By abetting the Vietnam War, institutional racism, student neglect, and the "military-industrial complex," the universities were pursuing evil ends.

In the 1960s critics other than students assailed universities. Some charged, for example, that the institutions had turned their backs upon urban America. While unprecedented problems faced urban leaders, university scholars, critics charged, were largely ignoring the problems. Not surprisingly, some planners, city managers, school superintendents, heads of social agencies, and other frustrated urban leaders joined the growing groups of university critics.

Critics battling on yet another front sought to puncture the century-old belief that science was the engine of human progress. By highlighting the negative results of technology, they tried to turn science on its head. Vividly reminding citizens of the deleterious effects of nuclear bombs, they also documented the damaging effects of poisonous chemicals upon the water, the land, and the air. Since the knowledge which had spawned these damaging effects emanated principally from universities, the latter were taken to task, as were the enterprises which produced the harmful products.

The attacks upon universities had their effects. The student protest movement, according to a well-known Berkeley sociologist, shook the beliefs of numerous professors in "their own moral and intellectual authority" and led some of them to question whether or not they had "a right to define a curriculum for their students or to set standards of performance..." (Trow, 1970, p. 35). Some, pondering the case against science, saw it in a less beneficent light. Concurrently, developments within the scientific community tended to undermine science's high authority. One very influential treatment of "revolutions" in the natural sciences highlighted the social character of scientific inquiry and underlined the impermanent nature of its theories (Kuhn, 1970). Many social scientists, after deciding in the 1940s that they could best advance their disciplines by aping the natural sciences, had by 1969 abandoned the strategy. One respected author summarized the conditions which were affecting social science inquiry in the mid-1970s as follows (Bernstein, 1976, p. xii):

> The initial impression one has in reading through the literature in and about the social disciplines ... is that of sheer chaos... There is little or no consensus—except by members of the same school or subschool—about what are the well-established results, the proper research procedures, the important problems, or even the most promising theoretical approaches ... There are claims and counterclaims, a virtual babble of voices demanding our attention.

Little wonder, then, that the editors of *Daedalus* chose the term "embattled" to depict the state of leading U. S. universities at the beginning of the 1969-74 period. Upset by unexpected student attacks, assailed by external critics, and shaken by collapsing assumptions about the beneficence and authority of science, university leaders carried heavy burdens. The critics spotlighted presumed inadequacies in university teaching, research, and service. Most departments, schools, and colleges could not escape the spotlight.·

Daunting Environmental Forces

During the 1969-74 period the nation's public schools were also targets of trenchant criticisms. Even the titles of books highlighted deep dissatisfactions with schooling. Note, for example, Charles Silverman's widely-read *Crisis in the Classroom* (1970), Ivan Ilich's radical book, *Deschooling Society* (1971), Peter Buckman's edited set of essays on *Education without Schools* (1973), and Ian Lister's probing collection of writings on *Deschooling* (1974).[2] The severest critics, ignoring education's past legacies, argued that new institutions were needed to replace the nation's "failed" schools. During the five-year cycle "decline" became a prominent negative watchword. After surging upward for two decades, school enrollments dropped sharply. One result was that school administrators had to close numerous unfilled schools. Since states typically used attendance figures to distribute monies to school districts, school leaders were not only faced with declining public confidence and enrollments but also with cutbacks in resources.

One of the most "embattled" units in universities were colleges of education. Graduates of these colleges, the critics said, were ill-prepared to teach or to administer schools. At the same time many working teachers and administrators were contending that university research on schooling was far removed from the world of practice.

Colleges of education were affected by changing demographics more than were other professional schools. In the 1950's and the 1960's these colleges, faced with accelerating demands for newly prepared school personnel, expanded rapidly. However, the trend slowed sharply as school enrollments declined. At that point the supply of certified teachers far exceeded the demand for them. Suffering from excess training capacities and from pressures to slash budgets, college of education leaders began using the term, "RIF" (reduction in force). Thus, the environments in which they functioned were much less friendly than were those of the "soaring sixties."

Enrollment decline in schools also affected those preparing school administrators. One result was that the discrepancy between the nation's capacities for preparing administrators and the diminishing demand for them had increased markedly. During the 1940-70 period the number of school administrators and of training institutions had surged upward (Culbertson, 1972). In 1940, for instance, there were approximately 32,000 school principalship positions. By 1970 the number had almost tripled to 92,000 (p. 87). Growing from 109 in 1940 to approximately 362 by 1970, the number of administrator training programs in higher education had more than tripled (p. 80). Attending the growth in training institutions were expansions in master's, specialist, Ed.D, and Ph.D programs for school administrators. The specialist or two-year program displayed incredible growth. In 1940 seven institutions offered such programs; by 1970 the number had grown more than twenty-fold to 145 (p. 82). Helping fuel the growth was a vote by the American Association of School Administrators (AASA) in the early 1960s that required future members to have two years of graduate work in school administration.

Master's and Ph.D programs grew relatively slowly, while the number of Ed.D programs grew more rapidly. Offering Ed.D programs in 1940 were 34 institutions; by 1970 the number had grown to 93 (Culbertson, 1972, p. 82). In the fifties and sixties the doctorate became a standard for newly-appointed school superintendents in urban and in many suburban districts and for personnel entering key positions in state and federal educational agencies, educational laboratories, professional associations, and other organizations. Acceptance of the standard fueled the increase in Ed. D. programs.

Given the striking quantitative growth in programs and the large oversupply of trained administrators, departments of educational administration were faced with excess training capacities. Ironically, the discrepancy in supply and demand was recognized about the time that many districts were closing schools. Concurrently, school districts were curtailing the training support they had traditionally provided school personnel. In the sixties many school districts offered selected personnel paid leaves of absence to pursue graduate degrees. However, because of declining resources and the declining number of administrative posts, most districts cut sharply the number of paid leaves they awarded for advanced study.

Professors of educational administration in the "elite" UCEA universities of the early seventies, then, found themselves in a much more daunting environment than that of the previous decade. Suffering from growing external criticism, they also faced a diminished demand for newly-prepared superintendents and principals and a relative decline in financial resources. Their over-riding challenge during the 1969-74 period as well as that which faced UCEA was adaptation.

Governors and The Governed: Issues of Control

Increasing criticism and declining resources were not the only factors stirring discontent among UCEA leaders. Plenary members were increasingly unhappy with UCEA's "strong" central governance and their limited role in making program decisions. I vividly remember talking about UCEA's programs in 1969 with James Applebury, then Plenary representative from Oklahoma State University and, in the latter part of the seventies, President of Pittsburgh College in Kansas. Speaking to me privately, he described his discontent. Disappointed with my response, he suddenly burst into anger. Spiritedly articulating the reasons for his anger, he made clear that Plenary members wanted a greater voice in determining UCEA's programs.

Impelled by strong desires to influence decisions about programs, Plenary members effected a major adaptation in UCEA's structure for making policy decisions. Aided by a Commission on Governance, the Plenary body, after divesting the UCEA Board of Trustees of its centralized policy functions, assumed final responsibility for making UCEA policy and program decisions. This shift in UCEA governance was attended by ambiguity, organizational struggle, redefinition of roles, drama, and even pain. A full account of the change is provided in Chapter Eleven. In this chapter only selected events which had special import for program development will be examined.

In the fall of 1970 the Plenary body formally stated its negative position about governance and program development. Two uncontested views the body expressed were (PS Min, 11/8-10/70, p. 2): "the UCEA central staff and projected Executive Committee" should be "more responsive to the general membership," and the "UCEA central staff" should "tone down" its "initiation of programs and provide more stimulation of ideas from member universities."

As I saw it, the press for greater participation in UCEA program development was salutary. In both the 1960's and the 1970's I stated to many UCEA groups that "individual initiative is one of the priceless features of organizational life." My aim was to legitimate and to nurture initiative within UCEA. However, the translation of ideas into inter-institutional practice proved to be a difficult endeavor in part because professorial views about inter-university cooperation differed significantly from those of the central staff. The point can be clarified through illustrative events.

During the development of UCEA's 1969-74 plan I traveled to about 30 universities. During university visits I asked several hundred professors the following question: "What problems should UCEA address during the next five years?" Respondents typically talked about problems related to the subjects they taught. Thus, a teacher of the politics of education would offer ideas very different from those provided by a specialist in personnel administration. Although some talked about broader concerns (e. g. improving the preparation of urban school leaders), they were in the minority.

The conversations helped illuminate the broad array of specialized interests in UCEA. However, they provided only beginning clues for UCEA programs. How a given UCEA professor's interests related to those of others was not always immediately apparent. Nor could program priorities be promptly determined. Finally, there was typically little analysis of how proffered ideas could be translated into inter-university research or development programs. Professors seldom were interested in the translation problem.

When UCEA staff members became involved in program development, a different set of difficulties arose. They typically began with broad statements of program purposes and means for achieving them. A five-page memo on "Plenary Session Leadership," which I prepared in 1971 for UCEA's fall governance meeting, provides pertinent examples. Stressing the need for "a broader base of leadership in UCEA" and "more varied instruments for its expression" (PS Mat, 10/31-11/2/71, p. 1)[3], the memo suggested that Plenary members could use commissions to produce useful outcomes for the field as, for example, ways UCEA might improve its five-year planning processes, recommendations to the National Institute of Education on needed research directions for the field, and guidelines for incorporating clinical experience into preparatory programs. Also described was a special commission in the form of a "Council of the Future."

The commission proposals, in the eyes of many Plenary members, had limitations. Since they were stated in general terms, they left many questions unanswered. In addition, most were not linked to the every day concerns of most Plenary representatives. Third, the roles of professors were not concretely specified. The ideas, then, were not unlike those articulated by professors in that they offered only beginning points for program development.

Another issue had to do with the number and scope of UCEA's programs. Some Plenary members wanted to increase the number of UCEA programs so that more professors could be active participants in them. Others, worried about "scarcity" issues in their institutions and the increased work loads they and other professors were carrying, wanted UCEA to decrease program offerings. Thus, pressures to expand UCEA programs were matched with pressures to limit them.

Faced with program counter pressures, the UCEA Board early in 1970 discussed whether or not "planning programming budgeting systems" (PPBS), if adopted by UCEA, might improve its program decisions. A planning model which the federal government had used extensively in the 1960s, PPBS was noted for its information gathering capacities, its well defined approaches to cost benefit and cost effectiveness analysis, and its abilities to generate new program ideas and to identify unproductive on-going programs. Harry Hartley, a specialist in PPBS and a member of the Board, helped the group assess the question. At a subsequent Board meeting the central staff outlined a pilot "control system" to monitor the "progress and costs" of three UCEA programs (Bd Mat, 4/30-5/2/70, p. 1). The pilot system was designed to shed light on the viability of applying PPBS to UCEA programs (p. 1). After discussing the system the Board decided that UCEA's executive director should "ask Hartley and two other professors to meet with the central staff to develop a viable PPBS system for UCEA" (p. 2). The Board also proposed that the staff present "a classification scheme, ... that reveals all major programs, sub-programs, and activities of the organization to ... the Board of Trustees as a basis for ... criticizing the program array" (p. 2).

Although I feared that the PPBS system would take time away from program development, we moved ahead on the task. Fortunately, Associate Director Alan Gaynor quickly grasped the import of the endeavor and with help from Harry Hartley began developing the desired system and "classification scheme." In a 17 page, single-spaced paper Alan depicted the relationships between UCEA's eight 1969-74 goals and its forty-four 1970-71 programs. After stating six objectives of the Monroe City Simulation program, he elaborated effectiveness measures for each objective. A PPBS system, he suggested, might help UCEA policy-makers confront priority problems, provide clients with better information about UCEA program operations, and offer better bases for evaluating programs.

At the next Plenary Session, held in September, 1971, the staff gave a progress report on the evolving PPBS system. I also described what, in my eyes, was a major value dilemma. This dilemma was rooted in the differing traditions of art and science. Dependent upon capacities for synthesis, program development, associated more with art, required qualitative and creative thought. Contrastingly, the evolving PPBS system was more of a scientific endeavor. Entailing extensive data-gathering and quantitative analysis, it provided useful information about programs, especially those already developed. Which of the two sets of values, I asked, would be most vital in UCEA's future, and how could the two best be kept in balance? I stressed that the staff needed to hear the views of the Plenary body on the value dilemma before it made final recommendations.

At the February, 1972, Plenary meeting the staff recommended that UCEA (1) develop annual or semi-annual displays of its "various programs and program elements" and distribute them to interested groups; (2) apply "cost-benefit and cost-effectiveness criteria in the making of program decisions;" and (3) "expand efforts to evaluate its programs" (PS Min, 2/10-13, 72, p. 3). Finally, the staff recommended that UCEA not develop "an accounting system which would provide specific data on the costs of its various programs" (p. 3). The Plenary body unanimously approved a motion by James Applebury, Oklahoma State, that UCEA adopt the recommendations.

The PPBS effort produced some good results. It enabled the staff to display, in an eight-page insert in the February 1972 issue of the UCEA Newsletter information on the full array of UCEA's goals and programs. Displayed, for instance, was information on each program's stage of development, the professor(s) responsible for executing it, the UCEA staff member assigned to monitor it, and the number of professors involved in it. Such displays helped UCEA professors get a better grasp of the meaning and scope of program development within UCEA. However, PPBS concepts did not resolve the conflicting judgments about program priorities!

The Shift Toward Specialized Training

In the 1969-74 cycle the thrust of UCEA's programs was significantly altered. Moving away from the earlier generalist bent, most
programs were designed to serve the specialized interests of scholars or
to address particular training needs. Even the names of UCEA's
programs pinpoint the shift. Implying that differing contexts spawned
special needs were the UCEA Urban Commission, the UCEA Non-
Urban Commission, the Complex for Leaders of Urban Education
(CLUE), and the "Monroe City" simulation; reflecting the new emphasis upon particular species of administration were the General-Special
Education Administration Consortium (GSEAC), the Non-Public School
Program, and the UCEA-NSPRA (National School Public Relations
Association) Commission; and initiatives designed to address the
needs of the underrepresented were the UCEA Native American Edu-
cational Administration Task Force, the UCEA-Black Institutions Project,
and the Native American Leadership Planning Conference.

Underlying the shifts in UCEA programs were opposing tendencies. The conflict between generalized and specialized thinking was
one of these tendencies. The early work of UCEA generalists on the
roles of theory, the humanities, and the social sciences in inquiry and
training was largely complete by 1969. Not only were new winds blowing;
professors, after exploring these subjects from numerous perspectives,
had expressed their best thoughts on them. Many of the general concepts
of the decade were applied in 1968-1969 in a staff study entitled *Preparing
Educational Leaders for the Seventies.* Through an analysis of six forces (e. g.
racism and the "business-education interface") and a study of prevailing
UCEA training programs, the federally-supported inquiry offered a
comprehensive set of recommendations.[4] Although we looked ahead, our
conclusions were informed more by the general concepts of the sixties
than by the more specialized ones of the seventies.

Most professors who opted to develop specialized training programs set aside the tenet of administration qua administration—a belief
which had undergirded general training programs for all administrators—as well as aspirations to achieve general theories of administration. Rather, they sought adaptations which would mesh with conditions in their markedly altered environments.

Several UCEA dissemination programs illuminated the trend toward more specialized training. The program which best depicted the

trend was a series of 25 articles on "Innovations in Preparations" which appeared either in the *UCEA Newletter* or the *UCEA Review*. Only a few of the 25 training initiatives were grounded in the "administration qua administration" concept. One example was the Stanford program jointly offered by the School of Business and the School of Education (Kirst, 1970). In almost all of the programs the dominant content was linked to particular functions, contexts, ethnic groups, or the interests of individual trainees.

Departing most markedly from tradition were four university programs whose content and learning modes were determined by the special interests of individual trainees. Illustrative of this approach was "An Individualized Learning System for Administrators" offered at New York University (Rose, 1971). Its purposes were to get its enrollees to think carefully about their "objectives" and "to approach the body of content" as searchers, or explorers with "experienced guides nearby" (i. e. professors) rather than as receivers "of a pre-packaged and pre-digested menu" (p. 18). After an orientation to the resources of the university, the trainees developed individual study plans, including means for evaluating them. When they completed their plans and obtained the approval of their advisors, they implemented them in their "own way and time" (p. 19).

The purposes of eight of the 25 programs were to provide trainees knowledge and skills needed to perform specialized functions (e.g. operations research) or to assume positions as specialists (e. g. directors of research in urban school districts). An example of this type of program was developed at the University of Iowa (Dusseldorp and Monahan, 1971). Its specific purpose was to prepare "administrators of research and/or information systems in large school districts, state education agencies," and related institutions (p. 15). Content requirements encompassed three areas: educational administration, research and statistics, and data processing and computer science. After obtaining their doctorates, almost all accepted posts for which their studies had prepared them.

Two of the 25 programs recruited and prepared leaders from particular racial groups. One at Harvard was designed to produce "Black" educational administrators (Cronin, 1970), while a Pennsylvania State program was implemented for "Red" administrators (Lynch, 1971). Concern for education in urban contexts was reflected in the "Philadelphia-Penn State Program" and the University of Wisconsin's initiative to produce newly trained administrators for inner-city schools (Fruth & Gregg, 1972).

The new emphases in university training was also reflected in a series of monographs which UCEA and the ERIC Clearinghouse on Educational Management at the University of Oregon cooperatively developed. One of the monographs, for instance, depicted and analyzed the trend toward preparing school administrators in quantitative analysis (Bruno, 1973). Another, focusing upon "new approaches" to the recruitment and selection of educational administrators, gave special attention to members of minority groups (Stout, 1973).

How did the content of UCEA Career Development seminars relate to the move toward more specialized training? Notably, only five of these seminars were sponsored during the five year time span in contrast to the ten and eight sponsored in the 1959-64 and 1964-69 periods, respectively. The reasons for the smaller number are not clear. Certainly, the funds needed to produce seminars and to publish their proceedings were much harder to find. Possibly a more important reason was that scholars, faced with unexpected changes, had not yet had the time to formulate fresh thoughts about them. In any case their content was related to the new emphasis upon particular contexts and positions, as the following titles indicate:

> "Alternative Models for Organizing Education in Metropolitan Areas," State University of New York at Buffalo, November, 1969.
> "Whither the School Principalship and Preparation Therefor?," University of Texas, 1970.
> "The New Politics and Educational Policy," Pennsylvania State University, October, 1970.
> "Imaging Alternative Future School Organizations," University of Minnesota, late October and early November, 1972.
> "Professional School-Urban Community Interface," Ontario Institute for Studies in Education, late October and early November, 1973.

The seminars at Buffalo, Pennsylvania State, and the Ontario Institute all reflected in yet another way the widespread concern with school administration in urban contexts. At the University of Texas attendees sought to re-think the nature of a particular position, while those at Minnesota looked at concepts and methods they might use to conceptualize alternative futures and, thereby, to attain means they could use to transcend the status quo.

In sum, an important feature of training during the five year cycle was its specialized bent. Earlier, leading scholars had focused more upon using generic theories to prepare all administrators. Leaders in the 1969-74 period chose content designed to prepare trainees to perform specialized functions, to deal with conditions in particular contexts, or to nurture the special interests of individuals. In the Iowa program, for instance, trainees acquired specialized content on the computer sciences from professors of mathematics and content on operations research from professors of industrial management (Dusseldorp and Monahan, 1971, p. 15). Such content differed markedly from that which students had acquired in the late 1950s and early 1960s from social science professors.

The new programs also placed a greater emphasis upon the application of knowledge. While generic theories presumably could be applied to phenomena in all organizations, specialized knowledge was designed to help managers and organizations become efficient and effective in particular ways or contexts. Thus, operations research offered trainees the knowledge and skills needed to achieve "optimal" solutions to various types of problems. An example of a solution would be a set of cafeteria menus for a particular school which was optimally responsive to the taste preferences of students, food costs, and the healthiest mix of foods. Another would be detailed outlines of the most efficient work schedules for building a new school.[4]

The emphasis upon application was also encouraged by innovative field experiences for trainees. New approaches to the design and evaluation of field experience were reflected in the titles of three of the 25 articles: "Field Stations and the Preparation of School Administrators" by M. Y. Nunnery and R. B. Kimbrough, "The Externship" by Fred Vescolani and Richard L. Featherstone, and "Rotating Internships and Situational Analysis" by Anthony M. Cresswell and Robert J. Goettel. These experiments also were responsive to the charges that training was too academic and impractical.

The shift toward specialized programs, it should be made clear, represented an incremental rather than a radical change in programs. Since most were funded in part by governmental agencies or foundations, they had difficulty surviving in the economic climate of the period. Their impact was also limited because most of them operated as "parallel" programs independently of established ones. Those who remained loyal to the theory movement, in other words, continued to teach content similar to that offered earlier. However, the professors who took part in the new programs continued to use their newly acquired knowledge and skills in re-designed or existing courses.

Regional seminars for UCEA graduate students was another new initiative. The originator of the seminar idea was Associate Director Bryce Fogarty. Bryce had served as a teacher and a school principal in Wisconsin and as the Associate Director of Admissions at Antioch College in Ohio. Later he obtained a Ph.D from the University of Wisconsin. An effective and articulate critic, he was a loyal pursuer of UCEA's mission. The seminar idea was pilot-tested at Syracuse and at Tennessee in 1967. Attending the Syracuse seminar were 80 persons from nine UCEA universities. Scattered throughout the audience were professors who had driven cars loaded with graduate students to the event. At the seminar participants engaged in a dialogue with Egon Guba of Indiana University, among others, on issues related to "Research in Educational Administration." The Tennessee seminar attracted 40 students from seven universities who heard expert views about "Collective Negotiations and the Educational Administrator."

At its May, 1969, meeting the UCEA Board approved a 1969-74 package of programs for graduate students. Included in the package, along with the seminars, was a projected UCEA National Graduate Student Council and an inter-university information service to help doctoral recipients find professorships. The "Student Council," whose membership consisted of one student from each UCEA university, met annually to examine issues related to training and practice.

During the seventies UCEA experimented with three types of seminars for graduate students. The first, a thematic one, enabled presenters to explore different facets of a stipulated subject. Later when the "Great Scholar" seminar was conceived, students asked leading thinkers to serve as seminar leaders. Finally, student-led seminars on dissertation design and research were implemented. The most popular of the three was the "Great Scholar" seminar.

From the beginning the seminars appealed to graduate students. They valued hearing and interacting with scholars they had not seen but whose writings they had read. They also found rewarding exchanges with one another about doctoral experiences and career opportunities in regions other than their own. Several times during the 1970's as many as three or four regional seminars were offered annually. Articles prepared by graduate students on the discussions appeared in the *UCEA Newsletter* and the *UCEA Review*. In the October 1977 *UCEA Review* for instance, Jeanne Campbell, Minnesota, and Ken Kempner, Oregon, summarized ideas discussed at their respective institutions on the "Management of Decline" and "Evolving Educational Policy in Foreign Countries." By 1980 the seminars had served an estimated 1,000 graduate students.

New Opportunities for Professors

The creation of new means for providing UCEA professors fresh learning opportunities was another major adaptation in UCEA programs. To respond to the specialized interests of UCEA professors the Board in 1968-69 approved an innovative means for encouraging R and D programs. Called special staffing patterns, the innovations enabled professors to conduct or manage programs and, in so doing, to enhance UCEA's outreach. Participating professors could become a UCEA Fellow, a UCEA Associate, or a UCEA Affiliate.[5] Professors who could obtain a nine month leave with pay to manage or execute an R or D project in UCEA's central office were eligible for the UCEA Fellow role. Troy McKelvey, State University of New York at Buffalo, served as a UCEA fellow in 1969-70. While at UCEA he helped more than 40 professors launch the Monroe City simulation project. UCEA benefited greatly from his work. However, the organization was unable to attract additional UCEA Fellows during the 1969-74 cycle.

The UCEA Associate role was designed for those who could obtain a leave of absence for a quarter or semester to conduct a UCEA project in their own university, at another university, or in the UCEA central office. Five UCEA Associates were appointed during the 1969-74 period. As a 1969-70 UCEA Associate, Gerald Rasmussen, Los Angeles State College, developed Monroe City's Janus Junior High simulation.[6] Completed in the summer of 1970, it was used widely in training programs. Joan Egner, Cornell University, an Associate in 1971-72, did research on one aspect of UCEA's "New Passageways to Leadership" project. Designed to illuminate the "barriers that discourage ... leaders in ... undergraduate populations ... from pursuing preparation for and careers in educational administration" (*UCEA Newsletter*, XII (4), p. 3), the project enabled Joan Egner to study the views of women and minorities.

In 1972-73 Associate Leslie Gue of Alberta examined how UCEA and the new Commonwealth Council for Educational Administration might jointly advance research on comparative educational administration. Herbert Rudman, Michigan State, an Associate in 1973-75, probed the problem of clinical learning by examining pertinent concepts and practices in such fields as medicine and law. In the spring of 1974 Robert Schweitzer, Pennsylvania State, became a UCEA Associate. Since the Plenary body had adopted "Knowledge Utilization" as a guiding theme for 1974-79, Schweitzer sought to elaborate models which could help program developers pursue the theme.

Easier to arrange than the UCEA Fellow and the Associate roles, the Affiliate role proved to be a popular one. Professors performed the role in their own universities, sometimes aided by reduced work loads. Launched in 1970-71 with 13 UCEA Affiliates, there were 16 in 1971-72, 11 in 1972-73, and eight in 1973-74. Information about illustrative Affiliate appointments follow:

A Study of the "Institutional Culture" of Preparatory Programs in Selected UCEA Universities. Carl Steinhoff and Lloyd Bishop, New York University, 1970-71.

The Simulation of Educational and Social Planning Problems Within Monroe City. Gordon McCloskey, Washington State University, 1970-71.

A Keyword-in-Context Index to Doctoral Dissertations in Educational Administration. Melvyn Robbins, Ontario Institute for Studies in Education, 1971-72.

Analytic Work on a Computer-Based UCEA Information System. Frank Banghart, Florida State University, 1971-72.

A Study of Professors of Educational Administration in the United States and Canada. Roald Campbell, Ohio State University, 1971-72.

The Impact of the "Janus Junior High" Simulation on the Learnings of Administrators. Ray Cross and Vernon Hendrix, University of Minnesota, 1971-72.

An Inter-Institutional Study of Relationships Between Urban

Schools and Universities. Brooklyn Derr, Harvard University, 1972-73.

Rural Educational Administration. Harold Goodwin, West Virginia   University, 1972-73.

Learning and Leadership Opportunities for Graduate Students in Educational Administration. Wayne Hoy, Rutgers University, 1972-73.

Implementation of a UCEA Student Data System. Charles Kline and   Richard Munsterman, Purdue University, 1973-74.

The Preparation of Native American Administrators. Patrick Lynch, Pennsylvania State University, 1973-74.

Doctorate Needs in Educational Administration During the 1970's and 1980's. S. J. Knezevich, University of Wisconsin, 1973-74.

Affiliate roles were initiated either by professors or staff. The study of culture and preparation by Steinhoff and Bishop, for instance, was conceived independently of the UCEA staff.[7] On the other hand, the study of professors by Roald Campbell was a staff-initiated one. In planning for 1969-74 I resolved to see if a comprehensive study of the professorship might be enacted. Believing that scholars external to the field might offer a more detached perspective, I turned first to sociologists. However, after talking with several scholars, I gave up on the idea and turned to Roald Campbell, who had long had a strong interest in the professorship. He immediately agreed to conduct the inquiry.[8] The study by S. J. Knezevich of doctorate needs was one of many projects which evolved from joint staff-professor discussions during university visits.[9]

How effective were the innovative staffing patterns? Most professors generated valued products in part because a quarter of the affiliates' appointments was extended from one to two years. However, more than a third of the appointees, for varied reasons, failed to complete their projects. Did the new roles diminish the amount of time the central staff devoted to program co-ordination, as some had hoped? Since only 10 per cent of those accepting special appointments chose to manage UCEA programs, the staffing patterns increased rather than decreased the work of the central staff.

Did the new patterns bring more focus to UCEA's activities? The general answer is "No." Since they were designed to serve the specialized interests of individuals, they fostered fragmented rather than inte-grated efforts. An exception was Frank Banghart's work on the UCEA Student Data System whose findings later shaped a major project for recruiting, preparing, and placing members of minority groups. (see Chapter Six). Signaling UCEA's strong interest in research and devel-opment, the special staffing program produced an array of visible R and D outcomes. Notably, the patterns continued to be used in the 1970s and early 1980s, though less frequently than in the 1969-74 period.

Another UCEA initiative designed to serve the special motivations of professors was the interest group program. The idea emanated from a board-staff planning meeting held at Chicago's O'Hare Inn in May, 1968. Shortly thereafter the central staff mailed five interest inventories to all UCEA professors. Each of the inventories was directed at a different use of knowledge: Form A at using knowledge to create new knowledge; Form B at employing knowledge to achieve new syntheses; Form C at using knowledge to update or design preparatory programs; Form D at using knowledge to develop new instructional materials; and Form E at using knowledge to derive solutions to school problems. Each form contained the same list of 20 categories of knowledge as, for example, disciplinary ones (e. g. the politics of education) and process ones (e. g. managing conflict). Professors were asked to choose the form(s) which denoted their major interest(s) in knowledge use and then to check the knowledge categories which best reflected their substantive interests.

After examining computer print-outs on professors' interests, the staff prepared a paper on "UCEA Interests Groups" (Bd Mat, 2/16/69). The purposes of interest groups, the paper stated, were to enable professors to (1) share and explore special ways of using knowledge, (2) establish communication channels which could continue to be used informally, and (3) design and conduct cooperative inter-institutional research and development projects. In February, 1969, the UCEA Board decided that the 23 staff recommendations "be adopted as a set of guidelines and a statement of developmental policies for use by staff and interest groups" (Bd Min, 2/13/69, p. 2).

In the spring of 1969 the staff activated 32 groups, each with a designated leader. Three groups, for example, were formed for each of the most popular domains: the economics of education, the politics of education, and the sociology of organization. After a list of all the groups was sent to UCEA professors (*UCEA Newsletter*, 10(4),12-13), some professors originated additional groups. Melvyn Robbins, Ontario Institute for Studies in Education, organized a group on "The Nature and Development of Educational Administration As a Discipline"; Robert Frossard, Florida, one on the "Design of Physical Facilities for Administrative Preparation"; and Leslie Gue, Alberta, a group on "Comparative Educational Administration."

During 1969-70 the interest groups, aided by their leaders, began to function. A few defined their objectives quickly. For instance, the "Higher Education" group, led by James Wattenbarger, University of Florida, chose to examine the governance of community colleges. Other groups began by exchanging information by mail. The group on the "Anthropology of Education," chaired by Donald Willower, Pennsylvania State, shared relevant references on theory, methodology, and research. Several groups explored issues in face-to-face meetings. Even though many groups had promising starts, some leaders soon reported that they were encountering problems. A widespread one was heterogeneity of interests in groups. Several leaders resigned their posts. However, when all the active ones were asked in the spring of 1970 if their groups should be disbanded, none answered "yes."

By mid-1972 most had ended their activities. A good proportion had attained, at least to some degree, the objectives of (1) sharing information and exploring uses of knowledge and (2) establishing new communication channels which could continue to be used informally. However, groups found it very difficult to generate inter-university R and D projects. Widely dispersed geographically and constrained by heavy work loads, most found it impracticable to become seriously involved in such projects. In fact, only one group succeeded in launching an externally-funded project. The project which dealt with general and special education administration is described below.

Designed as an "open" program for all UCEA professors, its leaders were confronted with the usual difficulties in bridging ideas and action. By studying carefully the written summaries of the hundreds of conversations the UCEA staff had held with professors during university visits, the staff very likely could have identified groups with more homogeneous interests than those in the 32 that had been launched. If so, the groups could likely have defined acceptable goals more easily. However, the "closed" process of selecting participants would undoubtedly have stirred discontent among those who were excluded from UCEA's inner circles. The project also enabled many professors to grasp more clearly the complexities faced by developers and implementers of inter-university R and D programs.

Another initiative was that of providing Plenary members specially arranged opportunities to hear scholars from outside UCEA present timely ideas. At the fall 1971 Plenary Session, for instance, William Walker, University of New England in Australia, spoke on "UCEA's Bright Son at Morning: The Commonwealth Council for Educational Administration." William Cody, Director of the National Institute of Education, spoke at the February 1972 session about the federal government's plans and aspirations for the "Problems," "Practices," and "Basic Research" divisions of the young Institute.

The endeavor also enabled Plenary members to confront issues currently before them. To stimulate thought and exchange, debates, individual presentations, and panel discussions. were sponsored At the 1969 Plenary Session, for instance, Chester Bumbarger, Alberta, and Robert Coughlin, Northwestern, debated the following question: "Should graduate students have voting rights similar to those of faculty members on matters concerning program change?" Another query which Samuel Goldman, Syracuse, and Neal Tracy, North Carolina, debated, was "Should forecasts of societal and educational futures be treated as central content in administrative preparation?"

Such offerings served a diverse professoriate. The diversity stretched across two nations; differing regional cultures; rural, suburban, and urban contexts; private and public universities; older and younger professors; and numerous specialized interests. In arranging debates, panels, and lectures for "captive" Plenary members, the UCEA staff, in the face of such diversity, often fell far short of finding subjects which appealed strongly to all participants. Nevertheless, the program apparently had its values. When I left UCEA in 1981, it was still in place.

When the Plenary body changed UCEA's governance, it decided that UCEA presidents should give annual addresses. These addresses, which began in 1972, provided Plenary members as well as UCEA presidents valued insights. Deliverer of the first address, "To Move A Profession," was President Samuel Goldman of Syracuse, a very loyal supporter of UCEA. Expressing strong concern about the "generalized 'depression of spirit' among" educators (Goldman, 1972, p. 1), he called upon his hearers to act more aggressively. To help repair the schools he argued that professors should reform training programs. Emphasizing the danger of allowing "ourselves to be overwhelmed by our critics so much so, that even our own confidence in our capabilities . . . seems to be deteriorating" (p. 3), he called upon Plenary members to translate "what we know and what we do into behavior that works" (p. 4). In his inspirational address Goldman sought to elevate the hopes of UCEA leaders.

The 1973 address was delivered by President Wailand Bessent of the University of Texas. A student of planning technologies, he chose the topic "Some Issues Underlying the Planning Process in UCEA." His aim was "to bring about some productive introspection in the frustrating task of planning" (Bessent, 1973, p. 13). In his paper he examined four issues. One was "Should UCEA have a focused or diffuse program?" Calling for more program focus, he stressed that UCEA's programs for several reasons were becoming more diffuse. First, professors faced with large membership fees were under pressure to justify UCEA's value. These pressures had encouraged some to adopt "a 'what's in it for me?' attitude," and UCEA through its own responses had contributed to the diffuseness of its offerings (p. 13).

A second reason for diffuseness stemmed from externally-funded programs. Such programs, driven by narrow aims, inevitably produced fragmented efforts. Third, "program elements created by the spin-offs from past successes" also contributed to the scattering of UCEA's activities (Bessent, 1973, p. 13): "The school simulation efforts . . . continue to generate new instructional products that require coordination . . . maintenance and distribution" (p. 13). Finally, UCEA was "prodded toward program diversity" because of specialization in the professoriate. Given the narrowing of "individual perspectives" among professors, it was "increasingly difficult to get consensus on a program focus in a department, let alone UCEA" (p. 13).

The 1974 address was delivered by Donald Willower, Pennsylvania State. A versatile scholar with interests in both theory and its relationships to practice, he spoke on "Educational Administration and the Uses of Knowledge." Calling upon UCEA to "keep alive and strong our visions of as yet uninvented theories and investigations that might add to, or even transform, knowledge about educational organizations" (Willower, 1974, p. 1), he also stressed the need for programmatic research to give focus to "inquiry . . . at a time when the dark shadow of decline clouds our future" (p 2). In his address he outlined seven changes in schools which could be abetted through knowledge use. Two of these, for instance, were "rearrangements and regroupings of organizational positions better to serve ends, . . ." and "interventions intended to reshape teacher norms" (p. 4).

Willower firmly believed that UCEA should devote its efforts principally to studying substantive questions. Observing that the "governance game seems ended and those toys are in the attic for now," he stressed that "in the rush, not to say stampede, into the field," we should "recall that UCEA is a council of universities and the distinctive contribution of universities is likely to be the scholarly examination of the nature of practice" (Willower, 1974, p. 5).

The presidential addresses added a fresh dimension to professorial exchange. They communicated the insights of thoughtful individuals and, as a collectivity, they reflected to some degree the infinite diversity within UCEA. In another sense they provided an increasingly specialized professoriate opportunities to examine the conflicting values espoused by generalists and specialists.

Mediating General and Special Interests

In conducting UCEA programs the UCEA staff was frequently involved in mediating the disparate expectations of specialists and generalists. The General-Special Education Consortium (GSEAC), perhaps better than any other program, required such mediation. Advocates of general theories of administration tended to oppose the GSEAC effort. Some even believed that the project denoted that UCEA had rejected general theories. However, the professors who created GSEAC wanted to make better use of such theories in the training of special education administrators. In addition, they wanted principals and superintendents to learn more about issues bearing upon the improvement of special education.

The seeds for GSEAC were planted in the spring of 1968 when four professors of special education administration traveled to UCEA's headquarters. From the University of Oregon came Melton Martinson; from Syracuse, Daniel Sage; from Texas, Charles Meisgeir; and from Pittsburgh, Godfrey Stevens. Expressing deep concern about the "separatism" between general and special education students, teachers, school administrators, and professors, they elaborated a vision for the future. Envisaging a wide-ranging attack upon separatism, they wanted more special education students moved out of separate facilities and into regular classrooms. They also wanted general and special education administrators to cooperate in effecting needed educational changes, and newly-designed training endeavors to help both types of administrators attain the hoped-for outcomes.

On-going efforts to improve the training of special education leaders suffered, the group stressed, from separatism. About four years earlier the Bureau of Education for the Handicapped of the U. S. Office of Education had made a series of training grants to improve the preparation of special education administrators. Significantly, the grants were awarded to departments of special education. As representatives of these departments, the visitors needed the help, they stressed, of professors of general educational administration.

The previous year the directors of the federally-funded programs had met in Washington, D. C., to assess their problems and prospects. Having formed a National Consortium of Universities Preparing Administrators of Special Education, they supported an enlarged program of cooperation. Toward this end the group had asked its elected executive committee to explore cooperative relations with an agency engaged in improving educational administration. As one of its members would later write (Meisgeier, 1969, p. 8-9): "The University Council for Educational Administration (UCEA) was selected as that agency. It had a . . . significant history of innovation, training, and curriculum design and development." The four travelers to Columbus constituted the consortium's elected executive committee.

Near the end of the meeting the group asked if I, as UCEA's executive director, would help them realize their objectives. The request generated ambivalent feelings within me. The improvement of special education and its leadership struck me as a compelling ideal. In addition, the unusual clarity of the vision articulated by the visitors impressed me greatly. However, since I was unacquainted with the special education network, I was not in a position to pretend that UCEA could fulfill the abounding aspirations of the four visitors. I also knew that the proposed endeavor, if implemented, would generate controversy within UCEA, and that organizational costs would be incurred. Thus, I temporized by agreeing that UCEA and the National Consortium would co-sponsor, if the UCEA Board approved, a conference in 1969 on the training of special education administrators.

The conference unfolded at the University of Texas in March, 1969. In attendance were pairs of general and special education administration professors from about 20 universities. At the conference I gained a keener understanding of the problems identified earlier. That both types of professors suffered from "separatism" was starkly apparent. Numerous pairs of them had not met one another previously. Several pairs had met for the first time, I was told, on their flight to Texas. Others got acquainted after they arrived in Austin. Few of those who had met previously had engaged in cooperative endeavors in their "home" institutions. On the neutral Texas territory, however, they began to show interest in each other's professional domains.

As I listened to the discussions, both formal and informal, I saw more potential in the proposed consortium project. I also realized that the operations envisaged by consortium leaders were within UCEA's capacities. Thus, I decided some weeks after the conference ended to cooperate fully with the group. By the end of 1969 selected professors had outlined a one-year planning proposal.

In February, 1970, the UCEA Board met in Atlantic City, New Jersey. Prior to the meeting I asked the four earlier travelers to Columbus if they could meet with and respond to questions from the Board. All agreed to do so. However, after landing in Philadelphia, they found that the buses were immobilized by icy highways. Not to be deterred, they found a cab driver who braved the hazardous roads toward Atlantic City. Hours later they arrived at the Traymore Hotel where UCEA Board members heard their case and asked them questions. Satisfied with their answers, the Board encouraged us to move ahead on the project. Later in the spring we learned from Kenneth Wyatt in the Bureau of Education for the Handicapped that his agency would award UCEA a planning grant for 1970-71 in the amount of $83,238.

Daniel Sage, a respected member of the consortium's executive committee, obtained a leave of absence from Syracuse to co-ordinate GSEAC's planning. As a Staff Affiliate at UCEA's headquarters, he began narrowing the psychological distance between general and special education administration. Assisting Dan in building an initial bridge between the two fields were associate directors Alan Gaynor, Michael Martin, and Jackson Newell. Earlier, Alan had been a Walter A. Anderson Fellow at New York University, where he earned a Ph.D. Still earlier he was a social studies teacher, a department head, and a director of adult education. A stimulating colleague at UCEA, he was a productive developer of ideas. Before he received his doctorate at UCLA, Michael Martin had taught social studies in a California high school. Later he was the coordinator of elementary and secondary education in Santa Barbara County. His charismatic personality and quick mind helped brighten and enlighten UCEA's activities. Jackson Newell attained his Ph.D. at Ohio State in higher education administration. Earlier he taught history at Deep Springs College and at Clemson University. He also served as an assistant dean at the University of New Hampshire. Known for his deep commitment to the liberal arts, Jack's UCEA interests spanned school and higher education administration.

In 1971 UCEA was awarded a three-year grant by the bureau to implement Sage's proposed plan. Support for 1971-72 was $98,188. Similar amounts were awarded to UCEA in 1972-73, and 1973-74. The project was designed to test the efficacy of an "inter-institutional change model" for improving the training of "specialized personnel." Its mission was to integrate training programs for general and special education administrators. Associate Director James Yates, a former school psychologist and a director of special education, coordinated the project. Recipient of a Ph.D. from the University of Texas, he became the hub in a wheel of national communication, where he skillfully managed GSEAC's varied activities.

The change model, a very complex one, can only be described here in simplified terms. Central to its dynamics were inter-university and intra-university teams, both composed of professors of general and special education administration. Inter-university teams generated R and D products (e. g. new program content) related to GSEAC's mission. Each GSEAC institution was asked to appoint a pair of professors—one from the special education department and the other from the department of educational administration—to serve as local change agents. The pairs performed two functions. They facilitated the adoption and use of products created by inter-university teams, and with the help of their colleagues effected internal ways and means for integrating the two training programs.

How effective was the "inter-institutional change model?" Before this question is addressed, some basic postulates underlying the "change model" need to be explicated. First, the model was presumed to be a generic one. If proven effective within GSEAC, it could integrate and improve programs in other fields (e. g. general and vocational education administration). Second, the model's capacity for effecting improvements depended upon whether it could move professors of general and special education administration away from segregated patterns of operation and toward more integrated approaches to training.

Finally, it could not generate improvements in training unless professors in GSEAC cooperatively developed program-related innovations and used them to change programs.

Implicit in the three postulates were evaluative criteria. Such questions as the following had to be affirmatively answered for the model to be effective. Did professors in the two fields cooperatively develop innovative products? Did GSEAC professors adopt and use the products? Did the products and locally created changes enable the professors to integrate their efforts in the training of school leaders? The criteria, it should be noted, were designed to test the model rather than specific training effects. GSEAC leaders presumed that if the model proved effective, improved training would result.

Did GSEAC's inter-university teams cooperatively develop innovative products? The general answer is "yes." For example, GSEAC teams, using telelectures at regional seminars, provided joint learning experiences for students of general and special education administration. They also added to the reservoir of available training materials, prepared fresh content for use in programs, and devised new means of transmitting information. An abbreviated description of selected GSEAC products will make the point clearer.

Telelectures were evaluated to determine their capacities for enhancing inter-institutional communication between the two fields of administration. In the spring of 1972, for instance, GSEAC tested the telelectures in four regions of the nation.[10] Universities which facilitated the telephonic tests were Alabama, California at Berkeley, New Mexico, and Teachers College, Columbia. The number of connected institutions ranged from two at Berkeley to six at Tuscaloosa.

The evaluator of the telelectures concluded that participants in multiple locations could effectively exchange ideas at a fraction of the usual costs of conferences, that the telelecture provided a helpful springboard for "increased communication . . . with colleagues in the complementary fields," and that the quality and amplitude of transmissions should be carefully pre-tested (Horn, 1973, p. 19). To enhance the learnings of GSEAC or UCEA students in the future, the respondents recommended that relevant reading materials be provided participants in advance of the telelectures.

Three GSEAC groups expanded the reservoir of training materials. One reviewed games and audio-visual materials available in other fields and identified those related to school administration. Six pairs of professors of general and special education administration conducted the reviews. Thurston Atkins and Vincent Aniello at Teachers College, Columbia, for instance, previewed films on education and race, while Melton Martinson, Oregon, and Charles Faber, Kentucky, examined materials on group processes. Other professors evaluated teaching tools on leadership, decision games, communication, and administrative techniques. Teams provided nine types of information on each audio-visual item and game as, for example, the developer of the item, its medium of transmission, its purpose, its length, and its quality. Information on about 175 items was programmed and sent to all GSEAC personnel for use (Yates, 1972).

Two other teams developed major simulations. Rooted in the "Monroe City" context, SEASIM was designed to help prepare directors of special education, while PSYSIM was developed for trainers of school psychologists. In SEASIM the problems simulated included the shortage of special education personnel, program ineffectiveness, and student classification. Simulated decision problems were presented through "in-basket" messages, films, and other media. The titles of three films illustrate the types of issues simulated: "The Unwanted Pupil," "The Placement Dilemma," and "Special Education Placement and the Law."

A third product was new substantive content. Aspiring to help leaders look beyond the status quo, GSEAC sponsored "futures" studies. One result was a series of trend analyses. Published by UCEA, the series, for example, included an essay by Maynard Reynolds, University of Minnesota, on "Changing Roles of Special Education Personnel," and another by David Kirp, California at Berkeley, on "The Special Child Goes to Court." A second achievement was a book on methods for studying the future. Between an introductory chapter and a final one entitled "Values and Forecasts" were 14 chapters, most of which depicted and analyzed a particular method for studying "futures." [11]

Another attainment of GSEAC leaders was the addition of a new section entitled "Special Education Administration" to the *Educational Administration Abstracts*. A more ambitious effort to meet the information needs of the two fields was led by Robert Ohm and Gerald Kowitz of the University of Oklahoma. Piloted with the help of 70 participants, the project featured a computer-based system for retrieving and transmitting information to GSEAC professors and students. However, the system failed largely because of its imprecise retrieval procedures and its limited information base.

Were the outcomes produced by inter-university groups used in GSEAC institutions? While the general answer is "Yes," some were used much more than others. SEASIM, for example, was employed widely within and beyond GSEAC while PSYSIM was used in less than one sixth of the consortium's 31 institutions. The book on methodologies for studying the future enabled professors in more than one fourth of the universities to spawn new courses on educational futurism, while the harvest from the audio-visual materials selected from other fields by the six pairs of GSEAC professors was a small one.

Did adopted R and D products facilitate the integration of GSEAC training endeavors for the two fields? Certainly, the numerous GSEAC conferences helped motivate professors to adopt the products. In addition, the experience, which the two types of professors gained through working with one another on teams, had its effects. They used the insights gleaned from each other to facilitate the dissemination, adoption, and use of the products they had jointly created.

Intra-university team members also helped ensure the use of GSEAC's R and D products. As activists, they encouraged professors and students to attend GSEAC conferences, seminars, and institutes to acquire needed information about the innovations. To make it easier for professors to use the products, some persuaded their university administrators to purchase GSEAC simulations and publications.

Intra-university teams did more than enhance the use of R and D products. They also worked with local professors in both fields to achieve more cooperative and integrated approaches to training. Jointly appointed committees worked to broaden learning options for doctoral students. Directing their efforts toward practice, others planned and offered workshops to serve both general and special education administrators. Other illustrative attainments were special seminars for students in the two fields, the design of new courses, the inclusion of new content on the management of special education in existing courses on general administration, and joint participation by both kinds of professors on dissertation committees. Such changes had their limitations. They tended, for example, to be incremental. In addition, a relatively small proportion of GSEAC's 31 institutions implemented even a majority of the changes. However, since some of them were attained in all the institutions, GSEAC changes were widespread. As a result, the walls of segregation between professors, students, and administrators in the two fields were breached.

One negative effect of the model was the divisiveness it activated. Almost half of the UCEA universities belonged to GSEAC, while the remainder did not. In addition, a half dozen GSEAC institutions were not members of UCEA. Since almost all GSEAC members had federal grants to prepare special education administrators, some UCEA professors outside the consortium resented their "have not" status. One department head reported that his university was dropping its membership because of UCEA's sponsorship of GSEAC.

The GSEAC "change model," as compared to other UCEA cooperative models, had a distinct advantage. It focused *directly* upon improving preparatory programs. Other UCEA cooperative patterns aimed *indirectly* at altering programs by generating R and D outcomes which professors presumably would employ in preparatory programs. By facilitating the R and D work of inter-university groups *and* by activating intra-university teams to effect specific changes in programs, the GSEAC model possessed dual strengths. The UCEA and GSEAC staff could have devoted more time to the intra-university teams. The functions of these teams might have been defined earlier and more clearly, and training might have increased the teams' competence. Two central staff members — one to facilitate the work of inter-university groups, and the other the work of intra-university teams—would have increased the model's effectiveness.

The GSEAC model, with its boundary-spanning capacities, has many potential applications. It could be used in fields less closely linked than were special and general education administration (e. g. curriculum and school administration). Given its versatility, the model could also help professors address problems in their own departments. Assume, for example, that professors of educational administration in eight universities wanted better ways of nurturing educational vision through training. The GSEAC model with its intra-university teams, its inter-university groups, and its central staff could be brought to bear on the problem. The resulting dynamic would generate much more learning and program change than would the workings of eight isolated staffs. Precisely because the relatively impermeable boundaries of departments constrain vision and action, change models are needed which span universities and departments. Otherwise, those who inhabit tradition-bound university isles will be deprived not only of needed stimuli but also of fresh perspectives.

Notes

1. See *Daedalus: Journal of the American Academy of Arts and Sciences.* (1970). The embattled university. 99(1), 1-224.

2. Lister's work contains selected essays from the sixties and early seventies and a "quotational" bibliography. See Lister, I. (Ed.). (1974). *Deschooling*. Cambridge: Cambridge University Press.

3. In this and other chapters the following abbreviations are used: Bd Mat, PS Mat, Ex Com Mat, and PCC Mat. These refer, respectively, to written materials prepared largely by the central staff for UCEA Board, Plenary Session, Executive Committee, and Partnership Co-ordinating Committee meetings.

4. See Culbertson, J., Farquhar, R. H., Gaynor, A. K., & Shibles, M. R. (1969). *Preparing educational leaders for the seventies.* Columbus, OH: University Council for Educational Administration.

5. For detailed information about the staffing roles, their purposes, and operations, see "Special UCEA staffing patterns for 1969-74: Policy guidelines." pp. 1-7. (Bd Mat, 5/15-17/69).

6. In 1959 UCEA began a policy which encouraged non-UCEA professors to submit cases to UCEA for possible publication. This policy was later expanded to encompass simulations.

7. For a description of the study see Steinhoff, C. R., & Bishop, L. K. (1974). Factors differentiating preparation programs in educational administration: UCEA study of student organizational environment. *Educational Administration Quarterly.* 10(2), 35-50.

8. Campbell later invited Jackson Newell, then UCEA administrative assistant and later a UCEA associate director, to assist him in the study. See Campbell, R. F., & Newell, L. J. (1973). *A study of professors of educational administration.* Columbus, OH: University Council for Educational Administration.

9. See Knezevich, S. J. (1974). *Doctorate needs in educational administration in the 1970's and 1980's.* Columbus, OH: University Council for Educational administration.

10. For a discussion of the experiment, along with suggested guidelines for using telelectures, see Horn, C. (1973). Telelecture series conducted by GSEAC. *UCEA Newsletter*, XIV(3), 17-20.

11. See Hencley, S. P., & Yates, J. R. (Eds.). (1974). *Futurism in education: Methodologies.* Berkeley, CA: McCutchan Publishing Corporation.

References

Bernstein, R. J. (1976). *The restructuring of social and political theory*. New York: Harcourt Brace Jovanovich.

Bessent, W. (1973). Some issues underlying the planning process in UCEA. *UCEA Newletter*, XIV(4), 12-16.

Bruno, J. E., & Fox, J. N. (1973). *Quantitative anaalysis in educational administrator preparation programs.* Columbus, OH: University Council for Educational Administration.

Cronin, J. M. (1970). Recruiting and training Black educational leaders: The Harvard experience. *UCEA Newsletter*, XI(5), 15-17.

Culbertson, J. A. (1972). Alternative strategies of program adaptation within the future time frame of the seventies. In S. H. Popper (Ed.), *Imaging alternative future school organizations* (pp. 79-92). Minneapolis: MN: College of Education, University of Minnesota.

Dusseldorp. R. V., & Monahan W. G. (1971). The Iowa "PAERIS" program. *UCEA Newsletter*, XII(3), 15-16.

Fruth, M. J., & Gregg, R. T. (1972). Preparing administrators of inner-city schools. *UCEA Newsletter*, XIII(5), 5-9.

Goldman, S. A. (1972). *To move a profession*. Columbus, OH: University Council for Educational Administration.

Horn, C. (1973). Telelecture series conducted by GSEAC. *UCEA Newsletter*, XIV(3), 17-20.

Kirst, M. W. (1970). Stanford joint program in educational administration. *UCEA Newsletter*, XI(4), 7-9.

Kuhn, T. S. (1970). *The structure of scientific revolutions*. Chicago: The University of Chicago Press.

Lynch, P. D. (1971). Preparing Red administrators. *UCEA Newsletter*, XII(3), 11-13.

Meisgeier, C. (1969). Special education leaders for a new era. In C. Meisgeier & R. Sloat (Eds.), *Common and specialized learnings, competencies, and experiences for special education administrators* (72-83). Austin, TX: College of Education, The University of Texas.

Rose, G. W. (1971). ILSA — An individualized learning system for administrators. *UCEA Newsletter*, XII(4), 17-20.

Stout, R. T. (1973). *New approaches to recruitment and selection of educational administrators. Columbus*, OH: University Council for Educational Administration.

Trow, M. (1970). Reflections on the transition from mass to universal higher education. *Daedalus: Journal of the American Academy of Arts and Sciences*, 99(1), 1-42.

Willower, D. J. (1974). Educational administration and the uses of knowledge. *UCEA Newsletter*, XV(4), 1-5.

Yates, J. R. (Ed.). (1972). *Selected instructional materials judged relevant to educational administration*. Columbus, OH: University Council for Educational Administration.

6

Crosswinds

"Those gazing on the stars are proverbially at the mercy of the puddles on the road."

Alexander Smith

During the 1974-81 period the navigators of UCEA encountered strong crosswinds.[1] New winds pushed UCEA toward greater equity for minorities, women, and the physically challenged, while opposing winds caused UCEA to cling to old moorings. Other winds propelled UCEA toward ports of renewal, while counter ones stirred entropic tendencies, as governance personnel became more involved in rule making, altering by-laws, and administrative matters. The counter tendencies activated by these and other crosswinds created an unusual challenge: Could UCEA's leaders keep the organization sailing toward new ports, or would they allow it to veer into tempestuous seas?

Dealing with the Drop-Out Problem

While developing their 1974-79 plan, some professors sought to chart new directions, while others questioned UCEA's capacity to survive. At a regional planning meeting in October, 1973, both Ray Nystrand, Ohio State, and Richard Wynn, Pittsburgh, predicted that UCEA would succumb by 1979. Most universities, they felt, would be unable to muster the membership fee. Numerous UCEA deans and department heads were concluding that the $2500 fee would produce more benefits and less conflict, if it were invested locally. Fueling the worries about UCEA's survival was a sharp drop in its membership— a drop accompanied by the increase in the fee from $1000 to $2500. In 1971-72 Nebraska, North Carolina, and Stanford withdrew. The next year California at Berkeley, Colorado, Massachusetts, and New Mexico departed. During 1973-74, Alabama, Chicago, Claremont, Florida State, George Peabody, Pennsylvania, and Temple left UCEA. Between 1971 and 1974 the membership dropped from 59 to 47 universities, even though several new universities entered UCEA.

Concerns about survival reached beyond UCEA. During the planning period some professors anxiously asked: "Will departments of educational administration survive?" Behind the query were economic forces which were depriving professors of colleagues, secretaries, xeroxing privileges, long-distance phone calls, travel funds, and student stipends. In addition, the drumbeat of criticism directed at professors persisted. One study concluded that professors were "alarmingly" homogeneous in outlook and relatively complacent about major problems in their field (Campbell and Newell, 1973, pp. 140-41). A Harvard student and two school superintendents rendered a harsher judgment (Merrow, Foster, and Estes, 1974, p. 50): "We are not optimistic. . . new initiatives are likely to be directed by the same parochial, complacent, personally ambitious, well-paid, white men."

In the spring of 1974 the Executive Committee reviewed the membership problem. Participating members were UCEA President, Loren Downey, Boston University; President-elect, Troy McKelvey, SUNY at Buffalo; James Applebury, Oklahoma State; John Brubacher, Connecticut; Peter Cistone, Ontario Institute for Studies in Education; Larry Hughes, Tennessee; Jay Scribner, UCLA; David Sperry, Utah; and Louis Zeyon (ex officio), American Association of School Administrators.[2] As the group probed the losses in membership, its mood turned somber. Several agreed to assess soon UCEA's future more thoroughly.

In June, 1974, Brubacher, Cistone, Downey, and McKelvey met in Boston where they examined the membership question at length. Three months later President McKelvey gave the Executive Committee a summary of the Boston discussion in a paper titled "Report of Regional Sub-Committee Meeting." Keenly aware of his responsibility, he stressed that "this Executive Committee does not want to be known for the demise of UCEA" (EC Mat, 9/8-10/74, p. 5). Desiring to "continue UCEA as a healthy and productive organization" (p. 2), he proposed that new "relationships between the Executive Committee and the central office staff" be developed and tested (p. 2). He wanted the Executive Committee to be more aggressive (p. 4).

In discussing UCEA's dwindling membership, McKelvey observed

(EC Mat, 9/8-10/74, p. 3): "We might scoff at the 'domino theory' but certainly a membership decline of nearly twenty per cent demands a 'new think.'" One solution, he thought, was to attract a more representative and larger group of universities into UCEA. Noting that the "operation of UCEA is a mystery" to many professors (p. 5), he also proposed that central staff and Executive Committee members visit universities and provide UCEA clients the feedback they needed.

As they probed the "drop-out" question, Executive Committee members called for more "involvement and commitment of member professors" and for "meaningful program activities" (EC Min, 9/8-10/74, p. 3). To achieve these ends, committee members decided they should make "visits to member institutions, with program charts, to discuss professorial involvement" (p. 3). The committee, it seemed, was initiating "new relationships" with the central staff. The group also activated two "Executive Task Forces"—one on "Membership, Fiscal Matters, and Dues Structure" and another on "Goals and Activities."

Although the Executive Committee struggled hard to resolve UCEA's problems, the latter proved to be more intractable than anticipated. The experiences of the committee appointed to promote UCEA's instructional materials (e.g. written and filmed cases, audio-recorded "Best Lectures," and simulations) are illustrative. Critical of UCEA's "soft sell" practices, the instructional materials committee believed that stronger promotion would produce greater revenues. The committee, after analyzing its mission, concluded "that the issues" demanded "a broader investigation" (EC Min, 10/3-5/74, p. 2). At a meeting one month later the Executive Committee specified a more limited mission "for the committee;" however, a new "leader" for the committee was "not specified" (EC Min, 11/10/74, p. 4).

Although the group's efforts stalled, the concern about UCEA's "soft sell" promotion policy did not go away. To test the effects of a more aggressive policy, I recommended "strategies to disseminate general information about UCEA materials to large audiences" and "strategies to promote specific materials" to particular audiences (EC Min, 9/18-20/75, p. 3). The group decreed that the strategies should be put "into effect" and that the staff at a later date should provide "a report on their impact" (p. 3).

Whether or not UCEA should lower its membership fee was a troublesome issue for both the Executive Committee and the central staff. In the materials prepared for the September, 1975, Executive

Committee meeting was a 23-page, single-spaced paper entitled "Reduced Fees and/or Expanded Membership: Some Alternatives." In the paper I estimated the stability of UCEA's membership by assigning each of 46 universities to one of three categories: very soft, soft, or stable. Seven universities, viewed as probable losses, fell into the "very soft" category. Nine, whose future decisions about membership were uncertain, were described as "soft," while 33 universities, including three new applicants, were judged to be "stable."

In addressing what some deans called the "exorbitant" fee problem, I offered four options: maintain the status quo, reduce the fee from $2500 to $1500 and retain the current membership criteria, reduce the fee to $1500 and expand membership via altered criteria, and reduce the fee to $1500 and establish affiliate memberships. Although some were worried about the impact of a $46,000 annual loss in UCEA income, the group decreed "that the UCEA membership dues be reduced from $2500 to $1500 per year" (EC Min, 9/18-20/75, p. 7).

In November, 1975, the recommended lowering of dues, along with projected cuts in programs, was presented to the Plenary body. In the ensuing discussion some, recognizing the "financial pinch that most universities were facing," spoke in favor of the reduction (PS Min, 11/6-8/75, p. 5). Others, stressing that the cut "would affect the size of the central staff and its ability" to involve "professors ... in projects," opposed it (p. 5). At the time the central staff consisted of the executive director and four associate directors. A few argued that the cut would impair UCEA's future risk-taking abilities. After Plenary members offered various motions and amendments to motions, all of which failed, the body decided that UCEA dues should "be reduced to $1500 per year." (p. 5). Of the 33 Plenary members in attendance 21 voted in favor of the motion, 11 voted against it, and one abstained.

After many months of discussion, then, UCEA's governing bodies lowered the membership fees. Though not an easy choice, the decision had a calming effect. While additional universities left UCEA during the 1976-81 period, new ones took their place, including some of the earlier drop-outs. As a result, the number remained at about the level which prevailed when the Plenary body reduced the fees.

About seventeen months after the testing of new "relationships" between the Executive Committee and the central staff began, the testing ended. The decision to end the experiment was precipitated by a hand-written memo prepared by Executive Committee member

Wailand Bessent. Early in his memo Bessent stated (EC Mat, 2/20-21/75):

> My major thesis is that UCEA program planning is made more difficult and less effective if the central staff is not given clear mandates to initiate and nurture program ideas... My concern is not so much for the formal governance structure and its operation as for the more subtle understandings which cast their influence on individual role performance. In other words, I would like for our central staff to feel a full vote of confidence over their administration. . . The distinction between policy making and administrative action is important to preserve in UCEA.

As they reacted to the memo, some committee members defended their previous actions by stressing their important responsibility "for UCEA projects and activities" (EC Min, 2/20-21/75, p 2). Obligated to address their constituents' concerns, they had responded to "questions and comments" made by "Plenary Session representatives" (p. 2). Later while probing their "primary role," they identified two high priority functions (p. 2): "to provide critical reactions to the ideas proposed by the central staff . . ." and "to apprise central staff and Executive Committee members of emerging interests and concerns in the field."

Bessent's observation that the experiment made "program planning . . . more difficult" was an accurate one. For one thing, the central staff spent an inordinate amount of time preparing for and attending governance meetings. Traditionally, executive committees met three times annually. However, the 1974 committee followed its September meeting with one in October, another in November, and two additional ones in February, 1975. During the September to February period two Plenary Sessions were also conducted. Harriet Ferrell, UCEA's able and industrious secretary, worked at full speed typing and re-typing materials for the seven meetings. Within a period of six months she mailed a total of 321 pages to Executive Committee members and about 200 pages to Plenary members. Though such demands diminished staff time for program planning, we were able during the period to prepare three new proposals which were designed to attract external funds.

While reassessing its own role the Executive Committee decided that the central staff should focus upon designing "new and creative 'edge cutting' projects . . " which reflected the "concerns of the UCEA members. . . " (EC Min, 2/20-21/75, p. 2). Inherent in this decision was a dilemma: how could programs be both edge cutting and supportive of the interests of all members. For example, the UCEA Computerized Research and Placement System for women and minorities, as described below, was an edge cutting effort; however, many professors initially perceived it to be antithetical to the interests of most of their students. Thus, the debate over programs continued. The large amounts of external monies acquired by UCEA during the period intensified the debate, because funded programs were directed at the needs of particular UCEA groups rather than at all professors.

In sum, the winds which propelled the experiment in new Executive Committee-staff relationships slowed UCEA's movements and at times moved it off course. Troubled by survival issues and faced with ambiguous conditions, the committee talked about holding regional meetings and visiting universities, tasks typically performed by the central staff. Luckily, the group, with special help from Wailand Bessent, returned to its policy-making role. In so doing it enabled UCEA to adjust its compass and move decisively toward new ports.

The Theory Movement: 1954-74

While working on UCEA's 1974-79 plan I met with the distinguished psychologist, Jacob Getzels, on a visit to The University of Chicago. During the visit I asked Getzels what should be on UCEA's agenda for the period ahead. His quick response was "stock taking." What had happened to the "theory movement", Getzels asked, and what crucial questions still remained? During our conversation he formulated an enduring title for an assessment project — "Educational Administration 20 Years Later: 1954-74." Promising Getzels that his idea would be placed on UCEA's agenda, I returned to Columbus much elated. The next day Roald Campbell and Ray Nystrand of Ohio State expressed to me their unhappy views about the quality of research in the field. Afterwards, I described Getzels' idea and asked if their concerns might be encompassed in it. Receiving a positive response, I promised to engage them in implementing the idea.

Early in 1973 I organized a group to plan the stock-taking project: Max Abbott, University of Oregon; Roald Campbell, Ohio State; Jacob Getzels, Chicago; Daniel Griffiths, New York University; Andrew Halpin, Georgia; Thomas James, The Spencer Foundation; and Donald

Willower, Pennsylvania State. After two meetings the group agreed that UCEA should produce a book which would describe the progress made during the 1954-74 period and delineate problems not yet resolved (*UCEA Newsletter*, XV(1), p. 2).

Since a search for external funds yielded negative results, I looked for internal resources. A few months later I asked Ray Nystrand if Ohio State might advance the project by sponsoring a Career Development Seminar which would also honor Roald Campbell, one of the field's influential leaders during the 1954-74 period. A few weeks later Ohio State officials responded favorably.

At the seminar, held on April 27-30, 1975, scholars examined the theory movement.[3] Jacob Getzels, the creator of the first theory in the field (Getzels, 1952), offered a relatively positive picture of the movement. Using his "social process" theory as an example, he documented the significant changes his theory had wrought in the content of textbooks. The very existence of the new periodicals, *Educational Administration Quarterly* and the *Journal of Educational Administration*, he suggested, reflected improvements in theory and research. Though the theory movement had slowed in the 1960s, it had produced "a significant change in the character of research and the literature" in the field (Getzels, 1977, p. 9).

In a jointly-prepared paper Andrew Halpin and Andrew Hayes offered a much less sanguine assessment. Theory in 1975, they said, was "treated as if it were a broken icon to be stored in a cobwebbed attic, along with a few scraps of late-Victorian furniture" (Halpin and Hayes, 1977, p. 263). The "crops of dissertations . . . that have come forth during the past decade most flagrantly violate the major principles of theory-oriented research" (p. 263). While noting that the theory movement had changed the language professors used, they felt the movement had failed resoundingly. The key question was "Why."

One reason the movement failed was that it was oversold (Halpin and Hayes, 1977, p. 271): "Because many of us had expected too much, too quickly, and too easily, we foredoomed ourselves to disappointment." Second, most professors never understood the concept of theory. Many, caught up in traditional advocacy roles, erroneously used the concept to prescribe what administrators ought to do. Third, since the field lacked the talent to advance knowledge, theory development took place only in social science departments. Finally, the movement could not "withstand the shock waves of the violent 1960s'"

(p. 273). Federal funding directed at effecting educational change promoted the wrong climate for research (p. 277): "The word was action, action, action; airport professors proliferated, and within the colleges of education private little empires appeared." Weakened by such conditions, theory based research suffocated.

The title of Donald Erickson's paper —"An Overdue Paradigm Shift in Educational Administration, Or How Can We Get That Idiot Off the Freeway?"—also signaled a negative view of the theory movement. The movement failed because of its unsound assumptions (Erickson,1977, p. 124): (1) scholars should use schools "as handy laboratories for testing, revising, and elaborating upon conceptual material valued by" social scientists; and (2) "research designed to produce implications for practice is necessarily inferior."

The field, Erickson contended, would not "get the idiot off the freeway" until it adopted a new paradigm to guide inquiry. The new paradigm should foster research on goal attainment in *educational* settings. Sorely required was "exciting new work on theories of *'educational* organization,' *'educational* production,' and the 'design and conduct of education'" (Erickson, 1977, p. 136). Needed was a two-pronged approach to research (p. 128-29): "inquiries into the consequences of various organizational arrangements, as largely exhibited in student behavior, and . . . investigations of the internal and environmental conditions . . . that produce and modify those organizational arrangements."

Countering the negative views of scholars was W. W. Charters, Jr., Center for the Advanced Study of Educational Administration at the University of Oregon. He rejected the seminar's dominant theme which he described as follows (Charters, 1977, p. 362):

The theme is expressed through phrases and observations of the following sort: anti-intellectualism is rampant; the Icon of theory is broken and stored away in the attic; the paradigm has run its course; only a fifth of the professors in the field even lay claim to engaging in research or scholarly writing; neither the quantity nor quality of published research has changed "all that much" in twenty years; the behavioral sciences have proven to be "a bust."

Charters asserted that the theme was "so utterly discordant" with his own observations that either "my senses have failed me or I am looking at a world different from that viewed by everyone else" (Charters, 1977, p. 362). In the face of such incongruity, he felt he had to "break the tacit unanimity before the study of administration is defined out of existence" (p. 362). Making the case that both the quantity and quality of research was significantly better in 1975 than in 1950, he contended that professors might better spend their time conducting research rather than in mourning the passing of the theory movement.

The large numbers of Chicago professors and students, both past and present, in attendance at the seminar likely contributed to the prevailing gloom. In a sense they were victims of the theory movement's strong backlash. The University of Chicago, as a theory movement leader, had prepared numerous professors of educational administration.[4] One Chicago alumni told me that as he talked to other alumni, he felt as if he were "attending a wake."

Notably, the presenters did not chart new directions. Erickson, recipient of a Chicago doctorate about the time the theory movement was at its height, did stir his listeners by outlining a new paradigm. Yet the paradigm's novelty stemmed more from its proposed focus than from new features. Nor did Halpin and Hayes point scholars toward new vistas. For them the tenets of the theory movement still pertained. A believer in science's capacity to correct its errors, Getzels favored the continuance of the theory movement, with needed mid-course corrections. Nor did Charters propose new approaches. Rather, he contended that scholars should address two problems: the field's paucity of facts and its inadequate theories.

The seminar's message, then, was a mixed one. Most presenters expressed disappointment with the results of the theory movement. However, none argued that theory development should cease or that its "scientific" premises should be discarded. The apparent inability of leading scholars to generate new directions was a measure of the success rather than of the failure of the theory movement. Its scientific tenets, which were based upon adapted versions of logical positivism, (see Chapter Two) were so deeply embedded in the scholarly community that seminar presenters, though dissatisfied with the theory movement's results, could not discard its tenets.

The Greenfield-Griffiths Debate Elicits a Dialogue

Nine months before the Ohio State seminar transpired, Thomas Greenfield, Ontario Institute for Studies in Education, vigorously rejected the tenets of the theory movement at the third International Inter-Visitation Program in London. His lecture, not yet available in published form at the time of the Ohio State seminar, was delivered to leading scholars and practitioners from five continents. His critique of the theory movement was a trenchant one. While recognizing that the movement had greatly influenced inquiry, he focused upon its "false" premises and its "misguided" approaches to research.

Greenfield's major thesis was that the theory movement's premises about organizations were grounded in faulty assumptions about reality. Organizations, he argued, are not objective entities as theory advocates presumed. Nor are they like natural systems which "'serve functions,' 'adapt to their environment,' 'clarify their goals,' or 'act to implement policy'" (Greenfield, 1975, p. 71). They are also not like houses which outlast the individuals who occupy them. Instead, they are the subjective creations of diverse individuals. As images in the minds of individuals, concepts of organizations vary from person to person and from one event to another. Greenfield saw organizations, then, "not as structures subject to universal laws but as cultural artifacts dependent upon the specific meaning and intention of people within them" (p. 74). Thus, any attempt to achieve a science of organization was doomed to failure.

Did Greenfield think that there could be theories when there are no fixed ways of construing reality? The answer is yes. However, he defined theory as "sets of meanings which people use to make sense of their world" . . . (Greenfield, 1975, p. 77). In investigating "sets of meanings," he had little use for "complex mathematical models, and bigger number crunchers" (p. 86). Rather, he advocated historical, comparative, and case methods of inquiry. Apparently his theories applied only to the subjects studied. Since the researchers and the researched are both constrained by their views of reality, the problem of "truth" is significant in Greenfield's formulation. Unfortunately, he chose not to address it systematically.

Certainly, Greenfield fired a shot at the theory movement which reverberated around the world. In his eye-witness account of the London conference Donald Layton observed that the paper was "beyond any doubt, one of the most provocative papers presented" (Layton, 1974, p. 10). It soon precipitated the "Greenfield-Griffiths debate" which stimulated an extended dialogue about theory. The debate was perceived by some to be about the relative merits of the logical positivistic and phenomenological views of knowledge. Logical positivists believed that knowledge is derived from objective observations about the external world; phenomenologists believed that knowledge is a human construction. As editor of the *UCEA Review*, Associate Director Paula Silver nurtured and helped give early expression to the "debate."

Before studying for the doctorate as a Walter A. Anderson Fellow at New York University, Paula taught English and French and had served as a department head in the New York City Schools. Deeply influenced by the theory movement, she viewed theories as esthetic objects as well as intellectual tools. During the 1976-78 period Associate Director Nicholas Nash continued to disseminate exchanges about theory as editor of the *Review*. After obtaining a B.A. at Harvard, Nicholas taught English, Latin, French, and ethics at a private school in Ohio and then became the school's principal. He brought to UCEA a rich educational background, a keen sense of humor, and a unique capacity for communicating ideas.

The exchange about theory began with the Griffiths-Greenfield debate. A participant in the London conference, Griffiths was the first to respond in writing to Greenfield's ideas. Noting that Greenfield's essay stimulated "a controversy on theory of the type not seen since the late 50's," Griffiths revealed that he was "quite surprised" that the paper provoked strong opposition (Griffiths, 1975, p. 12). He confessed that he had "always had a healthy skepticism" about achieving a general science of organizations, largely because of the inadequate practices of science by professors. Ignoring Greenfield's central argument that organizations are subjective constructions, he also did not question Greenfield's descriptions of the "scientific" tenets which guided the work of theorists. Instead, he discussed more traditional questions such as "Are administrative theories particular or general?" and, "Is theory a guide to action for administrators?" (p. 12). He concluded that the reason "theory has not achieved its promise .. is because we have not done our homework, not because the promise is unrealistic (p. 18).

In his rejoinder Greenfield implied that Griffiths' contention that the theory movement failed because professors did not do their "homework" was a weak response (Greenfield, 1976, p. 4): "Griffiths provides no new insight into how we are to improve our homework, . . ." or how the field could "develop theories which ... would inform a relevant and cogent corpus of research." Even more disappointing was the perception that Griffiths had ignored his primary arguments (pp. 4-5): "Griffiths' failure to deal with these arguments in my paper must surely have left his audience ... wondering what all the fuss at IIP 1974 had been about." The exchange, then, was not so much a debate as independently expressed views about disparate topics.

Next to contribute to the dialogue were two Australians: Allan Crane, University Fellow in the Centre for Administrative Studies at the University of New England, and William Walker, Dean of the Faculty of Education in the same institution. Among other things, the two Australians took exception to Griffiths' definition of theory (Griffiths, 1975, p. 15): "I would suggest that the Feigl definition that was generally accepted 15 years ago be reinstated, and that only work which approximates this definition be acceptable as theoretical." Feigl earlier had defined theory as "a set of assumptions from which can be derived by purely logico-mathematical procedures, a larger set of empirical laws" (quoted in Halpin, 1958, p. 7).

Contending that Feigl's definition, contrary to Griffiths' belief, was not a generally accepted one 15 years earlier, Crane and Walker quoted several American scholars who had written skeptically about its use in the early 1960s. They also argued that Griffiths by supporting the definition had avoided facing "some very significant developments in the field..." (Crane and Walker, 1976, p. 2). One was new evidence about the nature of science. They noted that Thomas Kuhn in his book, *The Structure of Scientific Revolutions* had shown that scientific theory simply reflects a "consensus amongst scientists," a definition that was far removed from that of Feigl (p. 1).

When Andrew Halpin introduced Feigl's definition to the field, he did not comment on its technical meanings, nor did the few professors who later re-quoted Feigl's definition. Thus, the complex edifice of rational procedures the logical positivists had elaborated for constructing theories or "hypothetico-deductive systems" was never transmitted into the literature of the field.[5] Since producers of "theories" were unaware of the rules for creating "hypothetico-deductive systems," they inevitably failed to use them. Employing the term "purely logico-mathematical procedures" and actually using the "procedures" in research were radically different things.

Halpin's use of Feigl's rhetoric can be viewed as a political act. Using UCEA as a platform, he helped set a new direction for the field. Had he presented in detail the technical meanings of Feigl's definition at the 1957 UCEA seminar, he might well have lost his audience;[6] or his hearers, repelled by strange concepts, might have rejected his call for theory development. Feigl's bare definition enabled Halpin to define a goal while leaving his hearers much room to interpret its meaning. The concept of theory, then, was applied to varying degrees and in diverse ways by professors. Guided by fragments of positivistic thought, users of the concept became a part of a new dynamic. Though the dynamic unfolded in ways which disappointed theory movement leaders, it did change inquiry.

By 1977 contentious exchanges had given way to more tolerant expressions. Oliver Gibson, a professor at the State University of New York at Buffalo, was the first to support both Griffiths' and Greenfield's views. A native-born Canadian, Gibson, as an undergraduate, had read the writings of the phenomenologist, Edmund Husserl, whose ideas had given him "a fresh perspective on the central importance of consciousness . .. " (Gibson, 1977, p. 36). While pursuing his doctorate at Harvard, he attended meetings of the Unity of Science group whose members included Philip Frank, one of the distinguished developers of logical positivism. Although Gibson adopted the phenomenological view, he stressed that "the binary opposition of naturalistic and phenomenological approaches is wrong-minded; a much more useful approach is to see them as complementary" (p. 38).

Jean Hills of the University of British Columbia offered a different rationale for embracing both views. After explaining how such concepts as experience, language, and creativity had affected his own ideas about theorizing, he noted that it was "extremely useful to think" of human beings as "creating and using a variety of conceptual codes to interpret experience and guide action" (Hills, 1977, p. 4). Unsure about which of the camps he inhabited, he suspected he leaned toward phenomenology. Yet he remained loyal to science. All scholarship, he insisted, should "in the name of science" meet "the dual criterion of logical and empirical validity" (p. 5).

Richard Kendell and David Byrne of the University of Utah maintained that "the Greenfield-Griffiths debate stands as an exemplar of . . . rigid polarizing..." (Kendell and Byrne, 1977, p. 7). The debate resembled a "political campaign" in which the contenders were competing for acknowledged leadership in the field (p. 6). However, as in most political campaigns the choice offered was an "either-or" one. Only after thorough analyses could scholars achieve needed "epistemological clarity" (p. 6). Rather than reject ideas that do not comply with established views, scholars should analyze them for what they have to offer. And it would be more fruitful "if more established views could be critiqued for what they have done and can continue to do" rather than castigating "them for . . . what they never pretended to accomplish" (p. 7).

In her essay, "The Phenomenological Appreciation of Theory," Paula Silver, University of Tulsa, sought to integrate the disparate views by positing two levels of organizational reality (Silver, 1978, p. 30): "that which is created by the participant and that which is observable to others." The reality of a class perceived by one teacher would differ from that of another teacher; however, observers of a class would agree that it was not a family or a corporation. Theory, then, does not elucidate any "objectively 'real' reality;" it is simply "a unique perception (invention) of reality . . ." (p. 30).

In sum, leading scholars during the period leveled harsh criticisms at the theory movement. Andrew Halpin and Andrew Hayes declared the movement a failure. Donald Erickson argued that its products had limited relevance to practice. Offering a more radical critique, Thomas Greenfield contended that the theory movement's tenets about reality and knowledge were false. In the debate which ensued Griffiths defended the movement's basic premises, while Greenfield opposed them. Finally, scholars constructed rationales to justify the use of both perspectives.

Greenfield's paper, I believe, stirred more discussion and thought than did any other one during my UCEA tenure. Opponents of the theory movement appreciated his incisive critique. His non-traditional premises about knowledge and inquiry provided a useful perspective to those who were skeptical about the value or viability of a science of administration. Yet Greenfield's impact upon research was limited. For one thing, he did not state his tenets about knowledge and inquiry as explicitly and as fully as had the leaders of the theory movement, nor did he generate a research exemplar which credibly demonstrated his views in practice. On the other hand, Jacob Getzels' "social process" theory and the research it spawned provided inspiring exemplars to those who helped advance the theory movement.[7]

Confronting Human Inequities

UCEA's efforts to enhance equity were partially rooted in earlier events. In 1972 Associate Director Michael Martin developed a UCEA Task Force on Native American Educational Administration. Among the programs generated by the task force was a federally-funded conference on Indian education. In 1973-74 UCEA had developed an information exchange project with professors in three institutions which specialized in training "Black" administrators: Atlanta University, Cheyney State College, and Howard University. An extensive project to integrate general and special education administration was described in Chapter Five. Such programs increased UCEA's awareness of human inequities in the field and provided a base for more far-reaching efforts during the last half of the 1970s.

In 1959 the number of women professors of educational administration in UCEA's 34 universities was fewer than six. The situation changed very little until the late sixties when numerous women began entering doctoral programs. Soon thereafter, some professors began nominating able women for UCEA associate director posts. In 1972 the "short list" of candidates for a UCEA post included a woman. When I reported this fact informally to a group of professors in Atlantic City, an awkward pause ensued. The silence was broken when an internationally known professor asserted that the employment of a female associate would be a mistake. She would not be able to function effectively during university visits, he said, because professors would be viewing her more as a sex object than as a professional colleague.

Though no one openly contested the professor's view, apparently some did not accept it. Later in the evening the view was assessed further, when a female staff member from a regional educational laboratory volunteered to play the role of an associate director on a UCEA university visit. After much role playing the group, according to a subsequent report from Troy McKelvey, concluded they could work professionally with a female staff member.

In the spring of 1973, UCEA employed Paula Silver—the first of three females who would serve UCEA in the 1970s. A confronter of discriminatory norms, Paula during university visits offered frank and often unpopular responses when asked about women's equity. She also helped sensitize UCEA's male staff members to inequitable practices. Very early she asserted that writers of UCEA's By-Laws had behaved as if women were non-existent in UCEA. Her observation, an undeniably accurate one, led to a re-writing of the By-Laws.

In May, 1974, the Executive Committee asked Paula Silver to assume the duties of "UCEA secretary." Before accepting the post, she requested that her title be changed to "administrative associate." Taking minutes, she noted, was not the only duty in the post. More importantly, some in UCEA were already presuming that she was a member of UCEA's clerical staff—a tendency she did not want to reinforce. The committee acceded to her request.

In early 1974 Paula Silver conceived the UCEA Computerized Research and Placement System (CORPS). This System was designed to gather and store data on all students completing doctoral and two-year programs in educational administration and to provide data to help women and members of minority groups obtain administrative posts. The general idea for a computerized student data system was outlined in 1969 by UCEA Associate Director Alan Gaynor. Then Frank Banghart of Florida State translated the idea into a specific plan. In 1973-74, Charles Kline and Richard Munsterman of Purdue University pilot tested the system. After Paula Silver outlined a three-year plan to assess the research and placement capacities of the system, the Ford Foundation provided UCEA a $150,000 grant to support the proposed plan.

In November, 1974, the UCEA Plenary Session had a lively discussion about CORPS. Two ideas proved to be very controversial: the exclusion of white males from the placement system and the inclusion of women and minority graduates from UCEA and non-UCEA institutions. Some Plenary members argued that the system promoted "reverse discrimination." Others felt it was unfair to include students from non-UCEA institutions. After a long discussion John Seger, a Plenary member from the University of Alberta, movingly argued that UCEA should implement CORPS, because it was morally correct to do so. He then made a motion that the Plenary Session "approve the spirit of the CORPS project and its . . . progress to date . . ." (PS Min, 11/11-12/74, p. 5). The body approved his motion.

The central staff worked diligently to make CORPS an effective system. More than 20,000 descriptive mailings were sent annually to school systems and other agencies in 1974, 1975, and 1976. Also, two directories—one featuring women and one minority candidates—were mailed widely yearly. Although the system helped some candidates obtain positions, its overall results were disappointing. CORPS simply could not compete with professors who used their own informal networks to place graduates. Further, placement was often influenced by male professors who were employed by school boards to recommend candidates for administrative posts. The impersonal computerized system meshed poorly with existing placement practices.

CORPS' data made their way into several articles on such questions as: how did the characteristics of candidates for professorships compare and contrast with those of candidates for administrative posts? What subjects did professorial candidates desire to teach? What were the differences in the experience backgrounds of white males, women, and members of minority groups?[8] Answers to such questions had import for the re-design of academic and clinical training experiences. An annually updated information system on all UCEA students would have provided a resource for research, program re-design, and placement efforts. Unfortunately, neither UCEA nor its members had the resources to continue the system.

CORPS had an important impact on UCEA norms. When the Executive Committee and the Plenary Session agreed, after much deliberation, that CORPS should be enacted, they gave professors an important message, namely: that it was morally correct to conduct programs to rectify the negative effects of long-standing discrimination against women and minorities. The decision made it easier for UCEA to address other equity problems. It also influenced equity decisions in universities. For example, by 1980 most of the UCEA universities had employed at least one female professor of educational administration. Discussions about CORPS helped pave the way for such actions.

In January, 1976, UCEA convened a task force on the advancement of women's equity in educational administration. Serving on the task force were five pairs of professors: Joan Dee and Don Davies, Boston University; Charlotte Robinson and James Maxey, Georgia State; Ann Engin and Russell Spillman, Ohio State; Virginia Nordin and Marvin Fruth, Wisconsin; and Gladys Johnston and Wayne Hoy, Rutgers. The group proposed that UCEA (1) develop training materials to enhance women's equity and (2) create a network of women and minorities to facilitate information exchange. The network, the group decided, might best be built through the launching of a new journal.

One month later the staff recommended to the Plenary Session that UCEA develop the desired training materials—a proposal the body debated and approved. Paula Silver then wrote a proposal for a two-year program. Later the U. S. Office of Education awarded UCEA about $250,000 to help implement the program. In 1976 Grace Butler, possessor of a newly acquired Ph.D from New York University, joined UCEA as an associate director and the coordinator of the project. Earlier she had taught music and had served as a department head and a project director in the New York City Schools. Sensitive to interpersonal relations and skilled in strategic thinking, she helped the project's leaders realize their aims.

Six teams composed of two or three professors and one or two graduate students developed the materials. Professorial team members were: Miriam Clasby, Joan Dee, and Don Davies, Boston University; Charlotte Robinson and James Maxey, Georgia State; Martha McCarthy, David Clark, and Marianne Mitchell, Indiana; Ann Engin and Russell Spillman, Ohio State; and Lillian Dean Webb and John McClure, Iowa. Paula Silver, aided by new colleagues at Tulsa University, developed a sixth set of materials.

Each of the six diverse sets complemented one another. The Boston team developed materials to train women for their first administrative post; the Iowa team, materials to sensitize all education trainees to important equity issues; the Georgia State team, materials to help professors change discriminatory practices in their departments; the Indiana team, materials for higher education administrators; the Ohio State team, materials to help K-12 leaders reduce inequitable school practices; and the Tulsa team summarized the basic content in the five other sets.

Each set offered both written and audio-visual components. The Georgia State set, for instance, contained a booklet on the status of women in administration, a self-study package for analyzing equity practices in departments; action guides for combating sex discrimination; a filmed case; and a group of role playing situations and games. At Indiana the team prepared a monograph on the effects of sex discrimination in higher education; a simulation; written and audio-recorded cases; a game; and a resource file. When the sets were nearly finished, Grace Butler arranged for the pilot testing of the materials at 18 university sites. Each team revised its materials after obtaining feedback from attendees at three sites.

The materials were arguably the richest ones ever created by UCEA. However, when judged by the use of its products, the project was a major failure. Early in the project I spoke with Washington officials about UCEA's strategies for disseminating materials. While my hosts listened politely, they displayed no interest. When I later learned that they had already awarded a large grant to a women's center in the Northeast to disseminate federally-funded materials on women's equity, I understood their reaction.

In the summer of 1978 UCEA shipped 46 training components to the United States Office of Education. Many months later we learned that the agency's evaluators had approved 44 of the 46 for distribution, and that most of the 44 had received the "highest" recommendation (PS Min, 10/16-18/80, p. 2). When I talked with the head of the women's center in the Northeast about distributing the materials, it was apparent that we had discrepant views. UCEA wanted to distribute materials to a special group; she wanted to reach more general populations. UCEA valued reality-oriented training materials, while she seemed more interested in concepts about ideal practices. Unfortunately, the center did not distribute the materials. One of my major regrets on leaving UCEA was that the materials were still not in use. Fueling my regret was the conviction that most of the training components could have had extensive use within and beyond UCEA.

The task force's proposal for a new journal posed special challenges. The two journals UCEA had launched a decade earlier were still not fully self-supporting. In addition, one study showed that only 10 per cent of the professoriate believed that the "problems minority groups" faced were "very serious" ones (Campbell & Newell, 1973, p. 87). Some who were relatively complacent about human inequities contended that the proposed journal was an unneeded competitor to UCEA's *Educational Administration Quarterly*. Only one female and no minority members had ever served on the board of UCEA's refereed *Educational Administration Quarterly*. Minorities and women resented the fact that their groups were excluded from the circle of white males who controlled the content of the *Quarterly*.

Efforts to create a new journal, then, were fraught with risk. Yet the staff believed that the initiative might diminish discrimination. On May 10-11, 1976, we convened several individuals to help conceptualize the project: Frank Brown, the State University of New York at Buffalo; Gerald Gipp, Pennsylvania State; James Maxey and Charlotte Robinson, Georgia State; and Leonard Valverde, Texas. Naming the medium *Emergent Leadership: A Focus on Minorities and Women in Educational Administration* the group decided that the purpose of the journal would be to help "educational leaders reduce sex and racial discrimination. . ." (*UCEA Review*, Vol. XVIII(1), p. 17). The group also agreed that leaders from the UCEA Partnership (see Chapter Nine) could serve on the journal's editorial board.

In the spring of 1976 the UCEA Executive Committee, after a lively debate, approved a four year trial period for the journal. Edited the first year by Charlotte Robinson and James Maxey of Georgia State, the periodical was designed to serve as a "vehicle" of exchange for those "traditionally underrepresented" in leadership positions (Robinson, 1976, p. 5). In its second year the journal was edited by Frank Brown at Buffalo; the third year by Leonard Valverde at Texas; and the fourth year by Grayson Noley at Pennsylvania State.

While planning for the 1979-84 period, the UCEA staff asked scholars not previously involved in the new journal to evaluate its first six issues. Noting that *Emergent Leadership* was the only journal written primarily for minority group members and women, the scholars recommended that UCEA continue the initiative. Suggestions for improving it were incorporated into UCEA's 1979-84 plan.

In October, 1979, the Executive Committee reviewed applications from four universities whose staffs wanted to assume editorial responsibility for the journal. After assessing the proposed editors, resources, and commitments of each university, the committee chose Arizona State. When I reported the decision the next day to Lillian Dean Webb, the new editor, and to Susan Paddock and Kay Hartwell, the new associate editors, they seemed elated. About a year later UCEA distributed the first issue. Although the periodical focused upon equity issues related to women, African Americans, Hispanics, Native Americans, and other groups, a new title appeared on its cover: *The Journal of Educational Equity and Leadership*.

For long-time supporters of the *Quarterly* (EAQ) the new journal was a negative symbol. One well-known UCEA professor expressed the view thusly: (Campbell, 1979, p. 16): "... it appears that UCEA gives little time and energy to EAQ and more time and energy to ... other journals that may compete with EAQ for at least some desirable manuscripts." Firmly expressing his priorities, he proposed that "UCEA should withdraw as soon as possible from its obligations to *Emergent Leadership*" (p. 18). A few months later the UCEA Executive Committee forthrightly voted to continue the journal. However, at its January, 1980, meeting the committee charged the staff and the editorial boards of UCEA's three journals to make them all "financially self-sustaining by June 30, 1983 ... " (EC Min, 1/3-5/80, p. 2). The decision put

UCEA's youngest journal at a greater risk than was the case with its two older ones. At the time that journal had about 300 subscribers.

UCEA's first major program to reduce inequities affecting the mentally and physically challenged was the General-Special Education Administration Consortium (GSEAC). (see Chapter Five). Through the leadership of James Yates, GSEAC's co-ordinator, UCEA originated the "National Level Internship Program." Emerging from a conversation between James Yates and Edward Sontag of the Bureau of Education for the Handicapped in the United States Office of Education, the program was designed to expand the pool of national leaders of special education. Sontag and Yates concluded that an internship program offered a promising means to expand the pool.

When Yates asked me for feedback on the idea, I supported it strongly. I also suggested that those with newly acquired doctorates in special education administration should become interns in national agencies concerned with general administration (e. g. the American Association of School Administrators), while interns with new doctorates in general administration should enter special education agencies (e. g. the National Association of State Directors of Special Education). Such arrangements, it seemed, should promote mutual understanding and cross-fertilization of ideas between interns and national agency leaders. The resulting insights should in turn help leaders in the two fields complement and cooperate with one another in subsequent efforts to improve education for the impaired.

In the summer of 1973 the Bureau of Education for the Handicapped approved a proposal written earlier by James Yates. In 1976 the program was extended for an additional two years. During the 1973-78 period UCEA received approximately $720,000 from the Bureau to help support the National Level Internship Program (NLIP). Associate Director Richard Podemski coordinated NLIP from 1973 to 1976, while Associate Director Peter Hackbert coordinated it from 1976 to 1978.

Richard joined UCEA at the age of 26 after acquiring a Ph.D from the University of Buffalo. Earlier he had shifted away from theological study to the study of educational administration. He brought to UCEA a fine intellect and a deep commitment to humanitarian values. After completing a B.A. at the University of Cincinnati, Peter Hackbert studied at the University of Oklahoma's Southwest Center for Human Relations Studies where he obtained a M.A. degree. Later he acquired a doctorate in school administration at Oklahoma. At UCEA he displayed a strong interest in theory and research.

In 1973-74 six interns took part in the program; in 1974-75 and in each of the three succeeding years eight interns participated. Between 1973 and 1978, thirty-eight individuals spent a year as interns in one of 15 national organizations located in Washington, D.C. Agencies which provided internships for those in special education administration included the American Association of School Administrators, the Council of Great City Schools, and the Office of the United States Commissioner of Education. Those with doctorates in general education administration entered such agencies as the National Association of State Directors of Special Education, the Council for Exceptional Children, and the Bureau of Education for the Handicapped.

Interns with doctorates in general education administration faced unique challenges. For example, Jeffrey Zettel, an intern in the Council for Exceptional Children, immediately found himself "enmeshed in a new world of terminology" (*UCEA Review*, XVIII(3), p. 17). David Rostetter, an intern in a special education agency, noted that the impact of the organization on the intern and vice versa depended largely upon how successful or unsuccessful the intern" was "at resolving the generalist-specialist dilemma" (p. 17). To build bridges between the differing specialists the interns, Rostetter wrote, had to "gain credibility"; otherwise, the prospect "for significant 'cross-fertilization' is decreased considerably" (p.16).

Since general education agencies were starting to respond to a new and far reaching federal law (The Education for All Handicapped Children Act), special education administration interns had special opportunities. Don Barbacovi, an intern in the American Association of School Administrators (AASA), served "as a catalyst in providing some initial direction to AASA's activities on behalf of handicapped children," . . . and increased "the organization's consciousness level concerning handicapped children in the public schools" (*UCEA Review*, XVIII(3), p. 19). Constance Halter, an intern in the Council of Chief State School Officers, conveyed to the Council's staff (p. 18):

> an awareness of management problems associated with providing special education services to all children, and the legal and moral obligation to provide those services... I do not agree with this position unequivocally, but now, at least, I understand it and can work to modify it...

The interns learned much from seminars led by NLIP co-ordinators. Gerald Griffin, an intern in the Bureau for the Education for the Handicapped, described the seminars' effects thusly (*UCEA Review*, XVIII(3), p. 16): "As interns share information about their various agencies, they. . . discover threads of commonality. . ." One of the threads was a deeper understanding of the concept of advocacy and its role in improving special education. Such threads were products of integrative thinking. They were also resources which interns could use in future leadership settings.

Did the program help integrate the two specialized fields? One indicator of integration was the degree to which interns with university training in one field accepted posts in the other field when the program ended. In the fall of 1976, 21 of the 22 previous interns were employed. Six of the 11 with backgrounds in general education administration had accepted posts in special education agencies. Three of the 10 interns with backgrounds in special education administration were employed by general education agencies. Certainly, the program helped interns make such shifts.

Why did more general than special education administration interns make a career shift into a new field? Perhaps there were more special education openings. Another explanation might lie in differences in training. Since doctoral programs for general education administrators often aimed at preparing personnel for varied leadership positions, their graduates may have found it easier to move into a new field. Whatever the explanation, the fact that more than 40 per cent of the interns accepted posts in their complementary field suggested that NLIP was relatively successful.

Proposed Changes Encounter Resistance

In 1975 David Sperry of the University of Utah proposed an initiative which would be affected both by winds of change and winds of resistance. At a UCEA Executive Committee meeting he noted that the group lacked "hard data" to make decisions (EC Min, 9/18-20/75, p. 8). The members did not know, for instance, whether "the loss in membership was due to the amount of the fees or some other variable such as . . . concern over the relevance of UCEA's program" (p. 8). He proposed that "an 'organizational analysis' of UCEA" be conducted (p. 8). Two months later the committee recommended to the Plenary

Session that such a study be initiated (PS Min, 11/6-8/75, p. 7). After approving the idea, the body decided that the study should be executed by "a blue-ribbon committee composed of individuals who have credibility with the Plenary body and relevant others; . . ." (p. 7).

Within a few months Francis Chase, former Dean of the Graduate School of Education at The University of Chicago, agreed to chair a "UCEA Evaluation and Planning Commission" composed of John Andrews, University of British Columbia; Luvern Cunningham, Ohio State University; John Davis, President of Macalester College; Aubrey McCutcheon, Executive Deputy Superintendent of the Detroit Public Schools; Edith Mosher, University of Virginia; Jay Scribner, Temple University; Edwin Whigham, Superintendent of Dade County Schools in Miami; and Donald Willower, Pennsylvania State University.

At a meeting in March, 1977, the commission discussed "the changing context of educational administration and the . . . need for re-examination" of training programs. Its members also noted that there was "no clear agreement" in the field "on strategies for increasing the knowledge base or knowledge utilization"—a condition which had created "unresolved implications for UCEA policy functions and activities" (*UCEA Review*, XVII(3), p. 17). Crucial questions which needed to be addressed included the following (p. 17):

Is UCEA's historic mission still relevant and important? If so, are the present provisions for organization, membership, finance, government, activities, and services appropriate to the mission? If the mission requires redefinition, what considerations should influence its policy changes and operations?

After conducting hearings at national meetings, sponsoring a report on the origins and evolution of UCEA, and soliciting ideas from professors about problems UCEA was neglecting, the most important contributions UCEA was making, and needed changes in UCEA, the commission prepared its report. In February, 1977, Francis Chase summarized the commission's findings and recommendations at a UCEA Plenary Session in Las Vegas. He began by offering the following assessment of the state of UCEA and of the field of educational administration (*UCEA Review*, XVIII(3), p. 7):

Because of its success in defining its mission and goals, obtaining highly competent leadership, and promoting the development and utilization of knowledge, UCEA was able to weather the loss of initial foundation support through increased membership fees and through grants to support special projects. It has continued as an unusually effective consortium and appeared to be in the ascendancy until university budgetary deficits and other developments in the 1970s led member institutions to re-examine their relationships to UCEA. In the meanwhile, new challenges to educational administration raised questions as to whether UCEA's historic mission and modes of operation would be adequate for the years ahead. . . It is especially important at this time to weigh the potential of UCEA for contribution to the future advancement of educational administration and the adaptation of education to the crucial needs posed by the last quarter of the twentieth century.

To develop an "effective response to the needs of education in the next two decades", the commission recommended that UCEA (*UCEA Review*, XVIII(3), p. 8-10):

1. Downplay its historic mission (i. e. improving the professional preparation of administrative personnel in education) and "give primary emphasis to serving a dual mediating function—between theory and practice and between professors and practitioners . . ."

2. Concentrate "its efforts on a small number of major thrusts designed to produce modifications in administration and to make education more responsive to .. needs and demands . . ."

3. Collaborate with such agencies as the Council of Great City Schools in the organization of "tasks to identify and examine phenomena encountered in the actual practice of educational administration. . ."

4. Sponsor symposia to identify the implications of the findings obtained through the previous recommendations for the "staffing and management of school districts," "the preparation of school administrators," and "theories of education administration . . ."

5. Establish "an independent council or commission of outstanding scholars and leaders and charge the new body" with such functions as recommending for UCEA membership "universities, state and local education agencies and other organizations. . ." and "making periodic assessments of UCEA's effectiveness. . ."

6. Make clear to new members that they have an obligation to co-sponsor UCEA programs.

7. Supplement its present staff by adding "at least two or three appointments on indefinite tenure . . ."

8.   Enlist the "help of national leaders in education to gain the support of private foundations and government agencies for studies, projects, and conferences."[9]

After Chase finished his summary, Plenary members peppered him (and me) with questions and reactions. They asked, for example, why UCEA needed a new "independent council or commission." Skeptical about the proposed "council," they questioned its capacity to serve "as a partial corrective" to UCEA's "weakness in governance." They also objected to the charge that Plenary members were more concerned about "their several institutions than about the national goals to which UCEA is, or should be, committed" (*UCEA Review*, XVIII(3), p. 10). Governance problems, some stated, should be addressed directly by existing governance bodies—not by an "independent council."

After the meeting the Executive Committee resolved to examine more thoroughly the commission's report at its May, 1977, meeting. Needing a plan for processing the commission's recommendations at the November, 1977, Plenary Session, the committee asked the staff to devise several ways Plenary members might process the recommendations, and to "spell out in . . . detail the operational implications" of the commission's proposed changes (EC Min, 2/27/77, p. 2).

At the May meeting the committee formulated its position on each recommendation. Concluding that the commission's recommendation on UCEA's membership criteria was insufficiently specific, the committee broke the statement into two parts: (1) UCEA should adopt less rigorous membership standards for higher education institutions, and

(2) it should accept as members selected local and state educational agencies. The committee also agreed to reveal to Plenary members its positions on all the recommendations before it asked the body to vote on the commission's proposed changes.

At the November Plenary meeting in Columbus, Ohio, the Executive Committee recommended that the body approve two of the commission's recommendations: "sponsor a series of symposia," and "enlist the help of national leaders in education" to acquire needed funds. It advised Plenary members to reject three recommendations: instituting an "independent council," accepting local and state educational agencies as UCEA members; and focusing upon a "small number of major" program thrusts. Deciding not to take a stand on the special "obligation" of new members to co-sponsor UCEA programs, the committee supported the commission's other four proposals in significantly revised forms.

By the end of the meeting the body had approved one of the original recommendations (i. e. "UCEA should enlist the help of national leaders" to acquire needed funds) and three others, after revising them. The effect of the revisions was to move UCEA away from change and toward the status quo. The movement can be seen in the body's responses to the proposal that "UCEA should give primary emphasis to serving a dual mediating function — between theory and practice and between professors and practitioners." The Executive Committee had altered it thusly: "UCEA, for the 1979-84 period, should adopt for its theme a 'dual mediating function . . .'" (PS Min, 11/17-18/77, p. 6). The Plenary body changed "its theme" to "a theme" and, after more discussion, to "a primary theme." It also endorsed the existing UCEA University-School System Partnership as a "structure through which to pursue the theme of mediation" (p. 13).

The Plenary body, then, approved one of the commission's proposed changes and three significantly altered ones. It rejected four and was neutral on one. Reflected in these actions were paradoxical meanings. Two years earlier many Plenary members had expressed dissatisfaction with UCEA's policies and programs and strong aspirations for change. However, the actions of Plenary members in Columbus seemed to signal that they were satisfied with UCEA's directions and policies. Perhaps the paradox was rooted in changed circumstances, especially the cut in membership fees and diminished pressures on professors.

A positive feature of the Columbus meeting was that its decisions were arrived at democratically after much discussion. Yet I felt dispirited. Although I had not supported all of the commission members' proposed changes, I shared their view about the urgent need "for imaginative rethinking in every aspect and area of education and for bold action to implement . .. the best that can be conceived" (*UCEA Review*, XVIII(3), p. 11). I also shared their hope that UCEA's past could "be a prelude to much more . . . pervasive contributions to the education of the future" (p. 11). Thus, I was disappointed that Plenary members had chosen to sail close to the shore rather than toward the horizon.

The experience brought forth a new question. For the first time in my eighteen years of attending Plenary meetings, I wondered at one point if I should resign my UCEA post. The discrepancy between my perspective and that of most of UCEA's governance personnel seemed to be widening. Although I was not in the best position to assess the soundness of either perspective, I was concerned about the gap between the two and the unhealthy results it might generate for both UCEA and for myself. However, my resilience re-asserted itself in a few days, and I turned once again to the formidable challenges within UCEA.

Notes

1. Chapter Six spans seven years (1974-81) in contrast to the three previous chapters which covered five-year periods.

2. Wailand Bessent, University of Texas, was unable to attend.

3. Perceptive studies of changes in training, research, and administrative practice are available in Cunningham, L. L., Hack, W. G., & Nystrand, R. O. (Eds.). (1977). *Educational administration: The developing decades*. Berkeley, CA: McCutchan Publishing Corporation. See especially Farquhar, R. H. Preparatory programs in educational administration, 1954-74 (pp. 329-357); Immegart, G. L. The study of educational administration, 1954-74 (pp. 298-328); and Watson, B. C. Issues confronting educational administrators, 1954-74 (pp. 67-94).

4. For information on the universities which were the major preparers of professors during the late 1950s and early 1960s see Shaplin, J. T. (1964). The professorship in educational administration: Attracting talented personnel. In D. Willower & J. Culbertson (Eds.), *The professorship in educational administration* (p. 1-14). Columbus, OH: University Council for Educational Administration.

5. For pertinent analyses see Achinstein, P., & Barker S. F. (Eds.). (1969). *The legacy of logical positivism*. Baltimore, MD: The Johns Hopkins Press. See especially "Logical positivism and the interpretation of scientific theories" by M.R. Hanson (pp. 57-84); and "Positivism and the logic of scientific theories" by H. B. Hesse (pp. 85-110).

6. Halpin first learned about logical positivism as an undergraduate at Columbia University in 1930-31. He summarized logical positivism's influence on him as follows (personal correspondence, March, 1980): "The import was strong enough to have stayed with me for half a century." However, he later reported via the telephone that his technical knowledge of logical positivism was limited.

7. UCEA offered only four Career Development seminars during the 1974-81 period. Following the Ohio State 1954-74 offering was a second seminar held at the University of Virginia in November, 1976. (see Mosher, E. K., & Wagoner, Jr., J. L. (Eds.). (1978). *The changing politics of education*. Berkeley, CA: McCutchan Publishing Corporation. In May, 1977, a third UCEA seminar was conducted at the University of Rochester. (see Immegart, G. L., & Boyd, W. L. (Eds.). (1979). *Problem-finding in educational administration*. Lexington, MA: D. C. Heath and Company. Finally, the Ontario Institute for Studies in Education in November, 1979, offered a seminar on "Deans As Individuals in Organization." Its proceedings were not published.

8. The following references written by Charles E. Kline and Richard E. Munsterman are pertinent: (1974). UCEA student data system, 1973-74; participation, references and positions. *UCEA Review*, XVI(2),19-22; (1975). Doctoral student characteristics: UCEA student data system, 1973-74. *UCEA Review*, XVI(3), 21-26; (1976). UCEA doctoral experience, competency and employment desire according to race and sex. *UCEA Review*, XVIII(1), 1-10.

9. *The Report of the UCEA Planning and Evaluation Commission* is available in the May, 26-28, 1977, Executive Committee materials.

References

Campbell, R. F. (1979). A critique of the *Educational Administration Quarterly*. *Educational Administration Quarterly*, XV(3), 1-19.

Campbell, R. F., & Newell, L. J. (1973). A *study of professors of educational administration*. Columbus, OH: University Council for Educational Administration.

Charters, Jr. W. W. (1977). The future (and a bit of the past) of research and theory. In L. L. Cunningham, W. G. Hack, & R. O. Nystrand (Eds.), *Educational administration: The developing decades* (pp. 362-375). Berkeley, CA: McCutchan Publishing Corporation.

Crane A. R., & Walker, W. G. (1976). Theory in the real world of the educational administrator. *UCEA Review*, XVII(3), 1-2; 37-38.

Erickson, D. A. (1977). An overdue paradigm shift in educational administration, or, how can we get that idiot off the freeway? In L. L. Cunningham et al (Eds.), *Educational administration: The developing decades* (pp. 119-144). Berkeley, CA: McCutchan Publishing Corporation.

Getzels, J. W. (1952). A psycho-sociological framework for the study of educational administration. *Harvard Educational Review*, 22(4), 235-246.

Getzels, J. W. (1977). Educational administration twenty years later, 1954-74. In L. L. Cunningham et al (Eds.), *Educational administration: The developing decades* (pp. 3-24). Berkeley, CA: McCutchan Publishing Corporation.

Gibson, R. O. (1977). Reflections on a dialogue. *UCEA Review*, XVIII(2), 35-39.

Greenfield, T. B. (1975). Theory about organization: A new perspective and its implications for schools. In M. Hughes (Ed.), *Administering education: International challenge* (pp. 71-79). London: The Athlone Press.

Greenfield, T. B. (1976). Theory about what? *UCEA Review*, XVII(2), 4-9.

Griffiths, D. E. (1975). Some thoughts about theory in educational administration — 1975. *UCEA Review*, XVII(1), 12-18.

Halpin, A. W. (1958). The development of theory in educational administration. In A. W.Halpin (Ed.), *Administrative theory in education* (pp. 1-19). New York: The Macmillan Company.

Halpin, A. W., & Hayes, A. E. (1977). The broken ikon, or, what ever happened to theory? In L. L. Cunningham et al (Eds.), *Educational administration: The developing decades* (pp. 261-297). Berkeley, CA: McCutchan Publishing Corporation.

Hills, J. (1977). A perspective on perspectives. *UCEA Review*, XIX(1), 1-5.

Kendell, R., & Byrne, D. R. (1977). Thinking about the Greenfield-Griffiths debate. *UCEA Review*, XIX(1), 6-16.

Layton, D. H. (1974). The third international intervisitation programme: An eyewitness account. *UCEA Review*, XVI(2), 8-11.

Merrow, J., Foster, R, & Estes, N. (1974). *The urban school superintendent of the future.* Durant, OK: Southeastern Foundation.

Robinson, C. (1976). Editorial. *Emergent Leadership: Focus upon Women and Minorities in Educational Administration,* I(1), 5.

Silver, P. F. (1978). The phenomenological appreciation of theory. *UCEA Review,* XIX(2), 30-31.

7

Reach Across the Seas

"Nothing happens unless first a dream."

Carl Sandburg

In 1966 UCEA launched the first International Inter-Visitation Program (IIP) — an undertaking which proved to be the initial link in a long chain of events. The Program was followed in 1970 with the second IIP in Australia, in 1974 with the third in the United Kingdom, and in 1978 with the fourth in Canada. These programs fostered the creation of international networks and facilitated the exchange of ideas about the training of educational administrators. More importantly, they provided settings in which leaders could generate new initiatives, including the formation of new transnational organizations. At the second IIP, for example, the Commonwealth Council for Educational Administration was founded—an organization whose reach would extend into more than 35 nations. In London at the third IIP the European Forum on Educational Administration was born.

The newly created transnational organizations in turn implemented programs. For example, their boards and staffs in the 1970s helped establish national professional associations for educational administrators in about 15 countries. To serve their clients the new associations conducted national conferences, founded new journals, published special studies, and encouraged those in higher education to design and offer new courses and training programs for administrators.

As the international and national offsprings carried out their expanding programs, they diffused ideas about administrative practice and training into many African, Asian, Australian, European, North American, and South American nations. One result was a rapid expansion of training opportunities around the globe. As the initiator of the first IIP, and the constant pursuer of ways and means to improve training, UCEA continued to play a central role in the international spread of training programs. Facilitating the spread were professors in UCEA universities who could draw upon a large reservoir of publications and insights gleaned from a century's search for effective patterns of training.

Building the Field's First International Network

In the summer of 1963, while sitting at my desk in Ohio State's Page Hall, I got an idea which would enable UCEA to set a new direction for the field. The idea emerged as I mused about a set of developments which at first seemed disconnected. "Down under" William Walker of the University of New England in Australia had launched in May, 1963, the first issue of the *Journal of Educational Administration*, whose introductory editorial had stressed the "demand" for a journal with an "international appeal" (Richardson, 1963, p. 1). Across the Atlantic William Taylor in England was employing simulated situations to teach school management at Oxford University's Institute of Education. North of the border at the University of Alberta Arthur Reeves and his colleagues were preparing educational leaders in a new doctoral program and placing them in key posts all across Canada. In one of Ohio's neighboring states professors Dan Cooper and Claude Eggertson at the University of Michigan had decided, while developing their institution's 1964-69 UCEA plan, to pilot a comparative study of school management in England during the summer of 1964.

As I thought about these widely dispersed developments, I recognized that path breakers around the world lacked formal opportunities to discuss their ideas with one another. More importantly, the field of educational administration had no structures for nurturing international development. The newly identified need, then, posed fresh possibilities. Could UCEA make a unique contribution to the internationalization of the field? Could it create modes of exchange which would enable nation spanning networks of leaders to effect new developments? Though the vision behind the questions was very compelling, the means for realizing it were not readily apparent. After pondering the problem, I wrote some able leaders and asked them if UCEA might help nurture future developments by sponsoring an extended international conference. William Walker in Australia responded quickly to my August, 1963, letter: "The sooner we have that international conference the better" (quoted in Culbertson, 1969, p. 4).

William Taylor at Oxford, Arthur Reeves at Alberta, Calvin Grieder at Colorado, and Theodore Reller at California in Berkeley also supported the conference idea.

During 1963-64 I conversed with leading UCEA professors about the projected endeavor. I learned that William Walker, who had completed his doctorate some years earlier at Illinois, had returned to the University of New England in New South Wales, where he and Allan Crane had developed the first university based Australian program for preparing educational leaders. Theodore Reller, who had spent several sabbaticals abroad, informed me about school administration in several nations, especially England.

In November, 1964, the UCEA Board of Trustees approved in principle my recommendation for an international program designed to serve leaders in Australia, Canada, New Zealand, the United Kingdom, and the United States. In early 1965 I traveled to Battle Creek, Michigan, to present the idea to Emory Morris, President of the W. K. Kellogg Foundation. As I described features of the proposal, he listened intently. When I finished, he remarked that I had a promising concept. However, he informed me that the foundation did not support conferences. He then asked if I could re-think the initiative in another format. When I agreed he suggested that I send him a written proposal when it was completed.

I soon concluded that Emory Morris had done UCEA a favor by pressing me to re-think the proposal. A conference, I recognized, was a conventional but inappropriate means for pursuing an unconventional end. Hence, I substituted the idea of an "International Inter-Visitation Program" (IIP) for that of a conference. Consisting of three phases, the IIP would begin with a one week seminar at a UCEA university, continue with a two week period of visits by international teams to selected UCEA universities, and end with a three day session devoted to evaluation and follow-up activities. Three outcomes were envisaged: an international exchange of ideas, the conception of future initiatives, and the creation of a network of leaders which would continue to generate new developments after the IIP had ended.

In mid-1965 when W. K. Kellogg Foundation officials reported their intent to support the proposal, I was faced with an imposing task. Keenly aware of my limited international experience, I knew that UCEA needed special help. As I thought about individuals who might provide needed assistance, the name of William Walker kept coming to the fore. A proven internationalist, he was acquainted with school management in Australia, Canada, New Zealand, the United Kingdom, and the United States. With his cross-national contacts he seemed uniquely equipped to assist UCEA. His earlier letter had also reflected an unmistakable enthusiasm for international development.

Recognizing how important it was to attain Walker's help, I wondered how to make the opportunity an appealing one. Presuming he would prefer to be located at a university during the UCEA project, I called Theodore Reller, Dean of the School of Education at California, Berkeley, to see if an appointment as a visiting professor might be available. When Reller responded positively, I invited Walker to assume the dual posts. Fortunately, he accepted the proffered invitation on short notice. In mid-September, 1965, I sent him a five page memo describing the challenges ahead. On September 29, 1965, he responded with a nine-page memo! His insights reinforced my belief in his capacity to assist UCEA. In late January, 1966, he stopped at UCEA's headquarters in Columbus on his way to Berkeley.

William Walker and George Baron, a specialist in comparative education at the University of London, represented Australia and the United Kingdom on the IIP advisory committee. Joining the group from Canada was the dynamic Arthur Reeves of Alberta, who a few years earlier had conducted a series of lectures in Australia. Other members were Dan Cooper of Michigan, who had close ties with his colleagues in comparative education; Russell Gregg, a respected scholar and teacher at Wisconsin; Calvin Grieder, a well-known writer at Colorado with international interests; Erich Lindmann, an able student of school finance at California, Los Angeles; and Theodore Reller at California, Berkeley, one of a small number of U. S. experts on comparative educational administration.

Meeting in Atlantic City, New Jersey, in February, 1966, the advisory group reviewed and approved plans for the IIP. During the day Dan Cooper, who had earlier requested that his university conduct the initial seminar, described Michigan's conference capabilities. The next day at a meeting of the UCEA Board of Trustees Walker reported on the previous day's discussion, and Cooper described plans for the October 9-14, 1966, seminar. After the Board approved several of the committee's recommendations, Baron described the state of training programs for school managers in England. Afterwards, he responded to some critical questions with wit and aplomb.

On his way to the United States William Walker had stopped in the

United Kingdom, where he identified potential IIP participants to supplement those on his "down under" list. In the spring of 1966 eight leaders from Australia, six from England, two from Scotland, and two from New Zealand agreed to take part in IIP. Most were members of higher education faculties. However, able practitioners also accepted invitations, including B. S. Braithwaite, Chief Education Officer, East Sussex County Council, England, and W. B. Russell, Assistant Director, Education Department of Victoria in Australia. Later nine Canadian and 42 U. S. professors agreed to take part in the IIP.

On October 9, 1966, with unmistakable expectancy, the first phase of the IIP began at the University of Michigan. Dan Cooper, Bill Walker, and I opened the session by describing briefly our plans and hopes for IIP. Then George Baron, Theodore Reller, and Bill Walker presented comparative analyses of educational issues, educational administration, and the training of school administrators in five nations. All three spoke on the limits of their analyses. Walker described the difficulty thusly (Walker, 1969b, p. 134): "It was Puck, I believe, who offered to put a girdle around the world in forty minutes. Having committed myself to a rather similar task I cannot now regard Puck as other than a very foolhardy fellow indeed."[1]

The audience also heard five presenters depict educational trends and issues in each of the five participating nations. Other topics addressed were uses of the behavioral sciences in training, theory, simulation, and strategies for change, including change in institutions of higher education. The new graduate school of administration at the University of California at Irvine was also discussed. William Taylor, a professor at the University of Bristol in England, called for a new approach to comparative research on administration. He then described how simulated situations could be constructed and used to illuminate values which shape school decisions in different cultures (Taylor, 1969, pp. 216-222).

The discussions vividly demonstrated that attendees defined such terms as "principal," "college," and "decentralization" in very different ways. Even the meaning of "educational administration" varied from country to country and even within countries as show by Taylor's comments about practices in England (Taylor, 1969, p. 211):

> Only a minority of the people concerned with the government and management of schools, colleges, and universities in

England are customarily regarded as educational administrators. The education officers and administrative assistants employed by local education authorities qualify for the title, as do the Registrars and Secretaries of some colleges and universities, but there is doubt regarding the proper term for the civil servants who man the Department of Education and Science. "The Office" and "Curzon Street" seem to be the preferred terms among teachers for the local and central administration respectively. Her Majesty's Inspectors; the local authority inspectors, organizers, and advisers; the members of the local education committee; the dean and heads of departments in a college or university; and the heads and deputy heads of schools—all do work that is largely administrative in character, but most of them seem to prefer not to be known as administrators. The head of a school is a head *teacher* —or master—or mistress; the chairman of a university department or a dean is still an academic man. . .

William Walker, cognizant of the problems created by uncommon meanings, agreed to help develop an international glossary of educational and management terms. Later assisting him were George Baron (United Kingdom), Calvin Grieder (United States), Ernest Hodgson (Canada), and William Renwick (New Zealand). Although the task proved to be an extended and demanding one, the group under Walker's leadership produced a glossary of terms whose multiple definitions shed light on facets of education and management in the five nations.[2]

At the end of the Michigan phase six teams, each composed of four individuals from Australia, Canada, New Zealand, or the United Kingdom, began their travels to UCEA institutions. Months earlier 25 universities had volunteered to host a visiting team. After on-site discussions with staffs in the 25 institutions, Walker recommended 17 hosts: Boston, Buffalo, California at Berkeley, Chicago, Colorado, Harvard, Illinois, Michigan State, Nebraska, New York University, Ohio State, Oregon, Stanford, Syracuse, Teachers College, Columbia, Texas, and Wisconsin. Each team typically visited two or three universities. During their visits they probed concepts and practices related to training, research, and university-school system relationships.

The contrasting views of the visitors and those visited made for stimulating exchanges. In the Commonwealth nations the belief that a liberal arts education provided the best preparation for society's leaders had long reigned. On each team, then, there was some skepticism about specialized training. On the other hand, since UCEA professors were grounded in a tradition which reached all the way back to the nineteenth century, they accepted the concept of professional training uncritically. Legitimated by state laws, the idea was a given. When visitors asked them what the rationale for their training programs was, they had to respond to a seldom asked query. Yet those who answered it effectively provided their visitors with arguments they could adapt for use in their own countries, if they chose.

Learning was also abetted by informal exchanges. As team members jointly assessed their university visits, they acquired fresh insights. Through discussions of management in their respective nations they acquired other insights. As they traveled, ate, and conversed with one another, they developed some of the human bonds needed for a network which would function after IIP had ended.

On the evening of October 30, 1966, Arthur Reeves welcomed the visitors to the University of Alberta for the program's final phase. The next day the conferees exchanged ideas about the preparation of administrators. As members of small groups, attendees on the second day brainstormed future possibilities. One warmly supported proposal was the international exchange of students and professors. Conferees also endorsed intercultural research, improved communication (e. g. the promotion of national journals), and the adoption of training programs by leaders in Commonwealth nations.

William Walker, in a summary of IIP's outcomes, stressed the breaking down of insularity and provincialism, the beginnings of an international concept of school administration, and a demonstration of the unexpected variety in U. S. university programs (Bd. Mat, 2/12/67, p. 4). He also suggested that IIP had stimulated leaders not previously interested in formal training to consider implementing programs in their own countries. Participants in IIP had agreed that committees to encourage training initiatives in Australia, New Zealand, and the United Kingdom should be instituted.

The conferees spent the final hours at IIP evaluating their experiences. Their recommendation that a variation of the first IIP be regularly re-enacted every three or four years somewhere on the international landscape reflected the high value they placed on the three-week program. Inherent in this decision were the seeds of important future international developments in the field.

As the first IIP closed, Bill Walker and I were indeed elated. Attained were the IIP outcomes envisaged two years earlier as, for example, the acquisition of fresh learnings by leaders from five nations and the articulation of aspirations for future developmental possibilities. Those who observed the restrained exchanges among conferees at the Michigan seminar and compared them with the warm and spontaneous ones at the University of Alberta would have recognized that important links in the hoped-for international network were already in place. However, few could have anticipated achievements which the network of leaders would realize in the years ahead.

IIPs Spawn International Organizations

As I complete this chapter, plans for the eighth IIP are unfolding. The first four occurred while I was at UCEA.[3] Although the second, third, and fourth took place in widely separated locales, served increasingly diverse audiences, and dealt with changing issues, their conduct was strongly influenced by the aims and format of the first IIP. Significantly, the IIP's flexible and floating structures and operation have enabled networks to pioneer important developments. What were the major ones spawned by the second, third, and fourth IIPs?

Twenty-four months after the first IIP ended, plans for the second one were already in place. Co-sponsored by the University of New England in Armidale, New South Wales, and UCEA, the program was held in Australia during August, 1970. Conceived largely by university professors and implemented with the help of high level Australian state leaders, the seminar dealt with the themes of bureaucracy and centralization, planning and systems analysis, accountability and assessment, and teacher negotiations.[4] During the visitation phase five teams traveled to Australian state capitals, where they observed new developments and discussed educational and management issues.

At the second IIP a unique organization was founded. Known as the Commonwealth Council for Educational Administration (CCEA), its impact would eventually be felt in nations around the globe. CCEA's founders, influenced by the first IIP, initially wanted a "plan for a council" which would "operate in much the same manner as the University Council for Educational Administration in North America"

(Walker, 1969a, p. 95). Envisaged before the second IIP began, the CCEA was conceived mainly by William Walker and George Baron of the University of London. Hoping that the new council might serve managers in "old" and "new" Commonwealth nations, program planners invited leaders from the nearest Commonwealth nations to attend the second IIP: East Pakistan (now Bangladesh), Fiji, The Gambia, Hong Kong, Malaysia, Singapore, Papua New Guinea, and Trinidad.

Robin Farquhar, UCEA's deputy director and a Canadian, was very excited when he heard about the proposed new organization. Before he traveled to the Australian IIP, he wrote a paper titled "Toward the Development of a Commonwealth Centre for Educational Leadership: An International UCEA?" His major thesis was that the projected new organization should *not* be an international UCEA. Rather, it should be defined by its differences—not its similarities to UCEA. The degree to which Farquhar's thesis influenced CCEA's founding fathers is unclear. Certainly, the UCEA model became much less salient as CCEA leaders grappled with the complex problem of serving school leaders in approximately 35 widely-separated and diverse Commonwealth nations.

Commonwealth conferees processed the CCEA proposal at the University of New England during the final phase of the IIP. The process began when the respected internationalist, William Walker, stepped to the podium and articulated his vision for CCEA. Other presentations followed, including a video-taped one by John Cheal of the University of Calgary in Canada. Thereafter, the body approved a constitution for CCEA and chose New England as the site for CCEA's secretariat. Weeks later a committee led by George Baron briefed John Chadwick, Director of the London-based Commonwealth Foundation, about CCEA and its potential. Subsequently, Chadwick, after visiting William Walker and others at New England, provided support for CCEA's initial development. John Ewing, formerly the Director of Primary Education in New Zealand, became CCEA's executive secretary. William Walker was chosen as CCEA's "founding president."

Shortly before he passed away, William Walker observed that CCEA was the "jewel in UCEA's crown" (personal correspondence, February, 1991). A good case can be made for his assertion. However, only examples of CCEA's attainments can be noted in this chapter.[5] One of its seven objectives was to help leaders in Commonwealth countries establish national associations of educational administrators. During the decade of the 1970s it nurtured the founding of numerous national associations. These associations offered seminars for school leaders, published journals, and stimulated the development of higher education courses and programs to prepare educational administrators.

To serve leaders in particular parts of the Commonwealth (e. g. the Pacific or the African arena), CCEA intermittently sponsored regional conferences. Designed to foster communication between and among administrators in different nations, they also transmitted fresh ideas to CCEA members. Among CCEA's publications were the *CCEA Newsletter* and *Studies in Educational Administration*. Illustrative titles of the *Studies* were "Commonwealth Directory of Qualifications and Courses in Educational Administration;" "A Teaching Bibliography for Educational Administration;" and "The Commonwealth Casebook for School Administrators." At the first IIP in 1966 Theodore Reller and William Walker had challenged their listeners to devote more attention to educational leadership in developing nations. To its credit CCEA responded in far-reaching ways to this challenge.

In November, 1971, William Walker, in an address to the UCEA Plenary Session in Columbus, Ohio, described the origins, nature, and functions of CCEA (Walker, 1972). His assessment of UCEA's role in the creation of CCEA was a very generous one as is evident from the title of his address: "UCEA's Bright Son at Morning: The Commonwealth Council for Educational Administration." In his remarks he affirmed the following (Walker, 1972, p. 19):

> Yet the real progenitor of the Commonwealth Council was clearly the University Council for Educational Administration itself, and no embarrassed maneuverings by Jack Culbertson or members of the UCEA Board of Trustees during the years 1963 to 1966 are going to hide the obvious fertility of that time of their lives! It was UCEA which conceived of the first International Intervisitation Program, held in 1966.

It is true that the vision for the first IIP emanated from UCEA, and that it was instrumental in shaping future path-breaking endeavors. However, vision was only a part of the story. Had it not been translated into new structures, networks, and developments, it would have had limited value. As I saw it, William Walker played an essential role in implementing the first IIP. By my lights, he and I were partners engaged in weaving together strands from dissimilar traditions. Within a month after he arrived in the United States the two of us were zealously seeking to ensure that the IIP would have fruitful follow-up endeavors. Our differing information bases complemented one another. I was intimately familiar with UCEA; Bill was not. Bill was knowledgeable about school management in Australia, Canada, New Zealand, and the United Kingdom; I was not. Very early I saw the importance of attracting to the program Commonwealth leaders who would significantly influence administration and training in the future; Bill identified these leaders.

Notably, the idea of CCEA was conceived on non-North American soil. I first heard about it in February, 1969, while meeting with Bill Walker, George Baron, and Robin Farquhar in Atlantic City. Though the CCEA concept was still somewhat inchoate, Walker's and Baron's intent to launch it at the second IIP was unmistakably clear. While UCEA provided Walker and Baron an inspiring developmental model, they and their Commonwealth colleagues conceived and implemented CCEA.

During the 1970 IIP George Baron expressed the hope that the United Kingdom might host the 1974 IIP. Within two years plans for the third IIP were in place. To begin in Bristol, England, and then move to Glasgow, Scotland, the program would end in London. At each of the three cities about half a week would be devoted to seminar activities and the other half to visiting local institutions.[6]

A number of important developments unfolded during the planning and conduct of the third IIP. One was the creation of the British Educational Administration Society. Designed to advance the field of educational management, its first function was to provide a structure for planning the IIP. Later the Society would sponsor annual conferences and publish the journal, *Educational Management & Administration*.[7] Its influence would spread rapidly and would soon extend into continental Europe as is documented below.

That 19 Commonwealth countries and several European ones sent representatives to the IIP reflected the growing diversity of its clientele. Unexpectedly, the European leaders sowed the seeds for another significant development: the European Forum on Educational Administration. In Europe, in contrast to North American and a goodly number of Commonwealth nations, there were no well established higher education training programs for school administrators. The

National Institute of School and University Management in France, established in 1962, had assumed the early lead in in-service training. During 1972-73, the year before the third IIP, it provided 9,175 days of instruction to practicing administrators (Bessoth, 1975, p. 39). Conducted through the Ministry of Education, the standardized training was far removed from university thought. In the 1970s Eskil Stegoe and his Swedish colleagues, through their ministry of education, implemented a large-scale and very different in-service training program for school administrators. Designed to improve Swedish schooling, the training, in contrast to that of the French, made considerable use of theory (e. g. concepts of change).

In the Federal Republic of Germany there were new stirrings. In 1974 Richard Bessoth and his colleagues at the Deutsches Institut fuer Internationale Paedagogische Erforschung in Frankfurt began an ambitious effort to develop an array of training materials. Aided by a grant from the Volkswagen Foundation, Bessoth and his staff tested the materials in courses for principals and supervisors.[8]

As they struggled to break tradition, the Europeans had a need for ideas. The dream of a Forum likely emerged from this need. First sketched at the third IIP, the dream was next seriously addressed in 1976 at the fifth annual conference of the British Educational Administration Society. At the conference European leaders invited the Society to help them found the European Forum on Educational Administration. The Society, chaired by Peter Browning, Chief Education Officer for Bedfordshire—and contributor of the name "forum"—accepted the invitation. In 1977, at the Sorbonne University in Paris, the Forum was officially born (Fonderie, 1986, p. 6).

Influenced by the IIP model, the Forum's major activity was "inter-visitation" programs. The leading implementer of the first one was Clive Hopes, of the Deutsches Institut fuer Internationale Paedagogische Erforschung in Frankfurt, and a recipient of a Master's degree in educational administration from McGill University in Canada. One week in length, the program, held in West Germany in 1980, enabled 70 participants from 10 European nations to explore the training needs of educational managers. Following the lead of CCEA, the Forum also helped found national associations for educational administrators. In 1978 and 1979 it helped beget associations in West Germany and France. The geographical reach of the European Forum was much more limited than that of CCEA. However, its programs were valued highly, in part because they emerged at a time when European interest in the theory and practice of training was in an upswing.

Yet another IIP outcome was an accepted plan to study training programs in Australia, Canada, New Zealand, the United Kingdom, and the United States. The idea emerged from a CCEA conference held in Suva, Fiji, in 1973. Responding to a request from Bill Walker, I presented a paper in Suva to stimulate the development of UCEA-CCEA cooperative research projects.[9] In the paper I described three structures which managers of international R and D projects might employ. Each of the three required a different approach to the definition, planning, and co-ordination of a project. The "parallel" structure, for instance, would help scholars set cross-national.goals, while individual researchers in each nation would be able to make decisions about methods. Staffs in each nation were also expected to share their research designs and provide critiques to one another.

The parallel structure, I suggested, could be used to study such phenomena as educational governance, training programs, and modes of knowledge utilization. Since the Suva conferees expressed an interest in a study of training, Bill Walker and I decided to see if such an inquiry could be implemented. After the governing bodies of UCEA and CCEA approved the idea, the following individuals agreed to undertake the parallel studies: Ross Thomas in Australia, Erwin Miklos in Canada, George Marshall in New Zealand, Ronald Glatter in the United Kingdom, and Seymour Evans, Jack Nagle, and Gary Alkire in the U. S.

At the third IIP individuals from each of the five nations exchanged ideas about plans for their respective inquiries on training. They also critically examined a research instrument developed by Seymour Evans of New York University. Four years later at the fourth IIP in Vancouver, Canada, they would report their findings. The third IIP, then, enabled the inquirers to share and refine their plans, while the fourth helped them disseminate their findings to assembled representatives from 31 nations.[10]

In May, 1978, the fourth IIP took place. Held in Canada, it was planned by a committee headed by Robin Farquhar, then Dean of the College of Education at the University of Saskatchewan. The plan was for attendees to meet in Montreal for an introductory session, then move westward and eastward with visitations along the way, and end in Vancouver for a one-week seminar. The seminar's theme was the role of leaders as mediators of conflicts between societal forces and school-ing tendencies.[11] About 300 leaders from 31 nations attended the 1978 IIP. Thus, the group was much larger and more diverse than the 1966 one, which had attracted 78 participants from five nations.

My functions as a corresponding member of the fourth IIP's plan-ning committee were affected by the growing number of training institutions which were dotting the global landscape. As more and more non-Commonwealth leaders traveled to UCEA's headquarters, we learned about the rapid growth of training institutions. Discussions and correspondence with leaders from such countries as Brazil, Egypt, France, Germany, Israel, Korea, Norway, Spain, Sweden, and Turkey revealed an interest in training not unlike that identified a decade earlier in Commonwealth nations. The leaders also wanted to be inside—not outside—the burgeoning international networks. In 1976 Heinz Dicker from West Germany visited UCEA's headquarters. A member of the above-described project headed by Richard Bessoth, he was studying U. S. training concepts and practices. Months later Bessoth invited me to speak in German about U. S. training programs for school administrators to an international audience at Oberwesel, a short train ride from Frankfurt.

Located on the Rhine River not far from the reputed location of the Lorelei, whom Heinrich Heine had made famous through his poetry about a century and a half earlier, Oberwesel provided a scenic setting for the conference. Attending were members of the Bessoth research group, scholars from universities and research institutes in the Federal Republic, and officials from state ministries of education. Six of us offered national perspectives on Canadian, English, French, Israeli, Swedish, and U. S. training programs.

My conversations during the conference and later at a meeting of the European Forum revealed views which differed from those expressed by non-Commonwealth visitors at UCEA's headquarters. The latter wanted to be a part of an established international network. Excluded from UCEA, CCEA, and the European Forum because of the membership criteria of the three organizations, they lacked profes-sional opportunities which others enjoyed. On the other hand, the Oberwesel conferees, as affiliates of the European Forum, had limited interests in helping create new international networks.

As a corresponding member of the Canadian IIP's planning com-mittee, I responded to the "exclusion" problem in two ways. One, a short term tactic, was to recommend to the committee that "outsiders" from about a dozen nations be invited to attend the IIP, and that several of them be asked to present papers in Vancouver. In accepting my suggestions, the planning committee increased the number of nations represented at the fourth IIP and made the task of scheduling the diverse array of program offerings more complex.

Shaped by a longer-term horizon, the second tactic was to invite leaders from each of the 31 nations at the Vancouver seminar to discuss the idea of establishing a World Council for Educational Administration. The brainchild of Franklin Stone of the University of Iowa, the concept was first assessed in 1976 by a UCEA committee comprised of Willard Lane and Frank Stone from Iowa, and Robin Farquhar from the Ontario Institute for Studies in Education. After reviewing Stone's position paper, the group explored such questions as: what unique functions would a World Council perform? How could it complement UCEA and CCEA? What language(s) might best promote international exchange? Agreeing on the merits of the concept, the group decided that UCEA should refine and seek to advance the idea. In February, 1977, the UCEA Plenary Session unanimously agreed that work on a World Council should proceed.

In Vancouver on May 22, 1978, representatives of 31 nations examined the proposal for a World Council. During the discussion some contended that the problems posed by the deep political divisions in the world presented insurmountable barriers. How, someone asked, could a World Council function, given such divisions as those existing between the East and the West, and the Arabs and the Israelis? Others expressed concern about the import of a World Council for existing international organizations. Already pressed to spend much energy searching for scarce resources, some members of these organizations were not eager to take on an imposing new endeavor.

Although some questioned the feasibility and even the desirability of the Council, most felt the "exclusion" problem should be addressed. As a result, the group formulated several recommendations: a standing IIP committee of representatives from UCEA, CCEA, and non-Commonwealth nations should be appointed; this committee should help plan the next IIP; non-Commonwealth leaders should develop national associations for school administrators in their countries; and both UCEA and CCEA should seek to open their programs to interested non-Commonwealth leaders. These actions, though limited, were reassuring to most non-Commonwealth leaders.

After the meeting Salah Kobt, former Rector of Ain Shams University in Cairo, Egypt, and Joseph Goldstein, Head of the Center for Educational Administration at the University of Haifa in Israel, transmitted a non-verbal message, as they walked with their arms around one another from the back to the front of the room. They then facetiously promised to improve relations in the Middle East by the next IIP! The incident made clear that the IIPs offered more than professional exchange; they also provided neutral grounds on which leaders could convey messages not easily conveyed in their home lands.

Although the Vancouver deliberations failed to bring a World Council into being, they provided discussants with insights into the expanding and changing field of educational administration. Newly crafted courses of action would help lower the communication barriers among leaders in Commonwealth and non-Commonwealth nations.

In sum, the IIPs provided settings for leaders to conceive, launch, and nurture novel undertakings. Newly created international organizations and networks were the most valuable and lasting of the IIP legacies. Spawned at the second IIP was the globe-girdling CCEA. Going beyond idea exchange, CCEA's leaders developed national associations and new training programs which helped advance educational management in many countries. Seeing much potential in CCEA's initiatives, leaders in non-Commonwealth countries adopted most of CCEA's innovations and applied them in their own practices.

Linking North and South American Scholars

Early in 1968 officials of the Pan American Union invited me to speak at an upcoming July conference of the Organization of American States (OAS). Issuing an unusual request, they asked if I would prepare a monograph on "Administration As A Basic Instrument for the Elaboration, Implementation, and Evaluation of Educational Development Plans." Given OAS' intent to publish and distribute the monograph, they asked that I summarize its major points at the opening session. After preparing a 72-page document, I sent it in late June to Brasilia, Brazil, site of the impending conference.

On entering the conference room on July 18, 1968, I was taken aback by the scene before me. Located around a partial circle of tables were the flags of the nations which comprised the OAS. Already sitting near

the U. S. flag was Arnold Spinner, a professor of educational administration at New York University, a fluent speaker of Spanish, and the
official representative of the U.S. Behind the tables were booths where
skilled linguists would translate conference messages into and out of
English, French, Spanish, and Portuguese.

Following a ceremonial beginning, I was introduced and asked to
summarize my ideas. Then a question period ensued which lasted until
nearly noon, when copies of four different translations of the "monograph" arrived. At that point the chair announced that OAS representatives would prepare themselves during the afternoon for the next
day's discussion by studying my monograph. In the meantime, I was
to speak about educational planning to a gathering of educators who
were also holding a conference in Brasilia.

At 10 a. m., on July 19, the OAS representatives reconvened.
Present were ministers of education and higher level government
officials from Latin American nations. From 10 to noon and from two
to four p. m. I responded to questions. Most had to do with the ideas
elaborated in the paper. However, at times queries went beyond the
paper's bounds to such issues as the purposes of education and the role
of schools in combating poverty. OAS leaders also posed questions
about the training of educational administrators. Through their pro-
longed questioning, they displayed considerable curiosity about administration and its instrumental values.

During the conference I conversed with Corlos Correa Mascaro, a
respected Brazilian who had served in both governmental and university settings. Dissatisfied with the quality of Brazilian school administration, he hoped to attain OAS support for improved university
training. He also asked for permission to translate the UCEA book,
Preparing Administrators: New Perspectives, into Portuguese. His letters
later revealed that he had been unable to translate and publish the book
or to launch new training initiatives.

For me the subject of training in Latin America lay dormant until
the mid-1970s, when Thomas Wiggins, a professor at Oklahoma, and
Patrick Lynch, a professor at Pennsylvania State, informed me that they
were concerned about the gulf which separated Latin American and
North American educational leaders. Wiggins, who had earlier refined
his Spanish speaking skills as a school administrator in San Diego,
California, had several Latin American experiences at the University of
Del Valle in Cali, Colombia, in the early 1970s. Working with Professor

Hernan Navarro, he helped implement a two year, OAS supported training program for school principals. At Cali he had also met Benno Sander who, as an OAS staff member, monitored the training program. In 1975 Sander would accept a post at the University of Brasilia. The recipient some years earlier of a doctorate in educational administration from the Catholic University in Washington, D.C., and later of a post-doctoral grant to study at Harvard, Sander would become an outstanding Latin American leader. He and Wiggins increasingly talked and wrote to one another about their dissatisfactions with the gulf between Latin and North American professors and practitioners.

Patrick Lynch obtained his first professional experience in Latin America in 1963, at the Autonomous University of Guadalajara. Intermittently traveling to Guadalajara from his location at the University of New Mexico, he helped the staff at the Autonomous University establish a Faculty of Education. He later worked in Colombia and Honduras on basic educational development programs. During the 1960s and 1970s he continued to acquire insights into Latin American education and culture in varied settings. His experiences ranged, for example, from that of teaching a course on educational research in Spanish at the University of Trujillo in Peru, to that of conducting a sector analysis of primary education in Ecuador. In the mid-seventies he tested his knowledge of Portuguese during a trip to Brazil—knowledge which he had acquired through independent study.

During his Latin American sojourns Lynch from time to time heard the name, Benno Sander. However, years passed before he actually met Sander at a meeting of the American Educational Research Association in the U.S. Sander, Lynch, and Wiggins all shared the view that rich learning opportunities could be afforded Latin and North American leaders, if the curtains which separated them could be opened. As Lynch and Wiggins thought about the problem, they decided to contact UCEA, because "it encouraged new scholars and scholarship" (Lynch, personal correspondence, December, 1990). When Wiggins and Lynch met with me in the mid-seventies, we all agreed that the problem might be probed initially through a UCEA Career Development Seminar. However, after several failed attempts to find a seminar sponsor, the idea collapsed.

In 1976 when Lynch, Sander, Wiggins, and I met, we took another tack: the establishment of an "InterAmerican Council for Educational Administration." We hoped that such an organization might help lower inter-continental barriers to exchange. Early in 1977 UCEA's governing bodies approved the goal of creating such a Council. Eight months later Lynch and Wiggins elaborated a rationale for the council (Wiggins and Lynch, 1977). Later, at Sander's suggestion, the name of the proposed organization was changed to the InterAmerican Society for Educational Administration. "Society," Sander said, had a more scholarly connotation in Latin American circles than did "council."

In the spring of 1978 Lynch, Sander, and I met again. Also present were Leslie Gue of the University of Alberta in Canada, and UCEA Associate Director, Peter Hackbert. Seeking a way to bring the Society into being, we agreed to implement an Inter-American Congress on Educational Administration and to involve its members in the founding of the Society. We concluded that the Congress should be held in Latin America, and that the National Association of Professionals in Educational Administration of Brazil and the Organization of American States should be major sponsors. We also elected Benno Sander to lead the initiative.

Held on December 10-14, 1979, in the strikingly designed Camara dos Diputados (Brazilian House of Representatives) in Brasilia, the Congress attracted more than 600 administrators, policy makers, and professors from 25 countries. Its theme was the role of educational policy and administration within political and cultural contexts.[12] Treated to a range of views, including Marxian ones, attendees heard five plenary addresses, six plenary symposia and 24 panel sessions. At mid-week Sander invited participants to discuss the inter-American initiative. At 5 p. m. on December 12 about 200 individuals gathered for a session chaired by Sander. An animated two hour discussion ensued. Mission, program, and financing were among the topics examined. The query, "Who will finance the Society?", produced the most dramatic event. A Costa Rican administrator, Lorenzo Gaudamuz Sandoval, ran from the back to the front of the room, threw a check in front of Sander, and exclaimed, "*We* will finance it."

In a display of impressive intercultural leadership, as he responded to participants in several different languages, Sander drew the meeting to a close around 7 p. m. After expressing their views about the Society, the participants agreed that it should be established by a declaration. Five individuals were asked to craft the declaration: Edirualdo De Mello (Brazil); Lorenzo Guadamuz Sandoval (Costa Rica); Richard Gordon Chambers (Jamaica); Carlos Ortiz Ramirez (Paraguay); and Jack Culbertson (United States). Serving as an interpreter, Ivan Barrientos

Monzon, a professor from the University of Kansas, skillfully helped the group understand the meanings of statements made in Spanish, Portuguese, and English.

On the final day of the Congress Lorenzo Guadamuz Sandoval read the "Declaration" to the assembled body. He began the official statement as follows (quoted in Culbertson, 1980, pp. 2-3):   The First InterAmerican Congress on Educational Administration, held in Brasilia, D. F., Brazil, from December 10 to 14, 1979 considers:

1.   That education, as a sector of society, constitutes a vital factor for the development and welfare of the people.

2.   That educational administration is of recognized importance for the full achievement of the goals and objectives of education.

3.   That for the effective attainment of educational objectives, it is necessary that the professionals in educational administration have systems of communication and association in order to diffuse and upgrade their knowledge and to facilitate the exchange of experience, research and innovative ideas.

Based on the above considerations, the participants of the First InterAmerican Congress on Educational Administration resolve:

To create the *InterAmerican Society for Educational Administration*, a professional organization of an autonomous and scholarly character, that brings together individuals, institutions and organizations with an interest in educational administration in the Americas.

When Lorenzo Guadamuz Sandoval finished reading the Declaration, expressions of elation could be seen on the faces of conferees. An elegant and memorable means for giving life to the InterAmerican Society for Educational Administration, the Declaration of Brasilia had special meaning to those from North America who were unaccustomed to seeing organizations created through declarative acts.

The final decision of the body was to elect the able architect of the First Inter American Congress, Benno Sander, president and executive officer of the new Society.

UCEA's International Impact

That internationally transmitted ideas had a far-reaching impact on training can be seen in the rapid adoption of programs in the 1960s and 1970s. When George Baron of the University of London helped plan the first IIP in early 1966, he was worried that formal training for school administrators in Great Britain would never be widely accepted. Little did he or his listeners suspect that by 1980 50 institutions of higher education in the United Kingdom would be offering courses or programs; or that in Canada and Australia in 1980 the comparable numbers would be 30 and 37, respectively.[13]

At the dawn of the 1960s Canada had one doctoral program; by 1980 it had 10. Even the diffusion of doctoral programs into developing nations moved with unanticipated speed. By 1980 universities in the following "new" Commonwealth nations had doctoral programs: Bangladesh, India, Kenya, Malaysia, and Nigeria. By then pioneers in non-Commonwealth nations (e. g. Brazil, Indonesia, Israel, and South Korea) had implemented doctoral programs. That the global flow of ideas proceeded speedily can also be seen in the adoption of other program offerings. By 1980 leaders in Ghana, Guyana, Japan, Argentina, Cambodia, Fiji, Panama, South Africa, Colombia, Chile, Mexico, El Salvador, New Zealand, Papua New Guinea, Turkey, Spain, Hong Kong, Venezuela, Malawi, Sierra Leone, Tanzania, Mauritius, Sri Lanka, West Germany, and the West Indies had implemented one or more of the following: courses, diploma offerings, or Master's programs.

What impact did UCEA have on the flow of training ideas and on their uses? Even though I have acquired much data on each of UCEA's international endeavors, any conclusions I might draw about impact would be limited. For one thing, my detachment could not match that of outside observers. More importantly, the problem of assessing impact is fraught with much complexity. A Korean professor, for example, reported he had based the design of his training program for educational administrators upon "conceptual, human, and technical" functions (Shin, 1978)—concepts which were originally disseminated from Harvard, a UCEA university. Recipient of a doctorate in 1975 from Minnesota, another member university, the professor had visited UCEA's headquarters where he had purchased several UCEA publications, one of which contained the three concepts he later used. What impact, then, did the Minnesota professors, the UCEA staff, the UCEA publications, and the creator of the three concepts have upon the Asian training program? The question highlights the difficulty of linking cause to effect in a world where many agents constantly compete and interact.

UCEA's primary instrument of change was ideas. In assessing UCEA's impact, the degree to which its international activities enabled professors to acquire valued ideas and to use them in training or inquiry is a key question. Ideas alone, however, are only a part of the story; infrastructures and media through which to transmit ideas, individuals or networks to receive them, and settings in which to apply them are also germane. The closer the ideas moved toward application, the more their destiny was shaped by local and national factors, and the less control UCEA had over them. Thus, it is especially difficult to assess UCEA's impact at the point where ideas affected the design, content, and methods of training programs.

Through newly formed organizations UCEA influenced the global spread of training and nurtured new developments. Since UCEA had conceived the first IIP and helped make it a quadrennial rather than a one-shot affair, UCEA's impact through the IIPs can be described as primary. The impact it had on founding new organizations, however, can best be described as secondary. In the case of CCEA its role was an enabling one, since the primary founders of CCEA were Commonwealth leaders who had attended the first IIP. To go one step further, UCEA's impact upon CCEA's achievements in advancing training in Malaysia, for example, might be described as tertiary. The line of influence, then, was through UCEA, IIP, CCEA and the new Malaysian training programs.

What can be said about UCEA's impact as an international transmitter of ideas? For one thing the conditions affecting the flow of ideas were favorable. Two relevant conditions were emphasized at the International Conference on the World Crisis in Education attended by 150 conferees from 50 nations in 1967, the year after the first IIP (Coombs, 1968, p. 168): educational innovation was sorely needed, and "unless educational systems are well equipped with appropriately trained modern managers—who in turn are well equipped with good information flows, . . .—the transition of education from its semihandicraft state to a modern condition is not likely to happen." Many of those who attended the first four IIPs were familiar with the themes sounded at the international conference. Since many came from nations where training was still in a developing state, they were motivated to acquire and assess IIP-transmitted concepts.

Because most of those at the first IIP were respected national leaders, their subsequent influence on training was substantial. The New Zealander, John Ewing, helped develop the first university training program in his country and later became CCEA's executive secretary. The admired leaders George Baron and William Taylor later influenced training in England in numerous ways. William Walker and A. R. Crane continued their pioneering work in Australia. A fellow countryman, R. W. McCulloch, developed a respected training program at Monash University. The impact of the first IIP on training in New Zealand, England, and Australia of course cannot neatly be separated from numerous other influences. However, informal reports from leaders in these nations suggest that the impact of the ideas they acquired at IIP exchanges, UCEA university visits, newly identified publications, and personal contacts had positive impacts.

The motivations of U. S. attendees at the IIPs differed from those of others. Since U. S. training programs were buttressed by a long tradition, some UCEA professors, as "expert" trainers, felt a limited need for "foreign" ideas. Clothing critique with wit, Walker, in discussing the expert role, affirmed that some U. S. professors approached training "with a hauteur which would have shamed Madame Pompadour" (Walker, 1969b, p. 145).[14] The problem surfaced in another way when U. S. professors sought to implant their training models in universities and cultures unlike their own. In 1979 Benno Sander, in discussing the future of the InterAmerican Society for Educational Administration, emphasized the need for transactional rather than interventionist roles and gently reminded his hearers of the need to respect cultural differences (Sander, 1980, p. 4):

> InterAmerican technical cooperation and comparative studies in the field of educational administration may become valuable instruments of educational development. In order to attain this goal, however, it is necessary to preserve the cultural identity, the political expression, and the peculiar national character of each nation. Otherwise, the builders of schools and educational systems run the historical risk of destroying national cultural values.

A related concern was UCEA's limited participation in the IIPs. Given the hundreds of professors who held posts in UCEA universities, leading Commonwealth professors were disappointed when only 14 and 15 U.S. professors, respectively, took part in the second and third IIPs. Commonwealth leaders were also frustrated because UCEA universities, as they saw it, did not send their most respected professors to the IIPs. The problem was further complicated by my own absence at the second and third IIPs, a fact which indicated to some that UCEA placed priority on its "domestic" activities.

The limited attendance of UCEA professors stemmed in part from conflicting schedules. During the months of July and August when the second and third IIPs were held, most UCEA professors were burdened by very heavy summer teaching loads. Additional reasons for the low attendance could be suggested. Still, they would not alter the fact that the IIPs had their least impact upon U. S. attendees, as measured by the proportions of professors affected in the various nations.

The second and third IIPs were led largely by Commonwealth participants, a fact which disturbed some UCEA attendees, especially professors at the third IIP in the United Kingdom. Robert Heller of the State University of New York at Buffalo stated the concerns of UCEA participants, thusly (EC Mat, 11/10/74, p. 40):

> There was a general feeling that UCEA has been underplayed at the conference and that the IIP is becoming a CCEA and host nation activity. The speculated reasons are many but perhaps can be explained to some degree by the high priority given to IIP by CCEA members and the relatively low priority given by UCEA member institutions and central staff.

The discontent of UCEA participants may have had a negative effect upon the exchange of ideas between Commonwealth and U.S. faculty. At the same time it generated insights which would not have emerged in more comfortable settings, as Oliver Gibson, a colleague of Heller's at Buffalo, has implied (EC Mat, 11/10/74, p. 35):

> There was a strong 'latent curriculum' component that I found useful privately (including some apparent cultural shock among those who came back very articulate about what was "wrong" and how it "should be done"). But just such cross-cultural contacts seem to me essential to the development of any real sense of international community.

Although the number of UCEA professors who took part in the IIPs was relatively small, those who did participate acquired new insights. Jay Scribner, University of California at Los Angeles, for example, described the information he and his U. S. colleagues gained from the three-week IIP in the United Kingdom (EC Mat, 11/10/74, p. 19-20):

> I felt the overall conference provided ample opportunity to become acquainted, if in some instances only superficially, with a variety of cultures, administrative perspectives, and educational developments among the several English-speaking countries. . . The trips to local educational authorities, colleges, institutes, central policy making agencies, and the like, gave all of us a much better view of Great Britain's educational system.

Undoubtedly, professors acquired their most valuable educational experiences through extended teaching and/or study leaves in an educational institution in another country. Typically facilitated by IIP leaders, such leaves enabled scores of professors from the United States (and other countries) to develop new perspectives. John L. Davis of the Anglian Regional Management Centre (ARMC) in Great Britain pioneered teaching exchanges which enabled numerous U. S. professors to join the ARMC staff in the 1970s, while ARMC staff served in positions vacated by their U. S. counterparts.[15] Bill Walker at the University of New England, and George Baron at the University of London, were among those who helped many U. S. professors find universities where they could spend their sabbaticals.

In assessing UCEA's impact as an international disseminator, one can usefully examine ideas which were transmitted through non-IIP channels. In 1966 the very large U. S. depository of publications on administration contained at least three classes of ideas. For pioneering researchers in other countries there were recorded ideas on the nature and conduct of inquiry. For program designers there were writings on the purpose, structure, content, and methods of training programs. For those looking for content there were numerous textbooks and articles they could consider. UCEA's publications dealt more with issues of inquiry and program design. However, textbooks tended to be produced independently of UCEA, mostly by professors in member universities. Although the distinction between IIP and non-IIP ideas is not an iron-clad one, it enables us to examine the impact of UCEA-transmitted ideas from another perspective.

Before the impact of non-IIP ideas on training is examined, some comments about the conditions which faced pioneers in the 1960s and 1970s are in order. Dispersed among many nations in which training was limited or non-existent, many of the pioneers had neither observed training programs nor had had opportunities to grapple systematically with purposive, structural, and methodological issues related to training. Since studies of school administration in their countries were typically few in number, they also faced the perplexing question of what content to use in training programs. As change agents who were critical of the status quo, they at times elicited unfriendly and even inimical responses. That they looked to other nations for ideas and moral support is understandable.

In the 1970s the UCEA staff had a steady stream of visitors from across the seas. Seeking ideas about training and inquiry, the majority came from developing countries. Visitors wanted to know about UCEA publications, on-going or completed research in UCEA universities, standards of preparation, and ideas about the design of training programs. Some reviewed UCEA cases, both written and filmed, and other training materials. Others sought advice on universities they might profitably visit or professors with whom they might best discuss research, program design, or content issues. Still others desired to visit school systems, and several sought specialized information as, for example, on the management of research centers.

Course content remained a troublesome issue for those launching new programs. School administrators and many trainers questioned the value of general theories about administration, especially since most of them were developed in the United States. In the early stages of program development, trainers usually made heavy use of descriptions of actual problems and issues faced by those in school systems. The experience of practicing administrators was another type of valued content.

As universities assumed a role in training, conceptual content became more prominent. Theories of administration, such as those developed by UCEA professors in the 1950s and 1960s, found a place in programs in developed and developing nations. In the 1960s general theories about such phenomena as bureaucracy and small group leadership were used in such universities as Alberta in Canada, and New England in Australia. Jacob Getzels' "social process" theory and

Andrew Halpin's studies of school climate were employed in training programs and in research endeavors in a half dozen nations at least. Nigerian professors informed me in the early 1980s that they included theories which originated in the U. S. in their offerings. The very generality of theories apparently enhanced their cross-national reach and their uses in markedly different cultural contexts.

The same Nigerian professors who valued theory indicated that U.S. textbooks on such topics as school law and school finance had little relevance in their country. However, the texts were not without value. For those struggling to write books on Nigerian school law and school finance, the U. S. texts provided potential examples of the defined scope of a subject, its major divisions, and its modes of exposition. The difficulty of creating "native" textbooks for new programs can easily be underestimated. Decades could pass before such texts emerged. Books on the principalship (or headship), often the first to appear, apparently were the easiest to produce.

Those developing program content in non-English speaking nations faced special problems. Perhaps the most unusual content development project of the 1970s was conducted by Richard Bessoth, Clive Hopes, and Berthold Killait in the Federal Republic of Germany. Called a "Learning System," the five-volume set of loose-leaf materials produced by the team covered school organization and school law, planning, personnel and school climate, innovation and development, and school supervision. Exhibiting the thoroughness characteristic of German scholarship, Bessoth and his colleagues evaluated and published more than 2000 pages of materials. Almost all the content was based upon excerpts from works in English, including some developed by professors under the auspices of UCEA. Most of the works underwent a double translation process: from a non-German language into German and sometimes from translated foreign concepts to altered ones chosen to fit conditions in the Republic. That professors of educational administration and social scientists in UCEA universities had a significant impact upon the materials was unmistakably evident.

Bessoth believed that knowledge generated in other nations should inform training initiatives in the Republic. A good summary of pertinent knowledge appeared in his monograph, *School Administration As a Profession: A Comparative Study of Educational Development and Training in Six Nations (Schulverwaltung Als Beruf: Ein Internationaler Vergleich)* (Bessoth, 1975). In this work he cited approximately 110 publications.

Seven, written by members of the Bessoth project, were in German. Six in French emanated from the National Institute of School and University Administration. Five were written by Australians, four by Canadians, four by Englishmen, and the remainder, slightly more than three-fourths of the total, were by U.S. authors. Two to four professors in each of three UCEA universities (Alberta, Harvard, and Oregon) were cited for research they had done independently of UCEA. The largest number of references (14) were ones produced through UCEA endeavors. The flow of ideas, then, from the United States and UCEA into the Republic was relatively heavy.

To sum up: the overall evidence suggests that UCEA's impact upon the diffusion of training ideas into developed and developing nations in the sixties and seventies was substantial and far-reaching. Originating in a vision formed in 1963, UCEA's initial impact was achieved through the creation of the IIP. Next, UCEA supported and helped leaders from different nations develop additional organizations for nurturing exchange and development. Employing ideas as the major means of influence, UCEA leaders and those in newly created organizations became international disseminators of concepts on training and inquiry. Among the channels through which ideas were disseminated were the IIPs and face-to-face discussions with visitors from roughly 30 nations at UCEA's headquarters. UCEA's influence was enhanced by the high status accorded it by program pioneers. One leader, for example, called UCEA that *"sanctum sanctorum"* (Walker, 1969b, p. 140). Another labeled it the *"Guetestempelvereinigung"* or the organization which bestowed "the stamp of approval" on training programs in America (Bessoth, 1975, p. 17).

As one who lived at the center of diverse cross-national networks, I had the good fortune to work with an ever-changing group of gifted leaders. As we strove to unfold path-breaking programs, I felt in my more elated moments that UCEA's international accomplishments alone were sufficient rewards for the 22 years I labored in its expanding vineyards.

Notes

1. For the Michigan seminar papers see Baron, G., Cooper, D. H., & Walker, W. G. (Eds.). (1969). *Educational administration: International perspectives*. Chicago: Rand McNally & Company.

2. See Walker, W. G., Steel, C., & Mumford, J. (1973). *A glossary of educational terms: Usage in five English speaking countries* St. Lucia, Queensland: University of Queensland Press.

3. The fifth IIP was conducted after I left UCEA. Developed largely by B. O. Ukeje, President of the Nigerian Association for Administration and Planning and Provost at the Anambra State College of Education in Awka, Nigeria, the program began on August 3, and ended on August 20, 1982. See Ukeje, B. O., Ocho, L. O., & Fagbamiye, E. O. (Eds.). 1986). *Issues and concerns in educational administration and planning.* Yaba, Lagos: Macmillan Nigeria Publishers Limited.

4. For the seminar proceedings see Thomas, A. R., Farquhar, R. H., & Taylor, W. (Eds.). (1975). *Educational administration in Australia and abroad*. St. Lucia, Queensland: University of Queensland Press.

5. For an early description of CCEA see Walker, W. G. (1972). UCEA's bright son at morning: The Commonwealth Council for Educational Administration. *Educational Administration Quarterly*, VIII(2), 16-25. For more recent data about CCEA's attainments see Walker, W., Farquhar, R., & Hughes, M. (Eds.). (1991). *Advancing education: School leadership in action*. Basingstoke, UK: Falmer Press.

6. For the seminar papers see Hughes, M. (Ed.). 1975). *Administering education: International challenge*. London: The Athlone Press.

7. The title of the Society's journal has changed several times. Its first name was *Educational Administration Bulletin*; its second was *Educational Administration*; and as of this writing it was *Educational Management &Administration*.

8. For additional details see Bessoth, R. (1978). First steps in an emerging field: Educational administrator preparation in West Germany. *UCEA Review*, XIX(2), 1-6.

9. A portion of the paper is available in Culbertson, J. (1974). UCEA-CCEA relationships. *UCEA Review*, XV(5), 15-20.

10. Two of the studies were published. See Miklos, E., & Nixon, M. (1978). *Educational administration programs in Canadian universities*. Edmonton, Alberta: University of Alberta; Silver, P. F., & Spuck D. W. (Eds.). (1978). *Preparatory programs for educational administrators in the*

United States. Columbus, OH: The University Council for Educational Administration.

11. For the papers presented at the fourth IIP see Farquhar, R. H., & Housego, I. E. (Eds.). (1980). *Canadian and comparative educational administration.* Vancouver: The University of British Columbia.

12. For details see Sander, B. (1980). Interamerican cooperation in educational administration: A doorway to development. *UCEA Review.* XXI(2), 4-6; Lynch, P. D., & Wiggins, T. (1980). The First Interamerican Congress on Educational Administration: A North American perspective. *UCEA Review,* XXI(2), 7-9; and Monzon, I. B. (1980). The First Interamerican Congress on Educational Administration and the Brasilia Declaration: A central American perspective. *UCEA Review,* XXI(2), 10-13.

13. See Culbertson, J. (1985). Administrative preparation: Pre-service. In G. Husen (Ed.), *International Encyclopedia of Education* (Vol. I, pp. 81-85). New York: Pergamon Press, Ltd.

14. For a more general picture of the progress made by U. S. leaders in becoming less provincial, see Walker, W. G. (1984). Administrative narcissism and the tyranny of isolation: Its decline and fall, 1954-84. *Educational Administration Quarterly,* XX(4), 6-23.

15. For a brief description of the Anglian Regional Management Centre and its exchange program see Layton, D. H. (1977). An interview with J. L. Davis of the Anglian Regional Management Centre in Great Britain. *UCEA Review,* XIX(1), 33-38.

References

Bessoth, R. (1975). Schulverwaltung als Beruf: Ein internationaler Vergleich. Saarbruecken: Institut fuer Sozialforschung und Sozialwirtschaft.

Coombs, P. H. (1968). *The world educational crisis.* New York: Oxford University Press.

Culbertson, J. A. (1969). A new initiative in educational administration. In G. Baron, D. H. Cooper, & W. G. Walker (Eds.), *Educational administration: International perspectives* (pp. 1-7). Chicago: Rand McNally & Company.

Culbertson, J. A. (1980). The Interamerican Society: An enlarged vista and new opportunity. *UCEA Review,* XXI(2) 1-2.

Fonderie, B. (1986). The European Forum on Educational Administration: Its achievements and aspirations. *European Forum on Educational Administration Newsletter,* I(1) 3-9.

Richardson, J. A. (1963). Editorial. *Journal of Educational Administration.*, 1(1), 1-2.

Sander, B. (1980). Interamerican cooperation in educational administration: A doorway to development. *UCEA Review*, XXI(2), 4-6.

Shin, C. S. (1978). A new program in Korea. *UCEA Review*, XIX(2), 11-12.

Taylor, W. (1969). Simulation and the comparative study of educational administration. In G. Baron et al (Eds.), *Educational administration: International perspectives* (pp. 207-222). Chicago: Rand McNally & Company.

Walker, W. G. (1969a). Editorial. *The Journal of Educational Administration*. VII(2), 95-96.

Walker, W. G. (1969b). Trends and issues in the preparation of educational administrators. In G. Baron et al (Eds.), *Educational administration: International perspectives* (pp. 134-153). Chicago: Rand McNally & Company.

Walker, W. G. (1972). UCEA's bright son at morning: The Commonwealth Council for Educational Administration. *Educational Administration Quarterly*, VIII(2), 16-25.

Wiggins, T., & Lynch, P. (1977). The Interamerican Council for Educational Administration. *UCEA Review*, XIX(1), 31-32.

8

The Monroe City Simulation

"First-hand knowledge is the ultimate basis of intellectual life. To a large extent book-learning conveys second-hand information, and as such can never rise to the importance of immediate practice... It is tame because it has never been scared by facts."

Alfred North Whitehead

In 1969 UCEA began a huge, six year developmental endeavor in Monroe City, the pseudonym for what at the time was one of America's twenty largest cities. Ending in 1975, the project was popularly known as the Monroe City simulation. Carrying out the endeavor were about 190 professors. Another 70 planned and managed institutes to demonstrate the instructional uses of new simulations, and scores of Monroe City educators and citizens provided professors the data needed to build the simulations. Each of 19 teams sought to build a simulation. Ten succeeded. An estimated 45,000 trainees experienced at least one of the ten new simulations in instructional settings.

Because of aggressive annexation policies and heavy immigration, especially from the south and the Appalachian region of the country, Monroe City's population grew rapidly in the 1950s and 1960s. In 1969 it had 589,555 inhabitants, of which 78 per cent were Caucasian, and 22 per cent were African American. For more than a century the city had served as a busy transportation center. During the Civil War, for instance, it became a focal military point. Possessing a relatively small manufacturing capability in 1969, its major economic activities other than transportation included contract construction, wholesale trade, insurance, and real estate transactions.

Although its problems were not as severe as those in America's largest cities, they were becoming increasingly salient. So were initiatives designed to ameliorate them. Although Monroe City had razed and rebuilt some of its slums, it still had blighted areas populated largely by African Americans and Appalachian migrants. The rehabilitation of poverty stricken areas was often attended by controversy. For example, some of Monroe City's more conservative citizens, fearing "federal controls," fought valiantly but vainly against accepting and using government funds to address problems of blight and poverty.

The school system faced a greater range of issues than did any of the city's institutions. Serving a student population in 1969, of 110,000, of which 30,000 were African Americans, it was affected by external and internal controversy. The schools faced six major challenges, according to data obtained from interviews with selected school and community leaders. Two illustrative challenges were "education and race" and "curriculum reform." Although the Board of Education had enacted desegregation policies, many African American as well as "liberal" white citizens were disillusioned with the results obtained. Many of those interviewed believed that the Board of Education had also assigned a low priority to curriculum reform.

Grounded in Monroe City's perceived challenges and the problems underlying them, the ten newly created UCEA simulations were "reality" oriented ones. Instead of being driven by computer models, they were shaped by a myriad of facts about an urban school system, its setting, and its problems. Undergirding the simulations was the belief that learning *about* administration and learning *to* administer are very different things. Effective training programs not only should transmit knowledge, but also they should provide trainees opportunities to apply it. By simulating decision problems, by showing professors how to use them, and by enabling higher education institutions to purchase them, UCEA afforded universities unique opportunities to strengthen the clinical dimensions of their training programs.

Launching the Monroe City Simulation

The need for the Monroe City simulation emerged from UCEA planning activities. Nurturing its conception were statements made by professors in 1968 at nine regional meetings. At each meeting professors identified problems they thought UCEA should address during the 1969-74 period. At the very first meeting in Seattle, Washington, professors highlighted the need to improve the training of urban school administrators. At subsequent meetings they repeatedly emphasized this need. Almost all had acquired their administrative experience in suburban or rural settings.

Such messages indicated that one of UCEA's 1969-74 goals should be improved training for urban school administrators. Less obvious and more perplexing was the strategy UCEA should employ to achieve the goal. After months of study and thought, I arrived at the urban simulation idea. Since the simulation would be an expensive, complex, and risky undertaking, I encountered skeptical views. One specialist in urban education asked me, during a breakfast conversation in February, 1969, why I believed that UCEA could gain entry into an urban school system to depict its problems. Even if entry were gained, what made me think that working relations could be maintained for five years? Concerned about the project's costs, he questioned UCEA's ability to obtain the funds needed for such a large scale and long term effort.

Fortunately, such concerns were not solidly grounded. The first school superintendent I invited to cooperate with UCEA responded positively and promptly. He wanted to see training programs for urban school administrators improved. In addition, he saw in the proposed simulation a promising strategy for effecting improvements. During the 1969-75 period Monroe City personnel helped scores and scores of professors acquire much information, while an associate superintendent "cleared" for UCEA's use thousands of pages, about eight hours of films and filmstrips, and more than two hours of audio recordings.

In the spring of 1969 the UCEA Board of Trustees approved staff plans for developing the simulation. In September, 1969, the staff launched the endeavor without external funds but with much contributed help from professors. Troy McKelvey of the State University of New York at Buffalo joined the central staff as a UCEA Fellow. Supported by a fully paid leave from his institution, Troy provided UCEA planning and management help during 1969-70. Joining the UCEA staff in the spring of 1970 was Gerald Rasmussen, a professor of school administration at California State College at Los Angeles. Recipient of a "creative" leave and an appointment as a UCEA Associate, he played the dominant role in creating the Janus Junior High simulation.

The Wilson Senior High Simulation

Six of the Monroe City simulations focused upon administrative positions. Three were school level ones: the Abraham Lincoln

Elementary, the Janus Junior High, and the Wilson Senior High principalships. The other three were central office positions: the School Psychologist, the School Superintendency, and the Special Education Director. Four of the ten simulations dealt with administrative functions: collective negotiations, curricular decision-making, problem sensing, and site budgeting. To shed light on the new training materials, I will describe selected features of the Wilson Senior High simulation.

The team which constructed the Wilson principalship had its first meeting in January, 1970. Chaired by Lloyd Duvall of the University of Rochester, the eight member team decided to simulate a high school located in a neighborhood which was undergoing major change. After choosing Monroe City's Wilson High School as the setting for its endeavor, the team began its work. Fifteen months after its initial meeting, the team had completed the simulation.

In April and May of 1971 selected members of the Wilson team demonstrated their new simulation at 11 UCEA institutes on "New Methods and Materials"—10 at U. S. universities and one at the University of Montreal in Canada. Subsequently, the simulation was demonstrated at a half dozen additional institutes.

Some of Wilson's components were designed to give trainees a "feel" for the Wilson community. Typically, trainees took a "tour" of the neighborhood through the medium of a 120-slide presentation with an accompanying commentary. As they viewed pictures of people, places, and things, they gained a feel for the Wilson community. Since the commentary illuminated how current scenes of people and places differed from those of the early 1960s, they also gained insights into the transitional nature of the Wilson community.

Wilson's principals-to-be also heard recorded interviews as, for example, with a poverty agency director, a youth social worker, a local businessman, and community-school workers. As trainees listened to the local business man and the poverty worker, they heard messages which were tinged with bitterness. The poverty agency director maintained that Wilson's teachers and administrators did not understand the culture from which their poverty stricken students came. Trained in an earlier era, most, he believed, neither accepted their students nor taught them effectively. On the other hand, the businessman was bitter because the newcomers, as he saw them, did not respect the community's long-time inhabitants, their properties, or their businesses. Put differently, they had diminished the value of his property and the volume of his business.

After they obtained a feel for the Wilson community, trainees were introduced to Monroe City and its school system (see below). Then, they became principals. Called "Chris Bush," a name applicable to both female and male trainees, each principal was assigned a particular desk or table. On each desk or table were two in-baskets which contained letters, memos, notes, and telegrams. Chris Bush's first task was to make decisions about the problems posed in 42 in-basket items. Two illustrative items follow. Sent to "Chris" in 1971, the first was written by Dorothy Prince, Wilson High's school nurse, while the second was penned by Carol Deke, a Wilson teacher.

1. I am very concerned about pregnancies at Wilson. We already have 14 known girls who are pregnant, and it is only October. I am aware of the policy of the board of education which prohibits me from dispensing birth control information to any student, but I must tell you that I have given out considerable referral information. I must do this out of my medical and professional conscience.

These policies are not helpful — either to the students' health (which is my concern) or to their education (which should be your main concern). I feel that I cannot do an adequate job of school nursing if these rules continue. Something must be done.

2. I think that Elijah Washington, the sweeper in our section of the building, is drinking during the school day. I have smelled alcohol on his breath several times. He does a good job, I know, but I would prefer that he not be cleaning up the locker room while the boys are still there. I have heard a couple of the boys joking about his drinking, and I don't think it's a good idea for him to be around them in that condition. I am not making any formal accusations, and I hope you won't carry me into this any further.

While the "principals" were making decisions about items such as those just noted, they were from time to time interrupted by Wilson's secretary who posed problems to them through audio recorded messages. Some of the problems were unusual ones (e.g. a reported bomb threat), while others were more routine (e.g. a request from the superintendent for data on student drop-out). At times trainees were also asked to view problems presented to them on one of the following films: "Karen and Yvonne," "Sally," "Chuck," "Frank," "Carlos," "Outside Advice," "The Outsider," and "A Sincere Proposal." For example, the film, "Sally," featured one of Sally's teachers, a white male; the Wilson vice principal, an African American male, and Sally, an eleventh grade African American student. Earlier in the day the teacher, after an emotional exchange with Sally, had sent her to the vice principal's office. Distracted along the way, she had arrived late. In the filmed discussion which took place in the office of the vice principal, the teacher argued that a harsher penalty should be imposed upon Sally than the one advocated by the vice principal. As the film ended, the teacher slammed his fist on the table and demanded that the problem be turned over to Principal Bush.

Other decision problems were transmitted to the "principals" via five written case studies. One, for example, involved the complaints of an unhappy parent about the secrecy surrounding Wilson's student files. Yet another way "interruption" problems were presented was through role playing situations (e.g. dealing with a student "walkout"). Finally, trainees made a series of sequential decisions about a problem presented in its different stages. One such problem involved a white teacher who had made negative comments about Wilson's students in a local TV interview. In such cases trainees initially received information only about the problem's first phase. In the subsequent phase they obtained information about the postulated results of their previous decision plus other relevant data. Such problems were presented in three to five phases.

As a rule, the trainees, after resolving "interruption" problems, resumed their work on the in-basket items. In all their decisions they had available a Faculty Handbook and a Student Handbook which contained many of Wilson's policies and procedures. They also possessed an information file on such subjects as school enrollment, faculty attitudes, student attitudes, and Wilson's course offerings.

When trainees completed each decision, they described in writing the solution they had reached and the reasons they had chosen it. By using written records and the experiences on which they were based, professors could pursue a variety of instructional objectives. Three popular ones were to help trainees (1) acquire needed administrative skills; (2) examine how concepts and theories could shed light on practice, and (3) understand and assess the values which shaped their decisions. For instance, by asking trainees to solve many problems in a brief period, they could be taught pertinent skills for handling information overload. How professors approached the objectives of theory use and value analysis can be clarified by examples. Those offered will show how one professor made use of the sequential case in which a Wilson teacher made the following comment on local television: "Most of the students do very well, but the pupils who are new to the school are inferior in their ability to learn."

The case had three choice points. The first was at a meeting of concerned parents who demanded that the teacher who made the negative comment be fired. After the trainees had made their choices, the professor would ask a sample of them to describe their decisions vis-a-vis the demand and the reasons for them. The reported choices were usually diverse. One trainee, for example, might have chosen to defend the teacher's action, another might have agreed to pursue the parents' demand, and a third might have opted for more time to study the problem. Reflected in the stated reasons for their choices were the differing values which undergirded their decisions. The trainee who defended the teacher could have valued highly improved teacher morale, given its sagging tendencies at Wilson. The trainee who agreed to pursue the parents' demand might have placed a high priority on the equal treatment of all students, given the alienation of the disadvantaged at Wilson. The third trainee, averse to conflict, might have placed a high value upon the skilled handling of public relations. By assessing the diverse courses of action, trainees could gain insight into the strengths and limitations of the crucial values which were influencing their actions.

Before illustrating how the professor used concepts in instruction, the phases of the case about the TV comments need to be described. The second phase was based on the premise that Dr. Bush, in the face of charges that he was "dodging the issue," chose to study the problem further. During his study of it, Chris met with a group of teachers who attested that the earlier comment about Wilson's students was accurate. The third phase presumed that the principal had decided to support the teacher. His decision was followed by rumors that a joint student-parent boycott was being planned, and that an article in a local paper titled "Racism Sweeps Wilson High" would appear the next day.

Among the concepts which the professor introduced into the

discussion was "decision trees." According to the concept, decisions have nodes and branches like trees. Over time the decision branches which grow from a node produce fresh ones which in turn generate new offspring. Initially, the trainees used the concept to map their decisions. By displaying actions taken at the three choice points in the sequential case, trainees could see clearly the various branches which grew from the three choice points. The result was a comprehensive map of their choices which they could study and analyze. Having learned how to apply the concept of "decision trees," they then could employ it in future situations to generate decision branches, to evaluate them, to choose the one judged most fruitful, and to formulate a sound rationale for their chosen actions.

The School System and Its Setting

Accompanying each of the 10 simulations were many facts and generalizations about Monroe City and its school system. The information was richer than that provided in the Jefferson Township (see Chapter Three) and the Madison simulations (see Chapter Four). Dimensions of the larger environment in which Monroe City's school administrators functioned were depicted through audio-visual and written components. A 30-minute film titled "Life in Monroe City" was designed to shed light on the "spirit" of the city. Viewers of the film gained a feel for the city's people and its dominant activities.

A second component consisted of eight "background" booklets. Describing the environment in which the school system was embedded, the booklets' titles and authors were:

1. *The Monroe City School System and Its Environment: An Overview* by Alan K. Gaynor.

2. *Monroe City: Its Setting and Demography* by Doris W. Ryan, John C. Walden, and Troy V. McKelvey.

3. *The Political Environment of the Monroe City School System* by John C. Walden.

4. *The Economic Environment of the Monroe City School System* by Walter G. Hack et al.

5. *Monroe City's Mass Media* by John Spiess.

6. *Patterns of Influence in Monroe City* by James Frasher.

7. *Inter-Agency Relations in Monroe City* by John Andes.

8. *Community Organizations and Their Demands Upon the School System* by H. James Mahan.

The booklets provided trainers and trainees much information about Monroe City. Booklet 6, for example, revealed that the "Fleet" and "Shillings" families along with some large real estate owners were dominant members of Monroe City's "power structure." The Fleet family, primarily Republican, and the Shillings family, largely Democratic, were especially influential. Although leaders of the two families often disagreed with one another, they influenced most of the city's major educational policies. Booklet 8, on the other hand, contained detailed information on the demands that Monroe City's community organizations were making on the schools. Thus, the Black Parents' League had demanded that the Board of Education make 27 changes to improve the school in its locality as, for example, mandatory human relations training for the school's teachers and administrators and special tutors for remedial readers. The Urban Education Coalition had a broader set of demands (e.g. the establishment of local assessment councils in all schools).

Also accompanying the 10 simulations was an array of information about Monroe City's school system. One segment of a filmstrip titled "Monroe City: Its Environment and Educational Setting," for instance, depicted changes in demographic data and described the import of the changes for Monroe City's schools. Eight "background" booklets provided detailed information about the school system:

1. *Monroe City's Board of Education* by Richard Saxe.

2. *Internal Organization and Decision Making in the School System* by Doris W. Ryan.

3. *Monroe City's Educational Program* by David K. Wiles.

4. *The School System's Professional Staff* by Alan K. Gaynor.

5. *Monroe City's Public Schools: Professional Negotiations* by Alan K. Gaynor.

6. *The Students of Monroe City* by Charles E. Kline.

7. *Special Education in Monroe City* by Lawrence W. Marrs et al.

8. *Perceived Challenges to Educational Leadership in Monroe City* by Mark Shibles.

Containing 3 maps, 66 tables, and 3 figures, Booklet 6, for example, provided copious data on such topics as student enrollment in each of Monroe City's 159 schools, enrollment trends in the city since the mid-1950s, and recent drop-out rates.

By publishing the data in 16 booklets rather than in one large volume, UCEA encouraged professors to use the information flexibly and experimentally. The booklets' uses varied from one simulation to another and from one professor to another. One user required trainees to develop a five year educational plan and, in so doing, to study all 16 booklets. On the other hand, many professors expected trainees to read booklets only when they needed to resolve specific decision problems. Still other uses were linked to specialized interests. Specialists in the politics of education, for example, were more likely to require trainees to read the booklet on the political environment than was a specialist in personnel administration.

"Interpretive" and "Conceptual" Content

Supplementing the simulation materials were "Interpretive" and "Conceptual" content. Interpretive content featured applications of concepts and theories to Monroe City's problems and/or their contexts. Paul Peterson, author of *Changing Power Relationships in Monroe City* , showed how Monroe City's political system affected schooling decisions. The school psychologist simulation offered a filmed example of interpretive content. This simulation by Ann W. Engin of Ohio State and Jane N. Miller of the Mishawaka, Indiana, school system, contained a 50-minute film called "The Three Faces of Theory". In the film a school psychologist and a teacher analyzed the learning disability of a student from three different theoretical perspectives: psychoanalytic, behaviorist, and phenomenological. The film showed how the disparate perspectives produced differing prescriptions for handling the student's disability.[1]

Interpretive pieces provided instructors teaching tools and models for developing their own content. Since only a dozen papers and one film were produced, the following question arises: Why did professors not develop more interpretive content? Scholars responded to the question usually with one of two answers. Some said they did not have enough facts about Monroe City to apply their favorite concepts. Others were skeptical about the cogency of theories and the feasibility of applying them meaningfully to Monroe City data.

"Conceptual content" had no direct links to descriptive or interpretive content. However, it had logical links to Monroe City's challenges and problems. One example was presented in the book, *The Principal in Metropolitan Schools* (Erickson and Reller, 1978). Offering content related to urban educational and management problems, the book's editors began by identifying major challenges faced by the principals of Monroe City's three simulated schools. They then invited authors to write chapters on chosen challenges as, for example, education and ethnicity, student rights, and the development of school programs.

Accompanying the director of special education simulation was a "book of readings." Assembled by Maynard Reynolds of the University of Minnesota and by Don Ray Hafner of the Educational Service Center in Austin, Texas, the book contained already published articles and chapters on financing special education, mainstreaming special education students, and other related problems. Two professors on the "Collective Negotiations" team also assembled a set of readings from already existing materials (Cresswell and Murphy, 1976). Distributed by a commercial publisher, the content was logically linked to Monroe City's simulated problems.

The extent to which the examples of conceptual content were used varied considerably. Since the book of readings on special education administration was distributed as a part of the simulation, it had extensive use by those who experienced the simulation. Because the collective negotiations and principalship books were not included in the Monroe City packages, they had limited use by the adopters of the two simulations. This was especially true for the principalship book whose authors prepared fresh content rather than assembled published materials. By the time the book appeared, UCEA had already ceased sponsoring institutes on the Monroe City simulations.[2] Thus, both of the commercially published books were used largely for purposes other than those pursued through the simulations.

Major Challenges Emerge

In January, 1970, 37 professors from 17 UCEA universities came together to plan the initial phases of the Monroe City simulation. Welcoming the group was UCEA Fellow, Troy McKelvey, co-ordinator of the three-day event. In his introductory remarks Troy facetiously observed that since UCEA neither paid the salaries of the participating professors nor determined their promotions, it had little power over their actions. He then stressed that UCEA was offering professors unique developmental opportunities.

Having volunteered to take part in the project, the 37 professors had already formulated ideas about the simulations for UCEA to consider and pursue. At the meeting they explored the ideas in some depth. Six individuals, led by Dean Bowles of Wisconsin, began defining what later came to be the "Abraham Lincoln Elementary" principalship. Another group of eight, chaired by Lloyd Duvall of the University of Rochester, focused upon the "Wilson Senior High" principalship. Gerald Rasmussen of California State College at Los Angeles led a six member group engaged in planning the "Janus Junior High" simulation. A ten member group, chaired by Jack Parker of the University of Oklahoma, focused upon Monroe City's superintendency. Finally, preparers of the "background booklets" reviewed their plans.

The January meeting set in motion a dynamic which would generate continuing challenges for the central staff. One was encouraging professors to launch Monroe City endeavors beyond those projected initially. At the meeting I outlined varied possibilities, including a school board simulation, a "school of the future," a set of planning problems, and inter-agency decisions. Stressing the need for newly simulated leadership problems, I pointed to such areas as race relations and curriculum reform in Monroe City. Several professors responded immediately to the proposals. For instance, after the meeting ended, Donald Piper, University of Rochester, and other professors explored the idea of a school board simulation.

Problems of priority were also ever present. For example, some argued that it would be wasteful to develop three principalship simulations. However, I recommended that three be developed so that more professors could learn about urban school administration. In addition, if UCEA had created only the Abraham Lincoln Elementary School, most junior and senior high principals would have viewed it as an irrelevant training vehicle.

The rapid growth of the enterprise created special demands for effective coordination. By November, 1971, ninety professors and another dozen local, state, and national leaders had helped advance at least one of the simulation efforts (Blough, Culbertson, Martin and Pirtle, 1971, pp. ix-xi). Forty-four professors had coordinated UCEA training institutes to demonstrate the new simulations (pp xi-xii). By 1975 eighty-four professors and/or school leaders had facilitated the demonstration of new simulations by coordinating institutes.

As the number of participants ballooned, financial support became a problem. Because of UCEA's cooperative ethic, professors and their universities contributed much time to the endeavor. Without such help the six year project could never have come to fruition. Yet UCEA needed funds to support the travel costs of professors who spent time in Monroe City and who attended meetings at UCEA's headquarters. Substantial UCEA funds were also required to produce audio-visual and other materials for distribution. In 1970 the U. S. Office of Education awarded UCEA a $65,000 grant—a timely event. Other efforts to obtain external monies failed.[3] Luckily, revenues from the sales of principalship simulations—the first ones completed—covered the travel costs incurred by future Monroe City developers.

The greatest challenge was to help teams realize their missions. Since the Monroe City simulation was only one of six goals UCEA pursued during the 1969-74 period, finding needed time to help team leaders resolve development issues was one dimension of the challenge. A more basic one was to ensure that teams moved beyond talk to action and transformed abstract ideas into concrete simulations. Because of the heavy demands most UCEA associate directors became involved in the project. For example, Associate Director John Blough played a major role in preparing simulations for distribution following their development, while Fred Frank coordinated the work of the team which developed the simulation on curricular decision making.

Holder of a Ph.D. from Ohio State, John Blough had earlier served as an advertising and marketing executive at Standard Oil, before he became a teacher and then an assistant superintendent of schools in Ohio. He brought to UCEA outstanding management skills and a capacity for probing critique. Earlier in his career Associate Director Fred Frank had received a B.A. and an M.A. degree from Syracuse University, where he specialized in the study of music. Before obtaining a Ph.D. from the University of Buffalo, he had taught music in the public schools of New York. Immediately after his appointment, he sought to understand UCEA by delving into documents about its past. In addition, he showed an intense interest in the political life of UCEA.

Successes and Failures

Chart I lists the names of completed and uncompleted simulations. Underlying the two lists is an important question: why did some teams complete their simulations, while others failed to do so? As I shared their satisfactions, frustrations, failures, and successes, I searched for pertinent answers. Unable to find a single or simple answer, I arrived at an array of possible explanations related to the nature of the simulations, the composition of teams, and team leadership.

CHART I
Completed and Uncompleted Simulations

Completed	Uncompleted
Abraham Lincoln Principalship	Computerized Simulation
Collective Negotiations	Curriculum Reform
Curricular Decision-Making	Education and Race
Janus Principalship	Educational Planning
Problem Sensing	Inter-Agency Relations
School Psychologist	Public Relations Director
School Superintendency	School Board
Site Budgeting	School Counselor
Special Education Director	School of the Future
Wilson Principalship	

The information in Chart I implies that it is easier to simulate well established posts (e. g. the principalship) than less established ones (e. g. the educational planner) or administrative functions (e. g. curriculum reform). Six of the ten completed simulations involved established positions, while two of the functions simulated (site budgeting and problem sensing) were embedded in the Wilson principalship. Why was it easier to simulate established positions? For one thing, the

Monroe City developers had only utilized the Jefferson and Madison materials—simulations which were centered in the principalship, the superintendency, and related positions. Since they had had no experience with simulated functions, they were better equipped to simulate well defined administrative posts.

Those who sought to simulate less established posts faced other difficulties. The educational planning team, for example, was unsure about where to locate the planning function. Should it be designed to serve all school personnel and, therefore, not be attached to any one position? Should it be linked principally to the associate superintendency for curriculum? Should it be placed in a newly created position? Given the resulting ambiguity, it was difficult for the team to agree upon the location of the planning function, a working definition of it, a taxonomy of its problems, and its short and long time frames.

A major determinant of a team's success or failure was its composition. Midway through the project I coined the terms "abstractitis" and "concretitis" to highlight two maladies (Culbertson, 1972, pp. 6-7). Teams which suffered from the latter focused largely upon specific problems and practices. Achieving a well conceived design to guide their actions was very difficult for such teams. On the other hand, teams which were afflicted by "abstractitis" focused mainly upon concepts per se and gave little attention to their application. While the latter usually failed to cross the divide between concepts and actions, the former had much difficulty building bridges between particulars and general concepts. Thus, both maladies often led to aborted efforts.

The best single predictor of a team's success or failure was whether or not its members had actually used simulations in instruction. If most of a team's members had done so, the probability of its success was heightened. Believing in the significance of theory-practice relationships, users of simulation had already gained insights into its design, purpose, potential, and impacts.

A team was also highly dependent upon the abilities of its leader. Because a team could falter or fail at many points on the way to a completed simulation, its leader needed numerous skills. As implied above, Lloyd Duvall, who headed the Wilson High team, was an effective leader. Why was he able to overcome problems which derailed the work of other teams? In addressing this question, I will describe selected aspects of his leadership. Members of his team were: Roland Barnes, University of Pittsburgh; Everett Nicholson, Don Tolliver, and

Ted Ulrich, Purdue; Powell Toth, West Virginia; John Trufant, Tennessee State; and David Wiles, Ontario Institute for Studies in Education.

Unless a team attained a viable set of objectives, it inevitably failed. The Wilson team, with Lloyd's help, formulated a mission statement at its first meeting (January, 1970), namely: to simulate a high school in a Monroe City neighborhood where there was white "flight" and a heavy influx of African Americans. At its next meeting in April the team determined the components it would develop. Informing the decisions about components were thoughtful ideas which were rooted in experiences Lloyd had gained during a three day visit to Wilson and in a careful assessment of these experiences.

At its April meeting the team moved past another crucial point, reaching an agreement on the tasks each member would perform in developing the simulation. Usually difficult to achieve, an effective division of labor was essential to a team's success. Because busy professors tended to be wary of taking on large UCEA tasks, a leader engaged in helping a team structure its work needed much sensitivity.

Team leaders confronted a range of bottlenecks. Common ones were member "drop-out" and unproductive members who remained with their groups. In its early months the Wilson team lost several members. In contrast to less successful team leaders, Lloyd, with the help of the UCEA staff, moved quickly to replace unproductive members with motivated ones. In the latter stages of the project the Wilson team faced an uncommon problem, when they failed to get the usual help from UCEA universities in film production. At that point Lloyd Duvall enlisted the aid of an outstanding drama teacher in a high school in his home city. A few months later the films and the other simulation components were all ready for demonstration. Without Duvall's entrepreneurial abilities, the simulation would either have fallen into the "uncompleted" category or not have fully attained its objectives.

An unusual outcome of the endeavor was a collection of materials assembled by Lloyd which, among other things, showed the crucial role which practice-related thinking played in the development effort. About two inches thick, the materials contain, for example, all the memos and letters Lloyd sent to his team, to its individual members, and to members of the UCEA staff as well as the responses he had received. The collection reflects an ever present tension between concepts and actions and at least three types of practice-related thinking. One type was directional in nature. It enabled the Wilson team to refine continuously its directions and to move steadily toward a completed simulation. For example, the team began with a general mission statement and moved to a specific set of objectives (i.e components to be developed). Deductive processes, while helpful, were not the only clarifiers of direction. The facts which Lloyd Duvall gathered during his early three-day visit at Wilson also shaped the objectives which guided the development effort.

Central to the second type of thinking were problem finding and problem solving. For instance, Lloyd identified a puzzling problem during his three day visit to Monroe City: what was "reality" at Wilson, and how could it best be represented in the simulation? His efforts to use data he had obtained to depict background features of the Wilson School ended in frustration. The approach, he concluded, inevitably produced biased views of "reality." He solved the problem by recommending that actual documents (e. g. Wilson's handbook for teachers) be used as "background" components.[4]

The third type of practice-related thinking was more wholistic and integrative. Lloyd recognized very early that as a team leader he needed a clear vision of the project's desired outcomes (personal telephone conversation, April, 1993). One facet of his vision was that each of the simulated decision problems should be complex and "rich" enough to generate multiple instructional "yields." During his first visit to Wilson he searched for problems which matched his vision. In a memo sent to his team members he described five problems of the type he hoped could be simulated.

Integrative thinking was also needed to achieve effective and accurate fits between and among the parts of the simulation. An example of such thinking dealt with the separate tasks of individual team members and how they could be performed in reinforcing ways. The memos reveal that Lloyd was often concerned about achieving harmonious team expressions. A second example of integrative thinking had to do with the different phases of the project. At given times the team focused upon a specified phase of the project. However, Wilson's team leader, while directing a given phase, was thinking about how future phases (e.g. the evaluation or the demonstration of the simulation) could be effectively executed.

By the time the Wilson team had completed its work, another team, which had begun its work when the Wilson team did, was still unclear about its objectives. Thus, I was pressed to find a new leader for the group who in turn failed to help the team achieve success. A third enabled the team to complete its simulation—four years after its initial meeting. Thus, the following question arises: why did the team's first two leaders fail? First, they were handicapped because neither had used simulations to instruct administrators. Second, they apparently lacked the entrepreneurial skills to cope with the uncommon challenges they faced. Third, at least one of the leaders was much more interested in exploring Monroe City's problems than in simulating them. His most valued experience was that of a dinner discussion about Monroe City's problems in the superintendent's home. Deeply interested in what administrators ought to do, he liked to project desirable courses of action. Professors who focused strongly upon advocating administrative solutions, I concluded, often lacked the motivation either to develop or to use simulations.

The curriculum reform team had strong beliefs about the functions trainers should perform —beliefs which affected its approach to goal setting. In its initial meeting the team set forth guiding objectives for a workshop. For instance, the group decided that the first day of a projected ten day workshop should focus upon "the techniques and values of simulation," while the fifth and sixth days should deal with "needs assessment, the evaluation of curriculum, planning and implementation" (*UCEA Newsletter*, XIV(1), p. 12). Such objectives were appropriate for a workshop. However, they were only tangentially related to objectives needed for developing a simulation. Thus, the team never attained a viable set of simulation objectives.

Since the attainment of a clearly stated set of objectives was crucial, the problem deserves some comment. Most teams grounded their objectives in the problems of the administrative post to be simulated. They acquired the needed data in various ways. The superintendency group asked UCEA professors in six urban universities to obtain data from their local superintendents about problems the latter were encountering. The Abraham Lincoln group "wired" a principal to obtain audio-recordings of all of the school-related messages he uttered during a five day period. The special education team drew upon an intensive study of problems in a very large school system.

After gathering pertinent information, teams usually classified their data into categories of problems. Categories identified by the superintendency and the director of special education teams, respectively, were "superintendent-school board relationships" and "mainstreaming." Implicit in a classification of problems was a set of viable objectives. The team's task was to simulate the problems in each of the categories in the classification scheme.

Although the strategy enabled teams to define objectives clearly, it had its limitations. First, problem statements could be biased and superficial. For example, members of school boards would have offered a different set of problems about superintendent-school board relationships than did the superintendents. An analysis by a third party would have produced a different list of problems. Second, since the objectives were stated in terms of the problems to be simulated, they left unclear the instructional outcomes to be attained.

Goals derived from idealized conceptions could be so grand that they soared far above the realities of Monroe City. Inherent in Samuel Popper's cutting-edge projections was a huge gap between guiding ideals and on-going Monroe City practices (Popper, 1972, p. 10). Arguing that past patterns of school organization had "led to our current preoccupation with expectations of disaster in American education," he rejected two widely-used approaches to educational change, namely: "ad-hocism" and "imitation" (p. 10). A "future-oriented model of school organization," he stressed, had "to be simulated as a comprehensive community resource for human development" rather than as "a conveyor of cognitive learning" (p. 10).

The in-basket approach had its value, Popper acknowledged. However, it was too provincial to guide the simulation of a "school of the future." Needed was the "global" concept of "system analysis" (Popper, 1972, p. 11). A system analysis approach could generate a simulation which would provide administrators needed insights into "the political and economic interchanges which bind the network of municipal agencies into a complex delivery system of human services" (p. 11). To produce such basic insights a school of the future should be set in "Newtown," or in "Monroe City Reconstructed" (p. 11).

Popper recommended that UCEA take ten years to simulate a school of the future. During the 1974-79 period UCEA should complete the project's first phase—a simulated "school of the extended present." Such a school would be based upon extrapolations of "future-bearing trends from the most promising innovations in contemporary public school systems. . . " (p. 11). The simulation would be a *composite* of forward-moving school systems" (p. 11). The "school of the extended present" would be a prelude to a "school of the future" as well as a means for alleviating the "future shock" which professors would experience as they gave up familiar training materials and created radically different ones.

In the second phase, projected for 1979-84, developers would simulate a school of the future. Its dominant objective would be sophisticated instruction in "system analysis" (Popper, 1972, p. 11):

> Simulation exercises could center around social system feasibility and trade-off analysis, social system design and development, social system management and control, social system evaluation and change... Included in such simulation exercises might be projective case analysis and futurological gaming...

Popper's projections aroused interests not stirred by the Monroe City simulations. Excited by the concept of a "school of the extended present," ten professors from Wayne, Michigan State, and Michigan universities began exploring the idea. After adding names of "lighthouse" schools to a list prepared by Popper, they gathered data about future-bearing trends. However, they were unable to meld their findings into a composite school of the extended present.

Although nine of the nineteen teams failed to complete their simulations, their work was not without benefit. Team members profited from the opportunities they had to gather, share, discuss, and apply facts and concepts about urban school administration and the training of urban school leaders. As teams succumbed to failure, their members likely grasped more fully the difficulties UCEA developers faced in the conduct of inter-university projects.

Changes in Image and Actions

As more and more institutions purchased Monroe City simulations, UCEA acquired a different image. Some suggested that UCEA's new mien reflected the disparate characteristics of "think-tank" and "mail order" enterprises. Not all were happy with UCEA's disjointed new look. As the Monroe City project moved into its last phases, Wailand Bessent expressed concern about UCEA's new features, though much more mildly than did some others (Bessent, 1973, p. 13):

I have heard it remarked that UCEA is like a combination of Sears and Roebuck Co. and the Rand Corporation. It may be that this duality is an inevitable or even desirable fact of organizational life for UCEA, or it may be that we have drifted into this state without having made a deliberate choice. I think the issue should be examined.

The UCEA central staff, some critics said, were devoting their energies to "low level" functions which were inappropriate for an academic organization. It was undeniably true that the rapid and rising acceptance of the simulations had created problems much more concrete than that of image. In the summer of 1972 I spent most of a month working to resolve some of these problems. Because UCEA Associate Director Jack Blough, who for several years had managed UCEA's instructional materials program, had accepted the school superintendency in Bexley, Ohio, the pressure was on, it seemed, to give UCEA a bureaucratic turn by producing a *UCEA Instructional Materials Handbook* (Culbertson, 1972).

The handbook contained an array of procedures for guiding the development, demonstration, evaluation, and revision of simulations and other UCEA materials. Other procedures dealt with the printing of written documents, the duplication of audio-visual components, promotion, and the distribution of materials. Encompassed in yet another set were storage, insurance, pricing, record-keeping, accounting, inventorying, re-printings, and re-duplications. Finally, there was information about how professors could use the materials.

Several external agencies helped UCEA produce and transmit the urban materials, most notably Interstate Printers and Publishers in Danville, Illinois. Professor Lee Garber of the University of Pennsylvania had recommended the printer to me in 1962, a few years after UCEA's failed search for a publisher of the Whitman simulation. When I wrote to Interstate, its president, Russell Guinn, promptly called. An ebullient entrepreneur, Guinn reported his intent to visit UCEA's Columbus headquarters. During his visit we agreed that Interstate would print, store, and ship the written parts of Whitman. Given its dependable past performance, we turned again to Interstate in the 1970s for help in disseminating the Monroe City materials. The Motion Picture Laboratories in Memphis, Tennessee, reproduced, stored, and shipped the audio-visual components of the simulations.

Essential links in the long chain which began with development plans and ended with uses of simulations were the UCEA institutes on "New Methods and Materials." Most of the 84 institutes at which the urban simulations were demonstrated were planned and co-ordinated by professors in a UCEA or a non-UCEA training institution.[5] About 12 of the 84 institutes were held at national meetings of such organizations as the American Association of School Administrators and the Council for Exceptional Children. Designed to help prospective adopters meet UCEA's "training-for-use" requirements, the institutes attracted professors, school administrators, and graduate students.

One or more of the original developers of a simulation conducted the institutes. Attendees viewed selected audio-visual components, examined written documents, made decisions about Monroe City's school management problems, and obtained specific ideas about how to use simulations. They also recorded their judgments about the degree to which the materials possessed teaching utility, technical quality, content credibility, and motivational appeal.

No one has studied the impact of institute activities on professorial decisions to use simulations. However, many participants reported to me that the institutes motivated them to adopt and use the materials. I surmised that the specific ideas they obtained influenced them less than did the overall experience. The institute, in other words, enabled professors to confront potential changes in their training practices. Since a simulation was a much larger, more complex, and more demanding instructional tool than a textbook, the institutes provided professors needed opportunities to contemplate change. The fact that a few attendees early in institute proceedings typically announced their intent to purchase a simulation likely tilted others toward adopting the new tools.

Since attendees at institutes already had an incipient interest in adopting a simulation, they were not representative of the UCEA population. In fact many in the latter group were critical of the simulations. Near the end of the six year project I heard professors at one of America's most distinguished universities express some of the prevailing criticisms. Troubling one professor was the "trivial" nature of the problems simulated. For example, in one principal's in-basket there was a hand-written letter signed by the school's two kindergarten teachers. Attached was a request that the letter be sent to the parents of all kindergarten students. The letter suggested how parents could use the kindergarten program advantageously. For most principals the letter posed a problem because of its ungrammatical and undiplomatic language. However, the concerned professor, a specialist in educational policy, would likely have viewed its content as trivial.

The aim of those who developed in-baskets was to capture some of the down-to-earth problems which made their way into the lives of principals. In practice it was important for principals to handle in-basket items with skill and dispatch. If they did not, the senders of the items could charge them with incompetence. Thus, in-basket users assumed that administrators should have opportunities during their training to address simulated problems and to acquire the skills needed to manage them. More importantly, most believed that simulated experiences enabled trainees to acquire and apply generic concepts to simulated administrative problems.

Trainers and trainees could view simulated decision problems singly or collectively. By viewing 50 in-basket problems as a collectivity, trainees could define and address problems which transcended single issues. For example, what tactics could a principal use to deal with information overload? An enlarged vista also enabled trainees, contrary to the beliefs of the critics of simulation, to address problems of change. For example, what changes might enable principals to break out of the "boxes" of administrative trivia in which they often resided and to address basic problems of schooling? A simulated school provided a meaningful context in which principals could identify and begin to think about such questions.

Another professor suggested that the content in simulations was of such a low order it had no place in a university. Indeed, the fit between the existing content in graduate programs and the raw information about Monroe City was an awkward one. Simulations posed questions while the usual textbook focused more upon answers. It was also understandable that the critics of Monroe City would argue that its content was inferior to that which they taught. After all they had spent their careers acquiring knowledge they deemed important. However, since few if any of the critics had fully read the Monroe City materials, they failed to see the intellectual challenge it posed: the fruitful application of knowledge to practice. By returning to the above-described letter penned by the two kindergarten teachers, a small aspect of the challenge can be delineated.

When I observed trainees discussing the letter, I noted that its facts soon took a back seat, while the values of the decision makers came to the fore. Although all the trainees began with the same stimulus (i. e. the letter), they disagreed about its significance. Those who valued harmonious school-community relations placed high priority upon re-writing the letter so as not to offend parents. Those who placed a higher value upon "good" human relations wanted to ensure that supportive links between themselves and the kindergarten teachers would be maintained. Those who assigned a heavy weight to efficiency might ask a secretary to revise and dispatch the letter. Thus, the seemingly simple letter brought to the surface contending community, interper-sonal, and organizational values. The result was that neither trainers nor trainees could craft absolutely correct decisions. In such situations, then, what knowledge could professors bring to bear on problems: modes of value analysis, problem-solving concepts, decision-making theories or what? Such questions afforded both trainers and trainees viable stimuli for assessing the degree to which and the manner in which existing knowledge could inform and buttress simulated deci-sion-making.

Impacts of the Monroe City Simulation

Was UCEA's urban simulation project a success? One way of answering this question is to determine whether the project met UCEA's three official "criteria of effectiveness," which were elaborated in the early 1970s. Set in different time frames, the criteria were categorized as immediate, intermediate, and long-range. The immediate criteria had to do with the completion of simulations and judgments about their instructional potential. Intermediate criteria related to the numbers of institutions which adopted and used the simulations. Long-range criteria dealt with the impact of simulations upon the learning and performance of school administrators.

Two questions pinpointed the immediate criteria. "Did teams complete their simulations?" was the first. As already noted, ten of the targeted simulations were completed, while nine were not. On this score, then, the project's results were mixed. The second question was: "Did those who observed and rated the simulations at UCEA training institutes believe that they met such standards as motivational appeal, content believability, technical quality, and instructional value?"

Data related to immediate criteria were obtained from attendees at 48 demonstrations of the Janus, Wilson, and Abraham Lincoln simulations.

Represented at these initial demonstrations were participants from all major regions of the U. S., 24 states, and two Canadian provinces. The participants gave different ratings to the "background" components (i. e. the film, "Monroe City," the filmstrip, "Introduction to Monroe City," and the 16 booklets on aspects of Monroe City and its school system).[6] Of the three the booklets were rated highest. Ninety-five per cent of the attendees at the Abraham Lincoln institutes "rated the background booklets high in instructional value. ..." (UCEA Newsletter, XIII(3), p. 3). The filmstrip was also highly valued (p. 3): "More than 90 per cent of the respondents rated the filmstrip good or outstanding in each of the evaluation categories." Ratings of the "Monroe City" film, however, were mixed. Recipient of a high rating on its technical quality, the film received a low rating on its instructional potential. As a result, UCEA made the film an optional component of the simulations.

Respondents accorded high ratings to in-basket problems. Ninety-nine per cent of those, who rated the Abraham Lincoln simulation, valued the in-basket items highly (UCEA Newsletter, XIII(3), p. 3), while "almost all the respondents" at the Janus institutes perceived the "in-basket items" to "be believable, significant, and potentially useful. . . " (UCEA Newsletter, XII(3), p. 3).

While filmed problems were highly approved, their overall ratings, on average, were somewhat lower than those given to in-basket problems. Since the reality depicted in films was more intricate and immediate than that in in-basket items, film producers faced a greater challenge than did letter writers. In addition, the content of in-basket items was one step removed from visible human action and, therefore, could be viewed with relative detachment. On the other hand, close-up shots of emotionally-laden incidents triggered strong emotional reactions among the respondents.

With one exception all components of the Janus, Wilson, and Abraham Lincoln simulations were rated either good or outstanding by most attendees. The exception was a set of videotapes in the Janus simulation which were rated very low on technical quality. As a result, UCEA delayed shipping the Janus simulation until its major developer had produced and evaluated a new set of videotapes.

UCEA's intermediate criteria of effectiveness were rooted in Everett Rogers' sociological work on the diffusion of innovations.[7] His ideas were consonant with UCEA's experience in disseminating the Whitman school simulation. His concepts of "innovators," "early adopters," and "laggards," for instance, pinpointed stages in the diffusion process. Thus, we assumed that if the urban simulations were widely adopted, they could be judged effective. However, to employ the criterion, we had to answer the following question: how many times did the simulations have to be adopted before UCEA could claim that the Monroe City project was effective?

The intermediate criterion established for each of the three principalship simulations was adoption by 40 training institutions within three years. A similar standard was set for the director of special education. The other targets established assumed that the demand for the remaining six simulations would be less than the demand for the simulated principalships. Thus, the standards ranged from 12 for the school psychologist simulation to 25 for the school superintendency. The standards were influenced by Rogers' views about the factors which affect adoption decisions. Negative factors, for example, were the size and complexity of the simulations, their relatively high costs, (ranging, for example, from about $1000 to $1400 for the principalship simulations) the heavy work demands they placed upon professors, and their awkward fit into the structure of higher education training programs. Positive factors included the strong demand for new approaches to the training of urban school administrators and the need for reality-based training materials.

Did the project meet its intermediate criteria of effectiveness? The general answer is "yes." Since one or more of the principalship simulations was adopted by an estimated 165 institutions, they met and exceeded their criteria. The director of special education simulation also easily went beyond its criterion in part because recently enacted federal legislation had created an urgent need for special training to help school leaders effect mandated changes in special education.

The other six simulations did not meet their targets. Notably, the site budgeting simulation had no adoptions. Developed largely by a single individual near the end of the project, it was a carefully structured simulation. However, it afforded professors limited opportunities to incorporate their own ideas into its uses. Only a few institutions adopted the school psychologist simulation. Even though it was highly rated by its evaluators, it did not make its way into training programs, in part because UCEA's network encompassed few leading professors of school psychology.

Because the earlier simulations exceeded their intermediate

targets, they more than compensated for those which did not. Although the adoption targets were arbitrary ones, they served useful purposes. They reminded the field that UCEA had an important diffusion role to perform. Pinpointing the objectives to be achieved, the criteria also signaled to UCEA developers and the central staff that simulations needed to be moved off the shelves and into training programs.

Two questions pinpointed UCEA's long-range evaluation criteria: did the simulations provide useful learnings, and if so, did the learnings change on-the-job behaviors? Student responses in surveys to simulation were positive.[8] However, little can be said empirically about how learning and performance were affected by simulated experiences. In fact, only a small number of researchers studied instructional effects.[9] In addition, actual studies involved relatively small numbers of the estimated 45,000 trainees who experienced one or more of the Monroe City simulations.

Determining the extent to which learnings acquired through simulated experiences were applied in action was an even more daunting problem than that of assessing the effects of simulation on learning. In fact, I concluded during the Monroe City experience that seekers of valid generalizations about the transfer of learning to administrative performance faced insurmountable difficulties. As far as I could see, no one had attained scientifically validated generalizations about the effects of university learnings upon the on-the-job performances of physicians, lawyers, or theologians. Yet training programs for these professionals were centuries older than those for school administrators. In addition, members of the three professions historically functioned in less complex, politicized, and expansive environments than those in which school leaders performed. How could scholars, even if well funded, establish and maintain the controls needed to cope with the many factors which affect the transfer of learning to on-the-job behaviors?

Ironically, then, UCEA was unable to demonstrate that the project met its important long range criteria. Thus, it had to rely upon logically derived generalizations. For example, if the postulate that simulations represented aspects of administrative reality is accepted, it would, or might, follow that simulations afford unique opportunities to apply knowledge to practice. If one assumes that the teacher is *the* determinant of effective instruction, then the potential of simulations is significantly diminished. If one posits that individuals learn best by doing, it logically follows that those who practice decision-making in simulated situations learn more about the process than do those who simply read about it. Such derivations were typical of those which scholars generated.[10]

The simulation project can be assessed by standards other than its official ones. Did it, for example, meet the need which spawned it: helping professors gain greater competence in preparing urban school administrators? About 185 professors served on simulation teams; more than 70 coordinated UCEA training institutes; about 50 demonstrated a simulation they had helped develop; an estimated 2500 attended one of the 84 training institutes offered; and an estimated 275 used a simulation. The Monroe City endeavor, then, can rightly be viewed as a six year, North American staff development program for professors of educational administration. Although no one has studied the learnings that professors acquired, it can be logically argued that the developers and users of simulations gained fresh insights into urban school administration, as they created simulations and used them in training programs. The same is likely true, though to a much lesser degree, for those who participated in training institutes.

Still another question can be asked about the project: to what extent did its implementers exhibit effective inter-university cooperation? Employing the "inter-university group" pattern of cooperation (see Chapter Three), its teams demonstrated through their many products the efficacy, power, and outreach of inter-university cooperation. A single university, even with a multi-million dollar grant, could not have produced outcomes comparable to those attained through inter-university cooperation. Guided by the ideals inherent in the cooperative ethic, UCEA brought to fruition, with very little external funding, one of the largest developmental projects in higher education's history. The endeavor enabled UCEA professors to escape temporarily from the ever present press in their institutions to compete for tenure, promotions, able students, research grants, and the esteem of school leaders, in order to take part in a far-reaching cooperative endeavor. Fusing their ideas, talents, and energies with those of others, they achieved an array of outcomes.

The impact of the Monroe City effort was enhanced because the tasks of developing, disseminating, and promoting the uses of the urban simulations were very closely integrated. Notably, the builders of the simulations both used and advocated their products. Their desires to see their creations contribute to training made it easy for them to advocate that professors use the simulations. Put differently, the physical and psychological distances between the developers, let us say, of a new drug and its potential users were much greater than those between developers and users of the Monroe City simulations.

The endeavor proved to be an unusually dynamic one. Completed simulations not only provided exemplars but also implicitly invited professors to create additional ones. Because new teams continued to be activated, as established ones dropped or completed their projects, the program possessed a self-renewing quality. Thus, the scope, the number of the project's outcomes, and the list of its participants continually expanded. Only at the end of the fifth year of its six-year life did it begin to lose vitality.

A distinctive feature of the project was its effective, cooperative linking with a large city school system over a six year period. By building bridges between leading universities and an urban school system, UCEA departed from its traditions. The newly forged pattern of cooperation with Monroe City personnel was absolutely essential to the project's success. Notably, the school system's leaders faithfully adhered to UCEA's cooperative ethic. Even in the face of incessant local demands, they contributed much time and talent to the project. In so doing they helped create benefits for professors and students of educational administration which reached far beyond the boundaries of Monroe City.

Notes

1. For a discussion of the theories employed in the film see Miller, J. N. (1974). Consumer response to theoretical role models in school psychology. *Journal of School Psychology*, 12(4), 310-17.

2. To provide trainers and trainees structured feedback on simulation experiences, UCEA staff helped professors develop and test four instruments: a value resolution scale, an action analysis profile, a means of communication profile, and a value assumptions profile. See Gaynor, A. K., & Newell, L. J. (1971). Structured feedback instruments. In J. A. Blough, J. A. Culbertson, W. M. Martin, & R. W. Pirtle (Eds.), *The simulation of an urban school system for use in preparing educational administrators* (pp. 137-153). Columbus, OH: University Council for Educational Administration.

3. Some of the federal funds obtained to support the General-Special Education Consortium (see Chapter Five) were used to simulate the director of special education post in Monroe City.

4. For more detail about the "reality" and related issues see Gaynor, A. K., & Duvall, L. A. (1973). Role simulation in educational administration: Some issues and developments. *The Journal of Educational Administration*, XI(1), 60-68.

5. Generalizations about UCEA's training institutes on "New Methods and Materials" draw heavily upon information published from 1971 to 1975 in the *UCEA Newsletter* and the *UCEA Review*.

6. A sixteenth booklet entitled *Special Education in Monroe City* was subsequently added to the fifteen published initially.

7. See Rogers, E. M. (1962). *Diffusion of innovations*. Glencoe, IL: The Free Press.

8. The first thorough survey of views about simulation was directed at professors and trainees who had experienced the Whitman School. Although both groups evaluated their experiences positively, trainees assigned a somewhat higher value to simulated decision making than did professors. See Weinberger, M. J. (1965). *The use of simulation in the teaching of school administration*. An unpublished doctoral dissertation. New York: Teachers College, Columbia.

9. For an illustrative study see Cross, R., & Hendrix V. (1972). Effects of instructional intervention on the behavior of participants in coping with information overload in simulated decision making situations. A paper presented to a Division A meeting of the American Educational Research Association in Chicago, Illinois.

10. For an early example of this type of analysis see Culbertson, J. A. (1960). Simulated situations and instruction: A critique. In J. A. Culbertson & W. A. Coffield (Eds,), *Simulation in administrative training* (pp. 39-46). Columbus, OH: University Council for Educational Administration.

References

Bessent, W. (1973). Some issues underlying the planning process in UCEA. *UCEA Newsletter*, XIV(4), 12-16.

Blough, J. A., Culbertson, J. A., Martin, W. M., & Pirtle, R. W. (Eds.). (1971). *The simulation of an urban school system for use in preparing educational administrators*. Columbus, OH: University Council for Educational Administration.

Cresswell, A. M., & Murphy, M. J. (Eds.). (1976). *Education and collective bargaining: Readings in policy and research*. Berkeley, CA: McCutchan Publishing Company.

Culbertson, J. (1972). *UCEA instructional materials handbook: Guiding concepts and procedures.* Columbus, OH: University Council for Educational Administration.

Erickson, D. A., & Reller, T. L. (Eds.). (1978). *The principal in metropolitan schools.* Berkeley, CA: McCutchan Publishing Company.

Popper, S. H. (1972). Suggested next steps for UCEA's urban simulation project. *UCEA Newsletter,* XIII(2), 10-12

9

The Partnership

"To divide the united and to unite the divided is the law of nature."

Johann Wolfgang von Goethe

Incorporated into UCEA's 1974-79 plan was the goal of creating a UCEA University-School System Partnership. Two conditions strongly influenced UCEA's decision to pursue this goal. The first was a widespread perception that the field needed to be more effective in "knowledge utilization." Participants at a University of Oregon seminar in the late 1960s had described different facets of this need and had identified various strategies for addressing it. (see Chapter Four). The second condition was rooted in a growing concern in the field about the gap between knowledge and practice. There were multiple reasons for this concern as, for example, beliefs, held by some, that tenets which had underlain the hoped-for science of administration, had widened that gap.

The Partnership was also rooted in fresh hopes. One was that it would provide a setting and a climate in which professors and administrators could work cooperatively. Another one was that over time the wide ranging human, organizational, and material resources of leading school systems and universities could be deployed in ways which would nurture the use and development of knowledge. Still another aspiration was that new approaches to knowledge development and its use would contribute to the renewal of the school systems and universities in the Partnership.

Attaining the hoped-for Partnership proved to be a daunting endeavor. Initially viewed skeptically by some school leaders and negatively by many professors, the idea sparked resistance. Nevertheless, by 1981 the Partnership had reached its pre-set goal of 30 school systems, including three Canadian ones. Possessing superior conceptual, planning, staff development, and research capacities, these systems and their leaders, along with motivated professors in UCEA's 47 universities, had achieved a viable mission, crafted needed governance arrangements, and formulated guiding policies. The Partnership had also demonstrated that its members could initiate and invest in jointly approved programs. By 1981 the new creation, though still suffering from growing pains, had served an estimated 2000 individuals in its sponsored programs.

Birth of the Partnership Concept

Brushing aside a few opposing comments, the UCEA Plenary body in February, 1973, quickly approved the theme of "Knowledge Utilization" as a guide for developing a 1974-79 plan. The theme succinctly encompassed two important but differing interests within UCEA. "Knowledge" appealed to those who wanted research to be placed high on UCEA's agenda. "Utilization" appealed to professors who wanted UCEA to focus upon using knowledge to improve school management practices.

The Executive Committee had chosen the theme ten months earlier at its 1972 spring meeting. Those involved in the decision were President Wailand Bessent, University of Texas; Vice President Ralph Kimbrough, Florida; Max Abbott, Oregon; John Brubacher, Connecticut; Dan Cooper, Michigan; Loren Downey, Boston; Samuel Goldman, Syracuse; Harry Hartley, Connecticut; and Donald Willower, Pennsylvania State. At the end of its discussion the group decided to probe the theme more deeply at its next meeting. President Bessent encouraged those present to write "background" papers to inform the upcoming discussions. Six papers were prepared for the meeting.

Drawing upon the extensive work of the University of Michigan's Center for Research on Utilization of Scientific Knowledge, UCEA Associate Director Rodney Pirtle delineated four models for using knowledge to change practice (EC Mat, 9/8-10/72).[1] Before Rodney earned a Ph.D. degree at New York University, he had taught high school English and physical education and had coached basketball. He also had served as athletic director at Lon Morris College in Texas for four years. An undergraduate major in journalism at the University of Texas, he brought to UCEA effective writing and editorial skills.

In another paper I described specialized uses of knowledge in research, decision making, synthesis, and development (EC Mat, 9/8-10/72).[2] Downey and Willower analyzed factors affecting the use of knowledge. Downey stressed that both universities and school systems can activate "latent forces" which severely fetter all efforts to change themselves by means of knowledge use (Downey, 1973, p. 8).[3] Two dominant fetters are the firmly held expectations of individuals and the organizational structures which constrain their behaviors.

Because the norms and reward systems which affect university and school personnel differ markedly, the two groups, Downey argued, cannot find objectives to which both together can fully commit themselves. Therefore, formal objectives are often pushed aside during knowledge use activities, as needs in the "home settings" of the two groups become the dominant forces (Downey, 1973, p. 7): "An example would be a credential-tuition trade-off where practitioner students need credits and degrees for professional advancement and salary increases, and the university needs tuition income for economic maintenance." In such trade-off situations using knowledge to effect change cannot be a priority for either school personnel or professors.

Willower reinforced Downey's somber message. Organizing his thoughts around the "domains" of inquiry, values, and practice, he argued that each is isolated from the others (Willower, 1973, p. 8): "The domain of practice is a world unto itself divorced from the realm of theory and research;" ... and "the domain of values is similarly isolated . . . ." However, he maintained that those who viewed a department of educational administration as "a haven of reflection, a sanctuary for scholarship," miss the mark (p. 3). Because such departments are professional rather than academic units, they contain two differing kinds of professors (p. 3):

> Such units ordinarily reflect the theory-practice dichotomy in the makeup of their faculties which are composed of both theory-oriented professors and practice-oriented ones. The theorists are thought to disdain practice while the practical professors are believed to take research lightly if not contemptuously.

In many UCEA institutions the relations between the two types were uneasy ones. Researchers, who typically had limited interests in helping practitioners apply knowledge, needed allies to apply their research findings. Since many practice oriented professors had direct links into school systems, they might have helped school leaders apply their colleagues' findings. However, given the harsh criticisms which theory advocates had leveled at their nakedly empirical research in the mid-1950s, most were neither motivated nor willing to do so. Those who adopted the knowledge utilization theme, then, faced a vexing question: how could new knowledge best be applied in the contexts of practice?

Ideals in school settings, Willower noted, "are often proclaimed, but the relation to goal achievement of such statements, largely nonoperational in nature, remains cloaked in blessed obscurity" (Willower, 1973, p. 5). To say that a school is advancing equal educational opportunity is one thing; to translate the concept into budgets, curriculums, and instruction is another. The pressures on school personnel are not directed at translating rhetoric into reality but at "control and order..." (p. 7). In such a culture explanatory theories of learning are "essentially abstruse, obtuse things properly housed in a distant land and not germane to the immediate and pressing problems peculiar to the world of practice" (p. 8).

Willower's and Downey's negative views about knowledge and change precipitated a lively discussion. Yet the group did not back off its chosen UCEA theme, nor did Downey and Willower for that matter. Downey proposed that UCEA professors address two problems (Downey, 1973, p. 9): "the need to develop knowledge for *changing* educational systems, rather than maintaining them, and the need to emphasize *utilization* rather than dissemination of such knowledge." Professors should first develop the knowledge required to change their own training programs and enact the needed changes. They could then credibly turn to the task of applying knowledge in school systems.

Willower saw a compelling need to enhance "organizational vitality and purpose by creating and reinforcing social structures that bring means and ends into closer concord" (Willower, 1973, p. 13). Recognizing that a "monumental undertaking" would be required, he suggested that UCEA should turn its energies to the task (p. 17): "That agency, which has done yeoman's service in transforming the profession by turning it toward inquiry should now make a major commitment to applications."

A second "background" paper which I had written began with a question (EC Mat, 9/8-10/72, p. 1): "How does one move 'knowledge utilization' as a concept on paper into a vital development effort?" My initial answer was an inferred given in the paper's title: "Knowledge Utilization in School Systems: A Projected Boundary Spanning Dynamic." The dynamic would be "rooted in inter-agency arrangements spanning UCEA universities and a number of public school systems" (p. 1). The endeavor "should encourage linkage between school districts and universities of a type which would lead to innovative processes in both of the systems spanned" (p. 2). I assumed, in other words, that neither system would have quick, sound, and acceptable answers for the other.

Several committee members supported the boundary spanning concept. Others, however, noting that the idea departed radically from tradition, were concerned that it might seriously damage UCEA. More than one asked why I had proposed the initiative. The response that it was logically designed to address the chosen theme of "Knowledge Utilization" was an unsatisfactory answer. Fortunately, I later had opportunities to articulate more carefully the reasons for launching a UCEA university-school system partnership.

Conditions Fostering the Partnership Concept

Near the end of the 1960s Professor Willard Goslin of George Peabody College came to the UCEA hotel suite in Atlantic City during an annual meeting of the American Association of School Administrators (AASA) to give me a message. A nationally recognized leader for almost three decades, Goslin had served as a superintendent of schools in Minneapolis, and in Pasadena, California. In 1946 he had chaired an AASA "Planning Committee" charged with projecting a ten year vision for improving the school superintendency. The committee's ideas set in motion a series of events which led to the W. K. Kellogg Foundation's decision to invest in a ten year program to improve the training of school administrators (see Chapter Two).

Professor Goslin courteously had come to inform me of his intent to deliver to AASA members a message which would be critical of UCEA. The time had come, he felt, to speak publicly against the perceived indifference of UCEA institutions to school practice. Later in the day I was told that Goslin had communicated to a large audience that UCEA professors should spend less time talking to one another and more time addressing problems which faced school leaders. School superintendents and others in the audience reportedly responded to Professor Goslin's remarks with applause. Undoubtedly, there were other "practitioner professors" in the audience who shared his view.

In the early 1960s at another AASA meeting I had heard Goslin speak favorably about UCEA's intent to develop new knowledge and to use it to improve training programs. Obviously, he later had arrived at a less happy view which many other practice oriented professors as well as school administrators shared. However, his presumption that the problem stemmed from excessive interactions of UCEA professors was a simplistic one. Put differently, the reasons for the growing press for more effective "knowledge utilization" and for constructive efforts to reduce the field's expanding theory-practice gap were multiple and complex.

The logical positivistic tenets undergirding the theory movement were among the factors which widened the gulf between knowledge and the practice of educational administration. To be sure these tenets affected the work of professors in certain UCEA universities in limited ways. However, their influence upon scholars in the leading research universities of UCEA was substantial. Scholars who advocated and used these tenets elevated the priority given to inquiry, made research more rigorous and scientific, and produced more intellectually challenging training content. At the same time they helped distance theory from practice, professors from school administrators, and leading universities from school systems. A few illustrations will make the point clearer.

One of the tenets of the theory movement was that the field should focus upon building an administrative science. Those who concentrated on this task allied themselves with theorists of business, government, hospital, and other fields of administrative science. The new alliances helped professors pursue the new science. However, it also made it easier for them to neglect particular aspects of educational administration and to ignore problems of school practice.

Pursuers of a science of administration embraced the logical positivistic tenet that scholars should describe and explain school management as it is; statements about how it ought to be lie outside the domain of science. The "is-ought" dichotomy placed science on a high pedestal and stigmatized non-scientific inquiry. By excluding from inquiry the study of policies which "ought" to guide schools, faithful users of the tenet helped enlarge the knowledge-practice gap.

Leading professors who worked to develop a science of administration faced heavy demands. For example, they had to grasp the content in new journals (e.g. *The Administrative Science Quarterly*) and master *generic* theories in various fields of administration and social science disciplines. Such demands often pressed scholars to look within their institutions for scholarly questions and stimuli rather than outward toward school practice.

School management presented the builders of an administrative science with a multi-faceted, wide ranging, and complex domain of study. One distinguished scholar derived from an explicitly stated set of assumptions the proposition that 50,000 types of decision problems confront school managers; further, the 50,000 types show an "astonishingly high degree of inter-dependence and interaction" (Schwab, 1964, p. 54). Noting that the number of constructs encompassed by mathematical equations in physics and economics ranged from three to five, and from 50 to 200, respectively, Schwab estimated that as many as 4000 constructs would be needed in school administration. His conclusions were based upon arbitrary though reasonable premises. Even if he overestimated the constructs by 100 per cent, inquirers would still be faced with great complexity.

Given the complexities and the problems which the relatively small number of pursuers of a science of administration faced, their research attainments were less than they had anticipated. Limited knowledge production constrained in another way their impact upon the practice of school management. Typically, their generalizations pertained to only a few dots on the large landscape of school administration. The results of a portion of the studies were published, usually in specialized journals such as the *Educational Administration Quarterly*. Since research results were expressed in the technical language of science, most who read them were professors. A leading school superintendent once told me that reading the *Quarterly* was a laborious task. He and other school leaders found it difficult to apply the generalizations to fragments of management. Forged at a site far removed from American school management (see Chapter Three), the logical positivistic tenets, then, which were based largely upon research practices in physics, fit awkwardly into the applied field of school administration. At best they provided the field an insufficient model. More precisely than any other model of inquiry, science prescribed for its followers how it should be practiced; yet it could say nothing about how school management ought to be practiced. Its appliers could produce trenchant critiques of research designs and methods; however, they could not produce critiques of school practice. They could use their imaginations to design ingenious research endeavors; however, as scientific scholars, they were forbidden to formulate needed school policies. Harsh critics of past approaches to inquiry, they did not foresee the limitations in their proposed new science. Little wonder, then, that the model's results disappointed many professors and school leaders.

Down-to-earth developments also had negative effects on the knowledge-practice gap. For one thing, leading universities in the 1960s faced an unprecedented demand for hundreds of newly prepared professors of educational administration. During the decade 26 new Ed.D programs were instituted in the U. S. as compared to 15 in the fifties (Culbertson, 1972, p. 82). Nineteen new Ph.D. programs were created in contrast to eight in the 1950s (p. 85). Established programs were also greatly expanded. Adherents of the new science, who were located largely in UCEA universities, were the major preparers and mentors of the new professors. As a rule, the latter, embued with the values of the theory movement and committed to the pursuit of a science of administration, were quickly employed. An eastern UCEA university in the mid-sixties, for example, employed four new professors with an eye toward developing scientific theory. Such large infusions of newly prepared professors into universities gave a fresh boost to the pursuit of a science of administration.

The new crop of professors widened the gap between universities and school systems. Considerably younger than beginning professors of the past, some of them had neither taught nor administered. Typically in their twenties or early thirties and sometimes lacking school experience, they often possessed a master's degree in such fields as operations research and economics. By casting their talent net widely, recruiters found a greater number of intellectually able candidates. Some recruiters also knew that many of the most dramatic discoveries in science had been made by scholars in their twenties or early thirties. Numerous employers, committed to the advancement of inquiry, recruited the younger professors (Shaplin, 1964, p. 9).

Most school administrators were not as tolerant of the younger professors as were the latter's employers. When I made university visits, I learned that some of the able young professors were upset because the practitioners in their classes questioned their credibility. Special knowledge, effective teaching, and intelligence were not always enough to dispel prevailing doubts. Over time some acquired the skills and credibility needed to apply knowledge in settings of practice. Most, however, concentrated upon using specialized knowledge in teaching and in inquiry.

Additional reasons could be given for the gap between knowledge and practice and for the growing interest in knowledge utilization. For example, educational leaders in the last half of the 1960s, faced with governmental and societal pressures to effect school innovations, needed knowledge more than did those who administered schools in the placid era which spawned the theory movement. Suffice it to say that the prevailing calls for improved uses of knowledge were generally supportive of the idea of a UCEA University-School System Partnership. The idea was also buttressed by the positive experiences UCEA had gained in working with school leaders during the 1969-74 time span. The Monroe City simulation provided one such set of experiences. (see Chapter Eight). Another set came from a conversation initiated by Curtis Henson, an assistant superintendent in the Atlanta Public Schools. He and his colleague, Ruel Morrison, Atlanta's director of continuing education, were searching for better ways to identify the training needs of school principals. Could UCEA, Henson asked, help Atlanta school personnel address this question?

With the aid of a group of Atlanta's school administrators and a national "Reaction Panel", a half dozen domains of principals' performance were identified. Illustrative ones were "Evaluating School Processes and Products" and "Initiating and Responding to Social Change." Selected UCEA professors elaborated performance objectives in each domain and developed instruments for gathering data about principals' performances. The data, it was hoped, would shed light on training needs. The findings from the project were set forth in *Performance Objectives for School Principals.*[4]

The Partnership was also grounded in new aspirations. One such aspiration was that UCEA could conduct some of its cooperative endeavors in school contexts and, in so doing, contribute to the renewal of UCEA universities and school systems. A related aspiration was that the Partnership would enable UCEA to assemble and deploy a broader mix of professional talent in its activities. By involving both professors and administrators in planning and executing Partnership activities, it was hoped that a better climate and more fruitful structures for applying and developing knowledge could be achieved. Reflected in such hopes was a dream as expansive as that of building a science of administration. Yet it seemed wise to move away from the ideology of logical positivism and to re-orient some of the field's inquiry toward problems within a new Partnership.

Initial Reactions to the Partnership

The proposed Partnership stirred strong emotions in many UCEA professors. While practice oriented professors embraced the idea, theory oriented ones tended to oppose it. The feelings of fear, anger, and threat evoked in those who opposed it did not disappear when UCEA finally approved the development of "new approaches to knowledge utilization within an especially created university-school system partnership" as one of its 1974-79 goals (Culbertson et al, 1973, p. 3). Five years later when UCEA voted to continue the Partnership for the 1979-84 period, some of the feelings were still apparent, if less intense.

As I listened to professors at meetings, and as I talked with them informally, I gained insight into their feelings. In December, 1978, I presented to UCEA's governing bodies a brief synopsis of 12 concerns which professors had articulated. The descriptions were introduced in part as follows (EC Mat, 12/7-9/78, p. 116):

In order to recognize these concerns and to afford more explicit opportunities for dealing with them, a brief report has been prepared elaborating the ideas professors have projected. We are not able to document how widespread the concerns are. . . However, all of those stated have been expressed by one or more professors.

Two of the 12 concerns were delineated by practice oriented professors only. Since many of these professors enhanced their incomes by working in school systems as consultants, several asked (EC Mat, 12/7-9/78, p. 118): "Will the Partnership interfere with or take away entrepreneurial opportunities from professors?" A few who were engaged in developing linkages with school systems in their regions asked a different question (p. 117): "Will the Partnership encroach upon the membership of school study councils?"

To some theory oriented professors the Partnership signaled that UCEA had turned its back on them at a time when the theory movement was being attacked. Viewing the Partnership as "a marriage of convenience," some argued that it would turn UCEA away from the task of building an administrative science (EC Mat, 12/7-9/78, p. 118).

Other professors, viewing UCEA as their "club," were afraid that the Partnership would damage opportunities for "informal communication ...., for friendship, and for social interaction" (EC Mat, 12/7-9/78, p. 117). They did not want "outsiders" coming "into their club" and creating "a less comfortable climate for interchange" (p. 117). Others feared that school administrators would "take over UCEA" (p. 117).

Some who had endorsed the Partnership nevertheless had misgivings about participating in it. They thought they would be "put in situations" and "not be able to deliver" (EC Mat, 12/7-9/78, p. 117). Some worried that UCEA might fail and "be dealt destructive blows" (p. 118). Questions they asked included the following (p. 118): "Can we collectively deliver? If we can't, will UCEA go under or be weakened? Will there be negative, unanticipated consequences?"

The ambiguity surrounding the Partnership also repelled professors. Since few activities emerged before 1979, the ambiguity persisted. Professors could not clearly conceive "micro" aspects of the Partnership until its central features were defined. Some, according me undeserved credit, maintained that I had a clear picture of what the Partnership would do but that I was not sharing it. Such perceptions spawned distrust (EC Mat, 12/7-9/78, p. 118): "What does Culbertson have in mind, ...?" "Isn't he being devious?"

As professors expressed their emotions and measured them against perceived realities, they tended to become more friendly toward the Partnership. However, many of their earlier concerns persisted—a condition which often slowed the development of the Partnership.

The first official discussion of the Partnership with school leaders took place in May, 1974. The participants were Robert Chisholm, Superintendent, and Henry Gardner, Director of Personnel in the Arlington County Schools (Virginia); Charlye Mae Edwards, Director of Staff Development, and Sidney Estes, Assistant Superintendent for Instruction in the Atlanta Public Schools; Edward Whigham, Superintendent of the Dade County Schools (Florida); James Singleton, Director, and Emerson Lavender, Assistant Director, of the Halton County Board of Education in Burlington, Ontario (Canada); John Peper, Assistant Superintendent, Division of Planning and Long-Range Development in the Milwaukee Public Schools; Randy Randles, Coordinator of

Professional Development, and Phyllis Shutt, Coordinator of Administrative Staff Development in the Nashville Metropolitan Schools; James Johnson, Associate Superintendent for Planning, Research, and Evaluation in the Washington, D. C., Public Schools; Stanly Schainker, Assistant Superintendent for Instruction, and Edward Vollbrecht, Director of Middle Schools in Yonkers (New York). Superintendents in Mesa, Arizona, and in Minneapolis, Minnesota, though invited, were unable to attend.

Six criteria for membership in the Partnership were elaborated before the meeting. Crafted to identify school districts which had the capacities to cooperate with UCEA in the development of knowledge and in its uses, the criteria were designed to identify school systems which had excellent research divisions, staff development programs, planning abilities, and whose leaders saw "positive potential in the application of ideas to practice" (EC Mat, 5/2-4/ 74, p. 2). Superior conceptual and visionary skills on the part of school superintendents or directors were deemed to be very important.

A minimum of 10-12 school systems was an early target for the Partnership. The criteria were sent to Plenary members and deans of colleges of education in all UCEA universities and to selected leaders in state education agencies, among others. Recipients of the criteria were asked to nominate a few school districts which they ranked highly. They responded with more than 80 nominations. Each of the ten school systems invited to send personnel to the May meeting had received multiple nominations. During the spring of 1974 I had met with personnel in eight of the ten school systems. In each case I had asked administrators to provide information about where their districts stood on the criteria.

Participants in the May meeting began by sharing information about the planning, research, development, evaluation, and staff development outcomes they had recently attained and about future challenges they would likely face. Thereafter, they raised a series of questions about the proposed Partnership (EC Mat, 9/8-10/74, pp. 21-22). Some were directed at the Partnership's rationale as, for example, "How will the Partnership be 'better' than the relationships which already exist between school systems and the surrounding institutions of higher education?" (p. 21). Others dealt with the motivations and abilities of professors: "What would professors be willing to learn through the Partnership?" and "Can universities and the professors . . . actually respond to school system needs?" (p. 21). One question focused upon the loyalties of the UCEA central staff: "Can the central unit of UCEA really be a third party in the projected Partnership, or will it be in the university group only?" (p. 21). Examples of feasibility questions included: "Can professors in the immediate environment of school districts be effective because of school system politics?" and "Is the Partnership feasible, given the different styles . . . of professors and school leaders?" (p. 21).

Reflected in the above questions were tough-mindedness and some skepticism. Lying behind another question was the problem of trust and possibly tinges of bitterness: "Will professors get the scholarly credit from efforts that emerge from the Partnership to the neglect of those in school systems?" (EC Mat, 9/8-10/ 74, pp. 21-22). With the advent of increased funding for research in the 1960s, school administrators had helped many professors acquire needed data. However, some thought that most professors had shown more interest in publishing their findings than in facilitating their use in schools. Perceptions that administrators had given more than they received had added to the strain between school and university staffs.

Following the assessment of the Partnership concept, the group examined the problem of governance. Its members agreed that "UCEA . . . and school system representatives in the Partnership" should have "full policy making responsibility" (EC Mat, 9/8-10/74, p. 22). Four years later UCEA would approve a formal structure which would approximate that proposed by the school leaders at the May meeting.

Near the end of the meeting the Partnership passed another test. The group decided to invest additional time and travel monies in the idea. Stressing the interdependence of colleges of education and school systems, Edward Whigham observed that neither could survive by a "go it alone" policy. For the second meeting the group asked John Peper, James Johnson, and me to prepare information on the Partnership's rationale and its modes of defining and analyzing problems. Other topics we were asked to address were knowledge use strategies, delivery structures, and costs and benefits. Peper volunteered to develop a statement on delivery structures, while Johnson agreed to elaborate ideas on problem definition and analysis.

The appointed planning group met in July to prepare for a September 1974 meeting. Initially, we set forth seven guidelines for conducting the September meeting. We decided, for example, that it was important that "progress in unfolding the program for the Partnership" be achieved, else attendees could lose interest in the concept (EC Mat, 9/8-10/74, p. 24). However, we also agreed that "every effort should be made to avoid an appearance of closure in thinking" in the prepared materials, and that the group should have abundant opportunities to "shape the scope and content of the projected Partnership program" (p. 25).

Taking part in the September meeting were most of those who had attended the May meeting plus John Davis and George Smith, superintendents of schools in Minneapolis and in Mesa, Arizona, respectively. Given the Partnership's incipient state, the concepts prepared for the meeting were general in nature. For example, I had prepared three charts, each of which depicted a distinctive knowledge utilization model. Attached to each chart were two pages of descriptive and cost-benefit information. Such materials did not spawn program proposals. Still the attendees did not give up on the Partnership idea. Calling for a third meeting, they decided that equal numbers of school leaders and professors should take part in it, and that the latter group should begin the meeting by sharing their recent achievements in teaching, research, and program updating, and by outlining challenges on the horizon. Thus, the group took yet another small step toward the creation of a Partnership.

Implementation: Small Steps

The idea for the Partnership's first program emanated from a meeting held on December 13-14, 1974. Six weeks before the meeting transpired, ten professors had agreed to serve on a Partnership Steering Commission with ten school administrators. All members of the Commission were invited to the December meeting. However, only six professors and five school leaders were able to attend. Participating professors were John Brubacher, Connecticut; Luvern Cunningham, Ohio State; Alan Gaynor, Boston; Kenneth McIntyre, Texas; Michael Nunnery, Florida; and Richard Weatherman, Minnesota. Attending administrators were John Peper, Milwaukee; Randy Randles and Phyllis Shutt, Nashville; James Singleton, Halton County Board of Education, Ontario, Canada; and Edward Whigham, Dade County, Florida.

The Commission projected a range of program possibilities: innovative staff development programs for school principals (Phyllis Shutt); an evaluation and updating of the Boston University training program for school administrators (Alan Gaynor); a conference on "Education in the Future" to be offered by the Milwaukee Public Schools (John Peper); a professional education program for leading U. S. and Canadian administrators and professors to be conducted by the Ontario Council for Leadership in Educational Administration (James Singleton); and the improvement of systems for evaluating school administrator performance in Dade County, Florida (Edward Whigham).

About four months after the Steering Commission had met, the Milwaukee Public Schools conducted a conference on "Education in the Future." Planned largely by John Peper with help from the UCEA staff and selected Milwaukee educators, the conference's purposes, as initially stated, were "to provide participants from universities and school systems opportunities to think about future-bearing trends and to explore possible follow-up activities. . ." (*UCEA Review*, XVI(3), p. 1). Attending were several hundred Milwaukee school personnel, the district's school board members, and a half dozen UCEA professors.

In his introduction John Peper announced that the conference would offer participants a "shirt sleeves ... session to develop an information base for planning" and "milestones which we can use in working with the staff and with the Board of School Directors" (Milwaukee Public Schools, 1975, p. 2). The "planning process," he noted, "is . . . involved in expanding the knowledge of alternative futures and in staging strategies for choosing the future" (p. 2). Pointing to impending societal changes, he stated (p. 3): "I am certain that the schools as they are presently structured are inadequate for providing sufficient psychological adaptability and technical knowledge for the future."

Luvern Cunningham was one of three professors who spoke to the conferees. Calling the meeting a "singular event among large city public schools," he stressed the need to "build a professional culture, . . . which has many members and within which planning and thinking and conjecturing are expected and really mean something" (Milwaukee Public Schools, 1975, p. 4). Recognizing that forces of inertia tend to paralyze large organizations, he urged that the "conference . . . give consideration to the setting in which it finds itself and to . . . the properties in its midst which support logical, rational, thoughtful views of the future" (p. 6).

The great majority of the presenters were school system staff. Offering thoughtful views about future-bearing trends, they discussed, for example, on-going and projected educational uses of television, radio, and computers. Also examined was the drop in Milwaukee's school enrollments (from 178,294 in 1967 to 146,865 in 1974), how it was related to urban housing, and its import for future student services, for staffing, and for staff evaluation.

The conference differed from past UCEA seminars. Employing ideas about the future, its primary aim was to change school practice. Thus, it compelled its members to address specific knowledge-practice problems. Notably, the conference not only provided school personnel with opportunities to think about the future of education, but it also generated ideas which found their way into recommended changes in school practice—changes which the Milwaukee Board of School Directors later approved for implementation. On the other hand, the ideas did not nurture the visions of Partnership school leaders outside Milwaukee, because these leaders were not present. Their impact upon universities was also limited since few professors had attended.

Of the half dozen program ideas which Partnership leaders proposed at their December 1974 meeting, only the Milwaukee conference was implemented. The requirement that Partnership programs involve *both* school system and university personnel multiplied and enlarged implementation problems as did differences in national cultures. James Singleton and the staff of the Ontario Council for Leadership in Educational Administration (OCLEA) were eager to offer a two-week professional development program for U. S. and Canadian school and university leaders within the context of a Canadian school system. Those involved would have observed problems of school practice and discussed views offered by external presenters about problem solutions. Canadian personnel were ready to attend. Unfortunately, U. S. invitees, faced by severe time and funding constraints, could not capitalize upon the opportunity.

At its December meeting the Partnership Steering Commission elected a sub-group to receive and to review program proposals. Chosen were John Brubacher, Connecticut; John Davis, Minneapolis; Stanley Schainker, Yonkers; and Edward Whigham, Dade County. The elected president was Edward Whigham.

Recipient of a doctorate from New York University, Whigham had taught at UCEA and non-UCEA universities in summer schools. An able conceptualizer, he was viewed by close colleagues as a "strong" superintendent. Sensitive both to university and school system problems, he provided crucial support for the Partnership during its infant years.

To encourage school leaders to assess their commitments to the Partnership, UCEA in 1975 established a $900 annual membership fee. Leaders in Arlington County, Atlanta, Halton County, and Washington, D. C. chose not to participate. Leaders in Dade County, Mesa, Milwaukee, and Nashville joined the endeavor as did Alex Sergienko, Superintendent of the Tacoma Public Schools in Washington. Because of unexpected career moves some leaders were unable to join the Partnership. Robert Alioto moved from the Yonkers superintendency to the superintendency in San Francisco, while John Davis moved from his Minneapolis post to the presidency of Macalester College.

A guiding UCEA theme for 1974-79 was the "mediation of theory-practice and professor-administrator relationships" (*UCEA Review*, XX(1), p. 20). UCEA staff members devoted much energy to the mediation of these relationships. To break down barriers between professors and school leaders, I sought ways to place them in communication with one another. In late 1975, for example, I arranged for Alen Sergienko, Superintendent of Schools in Tacoma, to attend a UCEA Executive Committee meeting. When I had first talked with Sergienko, he had displayed strong interests in the complex task of building the Partnership. Holder of bachelor's, master's, and doctoral degrees from Harvard, he had a keen appreciation of ideas and of their import for leaders. Thus, I hoped he might bring a fresh perspective to those centrally involved in framing the Partnership.

During the Executive Committee discussion a respected professor who was well known for his writings on theory and for his research activities angrily declared that the Partnership would not deter him from pursuing his scholarly interests. Immediately affirming his strong support for the concept of academic freedom, Sergienko suggested that scholarly findings and ideas were important not only for the Partnership but for the field of educational administration. The professor listened to Sergienko but did not respond to him.

Later during the dinner hour Superintendent Sergienko spoke about studies he had conducted and used while he had served as director of educational research in Tacoma. After listening to the exposition, the professor who had spoken angrily earlier in the day and who was sitting on Sergienko's left, wryly remarked: "You are confused about your role. Professors are the ones who are supposed to talk about theory and research!" As Sergienko and others around the table laughed, some of the tension evoked earlier seemed to disappear.

At the February, 1976, UCEA Plenary Session Superintendent Elbert Brooks of the Nashville Metropolitan Schools chaired a panel on the training of school administrators. Listening to panel presenters were about 80 UCEA professors. Speaking were three administrators from the Partnership. Superintendent Edward Whigham spoke about the key components of a university training program; Associate Superintendent Charles Frazier of the Nashville Metropolitan Schools focused upon in-service training issues; while Assistant Superintendent John Peper from Milwaukee talked about training within the Partnership.

During his talk Whigham pointed to "the hiatus between the practitioner and the professor" and stressed that it was "high time to get about the business" of addressing the hiatus (*UCEA Review*, XVII(3), p. 18). Recognizing that theories were "difficult to translate into realities," Frazier called for "an interdisciplinary approach" to in-service training (p. 18). He also noted that the "K-12 and higher education arenas need more systematic . . . cooperation," even though neither school systems nor universities "seem" to value it (p. 18). "Until recently," he observed, "there was no supportive environment for such endeavors" (18).

Peper sensed a "climate," he said, in which "those of us who practice . . . reach more frequently to join hands with those who teach educational administration. . ." (Peper, 1976, p. 22). This climate, he noted, could foster improvements in the "practice of our profession" (p. 22). Expressing a desire to "stimulate an initial line of thought," he declared that there was a need for a "national network" to support training (p. 23). To design a "lifelong plan" of "leadership education for current . . . and . . . prospective . . . administrators," he and his Milwaukee colleagues wanted "to open up avenues of exposure . . ." to "leadership staff in a broader set of institutions. . . " (p. 23). "Could this be done," he asked, "through . . . the University Council for Educational Administration?" (p. 23). A "National Catalogue" of approved UCEA courses could be helpful to planners as could specially designed mini-courses (e. g. a half or one semester hour of credit) to address particular school needs.

Peper also asked his listeners to consider becoming "Professors in Residence" in Milwaukee. Emphasizing that residencies would encourage problem solving and "promote reflective thinking," Peper delineated several options (Peper, 1976, p. 23):

Resident professors might operationalize the anthropological model of participant scholar. They might provide . . . 'point of need' education. They could participate in a continuous dialogue about causal problems and . . . hypothesize solutions. They could also provide knowledge resources at specific points of decision.

At the end of the presentations Professor Alan Gaynor, a member of the Partnership Steering Commission, thanked the school leaders for their ideas. Although the session ended without further comment, considerable exchange took place between the presenters and UCEA professors during the coffee break. Some professors were apparently reassured by the positive attitudes exhibited by the school leaders.

In 1974 I began inviting Partnership school executives to take part in established UCEA programs. Several attended the UCEA seminar, "Educational Administration Twenty Years Later: 1954-74," at The Ohio State University in 1975. Edward Whigham of Dade County attended the third International Inter-Visitation Program — a one month experience which took place in London, Bristol, and Glasgow, during the summer of 1974. As President of the Partnership, Alex Sergienko of Tacoma, in 1978 welcomed visitors from about 30 nations to the fourth International Inter-Visitation Program in Montreal, Canada. In 1979 Joseph Sweeney, Superintendent of Schools in East Brunswick, New Jersey, took part in the first InterAmerican Congress on Educational Administration in Brasilia, Brazil. The number of school leaders who attended UCEA programs was relatively limited. Those who did attend programs had opportunities to converse with UCEA professors and to look at school administration from new vantage points.

In the fall of 1978 personnel from 48 UCEA universities and 28 Partnership school districts were invited to help develop UCEA's 1979-84 plan. That school leaders influenced the plan can be gleaned from its content (*UCEA Review*, XX(2), pp 45-47). For example, one of its 10 goals was to realize the "learning and developmental potential" in the Partnership (p. 47). In addition, objectives listed under four other goals related directly to the Partnership. School leaders also helped evaluate the UCEA-sponsored journal, *Emergent Leadership: Focus on Minorities and Women*. Later the following Partnership members served on the editorial board of the journal: Elvira Dopico, Dade County Public Schools; Bethene LeMahieu, Montclair Public Schools; and Eileen Selick, Detroit Public Schools.

In 1978 the sub-committee of the Partnership Steering Commission began holding its meetings just before the UCEA Executive Committee sessions. This schedule enabled members of both groups to get acquainted at receptions held in between the two meetings. At the April 1978 meeting the sub-committee members began attending the Executive Committee sessions, a practice which continued for three meetings. During these sessions the groups jointly addressed governance issues

(EC Min, 4/18-20/78). Since there were more UCEA universities (48) than Partnership school systems (28), the following question arose: should there be equal or proportional representation on the governing body? After much discussion they decided that universities and school systems should each have five elected representatives on the body, and that all of the decisions about the Partnership should be approved by UCEA governing bodies. During my UCEA tenure all decisions made by the new body were promptly approved by UCEA bodies without ostensible misgivings. This new creation was an important milestone in the history of the Partnership. It signaled that influential UCEA professors and school leaders were beginning to place greater trust in one another. It also pinpointed channels through which leaders could initiate and unfold new programs.

The Partnership's Programs Expand

Early discussions taught me that Partnership R and D programs could not be enacted for some years. Other aims first had to be realized. A climate of trust was one aim. The meaning of the cooperative ethic within the Partnership also had to be diffused and understood. To legitimate R and D initiatives, a Partnership governance structure was needed. Thus, the staff focused largely upon dissemination rather than R and D programs initially.

Executives in the Partnership's five founding school systems wanted more effective in-service training programs. To pursue this interest UCEA obtained a three-year grant in 1976, from the Bureau of Education for the Handicapped, in the U. S. Office of Education. Called the Special and General Education Leadership Project (SAGE), its mission was "staff development innovations for integrating special and general education administration" (*UCEA Review*, XVIII(1), p. 19).

Associate Director Norman Ellis, who had earned a doctoral degree in educational sociology at the University of North Carolina, coordinated the SAGE project from 1976 to 1978. A former high school social science teacher in Indiana, he had also directed a special education project which provided technical assistance to 30 state education agencies. He brought to UCEA the requisite skills to coordinate a large inter-institutional project and knowledge of complex organizations.

Coordinating SAGE during its final year was Associate Director Ellen Herda, recipient of a doctorate from the University of Oregon.

Earlier Ellen had taught high school English and French, before she became coordinator of a reading and language program and of a multicultural endeavor in a California school district. She brought to SAGE needed management experience and to UCEA valuable insights about the foundations of knowledge and inquiry. Providing assistance to Ellen was Associate Director Walter Panko. A high school teacher and principal before he obtained a Ph.D at the University of Pittsburgh, he was committed to the cause of human equity. He also brought to UCEA considerable knowledge about policy research.

Elected to give direction to SAGE was an Executive Committee headed by George Smith, the Partnership's second president and the Superintendent of Public Schools in Mesa, Arizona. Smith was known for his ability to identify and attract talented educators to Mesa, which may explain why the school system there had received more than its share of national recognition.

In most of the participating school systems there was tension between general (e. g. principals) and special education administrators (e. g. directors of special education). The latter often felt that the former were not doing enough for the physically and mentally challenged. On the other hand, the former at times resented the pressures placed on them to effect changes—changes which were often advocated by directors of special education. Thus, SAGE sought to develop the common understandings which those in the two groups needed to improve special education.

Sage school systems offered staff development programs each year during the 1976-79 period. Norman Ellis and Ellen Herda provided designers of in-service programs data on training needs in the school systems. UCEA staff member, William Davis, had conducted the studies which produced the needs assessment data. After obtaining an engineering degree, Davis worked for the United Technologies Corporation. Finding engineering unfulfilling, he began conducting special studies of social and economic issues for a nearby "futures" organization. Later he obtained a doctorate at Oklahoma State University. Blessed with a superb mind, he brought to UCEA mathematical and analytical skills, a generous spirit, and a humane attitude.

Seeking to facilitate the flow of ideas across school boundaries, SAGE's managers encouraged the exchange of personnel between universities and school districts. Some movement from universities to school systems did take place. Daniel Sage, Syracuse University, spent three days a week for a year in the Dade County school system during a sabbatical leave. As a part-time member of the system's staff, he became immersed in the reality of urban school administration. Later he wrote that "fresh exposure to the day-to-day problems," after ten years in the professorship, provided him "invaluable material" to enrich his university's "training program for special education administrators" (Sage and Malloy, 1977, p. 20). A few years later, Michael Nunnery, University of Florida, acquired a similar experience. Working full time for 16 weeks in the Orange County, Florida, Public Schools, a Partnership member, Nunnery evaluated Orange County's system for assessing management performance. He and Linton Deck, the system's superintendent, delineated guidelines for future designers of similar experiences (Nunnery and Deck, 1978).

Did SAGE achieve its goal of "staff development innovations?" The answer is "yes" in the sense that the training programs were shaped in part by the staff of a national agency which had access to many sources of information and whose mission was to improve training programs. However, SAGE had very little success in helping personnel move back and forth between school systems and universities. Some professors did serve as trainers in Partnership school systems. While some school executives transmitted ideas about practice to professors through the UCEA Review, only a small number did so.

The Partnership's new governing body held its first official meeting in May, 1979. The five superintendents elected to the body were Albert Ayers, Norfolk Public Schools, Virginia; Jack Davidson, Austin Public Schools, Texas; Lee McMurrin, Milwaukee Public Schools, Wisconsin; Walter Marks, Montclair Public Schools, New Jersey; and Alex Sergienko, Tacoma Public Schools, Washington. The five elected professors were: Richard Gorton, University of Wisconsin in Milwaukee; John Hoyle, Texas A. and M.; John Pisapia, West Virginia; Richard Podemski, Arkansas; and Eugene Ratsoy, Alberta, Canada. During the meeting Jack Davidson recommended that "anticipatory leadership" be the Partnership "theme" for 1979-80 (PCC Min, 5/16-17/79, p. 3). The group asked the staff to develop activities related to the theme.

Six weeks after the Partnership's governing body met, I convened a task force to project activities for advancing "Anticipatory Leadership." The ideas formulated ranged from "temporary think tanks" to case studies of anticipatory leadership, to conferences (UCEA Review, XX(3), p. 43). Later I decided to focus largely upon developing conferences designed to advance anticipatory leadership. In so doing I encouraged school superintendents to take the lead in planning and financing conferences. To help ensure that school practices and ideas both received fair treatment, I also suggested that school leaders involve nearby UCEA universities in planning and supporting the conferences. The immediate results were the following:

"Financing Education in the 80's," March, 1980. The Institute for Public Finance at the University of Florida and the Orlando Public Schools, Florida.

"Preparing Educational Leaders for the 21st Century," May 8-10, 1980. The Montclair Public Schools, New Jersey.

"Children and Youth Within the Context of Changing Family Patterns: Implications for Education and Educational Leadership," November 2-4, 1980. The Lincoln Public Schools and the University of Nebraska.

"Urban Education Around the World," November 8-11, 1981. The Milwaukee Public Schools and the University of Wisconsin in Milwaukee.

Not everyone in the Partnership supported the use of "futures" content. Some professors, believing that it was seriously flawed, rejected it. Some school administrators shunned such content, because they were so caught up in the present, they could not attend to the future. On the other hand, most who attended the conferences were committed to studying and envisaging educational futures. As optimistic believers in human potential, they wanted alternatives which might transcend the status quo. Such alternatives, they believed, should be informed by futures content. Realizing they could not predict the future, they focused upon inventing and shaping it.

The four conferences suggested that it is easier to foresee problems than pertinent solutions. As they looked toward 1990, scholars at the conference on "Financing Education in the 1980s" gave detailed descriptions of various facets of three problems: the inadequacy of financial support, the inequality of school support, and the inefficient use of resources (Alexander, 1980). Salient throughout the 1980s, the problems still prevailed at the end of the decade. However, few of the recommended changes in funding eventuated. Speakers also found it easier to identify 1980 trends than to specify how school leaders would or should react to them. At the Nebraska conference on changing family patterns the trend toward greater numbers of female heads of households was correctly identified (Kelly and Sybouts, 1981, p. 13). Yet the proposal that districts offer before-school and after-school child care was not widely heeded.

Advanced by Walter Marks, Superintendent of the Montclair Public Schools and later President of the Partnership, the conference on the future preparation of leaders reflected in part Montclair's efforts to re-orient education. Holder of a doctorate from Ohio State, Marks had worked hard to give the Montclair schools a "futures" look. The curriculum of a "magnet" school, which conferees visited, was designed to help students think inventively about the future. Alan Peakes, a member of Montclair's central office staff, specialized in educational futurism. The conference also reflected the belief that close relationships between schools and communities should prevail. Not only did Montclair citizens offer their thoughts about leadership preparation at the conference, but also they hosted numerous "living room dialogues" and provided lodging in their residences for out-of-town guests (West and Marks, 1980, p. 4).

Initiated by Superintendent Lee McMurrin during his tenure as President of the Partnership, the Milwaukee conference was on "Urban Education Around the World." Possessor of a doctoral degree from Ohio State, McMurrin took great pride in Milwaukee's "specialty" schools, including two which featured global education programs. Conference presenters from Africa, Australia, Europe, South America, Asia, and North America observed the specialty schools before the conference began. One unanticipated result was that A\;io Nakajima, Director of Upper Secondary School Education in Japan, sent groups of Japanese educators annually over a period of several years to study the Milwaukee schools. Lee McMurrin was also invited to Japan to describe Milwaukee's specialty schools to various groups.

In contrast to earlier UCEA seminars most of the Partnership conferences were held in school settings, where both professors and school managers presented papers. Though cast in different language, the ideas of the two groups were often complementary. For example, at Montclair the renowned futurist, Willis Harmon, and the practitioner, Paul Shelley of the Paramus Public Schools (New Jersey), both

stressed the need for future leaders to rely more upon intuitive thinking. Harmon attested that every individual "has access to a
supraconscious, creative/intuitive mind whose capabilities are apparently unlimited" (quoted in West and Marks, 1980, p. 4). Shelley emphasized that the field should nurture the "kind of intuitive leader needed to
solve the exceedingly complex problems that face us in the future" (p. 4).

As the Partnership displayed its dissemination capacities, I began
to launch R and D endeavors. In 1980 a task force on the training of
anticipatory leaders was activated. Nancy Knapp, Northern Illinois
University, and Donald Steele, Superintendent of the Toledo Public
Schools, were asked to delineate major societal trends. Lee McMurrin,
Milwaukee Public Schools, and John Hoyle, Texas A. & M., agreed to
depict the challenges which societal trends posed to school leaders. A
delineation of the skills, understandings, and attitudes needed to
anticipate and manage trends was sought by Luvern Cunningham, Ohio
State, and Thomas Payzant, Superintendent of Schools in Oklahoma City.
Finally, Alan Peakes, Montclair Public Schools, and Laurence Haskew,
Texas, agreed to spell out implications of the previous papers for new
training programs. The task force's longer-term goal was "three or four"
university training programs to prepare "leaders to be more effective in
anticipating and managing the future" (PCC Min, 2/11/81, p. 1).

The last Partnership development I led originated in a "temporary
think tank" discussion sponsored by the Shawnee Mission Public
Schools in Kansas on November 8-9, 1979. Brainstormed were educational uses of microcomputers, laser discs, and satellites. Nicholas
Nash, manager of a six station radio network in Minnesota, and a
former UCEA associate director, challenged the group to test the
educational potential of satellite technology through the Partnership.

Confronted 18 months later with an exploding interest in microcomputers among Partnership personnel, I asked Ohio State professors
if they could offer a conference on the subject. They quickly acceded to
the request. In the fall of 1981, after having resigned the UCEA post and
accepted a position at Ohio State, I agreed to plan the conference.
Subsequently, Robert Burnham, Dean of the College of Education,
encouraged me to substitute a video teleconference for the conference
idea. I accepted his suggestion.

On October 29, 1982, the video teleconference came to pass. Originating from Ohio State's public television studio, the telecast transmitted images and ideas about school uses of microcomputers to about

7000 university and school personnel in the U. S. and Canada. Since the participants were located at 58 "down link" sites and in four time zones, the event was scheduled from 12:30 to 4:30 p. m. E.S.T., with a 45 minute break at 2:15 p. m. Individuals at 40 sites were listeners and observers. Persons at the other 18 sites posed scores of questions to and received answers from the nine experts at the originating site. Six of the interactive sites were located in Partnership districts, while 12 were at universities, including three in Canada. At most of the 18 sites the telecast was one of several activities offered at a day-and-a-half conference on microcomputers.

The teleconference focused initially upon innovations in one Canadian and two U. S. school systems. Executives from these systems provided filmed and verbal descriptions of microcomputer uses. Thereafter, those at the 18 interactive sites asked questions about the innovations. The second and third phases of the telecast featured a discussion of computer hardware and software and a debate on needed standards for "computer literacy." Experts on these two subjects included editors of journals, authors of books, and an evaluator of computer hardware and software.

Although a plan was developed to evaluate the "electronic learning" experience, it was not executed. However, pertinent cost-benefit observations can be made. If one assumes that the 7000 participants had traveled to Columbus, Ohio, to a conference on microcomputers and that their average travel and lodging costs were $300 for each, the total cost would have been $2,100,000, not counting lost work time. The "out-of-pocket" costs of the video teleconference were approximately $62,000, an amount covered principally by the $2,500 fees from interactive sites and the $300 ones from observer sites. Even though the two options cannot be equated, the cost-benefit ratio would still seem much in favor of the teleconference. More importantly, the Partnership, by pooling its resources, delivered a professional development program which a single school system or university would likely not have contemplated much less attained.

Assessment

At a New York City hotel in late 1979 I took part in a discussion of educational issues with a group of diverse leaders. During the session one discussant asked me to describe the Partnership. Later, during a coffee break the head of a small business enterprise posed a number of follow-up questions. At the end of his queries, he observed: "The Partnership is a major accomplishment." Taken aback by his generous assessment, I thanked him for the compliment although I had a less benevolent view of the Partnership's progress.

Stimulated by the businessman's remark, I compared the Partnership's progress with that of UCEA during the return flight to Columbus. Between 1972 and 1979 Partnership leaders had attained a mission, a governance structure, a membership, some external support, and had offered some programs. During the 1954-59 period the founders of UCEA produced comparable results. As I compared the two experiences and thought about the Partnership's hybrid nature, I arrived at an altered and more generous judgment about the progress made by participants in the Partnership.

By February, 1981, the Partnership's membership had reached the decreed limit of 30 school systems, including three in Canada. It was also experiencing a burst of dissemination activity with the Montclair and the Milwaukee conferences yet to come. At the same time the Partnership's potential for facilitating a flow of ideas had barely been tapped. The climate for research was also more supportive than earlier. The Task Force on Anticipatory Leadership had identified several areas of inquiry, including a study of the indicators of school systems' capacities to anticipate and manage the future. In late 1980 the Partnership's governing body endorsed research on the performance of school principals. On February 11, 1981, the day I announced my resignation as UCEA's executive director, the same body approved inquiry outlined in a paper by Ramona and James Frasher of Georgia State University. Thus, it seemed that a small number of participants were poised to tackle demanding R and D tasks.

Although the Partnership seemed ready to enter a new phase, its future was uncertain. Immediately, there was a need for resources (e.g. an five-year grant from a foundation with accompanying increases in the membership fees of school systems). Using UCEA as a standard, at least another decade of productive activity would be required to institutionalize the Partnership. A range of new R and D initiatives would need to be conceived and implemented. Outcomes helpful to both school leaders and professors would have to be accumulated. Values generated by these outcomes would have to be diffused and understood. The problem was not one of potential. Rather, it was finding the ways and means to deploy the Partnership's wide ranging organizational and human resources in the effective development, dissemination, and the use of knowledge. Turning my back on the challenges before the Partnership was the most difficult part of the decision to leave UCEA.

The experience of working with able professors and foresightful school executives on both sides of the border was a distinctive one. Both groups found it difficult to attain what was expected of them. At times I wondered which was more demanding: producing solid "truths" or effecting improvements in schooling. Since both parties pursued their ideals within contexts of contradictory expectations, they were often targets of criticism. However, untenured school superintendents were much more vulnerable than were professors. Unhappily, I saw able Partnership superintendents discharged and watched others make timely moves to new positions.

Notes

1. For detailed descriptions of the four models see Havelock, R. G. (1971). *Planning for innovation through dissemination and utilization of knowledge.* Ann Arbor, MI: Center for Research on Utilization of Scientific Knowledge, Institute for Social Research, University of Michigan.

2. For a thorough analysis of ten knowledge-related functions see Culbertson, J. (1977). Linking agents and the sources and uses of knowledge. In N. Nash & J. Culbertson (Eds.), *Linking processes in educational development: Concepts and applications* (pp. 74-117). Columbus, OH: University Council for Educational Administration.

3. Downey, who had accepted a new post at the University of Maine some months earlier, did not attend the September 8-10 meeting.

4. See Culbertson, J. A., Henson, C., & Morrison, R. (Eds.). (1974). *Performance objectives for school principals.* Berkeley, CA: McCutchan Publishing Company.

References

Alexander, K. (1980). Financing education in the 80's. *UCEA Review*, XXI(3), 8-10.

Culbertson, J. A. (1972). Alternative stragegies of program adaptation within the future time frame of the seventies. In S. H. Popper (Ed.),

Imaging alternative future school organizations (pp. 79-92). Minneapolis: Division of Educational Administration, University of Minnesota.

Culbertson, J. A. et. al. (1973). *UCEA: Alternative directions for 1974-79.* Columbus, OH: University Council for Educational Administration.

Downey, L. W. (1973). The context as crucible: An analysis of the knowledge utilization underground. *UCEA Newsletter,* XIV(3), 6-9.

Kelly, E., & Sybouts, W. (1981). Changing family patterns: Implications for educational leadership. *UCEA Review,* XXII(1), 13-16.

Milwaukee Public Schools. (1975). *Education in the future.* Milwaukee, WI.: The Milwaukee Public Schools.

Nunnery, M. Y., & Deck, L. L. (1978). The professor in an urban school district: A renewal/service option. *UCEA Review,* XIX(3), 7-12.

Peper, J. B. (1976). Preparing leadership teams for American schools of 1980-2000. *UCEA Review,* XVII(3), 22-24.

Sage, D. D., & Malloy, W. W. (1977). An experience in university-school system exchange. *UCEA Review,* XVIII(2), 18-20.

Schwab, J. J. (1964). The professorship in educational administration: Theory-art-practice. In D. J. Willower & J. A. Culbertson (Eds.), *The professorship in educational adminstration* (pp. 47-70). Columbus, OH: University Council for Educational Administration.

Shaplin, J. T. (1964). The professorship in educational administration: Attracting talented personnel. In D. J. Willower & J. A. Culbertson (Eds.), *The professorship in educational administration* (pp. 1-14). Columbus, OH: University Council for Educational Administration.

West, P., & Marks, D. (1980). Educational leadership in the 21st century. *UCEA Review,* XXI(3), 4-7.

Willower, D. J. (1973). Schools, values and educational inquiry. *Educational Administration Quarterly,* IX(2), 1-18.

10

The Renewers

"There are two ways of spreading light: to be the candle or the mirror that reflects it."

Edith Wharton

I was taken aback by a remark made to me in the mid-seventies by Francis Chase, former head of the Graduate School of Education at The University of Chicago. UCEA's greatest contribution, Chase affirmed, was that of providing a group of extremely able individuals a unique set of learning experiences. He was referring of course to UCEA's associate directors. Struck by his provocative assertion, I asked him how he justified it. The UCEA contribution to the field, he attested, could not be measured in the short term. Rather, it would accrue over time as former associate directors left UCEA and performed scholarly and leadership roles in other settings. Because they would bring perspectives to problems not possessed by others, their impact on the field, he declared, would be distinctive.

Since I viewed associate directors more as givers than as receivers, I did not share Chase's view. I knew that UCEA's unique environment fostered rich learning — a fact which many professors appreciated even though they had not worked at UCEA's headquarters. When they recommended recent recipients of doctorates for associate director posts, they were often excited about the options for learning which UCEA afforded. At the time Chase had made his remark, some were also calling associate directors "interns." Yet, UCEA's chief contribution, I thought, stemmed from the impacts of its most successful programs. Thus, the most basic functions associate directors performed were initiating, designing, and enacting new UCEA programs.

The Search for Talented Renewers

During the 1959-81 period 30 associate directors served UCEA.

Three had one year terms, 16 two year terms, 10 three year terms, and one a four year term. Hoping to achieve greater continuity in staffing, UCEA created a deputy director post in 1969 and appointed Robin Farquhar to the new position. However, its own life proved to be fleeting. After Robin had served with distinction for two years (1969-71), he left UCEA. The post was never re-filled.

UCEA's temporary staffing was a product of necessity—not invention. It persisted because UCEA's policy makers could not accurately predict the resources which would be available to UCEA. The organization, as a rule, could not employ associates until it had obtained external grants—grants which usually lasted for two or three years. Thus, 16 of UCEA's 30 associates were fully supported by governmental or foundation grants. Seven were partially funded by external grants, while seven were fully funded by internal resources (i.e. membership payments, revenues from the sale of instructional materials, or returns from investments in stocks or bonds).

Although the temporary staffing policy created major problems for UCEA, it also produced an unforeseen and valuable benefit: a continuing dynamic for renewing UCEA. Since new associates were inured neither in the traditions of UCEA nor the professoriate, they could look more critically at central office and university practices. Because they had just completed two or three years of intensive doctoral study, they also brought to UCEA the latest knowledge about educational administration—knowledge which contributed to my own continuing renewal and informed new UCEA program initiatives.

Temporary staffing was an ally of renewal in another way. At about the time that associates were developing vested interests in given UCEA projects or pursuits, they moved out and into new posts. This practice produced an organizational climate I had never experienced. One result was that changes in UCEA directions and activities were seldom ever stalled by protective associates.

Who were the renewers? Their names, the universities where they acquired their doctorates, and the dates of their tenure at UCEA are listed as follows:[1]

William Coffield, University of Iowa (1959-61).
Stephen Hencley, University of Chicago (1960-62).
Kenneth St. Clair, University of Texas (1962-64).
Glenn Immegart, The Ohio State University (1963-64).

Edwin Bridges, University of Chicago (1964-65).
Donald Anderson, University of Minnesota (1964-66).
Paul Cullinan, The Ohio State University (1964-66).
Loren Downey, University of Arizona (1964-66).
Robert Ruderman, Indiana University (1964-66).
Bryce Fogarty, University of Wisconsin (1964-68).
Terry Eidell, Pennsylvania State University (1965-67).
Robin Farquhar, University of Chicago (1966-71).
Mark Shibles, Cornell University (1967-70).
Alan Gaynor, New York University (1968-71).
John Blough, The Ohio State University (1971-72).
Michael Martin, University of California at Los Angeles (1970-73).
Rodney Pirtle, New York University (1971-73).
James Yates, University of Texas (1971-74).;
Jackson Newell, The Ohio State University (1972-74).
Fred Frank, State University of New York at Buffalo (1973-75).
Paula Silver, New York University (1973-76).
Richard Podemski, State University of New York at Buffalo (1973-76).
William Davis, Oklahoma State University (1975-78).
Nicholas Nash, University of Minnesota (1975-78).
Norman Ellis, University of North Carolina (1976-78).
Peter Hackbert, University of Oklahoma (1976-78).
Grace Butler, New York University (1976-78).
Martin Finkelstein, State University of New York at Buffalo (1976-79).
Ellen Herda, University of Oregon (1978-80).
Walter Panko, University of Pittsburgh (1978-80).

Since the selection of able associates was very important to UCEA, much time and thought were devoted to the process. Recognizing that associates needed stellar abilities, UCEA professors nominated only their most outstanding graduates. Typically, the pool of nominees for a position ranged from 30 to 35. Thus, in any given search for an associate a good proportion of the UCEA universities would not offer nominees. As a rule, professors whose candidates were chosen were filled with pride. However, some became disgruntled because a disproportionate number of those chosen came from midwestern and eastern UCEA universities. Even when I reminded professors in western, southern, and southwestern universities that the bulk of UCEA's members were in the midwest and the east, their concerns did not disappear.

Over time an explicit set of selection criteria was derived from UCEA's functions and was slowly refined. Since UCEA's mission was to improve university training, the capacity of candidates to function as change agents was of utmost importance. Since the major instruments for effecting change were ideas, criteria related to the cognitive capacities of candidates were central.

The selection process began with the usual collections of information about candidates, including two papers each had written. Staff members then read all the materials and independently ranked each candidate on a one-to-10 scale vis-a-vis such criteria as scholarly aptitude, conceptual ability, originality, writing skill, leadership capacity, and interpersonal skill.[2] After sharing their judgments with one another, staff members probed issues on which they had discrepant views. After acquiring and discussing additional information about the unresolved issues, the staff typically chose five to ten candidates for further study.

Staff members interviewed those on the abbreviated list during university visits or at national professional meetings. After further deliberation, they chose two or three candidates for more focused exchanges at UCEA's headquarters in Columbus. When candidates arrived, they were given two papers and were asked to be prepared to analyze them critically at a meeting the following day. Typically, one of the papers was written by me. The visitors' reactions to it shed light on their capacities to provide critique as well as on their interpersonal skills. The second paper was designed to illuminate the thought processes of candidates. A paper used often in the seventies dealt with four modes of thought: Lockean (inductive), Leibnitzean (deductive), Kantian (inductive and deductive), and systems analytic. At the meeting candidates analyzed the paper's content and stated how their own modes of thought were related to those outlined in the paper—a difficult assignment. One candidate described the task as a thinly disguised but powerful intelligence test!

While gathering data about candidates, I was constantly assessing their abilities to handle three types of thought, each of which was relevant to effective staff performance. One was abstract and conceptual.

Usually having little immediate import for UCEA programs, it was a type of thinking often expressed within UCEA. When associates interacted with professors about theoretical issues or responded to their requests for critiques of papers, they had to cope with abstract ideas. Since all candidates could think abstractly, the problem was to discern the ablest ones.

A second type of thought required strategic imagination. To express it, staff needed the capacity to conceive new objectives for UCEA and to project and assess relevant courses of action. To realize this type of thinking, candidates had to construct the right equations for merging ideas into UCEA actions. There were few if any reliable indicators of candidates' capacities for effective strategic thinking. Data about their past accomplishments could be suggestive. Asking them what action programs they would like to initiate in case they joined UCEA could also produce helpful clues. Yet some who were unable to cope with the question during interviews displayed strategic thinking skills after they joined UCEA.

A third type of thinking was reflected in operational decisions. If a professor asked an associate to see that a set of simulation materials was mailed to a specified location by a given date, did the associate respond effectively? Did an associate in charge of getting a UCEA monograph published identify and make needed corrections in the page proofs? Such decisions were important in the eyes of those served by them. Unable to observe the abstract and strategic thinking of associates at UCEA's headquarters, some professors used their perceptions about the quality of the staff's operational decisions to gauge the organization's effectiveness.

A relatively reliable indicator of a candidate's capacity to make effective operational decisions was previous administrative experience. However, after having engaged in two or three years of intensive doctoral study, UCEA associates in their new roles tended to value conceptual thinking highly. Strongly influenced by the priority placed on such thinking in elite research universities, some very bright associates early in their tenure looked askance at operational thinking. "Kicking around ideas" was a much more exciting activity.

Few associates were gifted in all three types of thinking. Thus, the goal was to achieve staff competence *not* in one candidate but in the staff as a whole. For example, we aimed to achieve an "appropriate balance" between (EC Mat, 9/13-15/73, p. 2): "inductive thinking and deductive thinking; . . . analysis . . . and . . . synthesis; . . . thinking and . . . doing;" thinking in "operational and tactical terms . . . and . . .in purposive and directional terms . . .;" and thinking critically about "the status quo" and thinking about "strategies to transcend the status quo."

All of the criteria just noted emerged from cumulative experience with the exception of the one dealing with inductive and deductive thinking. I obtained this idea in the mid-1960s from James Conant when I read his book, *Two Modes of Thought*. He summarized one of the book's theses as follows (Conant, 1964, p. xxxi):

> A free society requires today among its teachers, professors and practitioners two types of individuals: the one prefers the empirical-inductive method of inquiry; the other the theoretical-deductive outlook. Both modes of thought have their dangers; both have their advantages. In any given profession, in any single institution, in any particular country, the one mode may be underdeveloped or overdeveloped; if so, the balance will need redressing.

At the time I had read Conant's book, most UCEA staff members were deductive thinkers. However, one consistently practiced inductive thinking. As I observed him, I recognized that he made a unique contribution to staff thinking. He did this by providing deductivists critiques, which they could not provide themselves, and by designing UCEA initiatives which complemented those generated by deductivists.

During most of my UCEA tenure three to four associates took part in the selection of new staff members. They approached the final interviews with evident excitement. Early on I had decided that candidates for UCEA posts should not be employed unless they were supported by most of the existing staff. It seemed unfair both to current staff and to new appointees, if the latter received more negative than positive votes.

As in all domains of UCEA endeavor, there were tensions between conceptual criteria and their uses in practice. All staff members valued behaviors in candidates other than the rational ones described above. For example, they appreciated charm and scintillating wit, even when candidates used them to deflect or avoid difficult questions. Since UCEA associate directors were largely dependent upon one another for psychological support and colleagueship, they valued such personal factors as friendliness, empathy, and good will. Seldom did all staff members whole-heartedly agree on the "best" candidate. At times associates were employed who had only luke-warm support or even opposition from at least one UCEA staff member. The range of staff reactions to candidates can be pinpointed with some examples.

In the mid-sixties the staff quickly agreed to employ Robin Farquhar who was completing his doctoral work at The University of Chicago. The positive reaction was rooted partly in Robin's demonstrated thinking abilities. During his interview he was asked what he would like to accomplish at UCEA as an associate. In his response he displayed unusual clarity of vision about what he would like to achieve and why. For example, he projected a new UCEA initiative designed to improve preparatory programs for non-public school administrators. He also expressed his interests in building upon UCEA's existing activities on the role of the humanities in preparatory programs. Shortly after he described his program preferences, Associate Director Bryce Fogarty, who did not make decisions precipitately, passed me a written message: "Hire him. He is the brightest one I have seen coming down the pike." And we did!

An interview with Bruce Warren in 1970 produced an outcome which differed markedly from the one just noted. Warren was nominated for the UCEA post by Michael Nunnery of the University of Florida. Known for honest assessments of his students, Michael attested that the candidate was an extremely bright individual and an excellent student. Bruce's favorite question, the professor reported, was "Why." He also noted that the candidate could be argumentative. Held in connection with a national conference, the interview was a screening one. After an exchange about the candidate's background, the discussion turned to larger issues and soon escalated into a debate. In the exchange Bruce expressed strong views which were opposed by some UCEA associates. Undeterred by the rising emotion in the room, he skillfully held his ground. At the end of the exchange UCEA associates left for a pre-arranged appointment, while I spent another hour with the interviewee in a more subdued atmosphere.

In a staff discussion the next day no one questioned Bruce's intellectual abilities. Concerned about the chemistry of future UCEA staff relationships, most, however, believed that UCEA should look to others for a new associate. Some months later the candidate accepted a teaching post in political science at Manatee Community College in

Bradenton, Florida, where he soon became an associate dean of the College of Arts and Sciences. Later he reportedly obtained a law degree and began practicing law. Bruce Warren was one of many very able candidates who applied for but did not receive an associate post. Unsure that the interview had fairly reflected his abilities, I sometimes wondered what he would have done for UCEA, and what UCEA would have done for him had he served as a UCEA associate.

In the spring of 1973 UCEA invited Paula Silver, a highly recommended candidate from New York University, to Columbus for an interview. Though the interview had its emotional moments, it was more typical of staff-candidate exchanges than the two just described. When Paula left at the end of the day, the staff met to assess her candidacy. When we convened, one UCEA associate and I were seated on one side of the table, while three associates were located on the other side. Soon after our discussion began, it became apparent that the three seated on the opposite side of the table had reservations about inviting Paula Silver to become an associate. Having discussed informally her performance with two staff members earlier in the day, I was already aware of some of their reservations.

During the morning Paula had rendered an incisive critique of a paper I had recently written. Offering forthright and pointed views, she displayed a very critical mind—a quality I valued. I valued critique because it helped me improve both the quality of my ideas and their expression. Thus, I felt fortunate when at least one associate director could probingly analyze my writings. Since I also surmised that Paula had the mental acuity to perform other UCEA functions, I was supportive of her candidacy. My stance was also re-inforced by the need, as I saw it, for UCEA to act affirmatively in the employment of female staff members.

Since UCEA associate directors held temporary rather than permanent appointments, and since their responsibilities differed from my own, most did not feel as strong a need for critique as did I. In fact there were signs that Paula's sharp and pointed remarks were threatening to some associates. In addition, one shared with me his concern about whether the interviewee, if employed, could relate effectively to UCEA's existing staff and vice versa.

During the late afternoon discussion the staff exchanged views both pro and con. After a considerable exchange one of the three associates on the other side of the table moved to a seat at the end of the table. His subsequent comments made clear that he was adopting a more favorable view toward the candidate. At the end of the discussion some of the reservations expressed earlier by two UCEA associates were not yet expunged. However, the majority agreed that the candidate should be invited to serve as a UCEA associate.

In sum, UCEA had a carefully developed set of selection criteria. Yet when applied in practice, the criteria had limitations. At times informally sanctioned norms having to do with colleagueship and psychological support pushed formal ones aside. Non-threatening candidate behaviors which were supportive of staff needs could influence selection decisions even more than those linked to abstract, strategic, and operational thinking. Nor did the criteria neatly fit the actual behaviors of candidates. For example, since very few candidates were "pure" inductive or deductive thinkers, the usual problem was to assess the degree to which candidates thought inductively and deductively. Dichotomous categories did not fully capture actual behaviors. Finally, the criteria had logical but not empirical validity. That UCEA staff members needed the ability to think strategically could be logically demonstrated, but reliable empirical indicators of whether or not candidates would actually do so were lacking. Even though the selection criteria were incomplete, imprecise, and empirically unvalidated, they helped UCEA find associate directors who were perceived by many to possess stellar abilities. Since most of the candidates for associate posts later became professors in UCEA universities, the time and energy expended in getting acquainted with them were not lost. Knowing them as former candidates for UCEA posts, it was easy to involve many of them in R or D projects early in their professorial careers.

Fresh Ideas Renew the Director

How did associates abet UCEA's renewal? One important way was that of affording UCEA's executive director continuing learning opportunities. Very early I recognized that the life blood of UCEA was in ideas. Without fresh ideas to inform and guide research, development, and dissemination programs UCEA would be, I believed, largely impotent. I resolved early in my tenure, then, that if at any point I became unable to generate publishable ideas, I would leave the executive directorship. Although there were numerous sources of knowledge and diverse intellectual stimuli available to me, associate directors afforded me convenient and special ones.

Why were associate directors valuable sources of ideas? For one thing, the learnings they acquired before and during their doctoral studies were diverse. As a result, I was blessed with a constant but changing flow of ideas throughout my tenure. The diversity of their ideas stemmed in part from their dissimilar interests. Also reflected in their varied knowledge were the trends and values which influenced the study and the practice of educational administration at the time they were pursuing their doctorates. Since their ideas were in part products of shifting influences, they often had special import for UCEA program development. Some examples will help clarify the point.

Early in my tenure I noticed that university scholars and personnel in business organizations were increasingly using systems concepts. Believing that the trend toward greater use of the concepts was significant for the field, I spent a day in the early 1960s at Systems Development Corporation in Santa Monica, California. While there I learned more about applications of systems ideas by talking with the corporation's senior vice-president, Launor Carter, and with members of his staff. Shortly thereafter, I suggested to Daniel Griffiths that systems concepts would have a major impact on the study and practice of educational administration during the 1960s. Their impact had proved, in fact, to be greater than I had anticipated.

Some months before I traveled to Santa Monica, Glenn Immegart, a UCEA graduate assistant and a doctoral student, was learning about "systems theory" in a sociology course at Ohio State. By the time he had become a UCEA assistant director, he had read much about systems concepts and had written a paper on the subject. As I read his paper and some of the references in it, I learned more about the origins, spread, and uses of systems ideas. While planning three university seminars on educational research earlier in the 1960s, I asked Daniel Griffiths to present a paper on the role of "models" in inquiry. In his paper Dan used "systems-theory" to illustrate his views about models.[3] Later in the 1960s UCEA sponsored more comprehensive treatments of systems analysis, planning, and management.

In 1963 I had a conversation about taxonomic inquiry with Paul Cullinan, then a graduate student at Ohio State and later (1964-66) a UCEA associate director. During the exchange Paul told me about his study of the uses biologists were making of taxonomic inquiry. UCEA professors had not yet pursued such inquiry. Although the concept had entered the field, it was still used largely to refer to a set of loosely connected concepts. For example, professors employed "job," "know-how," and "theory"—one illustrative set—to think about training programs. They used these concepts to define administrative competencies and to design training programs.

Consisting of a set of logically and hierarchically related categories (e. g. order, family, genus, species), a taxonomy was an essential tool in biology. Paul Cullinan was enthusiastic about the results biologists had achieved by employing the concept. After our exchange I wondered if UCEA might sponsor a study to determine whether or not taxonomic inquiry could generate fruitful categories for observing administrative phenomena, for classifying empirical data, and for developing sound generalizations. With Paul's help I wrote a rough draft of a proposal early in 1964 which the two of us discussed with Daniel Griffiths. Several years earlier Dan had observed that taxonomies had "served useful purposes in practically all the sciences" (Griffiths, 1959, p. 18). Supporting the initiative, he agreed to develop a more refined proposal. In the fall of 1964 New York University received a federal grant to conduct a UCEA-sponsored, inter-university research project on taxonomic inquiry.[4]

In 1964 Robert Ruderman joined UCEA as an associate director and a staff member of the federally funded "Articulated Media Project (AMP)." In AMP he led an effort to develop a computer based simulation. Since Illinois only a decade earlier had become the first university to acquire a computer, the initiative was a pioneering one. While scholars had made progress in developing computer programs to facilitate learning, no one had simulated computer based decision problems in school administration.

During the conduct of AMP Bob taught me my first lessons about the nature of computer simulations and some of the problems involved in building them. He also helped me see how such simulations might be used in the future. For example, he postulated that simulations could be developed which would enable administrators to become more aware of the values which shaped their decisions. He also envisaged the development of computer based decisional analysis systems which could provide varied kinds of comparative data on the choice patterns of administrators. The learnings Bob provided helped me initiate subsequent UCEA simulation projects.

Constantly appearing in the oral rhetoric and the writings of the sixties was the word, "change." Among the influences which stimulated its uses were pressures to effect school innovations, to alter programs for preparing school leaders, and to employ new management technologies in school systems. In 1964, as the interest in change was surging upward, Loren Downey became a UCEA associate. At the University of Arizona he had studied change from the dual perspectives of cultural anthropology and systems theory. While at Arizona he had also tested his ideas in practice, as he participated in the re-design of the university's teacher training program.

In his UCEA role Loren offered tough minded views to me and to other staff members who were engaged in change activities. As a member of the UCEA Articulated Media Project in his second year at UCEA, he elaborated a set of ideas on planned change and presented the ideas to professors at each of three UCEA institutes.

Terry Eidell became a UCEA associate director in 1965. Earlier a student of the "hard" sciences, he had become a high school teacher of physics and chemistry. Recipient of a National Science Foundation Fellow award for 1960-61, he spent the year at Pennsylvania State studying his two teaching fields. After meeting Donald Willower a year afterward, he became intrigued with the new emphasis upon scientific research in educational administration.

When he arrived at UCEA, some already were criticizing the tenets underlying the hoped-for science of administration. One such tenet was that natural science modes of inquiry can and should be used to study social science phenomena. Fifteen years before Terry came to UCEA, I had adopted a very skeptical view toward the tenet. (see Chapter One). Yet I had not had an opportunity to probe the view with a thinker who had studied the hard sciences. Terry provided me the opportunity. He also advanced the work of the UCEA Task Force on the Social Sciences and the Preparation of Educational Administrators by developing a clearly conceived proposal for studying uses of social science content in administrator training (Eidell, 1966).

In 1973 *The Man in the Principal's Office* was published. Written by Harry Wolcott, an anthropologist at the University of Oregon, the book had meaning beyond that contained between its covers. It symbolized the growing interests of anthropologists in education and educators in anthropology. It was also a harbinger of an upcoming array of anthropological studies on school leaders. Later in the 1970s the National Institute of Education, for example, provided funds for about ten such studies. As a discipline which was noted for its commitment to field inquiry, and for its bent toward qualitative research, anthropology provided a haven for some of those who had become disenchanted with quantitative approaches to inquiry.

Fred Frank arrived as an associate director at UCEA the year Wolcott had published his influential book. While pursuing his doctorate at the State University of New York at Buffalo, Fred had served as an assistant to the anthropologist, Frederick Gearing, for about two years. While working with Gearing, he served as the assistant director of an anthropological inquiry which was designed to develop better methods of in-service education for teachers. When he arrived at UCEA, then, Fred was well equipped to inform me and others about anthropological concepts, their growing uses in educational contexts, and their import for the study of school leadership.

In the mid-seventies the *Educational Researcher* disseminated an article on "meta-analysis" to members of the American Educational Research Association (Glass, 1976). Informed by scholarly writings published in the early 1970s, the article caught the attention of many academicians. The interest it stirred likely stemmed from the fact that it offered a method for ordering and synthesizing the findings and conclusions of all the empirical studies related to a given subject. At the time thousands of "fragmented" studies on aspects of education and management were scattered in diverse and isolated publications. The need for a method to order and give meaning to the findings of extant studies on particular subjects was obvious.

In 1976, the year Glass's article appeared, Martin Finkelstein became a UCEA associate director. Earlier he had obtained a B. A. at Columbia before entering a doctoral program at Stanford where he studied the humanities. After a year at Stanford he returned to Columbia and began to study higher education. When he accepted the UCEA post, he was working on a doctorate in higher education administration at SUNY, Buffalo. At the time of his arrival I possessed a general understanding of meta-analysis. However, I had not yet seen an outstanding exemplar of it. His doctoral dissertation which contained a synthesis of more than 250 empirical studies on "American academics," provided me one. After reading the dissertation, I encouraged him to refine and publish it.[5] His scholarship enhanced my understanding of meta-analysis and stimulated me to think about its potential uses within UCEA.

As demonstrated in Chapter Five, Tom Greenfield's vehement rejection of the tenets underlying the theory movement precipitated an extended debate about the type of knowledge which would be of greatest value to the field. As the debate unfolded, advocates of diverse epistemologies contended with one another. When Ellen Herda joined UCEA in 1978, these advocates were debating the issue. Affected by some of the trends in inquiry noted above, Ellen had finished the required work at the University of Oregon for a doctorate in anthropology except for a thesis which she later completed. In her dissertation for the doctorate in educational administration, Ellen had investigated the field's foundations of knowledge.

Once again an able thinker had joined the UCEA staff with substantial knowledge about a salient problem of the time. Early in her interview for the associate post Ellen aggressively denounced the logical positivistic views of knowledge. As a UCEA staff member, she displayed an affinity for epistemological tenets which were rooted in the humanities. The tenets of critical theory and of hermeneutics, especially the latter, were appealing to her.

Since I had also been reading and thinking about the views of critical theorists and hermeneuticists, I shared Ellen's strong interests in epistemology. During her stay at UCEA we exchanged views about the foundations of knowledge. From time to time she also provided me copies of essays I had not read. An article on epistemology which appeared the year after Ellen left UCEA was influenced to some degree by our exchanges (Culbertson, 1981).

In sum, each of the eight associate directors mentioned above (and others not discussed) abetted my educational renewal. Their contribution was distinctive for at least two reasons. During their graduate and undergraduate studies each had acquired a constellation of learnings not possessed by me or other associates. As a result, their collective knowledge had a major impact on me. More importantly, most afforded me knowledge which was relevant to salient issues before UCEA at the time they served. Systems analysis emerged in the sixties—not the seventies, while competing epistemologies was a phenomenon of the seventies—not the sixties. New associates, then, helped me replenish the conceptual capital I had previously acquired and spent. In so doing they provided me ideas for the continuing renewal of UCEA and its programs.

Other Modes of Renewal

Associates also fostered my learning and UCEA's renewal by bringing knowledge to problems which were less current than those noted above. Mark Shibles, who during his doctoral studies took only three courses in Cornell's school of education and the rest in political science, public administration, and industrial labor relations, provided UCEA special knowledge about planning. Initially trained as an engineer with a heavy grounding in mathematics, William Davis offered me and others expert knowledge of statistics as well as research methods. Walter Panko, who had studied policy research at the University of Pittsburgh, helped me think about the Partnership's potential for policy studies. A former teacher of literature, Robin Farquhar provided UCEA ideas from the humanities; while co-ordinating UCEA's program on the use of the humanities in preparing school administrators (see Chapter Four), he also developed ideas about the outreach and the impact of the program.[6·]

Another way associate directors enhanced my learning was through critique. William Coffield, UCEA's first associate, and I frequently debated research and training questions. Possessor of a clearly defined set of values, Bill often challenged my views. As a result, he pressed me to clarify my positions on many issues *before* I discussed them with UCEA professors. Bryce Fogarty was also skilled in critique. Two weeks after he arrived at UCEA, I asked him to react to a proposal I had written. Blessed with a critical mind, he provided me a searching critique of the proposal. John Blough, who had majored in philosophy as an undergraduate, also had a capacity for trenchant critique. He once employed his knowledge of humanistic concepts to provide a strongly reasoned case against UCEA's participation in a proposed "career education" project.

Associate directors also helped renew UCEA by altering and im-proving its communication media. Two prominent publications were the *UCEA Newsletter* and its successor, the *UCEA Review*. The editors of these organs changed every two or three years as associates came and went. Such changes often brought renewal to the two outlets. I valued, for example, the succinct, witty, and sparkling style which Kenneth St. Clair expressed in the *UCEA Newsletter*. I also had great respect for the editorial abilities of Nicholas Nash. By applying his unique insights about format, his keen sense of esthetics, his eye for detail, and his imaginative thinking about content, he put a distinctive stamp on the *UCEA Review*. Ken and Nick also brought their special writing and editorial skills to other UCEA publications.

Some associates helped renew UCEA by shaping its five-year plans. Jackson Newell, whose doctorate was in higher education administration, used his knowledge in a study of programs for training higher education administrators (Newell, 1973). The information he acquired, along with ideas gathered through other planning activities, led UCEA to include in its 1974-79 plan the goal of developing new knowledge and new training materials for use in preparing higher education leaders. To help leaders design new programs related to "knowledge utilization"—UCEA's 1974-79 planning theme—Associate Director Rodney Pirtle synthesized key concepts pertinent to four basic modes of applying knowledge to practice (Pirtle, 1972).

Yet another way in which associates contributed to UCEA's renewal was by formulating fruitful UCEA research and development projects. This road to renewal was a rocky one, not easily traversed. To conceive new programs, associates not only needed special knowledge, but they also had to acquire an understanding of the UCEA culture, including modes of inter-university cooperation, and ways of building bridges between ideas and actions. They needed time to gain such insights. Thus, associates who remained at UCEA for three years were usually more successful in conceiving new programs than were those who served for one or two years.

Sometimes staff members cooperatively developed proposals. For example, three members helped Daniel Sage design the General-Special Education Administration proposal: Robin Farquhar, Alan Gaynor, and Michael Martin. Typically, individuals constructed proposals largely on their own. Illustrative examples of externally funded programs were the Politics of Education endeavor developed by Stephen Hencley, the National Level Internship Project formulated by James Yates, the Native American Planning Conference developed by Michael Martin, and the Women's Equity Project elaborated by Paula Silver.

Finally, associates effected organizational renewal through the coordination of inter-institutional research, development, and dissemination programs. While most of these programs were supported through UCEA resources, some were funded by governmental and foundation grants. Previous chapters have shown that Edwin Bridges, Donald Anderson, James Yates, Richard Podemski, Peter Hackbert, Paula Silver, Norman Ellis, Ellen Herda, and Grace Butler were among those associates who assumed full or partial responsibility for managing externally funded projects. Because such projects required wide ranging skills—conceptual, interpersonal, and tactical—they placed special demands upon their co-ordinators.

In sum, UCEA associates contributed to the renewal of UCEA in varied ways. They used their up-to-date knowledge to originate R and D projects. Bringing fresh perspectives to UCEA, they shed light on the field's problems. Some made UCEA's modes of dissemination more effective. Others utilized ideas to shape and give direction to UCEA's five-year plans. Most helped professors implement externally or internally funded R and D programs. In so doing they facilitated the creation of knowledge and products which professors could use to renew training practices in their own universities.

Coping with Complexity and Ambiguity

When new associates entered UCEA, they found themselves in an environment which differed radically from that of a single school, school system, or institution of higher education. Since UCEA universities were spread all across the U. S. and into Canada, the immediate environment was an expansive one. Lying beyond this primary environment was a much larger secondary one, which by 1980 encompassed hundreds of non-UCEA training institutions in North America, Asia, Africa, Australia, Europe, and South America. Other important external agencies with which UCEA had established links were approximately 12 national U. S. professional associations, a similar number of international organizations, 30 Partnership school systems, and several federal agencies. Extending outward from new staff, then, was a long and intricate chain of agencies.

Because the universities which belonged to UCEA were influenced by dissimilar settings, staffs, and objectives, they were a diverse lot. In the 1960s when I visited the University of Arkansas in Fayetteville, Arkansas, and Teachers College, Columbia, I could see the sharp differences in UCEA's membership. A salient feature of the University of Arkansas was its close links to state political institutions. An active member of the state Democratic political party and an Arkansas professor of school law, Roy Allen knew and frequently talked with members of the governor's staff, with state legislators, and with leaders of state associations, especially those which served teachers and school administrators. He worked hard to ensure that the university and his department were responsive to state interests, and that the state in turn supported his university.

Teachers College did not reside in a small town in a largely rural state, as did Arkansas. Located in the great urban center of New York

City, Teachers College early in the century had originated the first doctoral program in school administration. Its professors, in contrast to Roy Allen, talked infrequently with state politicians. Cultivating relations with officials in federal funding agencies was an activity to which they assigned a high priority. Rather than attracting doctoral students largely from its own state—as did the University of Arkansas—the institution's enrollees came from all regions of the nation.

Differences in settings, students, and professorial orientations inevitably influenced training programs in special ways. Marked dissimilarities could be seen even among private universities in urban contexts. During visits to Harvard and The University of Chicago in the early 1960s I identified major differences in training. Divergent practices were highlighted even in the conversations of students and professors in Chicago's cafeteria and in Harvard's student lounge. Subjects discussed often at Chicago, but seldom at Harvard, were linked to knowledge development: theoretical questions, research designs, statistical problems, and relevant social science concepts. At Harvard, on the other hand, the dominant subjects were educational policy issues and problems of school practice. As students talked about case studies of administrative behavior and about field studies in which they had examined such school problems as racial integration, they revealed a deep interest in social change and in the use of knowledge to improve school practice.[7]

The experiences acquired by Harvard and Chicago students were not products of random events. They were generated by disparate training rationales and purposes. The rationale at Harvard was based more upon a clinical model of training, while the Chicago one was based largely upon the disciplinary model of science. Not surprisingly, Chicago in the early sixties placed more of its doctoral graduates in professorships than any other UCEA university. On the other hand, Harvard prepared more than its share of "big city" superintendents.

One important way in which new associates confronted the ambiguity surrounding them was through university visits. Early in their tenure they usually traveled with me to three or four universities. At the first university an associate typically observed me interacting with groups and with individual professors. Afterwards we analyzed the purposes of my interactions, my approach to discovering the interests and the potential of UCEA professors to conduct R and D initiatives, and the means by which relevant findings and ideas could be promptly recorded for future use. As a rule, associates began their own search for program potential by interviewing professors at the second, third, and fourth universities visited. Thereafter, they traveled on their own to confront their ambiguous surroundings and to seek out program ideas.

Early in their tenure some associates were at times distracted from the task of program development during their university visits. Some were awed by renowned professors. Just before a new associate and I were to meet with The University of Chicago staff in the 1960s, my colleague was noticeably uncomfortable. Confessing that he felt more like returning to Columbus than attending the meeting, he was worried about his impending encounters with such "stars" as Jacob Getzels, Andrew Halpin, and Francis Chase. At the meeting he understandably thought little about potential R and D endeavors.

A few associates, curious about vexing questions they had identified during visits, focused heavily upon developing satisfying explanatory concepts. One associate was so intrigued with puzzling training issues that he struggled much more with the issues than with R or D projects during university visits. For some the visits increased rather than decreased the perceived ambiguity around them. One had firm views about the essential features of "quality" training programs when he joined UCEA. However, after seeing the varied approaches to training within UCEA, his earlier views about quality were shaken.

New associates also found it difficult to achieve clear definitions of their role and status at UCEA's headquarters. A prominent challenge, which was shared by the entire staff, was that of effecting desirable working relations between the associates and the executive director. Complicating this challenge was the fact that associates were temporary appointees, while I was a more permanent one. One result was that my UCEA experience and that of the associates became more and more discrepant as my tenure lengthened. When associate director Bill Coffield and I came to UCEA in 1959, our respective UCEA experiences were equal. So was our knowledge of UCEA and our influence in it. However, by the latter half of the 1960s the discrepancy in experience was noticeably affecting staff relations.

The fact that I had much, and new associates had little UCEA experience brought other issues to the fore. Some associates were uncomfortable with the fact that I was the major source of information about UCEA. Dependency was a condition not always welcomed by independent and able professionals. Sometimes the actions of professors further exacerbated their discomfort. Especially galling to some associates was the fact that some professors labeled them "interns." By regularly appending "Ph.D." after their names in all their correspondence, two UCEA associate directors in the 1970s sought to remind those in the UCEA community of their professional status.

Roles and Niches

Most new associates, especially during the last half of my tenure, tended to perceive me as a very influential figure. At the same time some felt that their powers were very limited—a belief which tended to affect those charged with developing new projects much more than those responsible for co-ordinating externally funded ones. Relatively independent co-ordinators not only had their "own" projects and budgets, but they also had much less ambiguous and more structured work tasks. At the same time their heavy work loads often deprived them of opportunities to explore ideas freely with project generators.

After assessing the limited powers which new associate directors felt they possessed, Associate Director Fred Frank proposed that UCEA's procedures for generating R and D projects be altered. Ordinarily, when staff members arrived at a general idea for a project, they elaborated it in writing. Typically, staff analyses produced suggestions for improving proposals. As authors refined their ideas, they received needed financial support to convene professors, to travel to foundations, or to execute other needed actions. Arguing that existing procedures were inappropriate, Fred offered a more decentralized mode of operation, namely: that associate directors be allocated each year a given amount of developmental money to control and expend as they saw fit. I undoubtedly added to Fred Frank's frustration, when I rejected his idea.

Another salient problem was that the role of project generators could not be defined with great precision, largely because it was a creative one. Although creativity could be nurtured, it could not be reduced to a set of specific prescriptions. Over time I did find ways of articulating values which could inform and shape the role. When I talked to new associates about UCEA's mission (i. e. improving training programs), I would pose the following question: "What is the largest room in the world?" The answer of course was the "room for improvement." I would emphasize that the concept applied both to training (and research) in UCEA universities and to UCEA's central office and inter-institutional practices. Within these domains of improvement, there were uncounted opportunities for associates to ameliorate practice. Undergirding these opportunities, I stressed, was unbounded human and organizational potential within UCEA—potential whose depths were yet to be plumbed.

Former UCEA associates will remember other role-related tenets I had elaborated such as: "individual initiative is a priceless expression in organizations," and "in setting objectives it is better to aim high than low." Ideas related to the darker side of change endeavors were: "failure can be a good teacher;" "it is all right to make mistakes as long as one learns from and does not repeat them;" and "those who cut the edge sometimes bleed." Telegraphing my esteem for the life of the mind and the importance of ideas in human affairs was a quotation from John Maynard Keynes which hung in my office for all to see: "It is ideas not vested interests which are dangerous for good or evil."

Some of the above ideas were embedded in the thoughts and actions of UCEA's founding fathers. Others were refinements and extensions of them. Still others seemed to fit the reality of my UCEA experiences. As guiding ideals and concepts, they reflected high expectations for UCEA associate directors. Other ideas which I transmitted to associates were related to efficient action. Two illustrative ideas, which emerged from my own thoughts about how to achieve more in less time, were "horizontal" and "vertical" integration.

The former concept referred to the efficient pursuit of multiple aims within a short time frame (e. g. two days). For example, when a staff member traveled to Washington, D. C. for a conference, did the staff member employ forethought in ways which produced results beyond those of the conference? Did the staff member before, during, or after the conference explore a projected joint endeavor with a national leader, acquire information from a federal agency about new funding possibilities, or solicit advice from selected conferees about an impending UCEA project?

"Vertical" integration involved projects with longer time frames (e. g. two years) in which a staff member kept one eye on a project's immediate phase and the other upon phases yet to come. By envisaging clearly all phases of a project and by thinking regularly about the execution of subsequent ones, more effective outcomes could be efficiently attained. A simulation's phases might be development, evaluation, revision, and demonstration. Did the simulation's leader regularly think about future problems and solutions including the disseminators, sponsors, and audiences which might best participate in demonstrations of the end products?

Fostering and managing creativity was complicated by human problems. In the last half of the 1960s the concept of "model" became a part of UCEA's culture. In the central office setting the concept referred to my own behavior. The term model, then, pertained to an actuality, not an ideal. Sometimes it enabled associates to acquire new and satisfying experiences. At other times it produced dissatisfaction and frustration. Months before I began writing this chapter, Alan Gaynor, a former UCEA associate, expressed the dual nature of the idea succinctly (personal correspondence, June, 1991): "I appreciate very much the model you set for me—even if I struggled against it." Surrounded by ambiguity and strong pressures to perform difficult tasks, associates, especially in their early months, looked to me for clues to guide their actions. However, at times most associates struggled against or with the "model." By the end of their first year typically most had clarified their roles and had put their initial struggles behind them. During their struggles I tried to help associates make their interests explicit, forge links between their ideas and new UCEA projects, and express *their* talents and individuality.

Modes of coping with the "model" were as diverse as were the associates. A few openly rebelled against aspects of it, while others, especially during UCEA's earlier years, entered into their roles with limited stress and with dispatch. The first to rebel openly was Bryce Fogarty. Rejecting my work ethic, he persuaded his colleagues that the practice of working on Saturday mornings should be abolished by the associates. I soon found myself alone on Saturdays except for one very conscientious associate director! In subsequent years associates seldom appeared at UCEA's headquarter's on Saturdays. Still their work schedule was a demanding one, since they often departed on or returned from UCEA trips during weekends.

Paula Silver openly opposed me because of perceptions about how I used my "power." Feeling that I had much and she had little control over UCEA events, she was unhappy with the "model." However, about seven months into her tenure the situation began to change when she asked me to discuss an idea. After she explained it, I asked if she could put it on paper in the form of a proposed UCEA project. She agreed to take on the task. The next morning she entered my office in a mood of elation. Stimulated by the idea outlined the previous day, she had spent the entire night at her typewriter. The result was a well-conceived plan for a UCEA project. My earlier expressions of faith in her ability had had no visible effects. However, by elaborating her own plan of action, she apparently had demonstrated to herself that she could also influence events. The incident proved to be a turning point in her UCEA career. In the remaining years of her tenure she conceived and helped implement varied projects.

Alan Gaynor, frustrated by the ambiguity surrounding his role, also expressed negative feelings at times toward the "model." However, as we learned more about each other, an effective working relationship emerged. In the process Alan implicitly taught me lessons which had import for others who faced ambiguous conditions. Over time I learned that Alan's most important question by far about any UCEA task was "why should it be performed?" Unwilling to settle for a cursory or general answer, he wanted a clearly elucidated statement of the reasons for conducting a given task. When he had obtained a satisfactory answer, he would pose a second question: "What is the desired outcome (s) of the endeavor?" Finally, Alan would ask for a deadline to complete the task. Answers to the three questions provided him the structure needed to perform his role with skill and dispatch. An able thinker, he left UCEA a legacy of published writings and of several new initiatives.

Associates sometimes came to grips with the "model" by studying its relationship to their own behavior. James Yates once told me that I offered a fine model, but that it was one he could not follow. A student of psychology, James apparently had arrived at his viewpoint after some introspection. Having recognized the discrepancy between our two modes of behavior, he had opted to respect both of them while employing and building upon his own. Known as a direct communicator, he worked with many leaders inside and outside UCEA. He also contributed to UCEA's renewal by conceiving and acquiring external support for a major national initiative.

Some associates incorporated certain features of the "model" into their own behavior. One such example began with a conversation I had with Robin Farquhar in the late 1960s. After reporting that he had received a proposal from Van Miller of the University of Illinois, he observed that there were several problems with it—problems which he lucidly delineated. Loyal to UCEA, Robin was concerned that support for Van Miller's idea would not square with past precedents. His inclination was to say "no" to the initiative. Complimenting him on his incisive analysis, I suggested that there were additional factors which might be considered. First, one could look beyond problems and probe more carefully the proposal's potential impact. Second, one could act upon the belief that keeping human aspirations alive is sometimes more important than adherence to precedent. I suggested that since Van had not asked for much, it seemed that a big organization like UCEA might find a way to help him.

The next day Robin told me that he had responded positively to the Illinois proposal. However, time passed before I learned the full impact of our conversation. Some years after he left his post, he confided that our exchange about the Van Miller incident had had a more profound effect upon him by far than any other UCEA event. As a result, he subsequently assigned much more importance to people and possibilities and relatively less to immediate problems and past precedents. In reviewing the incident with him while writing this chapter, he re-affirmed that it had "changed his life." He also noted that he still used the experience from time to time in his post as president of Carleton University. In so doing he sought to encourage those with whom he worked to attend more fully to human aspirations and potential in their decision-making.

The impact of temporary staffing reached beyond the associate directors to the executive director. An illustrative example had to do with organizational commitment. Because associates typically spent only two or three years at UCEA, the depth and intensity of their commitment to the organization, while strong, was inevitably less than my own. As a relatively permanent staff member, I could focus firmly on UCEA's long-range future. As temporary appointees, associates could not. During their final year, for example, they had to spend considerable time and energy finding a new position. Commitment was also reflected in work schedules. For some the number of hours I worked was excessive. When an associate once dropped by the UCEA office on Labor Day, he found me at work. Decades later I learned that he and his colleagues thought my action bordered on the preposterous! Only with time did I learn to accept the discrepant views about work schedules and organizational commitments.

Although the temporary staffing patterns afforded UCEA continuing options for renewal, they demanded much effort. I expended substantial time in recruiting, selecting, and serving as a mentor for new associates. During the last year of their tenure I also helped them find new positions. The continuing gaps in staffing brought other problems to the fore. For example, departing associates typically left behind unfinished projects. Most new associates were understandably more motivated to create and conduct their own projects than to finish ones initiated by others. In addition, uncompleted projects, especially those with complicated histories, usually proved easier for me to complete than to transfer to new associates.

Earlier I noted that UCEA required of its staff three types of thinking: abstract, strategic, and operational. Temporary staffing contributed to weaknesses in operational decision-making. Weaknesses exhibited themselves in large inter-institutional programs and in such functions as governance activities. One reason for the weakness was the unusual complexity of UCEA. Another stemmed from the fact that newly employed associate directors were largely unfamiliar with UCEA and with the current state of its existing programs. Early in their tenure some were also much more interested in abstract and strategic problems than in operational ones.

UCEA professors were tolerant of management errors. While I heard indirectly about negative responses of professors, I can remember only one professor who called an error to my attention directly. At a meeting in the 1970s a professor said that he wanted me to know that a UCEA associate during the previous nine months had sent Plenary members three different dates for their November meeting. Later the UCEA associate confirmed that the Plenary member's report was correct.

Such errors precipitated a discussion of staff "snafus" at an Executive Committee meeting in the mid-seventies. The discussion turned once again to problems of discontinuity in UCEA staffing. However, the problems generated by discontinuity continued to persist.

I easily identified with associates during their demanding first year. After all, I had also found that my initial year was in some ways the most difficult of the 22 years I spent at UCEA. Quickly making the unfamiliar sufficiently familiar to launch new and viable initiatives was not an easy task. I often felt frustrated because I seemingly could do so little to help associates originate new initiatives. Apparently, one of the most appropriate tactics was to exercise patience — a response which did not always come easy to me.

The experience of seeing associates leave their UCEA posts was emotionally-laden. I remember well a relevant occurrence from the

1960s. As we walked to the faculty club, an associate told me of his plans to leave at the end of the year—his second one at UCEA. Since the associate had worked closely with me on many projects and had initiated some of his own, I had hoped very much that he would spend a third year at UCEA. Thus, his message was a painful one. By the time we had seated ourselves for lunch, I had lost my appetite. Although I learned over time to view the departure of associates with some detachment, I always had difficulty living with the paradox that at the very time they were the best informed, the most competent, and the most confident, they left UCEA.

After making their marks upon UCEA, associates moved to new settings. Five-sixths of them accepted positions in higher education. Repelled by the ponderous movement of universities toward change, a few moved into the private sector. When this was written, Nicholas Nash and Walter Panko were presidents of their own corporations. On the other hand, Jack Blough and Rodney Pirtle accepted positions as public school administrators. Most of those who moved into higher education served as department heads, associate deans, or deans. At the time of this writing five had held or were holding administrative posts in the central offices of universities.

Former UCEA associates have produced many books and hundreds of articles. Most of them have maintained strong interests in idea-practice relationships. Some have concentrated more upon applying ideas. For many years Terry Eidell has performed as the Executive Director of the Appalachia Education Laboratory serving four states, while Loren Downey from 1985-1991 was Director of Professional Development for the University of Maine System of Higher Education. Many former associates during their careers have switched from roles of applying knowledge to roles of developing or acquiring knowledge and vice versa. For example, William Coffield moved from UCEA to the dual posts of professorship and department head, afterward to a deanship, then to a vice-presidency of academic affairs, then to a professorship, and ended his career in a deanship. Just before I wrote this chapter, he confided that he preferred to be remembered as a "proud professor." Rodney Pirtle, on the other hand, retired early from an associate superintendency of schools in Texas and entered the Perkins School of Theology at Southern Methodist University. At the time of this writing he had completed more than half of a Master's program in theology. By drawing upon his training in journalism, he hopes to disseminate selected theological ideas more widely.

Let me conclude by returning to Edith Wharton's observation about "spreading light". Thinkers have used "light" as a metaphor for knowledge and understanding for more than two thousand years. Though the 30 candle lights which associates brought to UCEA were of different hues, forms, and intensities, they all helped enlighten the organization's efforts. As the closest and most frequent viewer of the 30 lights, I gained the most from their illuminating effects. At times I helped associates focus their light beams upon new audiences. At my best I sometimes served as a mirror which reflected their rays, though at less than full strength, toward sites shrouded in shadows on UCEA's large landscape.

Notes

1. Glenn Immegart, who completed his doctoral dissertation while serving as a UCEA staff member, had the title of assistant director. William Davis, who worked on projects at UCEA's headquarters during summers and at Oklahoma State during the academic years of his UCEA tenure, was called a project associate director. Since both Immegart and Davis performed functions similar to those of associate directors, they are included in the group.

2. For a very detailed description of UCEA's selection processes see "Criteria and Procedures for Selecting Associate Directors" (EC Mat, 9/13-15/73).

3. See Griffiths, D. E. (1963). Some assumptions underlying the use of models in research. In J. A. Culbertson & S. P. Hencley (Eds.), *Educational research: New perspectives* (pp. 121-140). Danville, IL: The Interstate Printers & Publishers, Inc.

4. For a discussion of the uses of taxonomic concepts by scientists see Cullinan, P. (1969). Processes and problems in taxonomic studies. In D. E. Griffiths (Ed.), *Developing taxonomies of organizational behavior in educational administration* (pp. 3-25). Chicago: Rand McNally & Company.

5. Other readers of the dissertation also thought it should be published. Later an expanded version appeared. See Finkelstein, M. J. (1984). *The American academic profession: A synthesis of social scientific inquiry since World War II*. Columbus, OH: Ohio State University Press.

6. See Farquhar, R. H. (1970). *The humanities in preparing educational administrators*. Eugene, OR: The ERIC Clearinghouse on Educational Administration.

7. For comprehensive descriptions of Harvard's and Chicago's approaches to training see Cronin, J. M., & Iannaccone, L. (1973). The social sciences and the preparation of educational administrators at Harvard and Chicago. In J. Culbertson, R. H. Farquhar, B. M. Fogarty, & M. R. Shibles (Eds.), *Social science content for preparing educational leaders* (pp. 193-244). Columbus, OH: Charles E Merrill Publishing Company.

References

Conant, J. B. (1964). *Two modes of thought*. New York: Trident Press.

Culbertson, J. A. (1981). Three epistemologies and the study of educational administration. *UCEA Newsletter*, XXII(1), 1-7.

Eidell, T. L. (1966). The utilization of social science content in preparation programs for administrators. A paper prepared for the UCEA Task Force on the Social Sciences and the Preparation of Educational administrators.

Glass, G. V. (1976). Primary, secondary, and meta-analysis of research. *Educational Researcher*, 5(10), 3-8.

Griffiths, D. E. (1959). *Research in educational administration*. New York: Bureau of Publications, Teachers College, Columbia University.

Newell, L. J. (1973). A report on the higher education survey. *UCEA Newsletter*, XIV(3), 12-16.

Pirtle, R. (1972). "A synthesis of selected concepts produced by the Center for Research on Utilization of Scientific Knowledge." A paper prepared for a UCEA Executive Committee meeting (EC Mat, 9/8-10/72).

11

Governance

"If liberty and equality, as is thought by some, are to be found in democracy, they will be best attained when all persons alike share in the government to the utmost."

Aristotle

During the 1959-81 period UCEA's governance was affected by a lengthy struggle for power, considerable discontent among some professors, a major change in decision structures, and potent paradoxes. The struggle for power was rooted largely in UCEA's two unequal governance structures: the UCEA Board of Trustees and the Plenary Session. The latter body, made up of one professor from each UCEA university, elected the nine member Board. As the 1960s unfolded, some Plenary representatives became increasingly dissatisfied with the centralized decision-making of the "strong" UCEA Board. Unhappy with UCEA's programs, they not only desired to change them but also to increase the number of professors who participated in them. Thus, leading Plenary members rose up in the early 1970s and eliminated the UCEA Board of Trustees. Replacing the Board with a UCEA Executive Committee which had limited powers, the Plenary body assigned to itself the legal responsibility for making UCEA policy.

As the Plenary body struggled to realize the desired fruits of the changes in governance, it encountered severe problems. The size of its membership—ranging over the years from 34 to 59—made policy making at times cumbersome and inefficient. In addition, its governance personnel turned over frequently. Since an estimated 350 professors served as Plenary representatives during the 1959-81 period, many had limited knowledge of UCEA governance.

Paradoxical tendencies within UCEA also side tracked, slowed, or hampered policy making by Plenary members. For example, governance decisions were complicated by the fact that members of UCEA were institutions, not individuals. Diverse groups of professors in departments of educational administration often did not instruct Plenary members about how their universities should be represented at governance meetings. As a rule, the groups either remained mute or offered Plenary members conflicting views about impending UCEA decisions. Another illustrative barrier to effective policy making stemmed from the constant clashes between competitive forces and cooperative ideals. Such clashes made it difficult for Plenary members to appreciate, much less vigorously pursue, the ideals underlying UCEA's cooperative ethic. For example, many seemed more interested in competing for roles in emerging or ongoing UCEA programs than in cooperatively formulating policy designed to make programs more responsive to UCEA interests.

Given the problems it encountered, the Plenary body was unable to alter significantly UCEA's governance processes and outcomes. One result was disappointment among those who had worked to reform UCEA's governance. Another was a re-centralization of power. By the end of the seventies the Executive Committee was performing most of the functions performed earlier by the Board. The Plenary body *could* veto Executive Committee recommendations. However, it seldom did so. Although dissatisfactions remained, UCEA's adapted form of governance worked reasonably well for a far flung organization comprised of diverse universities and an even more diverse professoriate.

A Profile of UCEA's Policy Makers

Between 1959 and 1981 I had the distinctive experience of working with 18 UCEA presidents. Listed below in chronological order are their names and university affiliations:

Walter Anderson, New York University
Truman Pierce, Auburn
Van Miller, Illinois
Richard Lonsdale, Syracuse and New York University[1]
Kenneth McIntyre, Texas at Austin
Willard Lane, Iowa
Alan Thomas, Chicago
Samuel Goldman, Syracuse

Wailand Bessent, Texas at Austin
Donald Willower, Pennsylvania State
Loren Downey, Boston
Troy McKelvey, State University of New York at Buffalo
Peter Cistone, Ontario Institute for Studies in Education,
University of Toronto
Wayne Hoy, Rutgers
Larry Hillman, Wayne State
Carl Ashbaugh, Texas at Austin
Eugene Ratsoy, Alberta
James Maxey, Georgia State

Elected to UCEA's highest office, the above leaders all had unusual talents. The diversity they displayed in their styles, purposes, and performances impressed me greatly. To highlight their individuality, I will provide brief profiles of the first three with whom I worked throughout their full terms.

In 1959 Truman Pierce was arguably the most influential of all southern educational leaders. Reputedly the first southern educator to speak publicly in favor of school desegregation, he was deeply committed to improved community life through improved education. He had obtained a doctorate from Teachers College, Columbia, and among other things, had headed the Southern States CPEA Center. A task-oriented president, he encouraged all his colleagues to speak their minds. He focused upon getting decisions made while studiously refraining from offering his own ideas on the issues. Well versed in inter-university cooperation, he understood the challenges UCEA staff faced. He once volunteered to meet with the staff for a few days to project future UCEA initiatives. However, I declined the offer. I thought that an extended brainstorming session with only one board member might create problems.

Holder of a doctorate from Harvard, Van Miller had co-written a widely used text on school administration.[2] At the NCPEA some years earlier I had learned that we both had strong interests in communication theory. He, more than any other UCEA president, focused upon getting the board to approve the staff's proposals. Once when a board member moved that a staff recommendation "be buried as deep as possible," he seemed crestfallen. At the next recess he asked me to take a walk with him. During the walk he stressed that I should not take the board member's action too seriously. At the time I felt he was much more disturbed than I by the action.

I never fully understood why he was so loyal to the staff. I did know he was concerned about the competitive forces which interfered with cooperative UCEA action. Calling me a "navigator in the blue," he once remarked that if I did not get frustrated in my job, there was something wrong with me. Although he was protective of UCEA staff members, he did not hesitate to provide us critical feedback. Once he disapprovingly told me that I had handled an issue before the board like an aging county superintendent!

Richard Lonsdale, though younger than UCEA's earlier presidents, had already established his leadership abilities. He had headed NCPEA and had served as president of the Collegiate Association for the Development of Educational Administration in New York State. After obtaining a doctorate from Syracuse in 1946, he had joined the Syracuse staff. While there, he worked hard at applying social science concepts to administration. After his election to the UCEA Board, he and I served on the committee of the National Society for the Study of Education which planned the Society's 1964 yearbook on *Behavioral Science and Educational Administration.*[3] In a yearbook chapter, "Maintaining the Organization in Dynamic Equilibrium," he synthesized an array of concepts from several disciplines.

While chairing meetings, Lonsdale, in contrast to Pierce, became heavily involved with the issues. In fact, he addressed them with such enthusiasm that his colleagues had to remind him at times of his official role. He, more than any other president, concentrated on analyzing and generating ideas at meetings. After meetings he often provided me critiques. In doing so, he tended to analyze the semantics of words and phrases I had used. Although I did not always understand the rationale for his ideas, they were usually thought provoking.

Although very diverse behaviors could promote effective policy making, they did not always do so. As experts in analytic thought, some professors could become so immersed in the intelligent analysis of policy issues that they would forget or ignore the need to effect decisions. Choice making could be further complicated when several professors competitively displayed their analytical skills. The actions of UCEA policy makers, I observed, differed somewhat from those of Partnership policy makers. Composed of five professors and five school superintendents, the Partnership policy body was typically quite effective. (see Chapter Nine). The analytical bents of professors tended to be balanced by the superintendents' interests in moving discussions toward an effective conclusion.

That the qualities of UCEA policy makers changed over time can be seen by looking briefly at the first and the last governance meeting I attended. The initial one was in Urbana, Illinois, on November 18-19, 1959. Eight of the nine members of UCEA's Board of Trustees were present: President Walter Anderson, New York University; Francis Chase, Chicago; Russell Gregg, Wisconsin; Paul Jacobson, Oregon; Truman Pierce, Auburn; John Ramseyer, Ohio State; Theodore Reller, California at Berkeley; and Virgil Rogers, Syracuse. Also present was Hollis Moore, Executive Secretary of the Committee for the Advancement of School Administration and an ex officio member of the UCEA Board. Rounding out the group was Daniel Griffiths, the Secretary-Treasurer of UCEA. The ninth board member, John Norton of Teachers College, Columbia, was in India.

Twenty-two years later I attended my last governance meeting on May 20-23, 1981, in Columbus, Ohio. All nine members of UCEA's Executive Committee were present: President James Maxey, Georgia State University; Carl Ashbaugh, Texas at Austin; James Conway, SUNY at Buffalo; Gladys Johnston, Rutgers; Cecil Miskel, Kansas; Michael Murphy, Utah; Richard Podemski, Arkansas; Eugene Ratsoy, Alberta; and Dennis Spuck, Houston. Also in attendance was UCEA's Treasurer, Donald Anderson of Ohio State.

One of the 1959 board members had acquired his doctorate in the 1920s, four in the 1930s, three in the 1940s, and one in 1951. The two youngest members were born in 1908, three years after Elwood Cubberley and George Strayer—the two leading first generation professors of educational administration—obtained their Ph.D. at Teachers College, Columbia. Most of the 1959 members were third generation professors in that their instructors were largely students of first generation professors. Five of the 1981 Executive Committee members were born in the 1930s and four in the 1940s. Three and six members of the 1981 group obtained their doctorates in the 1960s and 1970s, respectively. Most were fifth generation professors.

The professional outlooks of the two groups were influenced by their university training. In the earlier era administrative experience was an important criterion for entry into doctoral programs and professorships. Those in the earlier group had met the criterion well. Virgil Rogers and

Paul Jacobson, for instance, were former city school superintendents. On the other hand, the 1981 members had acquired doctorates and entered professorships when the criterion of administrative experience was much less important. Four had served as principals and one as an assistant principal. Four had not held an administrative post in schools.

Having devoted much study to education and its societal contexts, the 1959 members viewed their field from a broad perspective. In the 1950s most of them co-authored general books on school administration. Jacobson co-wrote a text on the duties of school principals, Pierce a book on community leadership for education, Reller a reference on administrative problems, practices, and issues in education, and Ramseyer an introductory text on educational administration.[4] All were deeply interested in the concept of leadership. In an essay which described 10 societal trends and their import for school leaders, John Norton set forth a credo which the other board members shared (Norton, 1957, p. 80):

> Among the qualifications of the educational executive none is more essential than that he be a thoughtful student of the society which public education exists to serve. He should constantly seek to identify the factors and trends in the contemporary scene which hold implications for administrative leadership. From such study comes the social insight which is prerequisite to . . . leadership. Without such insight the educational executive will be a mere timeserver.

Since those in the 1981 group focused more on specialized content in their training (e. g. organizational and administrative behavior), their perspectives were less expansive. In the 1970s they had published articles on such topics as organizational behavior, the motivation of educators, the politics of education, women's equity, organizational structure, and computer-based simulation. Murphy was the co-author of an anthology of readings on collective bargaining.[5] When analyzing UCEA's actions, the 1981 group could apply organizational concepts which were unknown to their 1959 predecessors. The two professional associations they valued most were UCEA and the American Educational Research Association. Those in the 1959 group participated regularly in the National Conference of Professors of Educational Administration and the American Association of School Administrators.

To draw too fine a line between the two groups would be a mistake. Embedded in the thinking of the 1959 group were harbingers of things to come. Reller had introduced his readers to systems theory in his co-authored text. In the book on administrative behavior which Russell Gregg had co-edited, there were two chapters on theory.[6] As head of the Department of Education at The University of Chicago, Francis Chase had played a major role in nurturing theory development. Without such harbingers Cecil Miskel, a member of the 1981 group, might not have co-written a widely used text on theory.[7]

Differences in age and experience affected my relationships to the two groups. The 1959 board members ranged in age from 51 to 66. I was sixteen years younger than their average age of 57. Although I was reasonably familiar with their extensive accomplishments, I knew only Jacobson and Reller well. Keenly aware that all of them were much more experienced than I in inter-university endeavors, I was not entirely at ease with the group. At the same time I was excited by the opportunity to know and to work with these UCEA Board members.

The ages of the 1981 committee ranged from 34 to 48. On average, they were 20 years younger than I. Having conversed with them often and having read some of their writings, I knew their attainments well. By 1981 I was also highly experienced in inter-university practices. Thus, I was more at ease at the 1981 than at the 1959 meeting.

At the 1959 meeting the staff offered 12 policy recommendations, plus 10 reports in 74 single-spaced pages. Also presented were six applications for membership in UCEA (B Mat, 11/18-19/59). Since my ideas were set forth fully on paper, I spent most of the meeting listening. However, I did engage in some norm building. For example, after an extended discussion of what UCEA could provide its members, President Anderson asked how I had responded to the issue during visits to universities. My answer was that UCEA could provide professors unique opportunities to im-prove their field. My response was designed to re-inforce the norm of improvement. It was also directed at those who expected central office staff to generate UCEA's outcomes. I wanted professors to see that they had crucial UCEA roles to play. In addition, I was implicitly affirming the need for active, altruistic giving—not passive receiving.

At the May 1981 meeting, five weeks before I left UCEA, I offered only one program proposal. Devoted largely to issues posed by my impending UCEA exit, the meeting dealt, for example, with the future management of about $400,000 of UCEA surplus funds (EC Mat, 5/20-23/81). Since the committee's major task was to interview five candidates for UCEA's executive director post, my own role was limited. However, I did make one suggestion while the committee discussed its plans for a special conference to be held in 1982. When one of its members suggested that his university could sponsor the conference, I suggested that the planned event be announced and that all interested UCEA universities submit proposals to sponsor it. Such a procedure, I suggested, would ensure equality of opportunity and enhance the likelihood that fresh conference content would be generated for the field. Instead of engaging in norm building as I had in 1959, I thus lent my support to an established norm.

Changes during the 1959-1981 period made policy making more difficult for the younger group. For one thing, UCEA was a much more complex organization in part because it resided in a more turbulent environment than that of the earlier period. In addition, the 1981 policy makers were trained in doctoral programs which were more specialized that those experienced by the 1959 group. The latter group brought a broader perspective to policy making. As I saw it, the specialized views of those in the younger group (and in the UCEA Plenary members) made it more difficult for them to articulate general policy objectives.

A Crescendo of Discontent

UCEA's founders wanted the Board of Trustees to be a strong body. On the other hand, they saw Plenary members as "stock holders" in UCEA who would meet annually, receive "corporate" reports, elect board members, and approve budgets, new members, and changes in by-laws. Very early some Plenary members resented the lower status accorded them. They also decided informally that "powerful" deans of colleges of education should not serve on UCEA's Board. By 1963 they had replaced all the four deans on the 1959 Board with professors. They wanted to be governed by "their own kind."

As the Board and staff made more and more UCEA decisions during the 1960s, the resentment of Plenary members increased. Helping fuel ill feelings were frustrations created by the clashes between the ideals of cooperation and the realities of competition. The uneasy and paradoxical relations between the two can be clarified by looking at the founding and development of the *Educational Administration Quarterly*, an illustrative UCEA endeavor of the 1960s.

Undergirding the development of the *Quarterly* was the belief that if scholars from different UCEA universities cooperatively designed a journal, they would produce a better product than would a professor in a single university. Another crucial belief was that the journal's growth and continuance was more likely to be ensured through the cooperative pooling of UCEA resources. Initially, an official committee of able editors met to make plans for the journal. At the end of the meeting a question arose: who would edit it? Undoubtedly, most wanted to be the founding editor. However, in a cooperative endeavor they could not gracefully compete for the honor. Thus, an awkward situation arose. As an outsider, I asked the group if Roald Campbell might serve as the first editor. Although my idea likely disappointed most of those present, it was accepted by the committee.

During the 1965-81 period many professors competed for editorial posts and positions on the editorial board. When Roald Campbell and The University of Chicago were ending their three-year term, those in other universities began competing to host the journal. Later explicit procedures to enable all UCEA universities to compete for the editorship were approved. The journal's conception, then, was grounded in the cooperative ethic. However, its implementation took place in a milieu of competition. As institutions competed to host the *Quarterly*, scholars to edit it, and writers to have articles published in it, there were many more losers than winners.

As the numbers of unsuccessful competitors for UCEA roles grew, the resentment of Plenary members and those they represented increased. Winning competitors, UCEA Board members, and the central staff became targets of resentment. The content of UCEA programs also became a troublesome issue. The first time Plenary members discussed the issue publicly was at a "good of the order" exchange in 1965. One group concluded that in choosing "topics for future Career Development seminars and other UCEA work, some attention should be focused on the traditional subject areas, e. g. finance and law" (PS Min, 2/14/65, p. 3). Two years later at another Plenary meeting, a professor of school law angrily criticized UCEA's programs. By the end of the sixties numerous professors wanted changes in the content of UCEA programs.

Many professors wanted programs to be directly linked to the subjects they taught. However, most UCEA programs in the 1960s were directed at such broad objectives as new directions for improving training, more promising pathways to knowledge, uses of the social sciences, internationalization of the field, and ways of employing the humanities in training. Even such specific program outcomes as newly established journals transcended the specialized interests of given professors. Little wonder, then, that the specialist in school law was highly critical of UCEA's program offerings.

Another paradox affecting programs stemmed from the fact that the members of UCEA were universities, not individuals. Universities could fund Career Development seminars, instructional materials institutes, and task forces, while individuals could not. UCEA could also stimulate its members to develop five-year improvement plans, while organizations with individual membership could not. Yet UCEA was ultimately dependent upon individual professors who possessed much autonomy and whose objectives were very diverse.

The institution-individual paradox was further complicated by the fact that UCEA's key functions were research, development, and dissemination. Performers of these functions had to have unusual abilities. If planners of a UCEA Career Development Seminar did not have a cogent guiding conception as well as knowledge of pertinent research, they could easily produce a mediocre seminar. Expert knowledge and skill were even more essential in the performance of R and D functions. Thus, only a minority of professors could take part in R or D projects. The hundreds of professors who attended UCEA dissemination activities were not entirely satisfied with consumer roles. Many wanted to be involved in the higher status projects.   Over time, two classes of professors emerged who had divided loyalties to UCEA: participants and non-participants in R and D programs. Divisions were often reinforced by the uneasy relations between practice-oriented and theory-oriented professors in universities.

By the late 1960s some professors, afflicted with festering resentment, wanted to do more than change programs. In 1968 Keith Goldhammer, a friend with whom I had worked at the University of Oregon, warned me that some professors "were out to get me." The next year the UCEA Board dealt with the issue of my contract renewal. Afterward, UCEA President Willard Lane told me that one board member had made the case for my discharge. Ten years in the executive directorship, the board member maintained, was enough for one person. Eight of the nine members, however, voted to renew the contract.

The board member was undoubtedly influenced by professorial perceptions. Some thought that I was an overly aggressive program developer and that my "centrally" conceived programs did not reflect *their* interests. At one session Plenary members maintained that UCEA should "tone down some central staff initiation and provide more stimulation of ideas from . . . universities" (PS Min, 11/8-10/70, p. 2). One professor argued that the leaders of UCEA were the professors, not the central office staff. The role of the UCEA staff was to serve professors as, for example, by obtaining grants for professors to implement their programs.

Professors were also disturbed because, as they saw it, I opened the gate for participants in R and D programs and closed it on nonparticipants. Early in the 1960s I learned about the effects of my gatekeeping role when a professor who had experienced the pain of exclusion confronted me. He began in anger and ended in tears. Nationally known and respected, he charged that I had unjustly excluded his paper from a UCEA publication. After he made the case that I had acted unjustly, I apologized to him. He accepted my apology and forgave me. Four years later he was elected to the UCEA Board of Trustees. During his tenure as a board member the earlier events apparently had no effect upon his decision making.

Several reasons undergirded my admitted aggressiveness in program development. Without a constant stream of new programs UCEA could neither renew itself nor persistently pursue its mission. Keenly aware that many UCEA programs would not reach fruition and that failure would be as frequent a companion as success, I "loaded" the organization's agenda with initiatives. In addition, there was no UCEA function I enjoyed more than program development, nor was there one more challenging. Attaining well conceived programs was in a way like solving a jigsaw puzzle. A crucial difference, however, was that the pieces of program puzzles were not immediately given: they had to be discovered, adjusted, aggregated, and fused into a gestalt.

Program Development: Process and Policy

To shed light on the relations between professorial interests and UCEA programs, I will describe how I went about identifying interests and program possibilities. In doing so I will focus only upon three sources of program ideas: five year planning, conversing with professors during university visits, and reading materials.

Reflected in the goals and objectives of UCEA's five-year plans were numerous program possibilities. Yet written plans were not as helpful in the design of specific programs as was information which professors revealed about their abilities and interests during planning sessions. In developing five year plans, for example, about 200 professors typically attended one of nine regional planning meetings. There they talked about their departments' accomplishments, offered critiques of staff planning ideas, and advised UCEA about desirable objectives and programs for the next five year period.

The planning sessions uncovered numerous clues about human and program potential. Yet professors typically did not identify specific program ideas. Rather, one had to search for potential in the abilities they displayed. For instance, one professor spoke about his work on the "politics of innovation." His remarks showed me that he had a strong interest in his subject and a well ordered set of relevant concepts. Thus, I concluded that he had the capacity to work with others in the conception of a research endeavor.

Reflected in the professor's behavior, then, was one piece of a program puzzle. Would subsequent meetings uncover at least two or three other specialists in the politics of innovation? If so, could a group agree upon a problem to be investigated? Would universities support the planning of a research project? Would needed resources be found? At the meeting I asked the professor if he would send me some reprints dealing with his research. Since the actual implementation of a cooperative research program was so uncertain, I did not speak to the professor about it. Rather, I filed the idea in my memory and began a search for additional pieces of the program puzzle.

Planning processes uncovered scores of professors who might enact UCEA programs. However, I was frequently unable to find and fit together the requisite program pieces. In fact, the journey from identified possibilities to operating inter-university projects was treacherous. Fortunately, I could use my mental notes on potential for other purposes (e. g. informally linking individuals to others with similar interests or enabling professors to disseminate their ideas through UCEA seminars or other channels).

Planning meetings also produced valuable insights into institutional potential. University of Iowa staff displayed such potential at a meeting in 1962, when they described pioneering work their institution had achieved in advancing uses of the computer in education. Later I asked the professors if Iowa might sponsor a Career Development

Seminar on computers during the 1964-69 period. Reacting enthusiastically, they offered a UCEA seminar on "Computer Concepts and
Educational Administration" in the spring of 1965.

In my first year at UCEA I learned that university visits spawned
numerous program ideas. As professors talked to Bill Coffield and
myself during visits, we took notes on what we heard.   As we
accumulated written summaries of ideas, we identified eight interests
which cut across regions and universities — interests which we pursued the next year by activating eight task forces. (see Chapter Three).

Throughout my UCEA tenure I placed a high value on university
visits. They helped me grasp the changing "grass roots" interests in
UCEA and discover many program ideas.   During visits I asked
professors to specify the favorite subject they taught, UCEA programs
of interest to them, issues they thought UCEA should address, and
research they were engaged in or planned to conduct. Implicit in their
responses were ideas about how they might be involved in on-going or
new programs. In the 1970s I began summarizing in letters the ideas I
had gleaned. The following excerpts from a letter sent on December 5,
1975, to the University of Rochester's Plenary representative, Glenn
Immegart, are illustrative. Copies were sent to his dean, James Doi, and
his department head, Howard Bretsch.

I would like to summarize perceptions about points of tangency
between the interests of those in your department and the emergent or
on-going programs of UCEA.

1. William Boyd expressed an interest in attending the . . .
    career development seminar next fall at the University of
    Virginia on "The Politics of Education in a Time of Scar-
    city." He was also very interested in the computer-based
    simulation entitled "SAFE." We are sending him some
    special information in this area. Another possibility is for
    either Jerry Debenham or Mike Murphy to demonstrate
    the SAFE simulation at Rochester. . .
2. Both Mickie Garms and Guilbert Hentschke will be a part
    of the emergent network concerned with uses of computer-
    based simulation; this network will be generating . . . media
    for facilitating the flow of information and ideas in this area.
3. Tyll van Geel expressed a strong interest in the emergent
    network having to do with law and education and indicated

he would be willing to serve in a primary or secondary role as editor of a low-cost medium designed to transmit information of interest to professors teaching law; he has agreed to set forth some ideas about this topic and to write me.

4. We are pleased that you continue . . . to develop ideas and data on the 1954-74 period . . . related to the study of educational administration; when you have completed the draft . . ., we agreed that UCEA would find a . . . medium for disseminating the materials . . . to the profession of educational administration.

5. Jerry Lysaught gave me some interesting ideas about the relationships between medical and educational administration; I plan to follow-up on these conversations in visits to Washington during the coming months.

6. I am encouraging Howard Bretsch to consider writing a case on higher education decision making. Since he has had experience as a higher education administrator as well as experience in case writing, he could contribute to the UCEA Series.

7. We would be pleased if James Doi could attend the session at NYU in January . . . on research on the "Deanship." I am sure he could make a contribution to our thinking about research in this area. . . .

8. Finally, we are most pleased that we will be able to sponsor with the University of Rochester a seminar on research; clearly this is a very important topic, and we believe that significant contributions can be made to the field . . . through a seminar and the publication which results.

I hope the above perceptions prove useful to you. If you have further observations about how we can cooperate . . . to improve educational administration, please let me know.

Each year during my UCEA tenure I visited 15 to 20 universities on average. The pleasure I gleaned from discovering and identifying program possibilities during the visits never subsided. As I talked with professors, the objectives in prevailing five year plans were of enormous value. They provided foci for our discussions and frameworks within which to order new program ideas.

Another bounteous source of program ideas was the written word. Included in the large and constant flow of materials across my desk were unpublished papers, writings by scholars in other nations, journals on education and school management, reports from federal agencies and foundations, and writings by social scientists and humanists. From such sources I obtained many program ideas. As noted in Chapter Seven, UCEA's first International Inter-visitation Program was based mainly upon information obtained from reading written reports about English and Australian developments in training.

During most of my tenure at UCEA I skipped lunch when in Columbus and went to the reading room of the Ohio State Faculty Club. There I briefly escaped from the "firing line" to read about societal events and to think about their import for leadership. During the turbulent period of the late 1960s, for example, I examined societal events each week from three perspectives. By reading *Newsweek* I acquired a more liberal slant on events; from *U. S. News and World Report* a more conservative angle; and from *Time* a mixed view (i. e. conservative on economic issues and liberal on civic ones). The diverse slants on the news stimulated me to think about the conflicting values which society's leaders had to confront.

Insights about societal trends also shaped the design of UCEA programs. From analyses of six societal trends in the late 1960s the UCEA staff derived a set of guidelines for preparing future school leaders.[8] At the University of Texas in 1969, for example, I encouraged professors to think about the import for training of the expanding "business education interface" when I postulated the following development (Culbertson, 1969, p. 74):" . . . in Hegelian terms, education as a thesis and business as an antithesis will produce . . . a new synthesis during the decades ahead"—a synthesis shaped by clashes between the "economic rationality" of firms and the "human relations rationality" of schools (p. 74).

Sometimes I used ideas acquired from reading philosophical treatises to design programs. In the late 1970s I studied Juergen Habermas's *Knowledge and Human Interests* and Hans-Georg Gadamer's *Truth and Method*. At the time some professors were becoming more interested in the burgeoning controversy about which type(s) of knowledge was most valuable for the field. Since the two books illuminated the foundations of knowledge, they were relevant to the on-going discussions. Thus, I used ideas gleaned from the books to design a short seminar for Plenary and Executive Committee members.

My readings, consequently, helped inform my conversations with those in a diverse population of professors. By moving back and forth between reading and acting, I achieved needed balance. In fact the deeper I became immersed in UCEA activities, the greater the press to find my way back to the written word.

Did UCEA programs reflect the interests of professors? The answer is "yes" for some but not for all professors. Two of the three processes described above — developing five year plans and conversing with professors—produced a great deal of information about professorial interests—information which served as a crucial though beginning point in the design of scores and scores of UCEA programs. The third process—reading documents—also spawned ideas which helped me generate UCEA programs which appealed to some professors.

These conclusions do not square neatly with the fact that *many* professors felt that UCEA programs were disconnected from their interests. The discrepancy reflects the differing views of program participants and non-participants. Participants provided me with positive feedback about their experiences, while non-participants usually refrained from telling me directly about any discontents. Their Plenary representatives afforded them less threatening communication channels. Messages of dissatisfaction were usually transmitted to me by Plenary members in muted language as, for example: "Some members of my department want very much to be involved in UCEA's programs."

A Re-Ordering of Governmental Powers

In December, 1969, the Board unanimously recommended to the Plenary body that UCEA's annual membership fees be raised from $1000 to $2500. Although most Plenary members approved the proposal, the Board's action added to the already prevailing dissatisfaction. The resulting discontent gave rise to a major change in UCEA's governance. The end result was that the Plenary Session took over the final responsibility for making UCEA's policy.

Even though some Plenary members resented the limited "stock holder" role accorded them, they accepted it as long as the W. K. Kellogg Foundation met most of UCEA's funding needs. However, when member universities shouldered UCEA's financial burdens, the situation changed. More and more Plenary members decided that if their universities paid UCEA's bills, they should determine its policies.

Confronted with growing agitation within UCEA, I recommended to the UCEA Board that three Plenary members be invited to present solutions to the governance problem at their February 1970 meeting. After approving the proposal, the Board also appointed a commission to study UCEA's governance. Heading the Commission on the Governance of UCEA was Richard Lonsdale of New York University. Serving with him were Robert Coughlan, Northwestern; Oliver Gibson, State University of New York at Buffalo; Forbis Jordan, Indiana; Jay Scribner, California at Los Angeles; and Neal Tracy, North Carolina.

Speaking first at the February meeting was William Monahan of Iowa. An able thinker who used both "scientific" theory and humanistic content in his courses, he argued that a major change in governance was unnecessary and potentially damaging. Noting that the membership was now responsible for UCEA's survival, he asked whether his hearers were "truly willing to confront at all levels of the governing structure, and in a responsible and realistic fashion, a reassessment of UCEA's purposes, activities, commitments. . . . " (PS Min, 2/15/70, p. 4). Stressing that solutions to governance lay not in changed structure but in the behaviors of policy makers, he contended that Plenary members already had "the power to make wholesale changes" in UCEA's programs and to "become more active, more militant, more responsible, and more effective in performing their roles . . ." (p. 4). Using a metaphor from Voltaire's *Zadig*, he asserted that UCEA's governance problem was "about as serious as the abscess in Zadig's left eye—an abscess which healed in two days."[9]

The second presenter, Paul Fawley, read a paper prepared by Lloyd McCleary, a colleague of his at the University of Utah. McCleary, a frequent consultant on problems of organizational behavior, had attested that UCEA's primary problem lay in "the decision apparatus of the departments of educational administration and their . . . environments" (PS Min, 2/15/70, p. 4). His solution was closer links between Plenary and departmental actions. To effect the solution, he proposed that regional meetings attended by Plenary members and others from their departments be held to realign the "decision-making authority for the organization and participation in developmental activity, research and dissemination functions" (p. 4). Attendees would review the "program plans of both UCEA and member departments" (p. 4). The insights gained would enable Plenary members to be more effective at their national meetings.

The third presenter was Dan Cooper of Michigan. An effective writer and a strong believer in decentralized decision-making, Cooper argued that "the primary problem facing UCEA" ... was ... "the feeling that universities may be spending their money to support an agency which is supposed to be theirs but which in fact is . . . not owned by them" (PS Min, 2/15/70, p. 4). Noting that structure "rather than the quality of the UCEA program," was the crucial factor, Cooper attested that UCEA was "not an open" organization, even to Plenary members (p. 5). Thus, "Plenary Representatives" needed to "become the controlling Board of UCEA" (p. 5). The new goal, he contended, should be to "make each meeting of the Plenary Board . . . so exciting, so satisfying, so educative, and so productive that . . . deans and presidents will beg to create UCEA structures for all their faculty groups" (p. 5).

Though Cooper enthusiastically endorsed a "Plenary Board," he outlined eight "undesirable consequences" which could eventuate (PS Min, 2/15/70, p. 5). For instance, a larger board might be more wasteful of human resources, attract a lower quality of members, or be less motivated to solve problems. At the same time he noted 13 favorable consequences which could result, such as far better communication among UCEA personnel, a "surge of productivity in UCEA," an "emergence of new personalities in leadership roles in American education," and more "innovative" UCEA programs (p. 5).

Most of those who spoke following these three presentations contended that UCEA should follow the path outlined by Dan Cooper. As I later walked down a hotel corridor, Cooper caught up with me. Throwing his arm around my shoulders, he expressed the hope that I was not unhappy with his idea. I assured him that I would accept the solution which the majority of Plenary members favored.

After the meeting members of the governance commission met to develop plans. They decided to solicit information from about 1200 UCEA professors and deans. In May, after reviewing the responses they had obtained and analyzing the "respective powers of the Plenary Session and the Board of Trustees" (*UCEA Newsletter*, XI(5), p. 10),they made plans to submit their report at a fall meeting.

On November 8-10, 1970, UCEA members congregated in Minneapolis for a "Special Plenary Session." At an evening meeting the commission members gave an oral report. The main recommendations were that the UCEA Board of Trustees should be abolished, the Plenary Session should make UCEA policy, and an executive committee should be created to serve the Plenary Session. Plenary members reacted favorably to the proposed ideas. The first two respondents emphasized that the proposed changes would "increase participation by professors" (PS Min, 11/8-10/70, p. 2). The changes would also "make the UCEA central staff and projected executive committee more responsive to the general membership" (p. 2).

The next morning the body, among other things, approved two new programs, evaluated five, and analyzed a report on the past roles of Plenary members. At the afternoon session a motion to reject the governance report was made. Voting down the motion, the body by day's end had approved in principle all the commission's recommendations and had asked the commission to recommend requisite changes in UCEA's Code of Regulations and present them at the next Plenary meeting.

On the last morning Emil Haller, head of a committee charged with evaluating the Plenary Session, gave a report which was critical in tone. The body, he contended, had spent most of its time discussing nonpolicy issues. The "Quaker style" meeting, he maintained, was "inadequate to the needs of" UCEA. In addition, the "information provided" by the staff "was inadequate," because alternatives for action were not set forth" (PS Min, 11/8-10/70, p. 7).

The meeting ended on a positive note. All Plenary members, one professor said, "now have increased responsibility for participation not only in evaluating programs but in planning them as well" (PS, 11/8-10/70, p. 8). In looking ahead one member highlighted the need for setting "clearcut" agendas, conducting "business in a business-like manner," and finding an alternative to "take the place of the 'Quaker style' meeting" (P. 8). Plenary members left Minneapolis, then, feeling they had enhanced their governance powers.

In February, 1971, the Plenary body met in Atlantic City, at the Traymore Hotel. They brought with them proposed changes in UCEA's Code of Regulations. Commission members Richard Lonsdale and Jay Scribner, respectively, moved and seconded that the recommended revisions be accepted. Following a few opposing comments, Plenary members approved the proposed changes. The body then elected three professors to join six members of the abolished Board in a new Executive Committee. Two of the elected members were Samuel Goldman, Syracuse, and Donald Willower, Pennsylvania State, former board members. The third was Dan Cooper of Michigan.

Re-Defining Roles

After the Plenary Session ended, Executive Committee members met to assess their new status and to look ahead. Present were UCEA President Goldman and Vice-President Bessent; Max Abbott, Oregon; Dan Cooper, Michigan; Clifford Hooker, Minnesota; Harry Hartley, New York University; Ralph Kimbrough, Florida; Alan Thomas, Chicago; and Donald Willower, Pennsylvania State. Stripped of their former powers and status, most of the committee members appeared downcast.

Ralph Kimbrough began by asserting that since the new committee had no significant function to perform, it should be disbanded. Dismissing Kimbrough's idea, President Goldman proposed that the committee should perform functions that the UCEA Board had previously performed. No one supported either of the two polar positions. Rather, the group decided to define its new role at the next meeting.

At its May 1971 meeting the new committee probed the meaning of the new governance structure. After much discussion it adopted the following guiding principle (EC Min, 5/6-8/71, p. 2): "The Executive Committee . . . is seeking a more fluid system wherein decision-making is made in an atmosphere of trust and openness with all participants having access to the organization. . . ." The guideline was designed to "insure greater involvement, participation, and idea generation on the part of all concerned" (p. 2). Nine months later the group arrived at a more specific definition of its role (EC Min, 2/11/72, p. 3):

> Three basic roles were identified for the UCEA Executive Committee: (a) a *Visionary* role in which the Executive Committee would attempt to "reach for vision" by anticipating new developments and creative approaches in the field of educational administration; (b) a *Screening* role which would be an attempt by the Executive Committee to facilitate agendas for the Plenary Session meetings; and (c) a *Personnel* role wherein financial, budget, and personnel matters could be dealt with by the Executive Committee.

Sensitive to the Plenary members' negative views about centralized power, the committee expressed its guideline in restrained language. However, the statement provided the committee much room for discretion. "Facilitating agendas" came to mean that the committee determined what issues the Plenary session would address as well as recommendations to guide their actions. In so doing the Executive Committee could reject actions recommended by the UCEA staff. Since the Plenary body accepted the committee's screening and directive roles, a re-centralization of UCEA governance took place over time.

Not surprisingly, the first charge the Plenary Session gave to its Executive Committee dealt with program evaluation. In February, 1971, the body instructed the Executive Committee "to develop appropriate criteria and procedures by which the Plenary Session could thoroughly evaluate proposed UCEA programs" (PS Min, 2/18-20/71, p. 2). Three months later the Executive Committee addressed the criterion problem. To aid the committee the staff set forth both cost-benefit and cost-effectiveness criteria (EC Mat, 5/6-8/71, pp. 1-2). The cost-benefit criteria, which were related more to problems to be resolved, follow (p. 1):

1. How important is the problem compared to others?

2. How urgent is the problem? (e. g. Is the prior solution to this problem essential to the solution of other problems?)

3. How likely is it that the allocation of available resources will achieve a significant solution to the problem?

4. How central is the solution of the problem to the primary mission of UCEA?

5. How uniquely competent is UCEA in comparison to other available organizations to achieve a solution to the problem?

6. How will the implementation of a program to meet the problem affect the balance among programs?

7. How much of the cost can be offset by external funding?

Cost-effectiveness criteria were related more to solutions than to problems. The following questions pinpointed the content of these criteria (EC Mat, 5/6-8/71, p. 2):

1. What will alternative strategies cost in staff time and other direct expenditures?

2. What will be the costs of alternative strategies to the universities (in addition to staff costs)?

3. What strategy is most likely to achieve the best solution to the problem?

4. If a number of independent, but related, strategies are required for effective solution of the problem, in what sequence should they be implemented?

5. What effect, if any, will the implementation of one strategy, in comparison with potential others, have upon . . . future alternatives?

6. What political and policy implications does one strategy have in comparison to others?

After the Executive Committee approved the criteria, it recommended them to the Plenary body which in turn approved them. The body decided that "those submitting proposals for UCEA programs should be able to do so at either the exploratory development or planning stages" of their formulations (PS Min, 10/31-11/2/71. p. 2).

UCEA's accounting data relevant to the criteria were limited. Yet the criteria served important purposes. Providing an explicit set of standards for assessing UCEA programs, the criteria also were useful in reconciling general and particular interests. Admittedly, my estimates of costs and benefits were more intuitive than data based. Nevertheless, the criteria enabled me to think more systematically about UCEA programs. Ironically, UCEA's governing bodies never used the criteria to evaluate staff-proposed programs.

What changes did UCEA's new governance structure produce? The immediate effects of the changed structure were altered outlooks. Plenary members knew they could utter the final word on UCEA's policies and programs. Most believed the Plenary body could direct UCEA more effectively. Some thought they could control staff initiatives by crafting their own proposals. Thus, their immediate mood was one of elation tinged with hope for the future.

Shorn of their former status and powers, most of the Executive Committee members, as already noted, were initially downcast. Yet they gained fresh hope as they defined new roles for themselves. Over time they also acquired a noticeably higher status than that of their legal "bosses," the Plenary representatives.

Although my hopes for beneficial changes were less sweeping than those of the reformers, I thought that Plenary members had new options for leadership. In a paper entitled "Plenary Session Leadership: Some Alternatives" I stressed that the new structure could lead to a "broader base of leadership within UCEA and ... more varied instruments for its expression" (PS Mat, 10/31-11/2, 71, p. 1). I repeatedly emphasized to Executive Committee members that I saw no reason why they could not envisage and articulate new directions for UCEA.

Viewed within the longer time frame of the 1970s, the workings of UCEA's governance were not markedly different from those of the 1960s. Agendas for meetings were determined in the same way, and the scope and format of staff-prepared materials were comparable. The principal change was that Plenary members voted on all policy and program issues. Their informal influence on Executive Committee actions was also greater than Plenary members' influence on the UCEA Board in the 1960s. Yet most of the problems the new structure was designed to resolve were still visible in 1981. For instance, even though professorial participation in UCEA programs remained a lively issue, Plenary members seldom proposed new program initiatives.

Nor did Plenary members strengthen the tenuous relations between UCEA and its member departments. In my last years at UCEA Plenary members continued to talk about old problems. For example, they reportedly had difficulty getting UCEA issues on the agendas of their departmental meetings. Even when they did, urgent local concerns at times pushed the issues aside. Thus, some Plenary members chose to view themselves as delegates to the Plenary Session rather than as representatives. Relatively uninstructed by their departments, they performed their roles largely independently of them.

Since I valued initiative, I was at times disappointed because so few professors generated R and D proposals. How could I be responsive, I asked myself, if professors did not pinpoint problems they wanted to address? Over time I came to understand why professors seldom proposed ideas for cooperative R and D projects.

One reason professors initiated few programs was that they were busily engaged in other matters. The majority spent most of their time performing such functions as teaching, advising students, serving on committees, consulting, reading publications, and writing articles or books. Making changes in programs was seldom a priority. Even when they found the time to formulate change oriented UCEA programs, they faced special difficulties. For one thing, they lacked experience in creating inter-university R and D projects. Much easier to design were research projects they could conduct on their own.

Another obstacle to the full-fledged conduct of UCEA R and D projects was the isolation which specialization tended to foster. Specialists in school finance, for instance, usually had no one else in their departments with whom to share their interests. They tended to see unique opportunities in UCEA for exchanging ideas with their counterparts in other universities. Yet the central staff's priority was new initiatives for the improvement of training and inquiry. Differences in priority emerged when groups with similar interests came together. Focusing primarily upon the exchange of ideas and the making of new contacts, professors were less interested in generating for the field those deeper learnings which come from the conduct of R and D programs.

Barriers also resided in yet another one of UCEA's paradoxes: effecting change in institutions reputed to be the best. Professors believed that "elite" UCEA universities generated the most research, had the most knowledge, and trained the most outstanding school leaders. This view enhanced the status of UCEA professors. However, being the "best" could re-inforce the status quo. Resistance was implicit in questions professors sometimes posed as, for example: "Having achieved our current status after decades of effort, why should we opt for other alternatives?" Not infrequently, professors would suggest that UCEA should find ways to improve training in non-member institutions where the need for change was greatest.

Another reason why professors seldom initiated programs was that they lacked advantages which the UCEA staff possessed. Freed from professorial duties, we had the time, data, inter-university linkages, motivations, and experiences needed to launch cooperative endeavors. In addition, professors marched much more to the drumbeat of competition than to calls for cooperation. As I understood why professors seldom initiated programs, I became much more tolerant of their behavior. *Tout comprendre c'est tout pardonner!*

The major changes wrought by altered governance, then, were ones of mood and morale rather than of substance. Improved morale and brightened moods were not unimportant outcomes. Lying behind them was a more fundamental change: a freer Plenary Session. Though Plenary members seldom rejected the recommendations of the Executive Committee, they had the power to do so. Though they did little to alter UCEA's objectives and programs, they had the freedom to do so.

Though they rarely charged the Executive Committee with carrying out special tasks, they had the option to do so. Simply stated, the changes afforded Plenary members greater equality and freedom.

Tensions Between Policy-Making and Administration

An old saw is that executives should administer, and governance personnel should make policy. However, the dictum is seldom fully implemented, in part because working definitions of policy and administration are often imprecise. This point can be illustrated by looking at the actions taken at one UCEA governance meeting.

In November, 1969, the Board and I exchanged ideas about UCEA's 1969-74 program plans. Making sharp cutbacks in their own university offerings, some board members felt UCEA should also limit its programs. I argued against making immediate cuts. First, central office costs would be little affected by program cuts per se. Second, since I had discussed most of the proposed programs with interested professors, I felt obligated not to eliminate them arbitrarily.

Apparently exasperated by my resistance, one board member exclaimed: "The central staff must think it can develop any and all programs!" Shortly thereafter, the group authorized the staff "to recommend to the Board the dropping of projects which are determined after initial work . . . not to be desirable or feasible" and that "decisions take into consideration limitations upon . . . resources" (EC Min, 11/6-8/69, p. 2). I deemed the enacted guideline to be constructive. Thus, I was surprised when Stephen Knezevich, a member of the staff of the American Association of School Administrators and an ex officio board member, vehemently charged that board members were involved in administrative matters.

Was Knezevitch's charge correct? In answering the question a definition of policy making is needed. Some contend that the role of policy makers is to set goals and establish budgetary limits. Reflected in Knezevich'a remarks was this definition. Since the UCEA Board had approved goals for 1969-74 and would each year establish budgets to pursue them, it was making policy. However, when some members called for immediate program cuts, they had entered the domain of administration and, thereby, had limited the staff's discretion.

Others suggest that when board members approve (or disapprove) programs or courses of action for pursuing goals, they make policy. By

1963 I had adopted this concept of policy making. Since UCEA focused upon implementing research, development, and the dissemination of programs, the concept seemed to fit its functions well. Second, I learned that the Board could agree upon UCEA objectives but disagree about specific programs to achieve them.

In the fall of 1962 I met Arthur Gilbert, a staff member of the National Conference of Christians and Jews. Out of our conversation came the idea of a UCEA-sponsored institute for school superintendents and professors. To focus upon "Religion and the Public Schools," the institute was to be partially funded by the agency Gilbert served. When I presented the idea to the Board in February, 1963, I innocently presumed that a well established UCEA objective was that of offering learning opportunities to professors and school leaders. I quickly recognized, however, that the proposed program was a red flag. Suspicious of the motives of the provider of funds and deeply committed to the separation of church and state, some of the board members were very upset by my action.

Following a lively discussion President Van Miller observed: "You have slapped the wrists of the executive director. Do you want to do more?" After a brief pause a board member summarized the prevailing sentiment: "We want to make clear to the executive director that he is not to make policy for UCEA." Having made their point, the board members approved the proposed institute. Held at Purdue University, it attracted more than 200 attendees who discussed such topics as "Problems for Public Education Emerging from Our Religious Pluralism" and "Allocation of Funds to Non-Public Education in Canada, England, and Holland."

Policy making as program approval, though not encompassing all policy decisions, had its advantages. It required UCEA staff to think carefully about proposed programs. Discussions of descriptions of programs at meetings promoted board-staff understanding. They also highlighted the controversial facets of proposed programs. It was better to identify such facets before rather than during implementation. Finally, the unambiguous meaning of the concept made it easier to monitor the borders between policy and administration. If governance personnel specified ways to implement an approved program, for instance, they crossed the line into administration.

Board members in UCEA's earlier years had not become involved in administrative matters. At the first board meeting, for example, I presented a paper on cooperative research. At the time I was perplexed about what organizational structures might best advance such research. Since most of the board members had acquired much experience in cooperative endeavors, I would have welcomed their suggestions. Yet they chose not to provide advice. Instead, they "instructed" the "staff to exercise judgment in matters related to . . . cooperative research" (B Min, 11/18-19/59, p. 7).

The earlier board members seemed to accept and even at times to encourage aggressive staff action. After a controversial meeting in 1964, board member James Harlow approached me while I was browsing at a newsstand. Dean of the School of Education at the University of Oklahoma, he reassuringly stated: "Your role is to get through the Board all the proposals you can." I presumed that he accepted my role as an initiator and wanted me to perform it aggressively.

The Executive Committee was less successful than the former UCEA Board in staying out of administration. Yet its moves into administration tended to be self-correcting. In 1973 the committee asked the staff to describe its procedures for selecting UCEA associate directors. Behind the request were concerns within UCEA that a disproportionate number of UCEA's associate directors were graduates of eastern and midwestern universities. In discussing the selection procedures, a member proposed that "one or two Executive Committee members serve on the . . . committee" responsible for choosing UCEA staff (EC Min, 9/13-15/73, p. 3). Since the proposed action was clearly an administrative one, I was surprised. I was also relieved when the majority agreed "that current procedures were quite thorough and that no substantial changes should be made" (p. 3).

A few times the corrections evolved slowly, as witnessed by committee actions in 1974-75. Stirred by criticisms of UCEA's programs and worried about high membership fees, the committee proposed an array of actions, some of which were administrative in nature. For example, the group proposed that "Executive Committee" members make "visits to member universities, with program charts, to discuss professorial involvement" (EC Min, 9/8-10/74, p. 4) and become involved in "coordinating regional UCEA-related activities within a framework of alternative forms of UCEA membership" (EC Min, 2/20-21/75, p. 3). For a year the group tried to resolve UCEA's problems without distinguishing between policy and administration.

Wailand Bessent, an Executive Committee member, helped his

colleagues re-assume their policy making role. In a hand-written memo shared with Executive Committee members at a 1975 meeting, Bessent stressed that the "distinction between policy making and administrative action is important to preserve in UCEA" (EC Mat, 2/20-21/75, p. 1). He also stated that "our programs will be stalled if we rely on quarterly meetings of the Executive Committee to execute our program decisions" (p. 1). Though the committee did not openly discuss Bessent's memo, it began focusing upon policy making.

The Executive Committee seldom decreed ways to implement programs. However, the committee in 1980, after approving a plan to revise selected Monroe City simulations, did vote to "recommend to the Plenary Session the establishment of a committee to design a strategy to accomplish revision of the Monroe City simulation" (EC Min, 9/11-13/80, p. 9). I viewed the action as unwise. I had learned from years of experience with the Monroe City simulations that development teams, after pondering the specific constraints which faced them, needed to design their own strategies. Also troublesome were the months of delay the directive would produce. The work of UCEA moved slowly enough without artificially created obstacles!

Why did Executive Committee members become more involved in administration than did former UCEA Board members? Since most board members were much nearer the end of their careers than were committee members, they appeared more relaxed. The younger and upwardly mobile committee members seemed more eager to influence events. Second, since UCEA's trustees had had much more experience in working with governing boards than had committee members, they likely could recognize more easily the borders which separated policy from administration.

Board members were more interested in policy questions, while committee members tended to focus more upon organizational issues. In the mid-sixties UCEA boards held four two-hour seminars in which they discussed such issues as future "teacher-administrator roles" (B Min, 5/6-8/65, p. 5). Executive Committee members did not hold such seminars. They displayed greater interest in the organizational dynamics of UCEA. In addition, committee members were products of the theory movement whose tenets had excluded "ought" or policy issues from inquiry. The exclusion may have reduced the committee's interest in policy.

Dissimilarities in board and committee actions should not be overdrawn. For one thing, the differences in individuals *within* each group were significant. For another, both groups responded positively to the large majority of proposed UCEA programs, sometimes in the face of opposition. The Executive Committee, for instance, recommended to the Plenary Session that the very controversial UCEA Partnership be approved. Far outweighing the negative effects of occasional forays into the administrative realm were the positive responses to program recommendations. Without such responses UCEA could not have effectively pursued its mission.

Notes

1. Lonsdale was elected President of the UCEA Board in February, 1964. The next fall he moved from Syracuse to New York University.

2. See Miller, V., & Spalding, W. B. (1958). *The public administration of American schools.* Yonkers-on-Hudson, NY: World Book Company.

3. See Griffiths, D. E. (Ed.). (1964). *Behavioral science and educational administration.* Chicago: The University of Chicago Press.

4. See Jacobson, P. B., Reavis, W. C., & Logsdon, J. D. (1950). *Duties of school principals.* New York: Prentice-Hall, Inc; Pierce, T. M., Merrill, Jr., E. C. Wilson, C., & Kimbrough, R. B. (1955). *Community leadership for public education.* New York: Prentice-Hall, Inc; Campbell, R. F., Corbally, Jr., J. E., & Ramseyer, J. A. (1958). *Introduction to educational administration.* Boston: Allyn and Bacon, Inc; Morphet, E. L., Johns, R. L., & Reller, T. L. (1959). *Educational organization and administration.* Englewood Cliffs, NJ: Prentice-Hall, Inc.

5. See Cresswell, A. M., & Murphy, M. J. (Eds.). (1976). *Education and collective bargaining: Readings in policy and research.* Berkeley, CA: McCutchan Publishing Company.

6. See Campbell, R. F., & Gregg, R. T. (Eds.). (1957). *Administrative behavior in education.* New York: Harper & Brothers.

7. See Hoy, W. K., & Miskel, C. G. (1978). *Educational administration: Theory, research, and practice.* New York: Random House.

8. See Culbertson, J., Farquhar, R. H., Gaynor, A. K., & Shibles, M. R. (Eds.). (1969). *Preparing educational leaders for the seventies.* Columbus, OH: University Council for Educational Administration.

9. Even though the authors of the three papers presented to the Plenary Session searched for them, they were unable to find them. Fortunately, UCEA Associate Director, Michael Martin, took detailed notes on the presentations (EC Min, 2/15/70).

References

Culbertson, J. (1969). The business-education interface and the preparation of special and general educational administrators. In C. Meisgeir and R. Sloat (Eds.), *Common and specialized learnings, competencies, and experiences for special education administrators* (pp. 72-83). Austin, TX: University of Texas.

Norton, J. K. (1957). The contemporary scene. In R. F. Campbell & R. T. Gregg (Eds.), *Administrative behavior in education* (pp. 41-81). New York: Harper & Brothers.

12

Lessons Learned

"The years teach much which the days never knew."
Ralph Waldo Emerson

During my 22 years at UCEA ideas were ever-present sources of nourishment for the intellect. Residing at the center of an international network of scholars from many fields, I had ready access to both published and unpublished information and concepts. Disseminators and appliers of ideas in other organizations also supplied cognitive stimuli. The obtained ideas were immediately instructive. More importantly, many of them generated additional insights as I applied them to problems of program development and implementation.

Participation in the organizational life of UCEA also yielded understandings. As I listened to the statements of professors and observed their diverse behaviors, puzzling problems sometimes arose. Why, for example, did professors' perceptions of my status and actions at times clash sharply with my own? Such questions stirred my curiosity and made me search for explanations. The combination of searches for explanations, encounters with innumerable ideas, and struggles to apply them in cooperative, inter-university endeavors afforded me a cornucopia of learning opportunities.

Symbolism and Myth

During the first two years of my tenure some professors began calling me "Mr. UCEA." Although I typically was accorded the name in informal settings, I was introduced a few times as "Mr. UCEA" at formal meetings. Professors obviously enjoyed calling me "Mr. UCEA." However, I was puzzled and somewhat embarrassed by the appellation.

Clearly, there were major discrepancies in the ways professors and I perceived UCEA. By locating UCEA in a visible person, some professors achieved a simple but apparently functional view. However, I needed a more complex and expansive one. A quick look told me that UCEA was an organization of about 40 elite universities. A more intense look revealed hundreds of professors with multifarious motivations and talents who might become involved in cooperative endeavors. More probing looks produced an even more complex view—a plethora of possibilities for building bridges between ideas and practice.

Reflected in these discordant perceptions were opposing tendencies: the need for intricate conceptions of UCEA versus the need for simple, visible symbols to represent it. In performing my role I had to grasp UCEA as a many faceted phenomenon. Most professors, however, had neither the need nor the opportunity to grasp the complexities of UCEA. Since its central activities differed greatly from their own, and since its bounds reached far beyond their work settings, they needed defining symbols. In the early days my persona provided professors such a symbol.

Although professors ceased calling me "Mr. UCEA" around 1964, some continued to speak about the close links between the organization and me. A few years after my resignation a former UCEA Associate Director observed (Fogarty, 1983, pp. 141-142): " . . .in the minds of many, the man had long before transcended the role, and the distinction between Culbertson, the man, and UCEA, the organization, had become blurred."

In serving as a symbol for UCEA, I provided professors with meaning. Yet I often found myself situated in the gray area between legend and reality. A question which intrigued me was what made myths develop? Myths began, I concluded, in observations of unusual actions or events. As reports on the actions—often exaggerated—moved through the UCEA network, the actions came to be viewed as representative rather than unrepresentative. To illustrate the point I will turn to a concrete example, namely: perceptions about my energy and work patterns and how they were related to actualities. The perceptions, I believe, were rooted initially in observations of my behavior at UCEA Plenary Sessions, small group meetings, individual conferences, and informal activities in the early 1960s—events which took place during week-long annual conferences of the American Association of School Administrators.

By 1963 professors were speaking glowingly about my energy levels and speculating about the reasons for my stamina. In fact, Richard Lonsdale at a UCEA Plenary Session offered a public explanation for my energetic displays. Drawing upon a scientific study conducted by biochemists, he postulated reasons for my high energy output. As reports on my Atlantic City behavior spread, I gained a reputation for long work days. Writing two years after my retirement from UCEA, one close observer of my actions during the 1964-68 period offered the following view (Fogarty, 1983, p. 147):

> His stamina in following his grueling schedule of travels, meetings, administrative responsibilities, and scholarly productivity has become legendary. He appeared indefatigable. Constant activity of all kinds seemed to exhilarate rather than tire him. Eighteen-hour workdays and seven-day weeks were the rule rather than the exception, and while people who were trying to keep up with him were dropping from sheer exhaustion, he would be fitting still another dawn meeting or late night staff conference into his already overly tight schedule.

Bryce Fogarty's view was not an uncommon one. However, it was shaped more by fancy than fact. "Eighteen-hour workdays" rather than being "the rule rather than the exception" were in fact the exception rather than the rule. At the AASA conferences I did work 18 to 20 hour days. However, when I was away from the crowds and at home in Columbus, I labored considerably less. Typically, I worked in the office on weekdays from 8 a. m. to between 5:30 and 6. p. m. On most evenings I spent two to three hours on such tasks as dictating responses to letters, writing papers, formulating plans, and reading documents. When faced with deadlines, I occasionally worked at home from 6:00 to 7:00 a. m. editing UCEA materials (e. g. simulation components). Thus, I worked between 12 and 13 hours a day on average. On Saturdays and Sundays, respectively, I worked about seven and four hours. Obviously, legend outran reality. In the eyes of many the unrepresentative AASA workdays became the representative ones.

In my early UCEA years I was so deeply immersed in substantive problems that I did not see the importance of symbolism and myth. By the mid-sixties I was much less oblivious to these phenomena. I was also made aware of the negative effects of indifferent attitudes toward ceremony. When a well-known scholar invited me to represent UCEA at a celebration of his university's 100th birthday, I declined the request. Angry at my response, he did not speak to me for more than a year. Through such incidents I grasped the powerful influence of myth, symbolism, and ceremony in the life of organizations.

Power, Priorities, and Ethics

My single minded pursuit of program development helped create other discrepancies in perception. One had to do with the view that I was a "powerful" individual. This view, which developed in the last half of the sixties, struck me as erroneous. As a program developer and implementer, I was totally dependent, it seemed, upon the good will and the voluntary actions of others. Whatever power I had was rooted in ideas and persuasion. When professors called me a "powerful" person, I thought they were employing a false label.

As the years passed, I came to understand why professors and I had discrepant views about power: their views were grounded in observations of functions which to me were secondary. For example, UCEA personnel deemed my role in the placement of newly prepared and established professors to be very important. Because of my intimate knowledge of professors and of departments in UCEA universities, they often turned to me for help. I also became a handy writer of letters related to tenure decisions, promotions to full professorships, entries into associate deanships and deanships, and contests for grants and awards (e. g. Fulbright grants). Although I dutifully responded to the many requests, I did so with limited enthusiasm. As I responded to the thousands of requests for information about UCEA personnel, I felt I was neglecting my primary function: the creation of inter-university research, development, and dissemination programs.

Because of a conversation I had in the seventies with David Krathwohl, Dean of the School of Education at Syracuse University, I altered my view about the placement role. A few days before I was to visit Syracuse, I received a call that Dean Krathwohl wanted me to help him assess a number of candidates for an associate deanship post. I agreed to meet him for dinner at the Syracuse Faculty Club on the day of my arrival. After dinner we moved to a private room for the evaluation session. Fortunately, I was well acquainted, as I recall, with 14 of the 16 individuals on his list.

After Dean Krathwohl completed his thorough questioning, he noted that the field could never adequately reward me for the help I had rendered in personnel placement. Surprised by his remark, I confessed that I sometimes resented the fact that heavy placement demands diminished the time I had for UCEA's primary function. He then asked, "What could be more important for the field than helping get the right people into the right positions and institutions?" His question caused me to re-assess my attitude. As a result, I subsequently accepted the placement-related role with greater tolerance and equanimity.

Some contended my "power" was derived from a "system of patronage." They affirmed that professors who received "favors" from me (e. g. help in obtaining positions) loyally supported my UCEA actions. As I saw it, the view was an exaggerated perception. For one thing, I sought to serve the dual interests of candidates and employers. Not infrequently, I signaled to potential employers via very brief letters, letters which offered facts but not judgments, and sometimes by more direct means that particular candidates were unqualified. For another, university leaders often chose candidates for positions other than those I recommended highly. To be sure over time, I helped most of the hundreds of UCEA professors who chose me as one of their career "sponsors." Even so, the hundreds I helped to acquire positions and/ or promotions constituted a minority of the professors in UCEA.

Still another discrepancy between my views and those of professors stemmed from my intense commitment to the advancement of UCEA's mission (i. e. improved training). I was repeatedly reminded that most professors assigned a much lower priority to the mission than did I. The point can be illuminated with an illustration.

In February, 1973, the UCEA Plenary Session chose "knowledge utilization" for its 1974-79 theme. Thereafter, Plenary members were assigned to small groups and were asked to meet in hotel rooms to brainstorm program possibilities for 1974-79. As I walked toward these meeting sites, I observed two professors shaking hands and beginning a conversation. As they talked, their faces reflected a special radiance. As friends who likely had not seen one another recently, they were oblivious to the passers-by. As I approached a corner about a hundred feet from where they stood, they were still conversing. They would not make it to the UCEA discussions, I surmised. Their warm exchange was much more important to them than brainstorming ways and means to realize UCEA's mission.

That UCEA met needs which were tangential and even unrelated to its mission could be highlighted with many examples. Suffice it to say that the longer I stayed at UCEA, the more appreciation I had for its capacity to meet human needs. At times I thought that life would be easier if I struggled less with program development and more with nurturing the status and satisfaction of professors. However, had I adopted such a strategy, I would have had to turn my back on UCEA's founding fathers. In addition, my UCEA role would have been largely devoid of challenge. Thus, my intense commitment to UCEA program development was as strong in my last as in my first UCEA years. Yet I understood much better in 1981 than I did in 1959 UCEA's powerful non-programmatic ways of meeting human needs.

Another domain which generated questions was that of ethics. The issue was first raised at a non-UCEA sponsored seminar at the University of Oregon in the fall of 1964, where selected UCEA professors and I presented papers.[1] Afterwards, Daniel Griffiths, a seminar presenter, asked me if I had received an honorarium for my paper. When I answered, "yes," he expressed concern. He noted that an executive of an educational organization in New York had almost wrecked the agency he headed through excessive consulting. Concerned about UCEA's future, Griffiths was worried about my action. Two months later in November he presented the issue to the UCEA Board of Trustees. The Board listened to his statement but did not take action. Its members apparently felt I was adequately forewarned.

The honorarium issue was relatively simple. On those occasions when I was offered an honorarium by a UCEA university, I suggested that my service be viewed as a contribution. Some accepted the proposal, while others felt it was unfair to provide honoraria to UCEA presenters and not to me. If they insisted on providing me with an honorarium, I subtracted the time spent on the tasks from my vacation time. When I accepted honoraria for papers prepared for non-UCEA agencies, I charged my time similarly.

The most serious ethical issues were posed by individuals in non-UCEA agencies. Early in my UCEA career, for instance, sellers of textbooks came to my office and asked if I would write texts on educational administration for their companies. Such requests obviously clashed with the responsibilities UCEA had accorded me. But the visitors would argue that I could serve the interest of the field by providing leaders needed information and knowledge.

Other experiences reinforced the idea that individuals and their agencies not infrequently wanted to use UCEA (and me) to achieve ends which were alien to the organization's mission. For example, a publishing official asked me around 1967 if I would have dinner with him and the president and a vice-president of his company. At the time such buzzwords as the "business-education interface" and "education industries" were increasingly salient. Viewing education as a "growth industry," business leaders were acquiring and creating subsidiaries devoted to the development and marketing of films, video-tapes, computer software, and related materials. During the dinner hour my hosts reported their intent to establish a new subsidiary which would focus upon the creation and marketing of new educational technologies. Unexpectedly, they asked if I would chair the board of the impending enterprise. Explaining that I already had enough to do, I declined their offer.

Sometimes requests from non-member universities posed ethical issues. Occasionally, I was offered honoraria to evaluate or help design doctoral programs. On one occasion the proffered honorarium was almost three times higher than the going rate. Since I already knew the institution wanted to become a member of UCEA, I had more than one reason to reject the invitation.

About 5:30 p. m. on my last day at UCEA I received my final official telephone call. On the other end of the line was Eugene Ratsoy, the immediate past president of UCEA and a professor at the University of Alberta. During our conversation Eugene mentioned that the ethical behavior I had exhibited had impressed him favorably. Since Griffiths and Ratsoy were the only professors I can remember who commented on my ethics, I do not know how others felt. Yet I do know that in my efforts to avoid tarnishing UCEA's reputation and impairing its effectiveness, I had to examine skeptically all entreaties to perform non-UCEA tasks.

Giving Away Ideas

As a practitioner of "inter-institutional cooperation," I learned varied lessons. One was the "giving away" of ideas. In late 1964 I conceived the International Inter-visitation Program (IIP). The IIP, I projected, would begin with a seminar at the University of Michigan. In the written proposal I suggested titles for seminar papers. Later

William Walker and I made plans to publish the papers. When I suggested that Walker, Dan Cooper of the University of Michigan, and I might edit the volume, Walker astutely observed that it would be a mistake to feature two U. S. and one Australian editor of a book directed largely at administrators and professors in five nations. Recognizing the wisdom in Bill's remark, I uncomfortably stepped aside for another editor. George Baron of the University of London joined Bill and Dan as editors of *Educational Administration: International Perspectives.*

By the end of the sixties I had learned not only to live with my "proprietary" propensities, but I also was obtaining much satisfaction from envisaging programs, putting them on paper, transferring them to others for implementation, and seeing uses of their outcomes. Such activities helped me to see the crucial role of ideas in cooperative practice. To pinpoint the major satisfactions I acquired from developing and giving away ideas, I will describe how a program conception was crafted and moved into practice.

Members of the General-Special Education Administration Consortium (GSEAC) in 1972 evaluated a list of proposed 1972-74 objectives. One highly ranked objective was the attainment of "data and methods" for understanding "future trends" (*UCEA Newsletter* XIV(2), p. 7). To help professors pursue the objective, I constructed in the summer of 1972 a plan for a book on methods for studying the future. In grappling with the question of what methods could help professors study "educational futures," I found two books to be especially helpful: Bertrand de Jouvenel's *The Art of Conjecture* and Erich Jantsch's *Technological Forecasting in Perspective.* Rooted in the humanistic tradition, Jouvenel's book was more skeptical in tone and more qualitative in thought. Jantsch's book tended to reflect quantitative ways of studying the future; less critical in tone, it described more than a hundred "forecasting" methods.

One major problem was that of identifying and resolving key conceptual issues. For example, to what extent should qualitative and to what extent should quantitative methods be featured? After analyzing many methods, I decided the book should feature eight qualitative and four quantitative methods. Feeling uncertain about the four quantitative methods I had tentatively chosen, I called James Bruno, a specialist in quantitative forecasting methods at the University of California in Los Angeles. Quickly responding to the issue, he suggested that four quantitative methods should be featured: trend analysis, Markov chains, Monte Carlo techniques, and Baysian statistical models. His four suggested methods were the ones on my list! I cannot remember another occasion at UCEA when my generalist judgment matched so well that of a specialist. In selecting qualitative methods I emphasized those already utilized by educators such as contextual mapping, cross impact analysis, the Delphi technique, force analysis, and scenario development.[2]

The ideation phase ended in a plan for a book. In most of the book's chapters a particular method was to be depicted and analyzed. The remaining chapters would contain introductory, comparative, and critical content. The intellectual challenge of mastering the requisite knowledge to move from an ambiguously stated need to an unambiguous plan had produced great satisfaction for me.

While conceiving the plan, I was also thinking about how it could be implemented. With the help of GSEAC's co-ordinator, James Yates, I sought to identify those professors of general and special educational administration who could best describe and analyze the various methods. When we arrived at a satisfactory list, James Yates began implementing the plan by inviting professors to prepare chapters. The authors who accepted invitations met in Minneapolis in November, 1972, to review the plans. Providing help to the group was Earl Joseph, a long range planner at the Sperry Univac Corporation.

I enjoyed the entire process of envisioning projects. However, the satisfaction gained from implementing projects occurred largely when their conceptions were effectively transferred into actions. When I confidently felt I could walk away from a project knowing that it would be completed, I experienced immense satisfaction. By the end of the November GSEAC meeting, for instance, I was sure that the authors and editors would produce a new book. Thus, I was free to search for new conceptions to meet needs not yet addressed.

The final major satisfaction came from seeing professors adopt and use the products produced through UCEA projects. Fifteen months after *Futurism in Education: Methodologies* was published, a half dozen writers of its chapters were already using it as a text in newly-designed courses. When I observed one of the class discussions, I saw that students were acquiring content which might enhance their roles as visionary school leaders.

Trust and Cooperation

Cooperative practice was also significantly affected by the presence or absence of trust among professors whose institutions for decades had competed with one another for students, staff, research grants, and national and international reputations. Chapter Two reveals how the competitive drives of UCEA's founders almost derailed their efforts. Chapter Three shows that UCEA's executive director was also distrusted by some professors. I soon realized that the soil in which UCEA was rooted was relatively shallow. The problem was how to build a cooperative organization in the face of such inter-university competition and distrust.

Given such conditions, what could I do to enhance trust? Knowing that distrust tends to beget distrust, I sought to follow an Emersonian dictum which I had long cherished: trust people, and they will be true to you; treat them greatly, and they will show themselves great. Emerson's grand ideal, like other noble precepts, could be sought but never entirely realized, nor could it fully deliver its promise even when it was effectively pursued.

While interacting with UCEA professors and deans, I could almost always trust the intent of their messages but not infrequently I distrusted the soundness of their views. Long-standing competition between universities which were located close to one another, for example, inevitably warped the attitudes and views of professors. From many university visits I learned not to take at face value the comments professors made about their competing neighbors. Many tended to downgrade the offerings of their nearby rivals while speaking in inflated ways about their own. At national meetings I observed similar tendencies, if to a lesser degree, among leaders of widely dispersed elite universities.

When professors proposed ideas to me, I tried hard to dispel any concerns about theft. Among other things, I repeatedly gave them full credit for their ideas orally and, when feasible, in writing. I also tried to clarify potential UCEA actions involving a proffered idea and to "clear" the actions with the idea's author. Involvement of the idea's owner in planning and in implementing projects was another important tactic. Admittedly, I did not always succeed in meeting the expectations of professors, largely because I was at times unable to involve them from the beginning to the end of projects.

During my UCEA tenure I received thousands of statements about what I or UCEA leaders "ought" to do. Authors of such statements were often dissatisfied with aspects of UCEA's performance or with facets of my own behavior. At a luncheon meeting in the early sixties an influential dean of a UCEA university told me that I "ought" to exercise more leadership. As we left the restaurant, he forcefully stated that I should either start taking firm public positions on training issues or get out of the UCEA job.

When I received blunt messages such as that just noted, I faced two questions related to trust. The first was whether I trusted the intent of the messenger. In the case of the dean I had no compelling reason to question his motives. His propensity for speaking candidly was well known. In addition, he may well have thought that his junior companion needed advice! In any case I evaluated his intent positively. The second question was whether or not I could trust the soundness of his message. I was not persuaded that the dean had given me wise advice. If a time came when I could presume to speak authoritatively on the field's wide-ranging training issues, I believed I would be obsolescent. My role was to help professors find new answers—not delineate existing ones. The dean acted as did many others. He wanted me to adopt behaviors he displayed and valued, even though my role differed markedly from his own.

Frequently, I received contradictory messages. In the late 1960s one professor told me that the reason for UCEA's "success" resided in my unusual openness to ideas. Shortly thereafter, another professor irritably stated that I had such a closed mind I was excluding many professors from UCEA activities. Even though both messages seemed greatly over simplified, there was some truth in each. The first professor had taken part in several UCEA activities as had many of his friends and acquaintances. The second professor, however, had not participated in UCEA R and D programs. The discordant views, it seemed, were rooted in different experiences. By trusting the intent of both professors, I could continue to relate to them.

By the mid-sixties there were signs of growing trust within UCEA. For example, by 1966 the flow of skeptical questions from professors about whether or not The Ohio State University was meeting its commitments as the provider of UCEA's headquarters had finally ceased. During visits to universities I also found that professors were less guarded than earlier in sharing their ideas with me. Their opportunities to see and experience the benefits of cooperative action were apparently building a climate of greater trust. Yet the forces of competition were always present and ready to inhibit or affect negatively UCEA's inter-university actions.

Linking Programs to Human Potential

Another arena rich in learnings was that of program development and enactment. Within this arena the most crucial challenge was that of envisaging programs. A very important requirement was that program conceptions be grounded in realities. Visions which were rooted in or deduced from abstract formulations could provide professors insights and stimuli for thought, but they were much less likely than grounded visions to foster effective actions.

Since program outcomes could only be attained through the concentrated efforts of talented individuals and groups, the most important thread in the texture of a grounded vision was that of human potential. As previous chapters have demonstrated, I worked constantly to understand how the dormant potential of individuals and institutions could be identified, harnessed, and expressed.

Sometimes the beginning point in conceiving a new program was a perceived constellation of talents. The international initiative of the 1964-69 period began in a perception of the interrelated talents, motivations, and achievements of outstanding thinkers in Australia, Canada, the United States, and the United Kingdom. Had I not escaped from the initial impression that the thinkers' actions were only isolated events in widely separated contexts, I would not have been able to conceive the International Inter-visitation Program (IIP).

The identified potential from which the IIP sprang was grounded largely in published ideas and information. Notably, the goal of the IIP (and other UCEA projects which were rooted in perceptions of potential) was arrived at in a non-traditional way. Instead of deriving IIP's goal from a defined problem, I simply made explicit a goal which was implicit in a perceived possibility, namely: the creation of new transnational structures and networks to help internationalize the field. (see Chapter Seven).

The practice of developing program goals from identified potential had distinct advantages. It helped ensure that program participants would have the requisite freshness in perspective to generate new program outcomes. In addition, the practice accentuated the positive, in contrast to that of deriving goals from problems which tended to highlight human shortcomings and foster resistance to change. Thus, less time and energy were usually required to pursue goals which were rooted in identified potential. In addition, goals grounded in potential were more often likely to be attained than were those derived from described inadequacies in the field.

Eliciting goals from human potential also had shortcomings. If UCEA had limited its projects to those rooted in potential, core problems in the field would have been neglected. Since this focus upon goal setting usually involved professors who were thinking about frontier issues, it often screened out those who were more concerned about improving traditional aspects of practice. For example some, dissatisfied with the international effort, argued that UCEA should concentrate its efforts upon "domestic" issues.

Even when program conceptions were grounded in explicit problems, I still had to search intensively for potential ways to address the problems. Chapter Eight indicates how various professors revealed during planning activities that their abilities to teach urban school administration were inadequate. Any successful endeavor had to be grounded in information about the capacities of UCEA professors and their institutions to meet the identified need.

Shortly after I had announced my UCEA departure, Gordon McCloskey of Washington State University gave me a compliment. A participant in UCEA's early task forces and a gifted turner of phrases, he called me "the great potential finder." I am not in a position to evaluate his judgment. However, I do know that no other function afforded me greater enjoyment than that of searching for and finding human and organizational potential. In pursuing program possibilities during my tenure, I was able to talk at length and often many times with more than 1600 professors from many nations. In addition, I conversed with leaders in numerous other groups as, for example, an estimated 200 leading U. S. and Canadian school administrators in the UCEA 'University-School System Partnership.

There was always a yawning gap between identified potential and its expression in program outcomes. This gap was conspicuously highlighted when groups and individuals reacted to newly proposed programs. In their reactions participants typically focused upon problems UCEA would encounter in implementing programs. Positive potential tended to be ignored. When members of the Board of Trustees discussed the recommended launching of a new journal, they spent more than an hour talking about such problems as scarcity of scholarly articles, financing difficulties, and the growing costs of printing. In the exchange no one spoke about the journal's capacity for influencing the field. (see Chapter Four). Most UCEA Board members ably identified problems on the road ahead. Yet positive possibilities seemingly had to demonstrate themselves in concrete outcomes before most professors could appreciate them.

Inventories of problems were valuable to the staff. Since inventories provided a map of possible barriers on the road ahead, I listened carefully to descriptions of problems. Yet I learned not to take them too seriously. While many projections proved to be accurate, others did not. Sometimes errors arose because professors identified problems more from the purview of their own universities than from a central UCEA perspective. An exchange about the Monroe City simulation with a professor from a large city is illustrative. When I told the professor about the simulation, he asked two questions: "What makes you think that a school system will permit dozens of professors to depict in writing and on film events which highlight its decision problems?", and "If you do gain entry, how can you remain there for five years?" As Chapter Eight makes clear, the first urban school system invited to cooperate with UCEA responded positively and with alacrity. Further, the cooperative effort endured for six years. The professor's biased view was undoubtedly influenced by difficulties he had encountered in building relations between his own university and a surrounding urban school system.

Errors in projecting problems were often linked to threats posed by impending change. Therefore, I tried to differentiate between analytical and emotionally-laden descriptions of problems. When I proposed the UCEA University-School System Partnership, professors who directed local school study councils feared that the Partnership might weaken their agencies. Yet neither the professors nor I could identify clear and compelling reasons to support their concern. Thus, I did not take the perceived problem seriously.

UCEA's Core Strategies: Some Observations

UCEA's potential, as perceived by its founders, was to be realized through *cooperative, inter-institutional* programs. UCEA's experience attested to the soundness of their vision. Through UCEA hundreds of professors altruistically contributed their time and talents to the enactment of programs. Further, cooperation was effected through a variety of patterns, including centralized and decentralized as well as individual, group, and institutional patterns. (see Chapter Three). UCEA's founding fathers also presumed that their offspring could realize its potential through the three strategies of cooperative research, development, and dissemination. To what extent did the outcomes effected through the use of these strategies fulfill the aspirations of UCEA's founders?

In the early sixties I sought to implement large scale, theory based programs of inquiry. While working with UCEA task forces, I learned some painful lessons. The insights I gained from a task force on the "Politics of Education" were especially telling. Aided by a federal grant, the task force—composed of six political scientists, four professors of school administration, and a sociologist—sought to develop a conceptually integrated, large scale research plan during the summer of 1963. For varied reasons this multi-disciplinary group failed to achieve its mission. A prominent reason for its failure was that available theories were simply too narrow in scope and too weak in content to buttress a large and long range inter-university project. In addition, individual professors shied away from giving up their cherished "islands" of theory on which they had resided for many years. UCEA task force efforts also revealed that highly creative researchers typically preferred to pursue their work autonomously. Thus, in the mid-sixties I reluctantly relinquished my dreams (and those of UCEA's founders) for cooperative, theory based, and large scale research endeavors.

UCEA did facilitate certain types of cooperative inquiry. The taxonomic inquiry is an example (see Chapter Three). Conceived without the aid of most of those who conducted it, the project was grounded in four separate domains of theory: bureaucratic behavior, compliance, decision making, and organizational behavior. Aided by federal funds, an inter-university team conducted the inquiry. Since the theories which guided the inquiry differed markedly, the members of the team pursued their work relatively independently. Certainly, the research talent on the inter-university group was superior to that possessed by any one of the universities from which individual members came. Yet the team produced relatively fragmented findings—results which UCEA's founders hoped the organization would surpass.

UCEA found it relatively easy to perform inductively based, cooperative research. The extensive study of U. S. training programs for school administrators is illustrative. (see Chapter Seven). In this study scholars from six universities gathered data on training practices in doctoral, Master's, specialist, and certification programs. An advantage of the cooperative approach, as used in this and similar studies, was that members of the team could provide one another critiques of proposed data-gathering instruments and initial drafts of chapters.

Inter-university teams of UCEA scholars also had special capacities for ordering and synthesizing existing knowledge. By tracking new developments and by monitoring the changing interests and outlooks of professors, the central staff helped groups of professors effect two somewhat different types of synthesis. One organized existing knowledge related to policy questions in the field. An early example of this type is found in the book *Educational Research: New Perspectives*. Offering forward-looking perspectives, leading UCEA scholars synthesized "state-of-the-art" knowledge related to ways and means for improving training, recruiting, and nurturing the development of inquirers, and for advancing theory based research. (see Chapter Three). A second type involved the synthesis of bodies of knowledge. The book described above—*Educational Futurism: Methodologies*—provides a relevant example.

Scholars in UCEA universities also led efforts to synthesize knowledge. In planning and implementing Career Development seminars, for instance, they involved professors from different universities in the synthesis of findings and ideas about particular topics. The following publications from among the many which emanated from Career Development seminars are illustrative: *The Changing Politics of Education; The Professorship in Educational Administration;* and *Educational Administration: The Developing Decades.*

How successful was UCEA in implementing cooperative development endeavors? Its most widely-used developments were newly created methods and materials for preparing school administrators. Especially significant were UCEA's rural, suburban, and urban school simulations. By enabling professors to bring "slices" of administrative reality into classrooms, UCEA helped tens of thousands of practicing and prospective school leaders experience simulated decision-making. The simulations added a needed clinical component to preparatory programs. Also widely used were the written cases, filmed cases, and audio-recorded "Best Lectures" which UCEA developed and distributed.

Other important expressions of UCEA's developmental capability were newly created institutions. Undoubtedly, the most productive one was the International Inter-visitation Program (IIP). The creation of this program and the various organizations it later spawned continues to influence the study and practice of educational administration around the globe. A very different type of institution which UCEA launched in the 1970s was the University-School System Partnership.

UCEA failed to realize many of its hoped-for developments. Especially notable was its inability to achieve effective new systems, technologies, and instruments for the use of managers in school systems.[3] Why did UCEA fail to attain such products? For one thing, professors were understandably more motivated to develop means for improving training than means for improving school management. For another, the task of developing management tools which could be employed effectively in the complex environments of diverse school systems was difficult and daunting.

UCEA's dissemination programs were significant for several reasons. First, since UCEA's core strategies were research and development, its clients profited from a steady stream of fresh ideas and newly developed training materials. Secondly, since UCEA produced much of the content it diffused, it could make its dissemination programs more effective through pre-planning. Because most of the leading scholars in administration and in related fields were faculty members in UCEA universities, much knowledge beyond that generated through UCEA's R and D programs was always available for distribution.

Finally, the variety in UCEA's offerings enhanced its outreach. Institutes which featured demonstrations of freshly created training materials and their applications in instructional settings helped hundreds of professors acquire new teaching skills. Career Development seminars provided professors with fresh ideas for use in research and training. Seminars usually were designed to include presenters from both inside and outside the field. Outside presenters included social scientists, humanists, professors of public and business administration, scholars from other nations, and leading school administrators. By constantly offering "outside" perspectives, UCEA sought to expose UCEA professors to content they were unlikely to encounter in their work settings and to stimulate them to evaluate and update their training and research practices.

Knowledge: Its Power and Weakness

The over-riding learning I obtained from two decades of observing the uses and benefits of knowledge and of examining its foundations can be stated in the form of a paradox. On the one hand, I could not have functioned without generalizations, concepts, and information; on the other, the available knowledge suffered from severe weaknesses. In describing and analyzing this paradox, I will reveal some of my presuppositions about knowledge and will indicate how they were related to my UCEA experiences.

My basic views about knowledge are rooted in epistemologies which hermeneuticists have delineated. Since not all hermeneuticists share the same beliefs, I shall ground my statements in a specific historical and analytical treatment of knowledge (Gadamer, 1975). In his comprehensive study Gadamer examined postulates about knowledge as well as tenets about its uses. Included in his purview were philosophical and historical works as well as studies of how practitioners (e.g. lawyers and theologians) had used knowledge.

Hermeneutics did not originate in an abstract problem. Rather, it emerged from a concrete one faced by theologians: how to understand accurately the meaning of Biblical texts. Later, hermeneutics expanded to encompass other texts as, for example, those used by literary critics, philosophers, and judges. Still later the domain widened again to encompass oral texts. Rather than spanning metaphysics, ontology, and other domains of philosophy, hermeneuticists have concentrated largely upon the problem of "truth."

According to Gadamer, hermeneutics, when viewed conceptually, is rooted in the nineteenth century debate in Germany about the relations between the human and the natural sciences. This debate preceded the one later in the century over the links between the natural and social sciences. Scholars have frequently used the term "human sciences" to translate the German word, "Geisteswissenschaften," into English. However, the latter term, rooted in older meanings of science, included such disciplines as history and literature.

During the nineteenth century such German scholars as Hermann Helmholtz, an expert in both the human and natural sciences, argued that the methods used in the natural sciences could be applied fruitfully to the human sciences. However, Gadamer maintained that the view was erroneous (1975, p. 7): "For Helmholtz the methodological ideal of

the natural sciences needed neither historical derivation nor epistemological restriction, and that is why he could not logically comprehend
the method of the human sciences any differently." Believing that
individuals and institutions are constantly growing and changing,
Gadamer argued that human scientists should produce understandings about the "unique and historical concreteness" of human phenomena (p. 6). Their goal should be grounded understandings—not predictions or laws. The essential "truth" question is the following (p. 6):
"What kind of knowledge is it that understands that something is so
because it understands that it has so come about?"

For me the hermeneutic view meshed well with the complex
dynamics of UCEA. The belief, that the primary outcome of inquiry
should be understanding, supported my constant need to grasp accurately the meaning of written texts prepared by university scholars and
others. Daily I also spent hours grappling with orally stated concepts and
generalizations with nearby colleagues and with distant professionals in
telephone exchanges. Understandings began and ended in language.

A major expression of understanding, hermaneuticists maintain, is
that of interpretation. The application of interpretations is a second
important ingredient. All three aspects of the process were salient in my
work at UCEA. To take a simple example, when I accepted the post I
read a mission statement in a text prepared by UCEA's founders. On
many occasions I made my understanding of UCEA's mission explicit
by interpreting its meaning to others. As I developed and helped
implement UCEA programs, I moved my linguistic interpretation of
UCEA's mission into practice. Significantly, Gadamer did not pretend
to prescribe specific methods for effecting understanding, interpretation, and application (1975, p. 274): "It is notable that all three . . .are not
considered so much methods that we have at our disposal as a talent
that requires particular finesse of mind." Gadamer's view about
methods, therefore, struck me as sensible.

Although hermeneuticists offer no specific rules for understanding, interpreting, and applying knowledge, they suggest ways of ap-
proaching the processes. For one thing, effective interpretation can
only be attained by peering beyond immediate statements to the
contexts from which they come. When Friederich Schleirmacher applied this idea to the study of Biblical texts, he looked for meaning in the
ancient cultural contexts in which the texts were imbedded. Setting
aside translations of texts, he studied the original ones in Greek and

Hebrew. To acquire accurate meanings about such concepts as sin and salvation, scholars had to "recapture the perspective within which" the concepts were originally elaborated. (Gadamer, 1975, p. 259)

To understand phenomena accurately, scholars need to use the concept of the "hermeneutical circle." Shortly before leaving UCEA, I described this concept as follows (Culbertson, 1981b, p. 3):

> What came to be called the "hermeneutic circle" was vital for the achievement of understanding and interpretation. More specifically, the researcher, in the pursuit of understanding, circled back and forth between the part and the whole. A word, for example, is understood . . .in relationship to the sentence in which it is located. . . As the researcher pursues understanding of the object studied, the circle addressed tends to expand. Gadamer has expressed the general aspiration of scholars in the hermeneutic tradition as follows (1975, p. 259): "The harmony of all the details with the whole is the criterion of correct understanding."

While at UCEA I was always skeptical about the logical positivistic claim that inquiry can be "value free." Thus, the relatively modest "truth" claims of hermeneuticists appealed to me. Gadamer, who viewed historical inquiry as a major avenue to understanding, observed (1975, p. 253): "it is senseless to speak of a perfect knowledge of history. . ." Attainable understandings, he thought, were finite and changing.

Stressing the significance of the "fore-conceptions" which researchers bring to the subjects they study, Gadamer believed that scholars should become more self-conscious about these conceptions (1975, pp. 235-40). In my early days at UCEA I was impressed with how the disparate "fore-conceptions" of professors of school administration and political science influenced their studies of the "politics of education." For the latter group such concepts as "power structure" and "vested interests" were salient. Most professors of school administration held views which were rooted more in education than in raw political facts. Viewing politics often as a process of education and indoctrination, they used such phrases as "educating the public" and "selling bond issues." UCEA projects in the 1960s enabled selected professors in both groups to become more aware of the fore-conceptions which influenced their respective research outlooks. However, neither the conceptions nor their effects disappeared.

Creators of "scientific" theories within UCEA worked hard to achieve objective formulations. However, since their choices of the constructs in theories and the fore-meanings they brought to them could not be fully controlled by logic, their formulations inevitably reflected personal predilections. By conducting empirical studies, they sought to validate theories. However, in the dynamic milieu of educational organizations testers of theory constantly settled for feasible rather than ideal research designs. The more sophisticated opted for standards in addition to scientific validation. One suggested that "in the long run the best test of the usefulness of a theoretical formulation is whether or not it generates research and inquiry" (Getzels, 1958, p. 150).

Gadamer posited that prejudice, another subjective influence, could have positive or negative impacts upon inquiry (1975, pp. 240ff). For example, negative effects result from biased preferences for one authority over others, mistaken understandings derived from unexamined opinions, and distortions arrived at through hasty judgment. Prejudice can play a fruitful role in inquiry when it spawns fresh research questions. Because bias has a double edge, the following epistemological questions are fundamental (Gadamer, 1975, p. 246): "What is the ground of the legitimacy of prejudice? What distinguishes legitimate prejudices from all the countless ones which it is the undeniable task of the critical reason to overcome?"

Even as a graduate student I perceived countless examples of the negative effects of prejudice upon inquiry. For instance, during the third quarter of the century most professors of public administration and professors of school administration expressed prejudicial views about which governance bodies should make fiscal decisions for school systems. The former contended that school systems should be fiscally dependent, while the latter argued that school systems should be fiscally independent. Empirical findings of the two groups tended to support their respective biases.

At UCEA I sometimes observed that prejudice could fruitfully influence inquiry. In the late 1960s I began to see the impact of a "legitimate" prejudice, namely: that women in educational administration were treated inequitably. Over time this prejudice spawned numerous studies of the practices of universities and school systems. First pursued by women who were newcomers to the field, the studies documented inequitable practices and provided reasons for their existence. Over time the findings helped more and more women to enter professorial and school leadership posts.

The field's generalizations were not only colored by prejudices and "fore-conceptions," but they were also shaped by societal values. In the late 1940s the concept of "democratic school administration," formulated earlier in the century, pervaded textbooks. This concept's unusual popularity stemmed in part from the euphoria which surged through society immediately after World War II. Fanned by the successful conclusion of a deathly struggle to make the world "safe for democracy," the euphoria lent support to the idea of democratic decision making by school leaders. In the 1950s this societally valued concept of science was influencing inquiry in the field (see Chapter Two). Thus, the nature of knowledge is continually affected by the ebb and flow of changing societal values.

Professors of educational administration, in contrast to those in academic disciplines, were charged with *improving* practices in systems of education. When they prescribed ideal training programs or set forth their ideal images of administrators, they inevitably expressed values. In the early 1960s, for instance, I proposed that administrators should be "perceptive generalists." The image influenced my views about the desirable aims and content of training programs. Implied in the image, for example, was the need for a broadly based curriculum. Other scholars opted for such differing images of the "good" administrator as "human relations expert," "social engineer," "systems analyst," and "coalition builder." Implicit in these images were disparate values which inevitably shaped scholarly views about ways of improving training.

Because the field's knowledge was heavily infused with subjective and social influences, its base was soft, uncertain, and impermanent as was the base of behavioral science knowledge. Ironically, many creative works of the past now lie largely dormant, in part because they captured so well the ascendant norms of their time. The book, *Mathematico-Deductive Theory of Rote Learning*, written by Clark Hull and his colleagues (see Chapter Three), contains a pioneering application of "hypothetico-deductive systems"—a concept which was central to logical positivism—to problems of psychology. Although the volume received considerable acclaim in its time, it now lies in the book bins of history.

Even though knowledge suffered from serious shortcomings, I was constantly dependent upon generalizations, concepts, and information.

Since my most crucial function, as I saw it, was envisaging new directions and programs for UCEA, I will use this function to highlight selected relationships between knowledge and practice.

An expansive vision, I believed, spawned more fruitful directions than did a narrow one. Thus, I constantly sought vistas which spanned UCEA events, educational developments, and societal conditions. The need for a broadened outlook was rooted in the idea of interdependency; departments of school administration were created to serve educational institutions, and the latter were established to serve society. By viewing as many threads as I could in the tapestry of inter-institutional relationships, I could more capably identify sound directions.

Knowledge was an essential ingredient of an expanded perspective. Therefore, I constantly read various materials for clues about needed turns in UCEA's directions. When staff members in the late 1960s projected guidelines for preparing school leaders, we studied many references on societal conditions which had import for education and its management (e. g. "racial unrest" and "the business-education interface"). Concurrently, we conducted a study of on-going training programs in UCEA universities and probed selected problems in school systems (i.e. "teacher militancy"). The studies illuminated some of the boundaries between society, schools, and universities. Although our knowledge base was limited, it helped us think about desirable changes in training from an expansive rather than a narrow perspective.

Since UCEA relied heavily upon planning, a vision which reached into the future was preferable to a shortened one. While knowledge about the present and the past was indispensable for sound five year planning, it provided an insufficient base for charting fresh paths into the future. Luckily, when I came to UCEA, the number of scholars who were studying the future was growing. The World Future Society was founded in 1964, shortly after UCEA completed its 1964-69 plan. Ideas presented in the journal, *The Futurist*, stimulated me to think about UCEA possibilities. From time to time I synthesized future-oriented studies and spelled out their implications for UCEA. The last paper I read at a UCEA seminar—"Moving Education and Its Administration into the Microelectronic Age"—is illustrative. The paper was informed, for instance, by Yoneji Masuda's *The Information Society* and *The Microelectronics Revolution* edited by Tom Forester. Such syntheses helped me attain a more elongated vision.[4]

Professors imbued with the methods of science were often critical of studies of the future. However, "scientific" predictions of regularities in human affairs were, in my view, just as vulnerable to error as were generalizations about societal trends or projections derived from cross impact analysis. In any case well reasoned and informed studies abetted my search for promising possibilities.

Effective vision not only needed to be broad gauged and elongated but also to be grounded in the reality of UCEA's traditions, constraints, capacities, and the forces which were impinging upon it. Such groundings made initiatives less vulnerable to failure. Knowledge of the fears, aspirations, reasoned objections, and other pertinent phenomena activated by a given initiative was essential to its effective implementation.

Occasionally, UCEA professors asked me about my use of theories (i.e. science-based descriptions, explanations, and predictions of administrative events). The number of theories I repeatedly employed was fewer than six. Since those theories tended to encompass a small number of factors, their reach into the more complex expressions of UCEA was limited. Generalizations about simpler UCEA expressions (e.g. small group behavior) were easier to apply than were those about more complex and expansive ones (e.g. organizational behavior). Well-defined and loosely related concepts were often more useful than theoretical postulates. Such concepts as "linking agencies," "temporary systems," "networks," and "learning systems," for instance, helped me to grasp and capitalize upon aspects of UCEA's capacities.

A theoretical postulate I sometimes used was that two-person coalitions tend to develop within three-person groups. Experiences I had early in my UCEA career supported the idea. Sensitized to the tendency of two persons to "gang up" on the third, I developed a more even-handed approach to group discussions. Notably, members of groups could invalidate the postulate by grasping its import and changing their behavior. When they did so, they highlighted the fragility of "scientific" generalizations.

In sum, the conceptual coins available to me for investment in UCEA programs had two sides. On one side were pictures depicting knowledge's limited reach, its uncertain foundations, its soft substance, and its relatively fleeting life span. Displayed on the other side were messages about knowledge's essential role in research and development, in individual and organizational renewal, in broadening, extending, and grounding visions, and in making organizational decisions. Of the persistent paradoxes I lived with at UCEA, none was more salient than that imprinted on the two faces of knowledge.

A Friendly Departure

Shortly after I announced my departure from UCEA, Ralph Kimbrough of the University of Florida teasingly told me that I was a "slow earner." Implicit in his remark was a question: Why had I not vacated the UCEA post long before 1981? My extended tenure was rooted in decisions made in the early UCEA years. As attractive non-UCEA positions came my way, I had to decide what career outcomes were most important to me. Two questions pinpointed the crucial ones: in what position could I contribute most to my field, and what post would afford me the greatest personal satisfaction? For two decades no post could compete with the UCEA one on either count.

The unusual opportunities UCEA provided me stemmed largely from three conditions. First, the scope of UCEA's outreach was not limited by national boundaries. As a result, the number of opportunities afforded me was greatly increased. Second, since I could work with and through the field's most outstanding scholars and leaders, I felt my contribution was further enhanced. Finally, by pooling and harnessing the specialized talents of professors in cooperative endeavors, one could often realize "multiplier" effects.

The personal satisfaction UCEA rendered me stemmed largely from the unique and immense challenges I continually faced. On the one hand, there was the intellectual challenge of understanding complex arrays of changing issues, developments, specializations, scholarly writings, and emergent training needs. On the other, the leadership challenges I faced were just as daunting. Building and institutionalizing a new and far-flung organization was one example. Another was the continuous launching of fresh UCEA programs. A third was advancing the altruistic ideals of the cooperative ethic in a highly competitive milieu. Effectively addressing such challenges gave me immense satisfaction.

What developments and insights changed my career equation? In answering this query I will use the concepts of "hedgehog" and "fox" — terms originally elaborated by the Greek poet, Archilochus.[5] The fox, Archilochus noted, is one who knows many things in breadth, while the hedgehog knows one or a few things in depth. The UCEA role pressed me to be an arch fox. For two decades I enjoyed grappling with the unending variety of "things" within and beyond UCEA and of understanding what one scholar has called the "requisite variety" to facilitate policy and program development (Weick, 1978, p. 41). However, as UCEA's programs increased in diversity and number, and as its links to other agencies and leaders grew markedly in scope and quantity, my "foxy" role became more and more burdensome. In 1979-80, I began experiencing malaise. Its most salient symptom was a growing desire to focus upon fewer things. Another was a sharply reduced gusto for responding to queries I had answered many times in the past. The keen satisfaction the role had long given me was waning.

Throughout my UCEA career governance personnel and I at times had conflicting views about issues before us. Such conflicts in view I deemed to be healthy and functional. However, in the last half of the 1970s, I began to wonder if differences were nearing the point of an unhealthy state, both for UCEA and for me. Most conflicts, it seemed, were rooted in generational differences.

Because almost all of UCEA's governance personnel had acquired their doctorates 10 to 15 years after I had obtained mine, our respective patterns of experience and training differed significantly. At times discrepancies in the scope and the depth of our respective information bases about UCEA's traditions and operations frustrated me. These discrepancies also seemed at times to create discomfort for newly elected Plenary members and even for Executive Committee personnel. We also tended to employ dissimilar lenses when we looked at policy issues. Assuredly, the gap in our views would continue to widen. The time had come, I concluded, for me to leave UCEA in a friendly and voluntary manner.

In a "mood of thanksgiving" on the occasion of my farewell address to Plenary members, I observed (Culbertson, 1981a, p. 7): "I am especially grateful to that brave band of board members who in the spring of 1959 provided me the opportunity to move from an assistant professorship at the University of Oregon to the executive directorship of UCEA."

The reasons for my gratitude to the "brave...board members" and their many successors were many. I was most appreciative to them for placing and keeping me in a position where I could "observe, listen, initiate, learn, invent, and achieve" (p. 7). I was also grateful that they and I, even when we disagreed, had behaved respectfully toward one another for more that two decades. Indeed, my greatest gratitude to UCEA's governors came from their approval of most of my program recommendations. In so doing they enabled me to take the lead in building many, many bridges on UCEA's landscape—bridges which made it possible for hundreds and hundreds of professors to travel into and to explore new territories. From their explorations continually came new insights, useful products, and thoughtful generalizations— outcomes which had significant impacts upon the training and research practices of professors of educational administration.

Notes

1. See Pellegrin. R. J. (Ed.). (1965). *Perspectives on educational administration and the behavioral sciences.* Eugene, OR: The Center for the Advanced Study of Educational Administration, University of Oregon.

2. For detailed treatments of the methods and their uses see Hencley, S. P., & Yates, J. R. (Eds.). (1974). *Futurism in education: Methodologies.* Berkeley, CA: McCutchan Publishing Corporation.

3. In the UCEA "Atlanta Project" a group of professors developed a number of instruments for gathering data from principals about their specific needs for continuing education. However, the instruments had limited use. For details see Culbertson, J. A., Henson, C., & Morrison, R. (Eds.). (1974). *Performance objectives for school principals.* Berkeley, CA: McCutchan Publishing Corporation.

4. For ideas related to the nurturing of vision through university training see Culbertson, J. A. (1991). Leadership and vision. In D. L. Burleson (Ed.), *Reflections: Personal essays by 33 distinguished educators* (pp. 112-122). Bloomington, IN: Phi Delta Kappa Educational Foundation.

5. For an insightful application of the two concepts see Berlin, I. (1953). *The hedgehog and the fox: An essay on Tolstoy's view of history.* New York: Simon and Schuster.

References

Culbertson, J. A. (1981a). The state of UCEA in 1981. *UCEA Review,* XXII(2), 7-11.

Culbertson, J. A. (1981b). Three epistemologies and the study of educational administration. *UCEA Review,* XXII(1), 1-7.

Fogarty, B. M. (1983). Dedication and introduction. *Educational Administration Quarterly,* XIX(3), 141-152.

Gadamer, H. (1975). *Truth and method.* New York: The Seabury Press.

Getzels, J. W. (1958). Administration as a social process. In A. W. Halpin. (Ed.), *Administrative theory in education* (pp. 1-19) New York: The Macmillian Company.

Weick, K. (1978). The spines of leaders. In M. W. McCall, Jr. & M. M. Lombardo (Eds.), *Leadership, where else do we go?* (pp.37-61). Durham, NC: Duke University Press.

Name Index

Subject Index